FULLER E. CALLAWAY

PORTRAIT *of a* NEW SOUTH CITIZEN

FULLER E. CALLAWAY

PORTRAIT *of a* NEW SOUTH CITIZEN

BUCKNER F. MELTON, JR.
&
CAROL WILLCOX MELTON

LOOKING GLASS BOOKS

AUTHORS' ACKNOWLEDGEMENTS

As Fuller Callaway knew and often pointed out, large projects are a collaborative effort, and this book has been no exception. We are indebted to the staff of the Troup County Archives, who went above the call of duty in accommodating our research requests and granting us access to everything we needed, even while the Archive was being renovated; Kaye Lanning Minchew, Cindy Pendleton, and Forrest Clark Johnson III, who made his extensive knowledge of the Callaways and West Georgia available whenever needed. Beth Van Norman at the Callaway Family Office allowed Carol to set up her research in the office and produced a wealth of documents and memorabilia that was essential to the writing of this book. Our thanks also to Natalie Edison, who as a Macon State College student, traveled to LaGrange to help with research. For their hospitality, patience and diligent research we would like to express our gratitude to the staff of Hills and Dales Estate. The staff made every facility available during the research phase of this project. Our heartfelt thanks to Carleton Wood and Judy Edmonds, who labored for hundreds of hours collecting and obtaining the photographs that bring this story to life. For their help in proofreading and correcting the manuscript we are deeply indebted to: Judy Edmonds, Laura Jennings, Jo Phillips, Stephanie Preston, Maggy Shannon, Lorraine Thompson, and Carleton Wood. For their expertise and advice we are grateful to our colleagues at Middle Georgia State University who allowed us to bounce questions and ideas off of them, especially Stephen W. Taylor and Matthew Jennings. For herding this project to completion we are very grateful to Stephanie Joseph Preston for her tact, patience and persistence. Most of all we would like to express our thanks to the Fuller E. Callaway Foundation and the Callaway family, who, at the urging of others, commissioned this biography, and without whose unstinting support it could not have been completed.

Buckner F. Melton, Jr., and Carol Willcox Melton

❧

ILLUSTRATION & PHOTO ACKNOWLEDGEMENTS

I wish to extend a special thanks to the all organizations, collections and individuals who generously provided permission to use their images in this book. Kaye Lanning Minchew, Director of the Troup County Archives, provided much help and guidance throughout the process. Troup County Historian Forrest Clark Johnson III provided invaluable historical information and assisted with identifying and locating images. Cindy Berman and Shannon Gavin Johnson scanned many of the images that are included in the book. Judy Edmonds of Hills & Dales Estate and Stephanie Preston, the project coordinator, obtained permissions, assisted with locating images and helped bring order to the image collection process. Unless otherwise noted, Lee Cathey of Multi-Image Studio took all photographs of portraits and objects, and Chris Timms generously provided images of St. Neot Church. The rich imagery in this book would not have been possible without the help of everyone above, as well as the numerous organizations and people mentioned in the photo credits. Most sincere thanks are due to everyone who contributed images to this book.

Carleton B. Wood, Photo Editor

Fuller E. Callaway: Portrait of a New South Citizen

Published by Looking Glass Books, Inc. in association with
The Georgia Humanities Council and Fuller E. Callaway Foundation
Distributed by John F. Blair, Publisher
Winston-Salem, N.C.

ISBN: 978-1-929619-60-3

Photo Editor: Carleton B. Wood
Book and jacket design by Burtch Hunter Design

Cover portrait: Unsigned portrait of Fuller Earle Callaway, courtesy of Fuller E. Callaway Foundation
Back cover photograph: Fuller E. Callaway with a cane in the historic Ferrell Gardens

Printed in Canada

CONTENTS

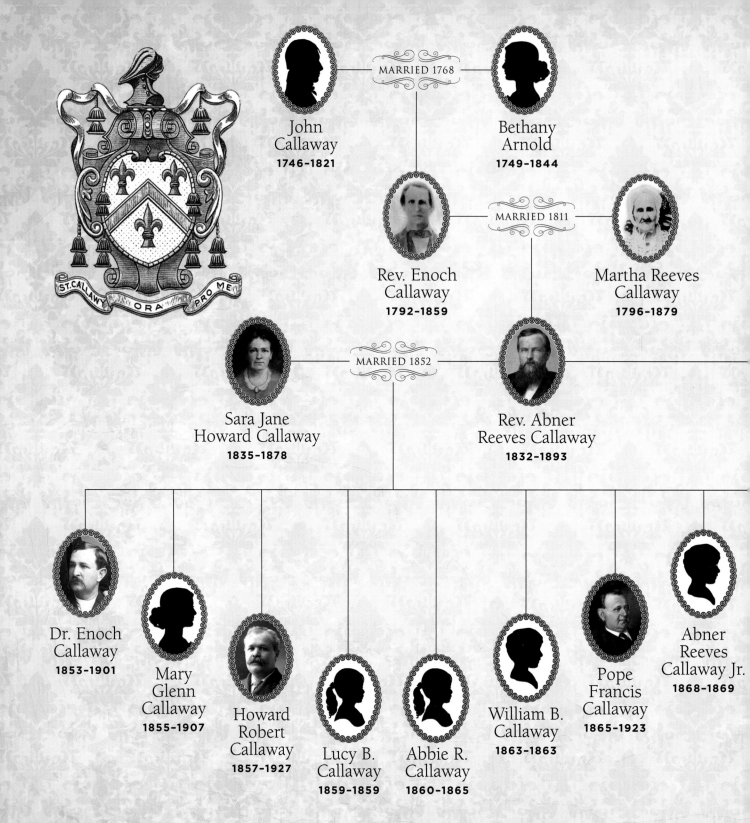

ST.CALLAWY ORA PRO ME

John
Callaway
1746–1821

MARRIED 1768

Bethany
Arnold
1749–1844

MARRIED 1811

Rev. Enoch
Callaway
1792–1859

Martha Reeves
Callaway
1796–1879

MARRIED 1852

Sara Jane
Howard Callaway
1835–1878

Rev. Abner
Reeves Callaway
1832–1893

Dr. Enoch
Callaway
1853–1901

Mary
Glenn
Callaway
1855–1907

Howard
Robert
Callaway
1857–1927

Lucy B.
Callaway
1859–1859

Abbie R.
Callaway
1860–1865

William B.
Callaway
1863–1863

Pope
Francis
Callaway
1865–1923

Abner
Reeves
Callaway Jr.
1868–1869

THE
FULLER E. CALLAWAY
Family Genealogy

MARRIED 1879

Mary Wilbourne
Ely Callaway
1842–1915

MARRIED 1891

Fuller Earle
Callaway
1870–1928

Ida Jane
Cason Callaway
1872–1936

Ely
Reeves
Callaway
1880–1956

Abbie
Callaway
1883–1974

Harry
Wilbourne
Callaway
1884–1950

MARRIED 1930

Fuller Earle
Callaway Jr.
1907–1992

Alice Hinman
Hand Callaway
1912–1998

MARRIED 1920

Cason Jewell
Callaway
1894–1961

Virginia Hollis
Hand Callaway
1900–1995

Fuller Earle
Callaway III
1931–1971

Ida Cason
Callaway Hudson
1935–2009

Virginia Hand
(Jinks) Callaway
1921–1984

Cason Jewell
(Caso)
Callaway Jr.
1924–2011

Howard Hollis
(Bo) Callaway
1927–2014

KEY EVENTS
in Callaway Family History

1577 ～ John Callaway presents St. Neot Church with the St. Callaway window

1712 ～ Thomas Callaway, progenitor of American Callaways, born in Bedford, Virginia

1764 ～ Richard Callaway, brother of Thomas Callaway, goes west with Daniel Boone

1776 ～ Elizabeth and Francis Callaway captured by Indians along with Jemima Boone (a probable basis for James Fenimore Cooper's *The Last of the Mohicans*)

1783 ～ Four sons of Thomas Callaway of Virginia settle in Wilkes County, Georgia

1792 ～ Enoch Callaway, father of Abner, born in Wilkes County Georgia

1826 ～ Troup County established

1828 ～ LaGrange incorporated and named the county seat

1832 ～ Abner Callaway, son of Enoch Callaway, born

1852 ～ Abner Callaway marries Sarah Jane Howard

1853 ～ Enoch Callaway II born

1853 ～ Abner Callaway ordained, shortly thereafter moving to Meriwether County and beginning to teach a boys' school as well as preaching

1856 ～ LaGrange borders expanded to reflect growth

1857 ～ Howard R. Callaway born

1857 ～ Atlanta and LaGrange Railroad extended to West Point and renamed Atlanta & West Point Railroad

1865 ～ Pope F. Callaway born

1865 ～ Abner Callaway uses gold from cotton sales to buy farms and tracts of land in Troup County

1866 ～ Abner Callaway moves his family to his new house in LaGrange

1870 ～ Fuller Earle Callaway (FEC) born on July 15

1872 ～ Ida Jane Cason born on July 17

1872 ～ Roy Dallis born on September 15

1877 ～ Hatton Lovejoy born on March 19

1878 ～ Sarah Callaway dies on September 10

1879 ～ Abner Callaway marries Mary Wilbourne Ely at governor's mansion on June 24

1879 ～ Shittim wood tree planted in Ferrell gardens; still flourishing in 1929

1880 ～ Ely R. Callaway born on June 5

1883 ～ FEC goes to work at Bradfield's Clothing Company

1884 ～ FEC drives livestock from Long Cane to LaGrange for fifty cents, where he is spotted by his sister-in-law Fannie Banks Callaway and invited to live with her and Enoch Callaway

1885 ～ FEC meets Ida Jane Cason

1887 ～ Abner Callaway deeds to Pope Callaway and FEC a farm near Cuthbert, Georgia

1888 ～ FEC and Pope Callaway sell their farm, providing FEC with money to start a business

1890 ～ LaGrange electric system first set up

1891 ～ FEC marries Ida Jane Cason on April 28

1893 ～ Abner Callaway dies on September 23

1894 ～ FEC begins first of many terms on LaGrange Town Council

1894 ～ Cason Jewell Callaway born on November 6

1895 ～ Dixie Cotton Mills incorporated and built with substandard plans and machinery

1895 ～ FEC turns down offer to move to Atlanta and build/manage new department store for $25,000/year, perhaps because of Dixie Mill opportunity

1899 ～ J. H. Lane Company plans to invest money in new LaGrange mill provided LaGrange citizens help pay for it and FEC helps manage it

1900 ～ Unity Cotton Mills built

1902 ～ Milstead Mill organized

1903 ～ FEC's wholesale operation is incorporated as the Fuller E. Callaway Company

1904 ～ FEC testifies before Congress regarding an eight-hour workday

1904 ～ FEC voted out and back in at Unity Mills

1905 ～ Elm City Mill chartered

1905 ～ Atlanta, Birmingham & Atlantic Railroad organized

1905 ～ LaGrange National Bank, a forerunner of C&S, founded

1906 ～ Callaway Development Company chartered to develop the new town of Wadley, Alabama

1906 ～ Governor Hoke Smith appoints FEC to Georgia Railroad Commission

1906 ～ FEC creates the Union Brokerage Company, a company specializing in wholesale brokerage

1906 ～ Elm City Mills opens in Southwest LaGrange

1906 ～ Manchester Development Company chartered (originally as Chalybente Development Company)

1906 ～ LaGrange Savings Bank chartered

1906 ～ Security Warehouse Company chartered

1906 ～ LaGrange Grocery Company established

1907 ～ FEC travels to Europe

1907 ～ Calumet Company, FEC's holding company for Unity shares, chartered

1907 ～ Atlanta, Birmingham & Atlantic Railroad begins freight and passenger service through LaGrange

1907 ～ Electric Ginnery chartered

1907 ～ Fuller Earle Callaway Jr. born on January 1

1908 ～ LaGrange Insurance Agency established

1908 ～ FEC runs for new term on Georgia Railroad Commission

1908 ∾ Callaway's Department Stores incorporated, ending the organization's many name changes	**1917** ∾ FEC announces his plans to request incorporation of Southwest LaGrange as a separate town on temporary basis
1908 ∾ Unity Spinning Mills constructed	
1909 ∾ Unity Spinning Mills built (Unity Cotton Mills expansion)	**1917** ∾ General Assembly incorporates Southwest LaGrange for 28 months
1909 ∾ FEC resigns from Georgia Railroad Commission	**1917** ∾ FEC elected president of the American Cotton Manufacturers Association on May 23
1909 ∾ Manchester Mills organized	
1909 ∾ FEC declines gubernatorial appointment as delegate to Southern Commercial Congress	**1917** ∾ President Woodrow Wilson meets FEC and other members of the American Cotton Manufacturers Association on May 23 in the East Room of White House
1909 ∾ The Callaways put their home at corner of Haralson and Lewis Streets up for sale on December 24	
	1918 ∾ FEC becomes a member of the governing board of the Field Division of the Council of National Defense
1910 ∾ The Callaways move into a new home on Broad Street on February 23	
	1919 ∾ FEC tours Europe in the summer of 1919 as committee chairman of the World Cotton Conference
1911 ∾ FEC taken ill in NYC with facial erysipelas	
1911 ∾ FEC travels to Europe, interested in finding new ways of using textile waste	**1919** ∾ LaGrange Realty Company established
	1919 ∾ FEC steps down as president of LaGrange National Bank, succeeded by Ely Callaway
1911 ∾ FEC buys Ferrell Gardens	
1912 ∾ LaGrange Development Company chartered	**1919** ∾ FEC sends postcard from treaty signing at Versailles on June 28
1913 ∾ FEC declines appointment as federal Commissioner of Indian Affairs	
	1919 ∾ FEC serves as a delegate to President Wilson's First Conference on Industrial Relations in Washington in October
1913 ∾ FEC meets Lord Kitchener on February 1	
1913 ∾ Fuller Callaway hires Neel Reid and Hal Hentz to design a new home adjacent to Ferrell Gardens	**1919** ∾ World Cotton Conference delegates visit LaGrange on October 11
	1920 ∾ FEC is first treated at Johns Hopkins Hospital
1914 ∾ FEC testifies before Congress on the subject of regulation of cotton exchanges	
	1920 ∾ FEC steps down as corporate officer of the mills and becomes chairman of the boards; Cason Callaway becomes treasurer of Unity and Elm City Mills, president of Hillside and Milstead Mills
1914 ∾ The Callaways announce a plan to build their new home adjacent to Ferrell Gardens	
1914 ∾ Callaway's Department Store destroyed by fire; relocation and rebuilding begin immediately	
	1920 ∾ Ida Tarbell publishes profile of FEC in *Red Cross Magazine*
1914 ∾ FEC, Howard Callaway, and S. Y. Austin travel to Europe; are separated, reunited, and then temporarily trapped in England by outbreak of World War I	
	1920 ∾ FEC mentioned as the probable successor to Secretary of the Interior Frank K. Lane but declines to be considered
1914 ∾ Assassination of Archduke Franz Ferdinand on June 28	
1914 ∾ Austria-Hungary declares war on Serbia/World War I begins on July 28	**1920** ∾ Cason Callaway marries Virginia Hollis Hand on April 3
	1921 ∾ The Callaway family tours Europe
1914 ∾ Germany declares war on France on August 3	**1921** ∾ Virginia Hand Callaway born on August 21
1914 ∾ Germany invades Belgium; Britain declares war on Germany on August 4	**1922** ∾ Callaway Mills Inc. establishes its own selling agency; Cason Callaway becomes agency's first president
1914 ∾ FEC, Howard Callaway, and Austin sail for America on August 5	**1922** ∾ Highland Country Club chartered
	1923 ∾ FEC declines to serve on state tax committee
1915 ∾ Mary Wilbourne Ely Callaway dies on March 27	**1923** ∾ Pope Callaway dies on July 31
1915 ∾ Cason becomes manager of Valley Waste Mills	**1923** ∾ FEC and Ida invite Howard Callaway to come live with them
1915 ∾ Hillside Cotton Mills built	
1915 ∾ LaGrange National Bank builds new building at Main and Broome Streets	**1924** ∾ Alfred Pearce Dennis publishes profile of FEC in *Country Gentleman Magazine*
1916 ∾ FEC testifies before Congress on dyestuff issue	**1924** ∾ Cason Jewell Callaway Jr. born on July 17
1916 ∾ FEC elected chairman of the American Cotton Manufacturers Association's Board of Governors	**1927** ∾ Valway Rug Mill created in Southwest LaGrange
	1927 ∾ Howard Hollis Callaway born on April 2
1916 ∾ The Callaways belatedly celebrate their silver wedding anniversary at the newly completed Hills and Dales on June 15	**1927** ∾ Howard R. Callaway dies on May 4
	1928 ∾ Roy Dallis dies on January 19
	1928 ∾ FEC dies on February 11
1916 ∾ Cason Callaway becomes a director of Unity Mills	**1930** ∾ Marriage of Fuller Callaway Jr. and Alice Hand
1917 ∾ Cason Callaway volunteers for the United States Navy, assigned to division of purchase and supply	**1936** ∾ Ida Callaway dies on April 10

LaGrange

TROUP COUNTY GEORGIA

KEY

Map adapted from the 1938 LaGrange City Directory Map.
Points of interest related to Fuller E. Callaway are highlighted.

MILLS

1. DIXIE MILL
2. DUNSON MILL
3. ELM CITY MILL
4. HILLSIDE MILL (OAKLEAF & ROCKWEAVE)
5. LAGRANGE MILL / CALUMET MILL
6. UNITY MILL
7. UNITY SPINNING MILL
8. VALLEY WASTE MILL

RAILROADS

- ATLANTA & WEST POINT RAILROAD
- ATLANTA BIRMINGHAM & COAST RAILROAD
- MACON & BIRMINGHAM RAILROAD
- RAIL SPUR

OTHER SITES

A. BENJAMIN FRANKLIN INN
B. CALLAWAY MEMORIAL TOWER
C. CALLAWAY WHOLESALE DRY GOODS
D. CALLAWAY'S BROAD STREET HOME
E. CALLAWAY'S HARALSON STREET HOME
F. CALLAWAY'S RETAIL STORE
G. CHURCH OF THE GOOD SHEPHERD
H. COURTHOUSE SQUARE
I. HILLS & DALES / FERRELL GARDENS
J. HILLVIEW CEMETERY
K. LAGRANGE FEMALE COLLEGE
L. LAGRANGE NATIONAL BANK
M. MARTHA WASHINGTON INN
N. SECURITY WAREHOUSE COMPANY
O. SOUTHERN FEMALE COLLEGE
P. SOUTHWEST LAGRANGE PUBLIC SCHOOL

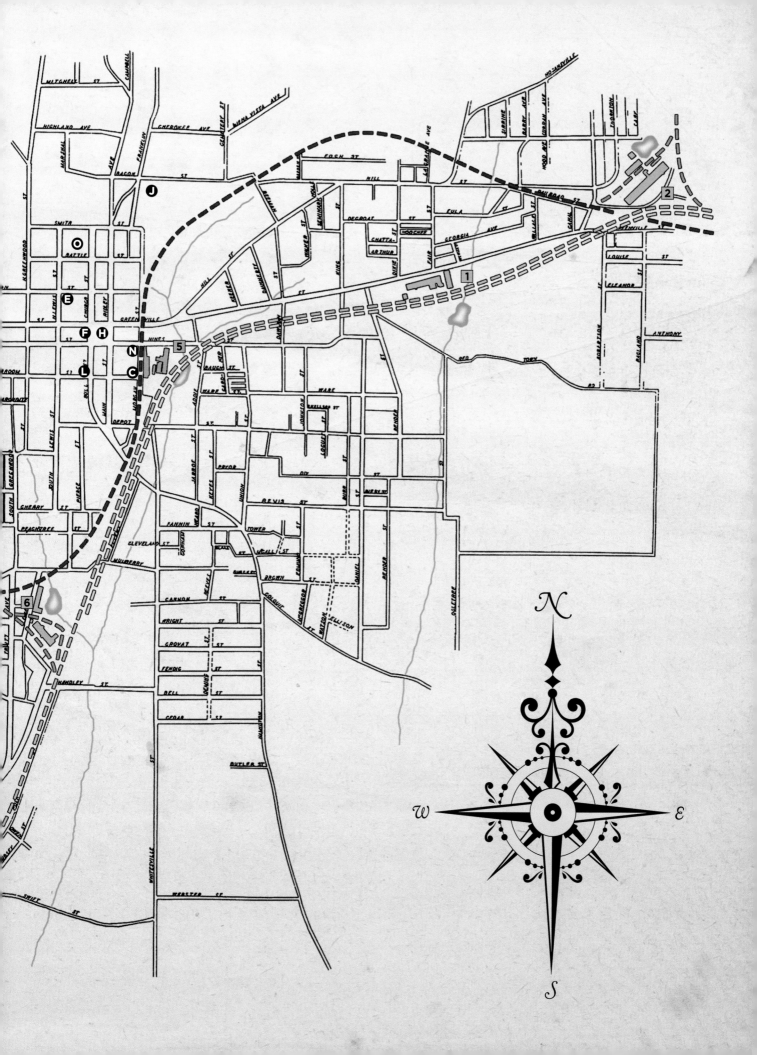

FULLER E. CALLAWAY

PORTRAIT *of a* NEW SOUTH CITIZEN

FULLER E. CALLAWAY AS A YOUNG MAN

· 1 ·

THE YOUNG ENTREPRENEUR

The boy walked down the long Georgia road in the morning light of late autumn. The town lay ten miles distant, quite a way for an eight-year-old to travel. But he'd come a long way already this year; at summer's end his mother had died, and without her to encourage him, he'd pretty much dropped out of school. The youngest of more than a half dozen children, he easily got lost in the shuffle, despite his father's intentions. The family wasn't well off; first the war, and then the recent financial panic, had seen to that. There wasn't a lot to go around. Even at his age, he seemed to sense that he would have to make a way for himself—and soon.

That was what he was doing this morning, as he set out on a twenty-mile round trip to town and back. Today, something had changed. He had a nickel in his pocket.

It was the first money he'd ever had. Nobody knows where he got it; one tale has him earning it by helping a neighbor put an oak shingle roof on his barn a day or two earlier. Another says that it was a gift from someone at the church where his father preached. But whatever its provenance, it was his now. And he meant to make use of it.

A nickel doesn't sound like too much to

twenty-first-century ears. Adjusting for inflation, a boy walking down that same road today would be carrying closer to two dollars. But that was still a lot. This was the rural South, and cash was a rarity. The economy was barely set up to handle it. Sharecropping; tenant farming; poor farm workers, black and white, found many ways to pay their way in the absence of money. For an eight-year-old, he was practically rich.

Perhaps, as he gamely trudged closer to town, he'd not yet decided how he would use it. Maybe he didn't decide until later. But whenever he made his choice, he had no way of knowing that his nickel was a seed from which a new way of life—for him, for his family, for his community, and for thousands of fellow Georgians—would in time start to blossom.

"Such is the unity of all history," wrote a famous English historian of the late nineteenth century—Fuller Earle Callaway's era— "that any one who endeavors to tell a piece of it must feel that his first sentence tears a seamless web." The same is true today. The beginnings of the Callaway story are ancient and varied. Although Fuller Callaway, armed with his nickel, was to change that story forever, he had a heritage that stretched back through centuries.

The name Callaway appears to have Celtic roots. An English strain exists, imported from France by the Normans, referring to Caillouet-Orgeville, a settlement with a population that even today numbers well under a thousand. The medieval records speak of a Walter Calewey of Buckinghamshire as early as 1273, and of a William Callewey of Devonshire around the same

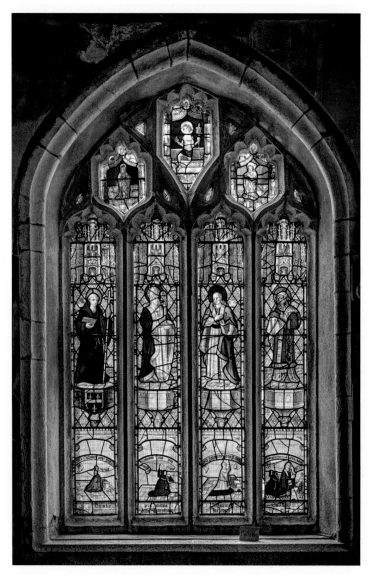

The Callaway stained-glass window at St. Neot Parish Church, Cornwall, England.

time. William Caloway's name appears on a London marriage license in 1524, and in a registry of 1549 we find yet another version with the name Robert Calwaie. But early versions of the name are prolific in and near Cornwall, one of the Celtic regions; perhaps the name came from a settlement in Cornwall or neighboring Devon. Wiltshire, near Devon but not far from Wales, boasted a Cassandra Cayllewey, a suspiciously Welsh-sounding name, in the late thirteenth century, the era of Edward I's wars against Celtic Wales. Cornwall was home to one John Callway in 1500. After that the name pops up more and more often among England's yeomanry and landed gentry, especially in Cornwall and London.

One intriguing bit of evidence is to be found in St. Neot Church in Cornwall. There, a stained glass window dating from 1577 reads, in Latin, "St. Callaway, pray for me." Doubtless sponsored by the Callaway family, the window depicts, among others, the local Cornish saint Lalluwy, patron saint of a nearby village. He was likely chosen to appear in the Callaway window because his name so closely resembled that of the donor family. The similarity resulted in some confusion when the windows were heavily restored in the nineteenth century and the artisan substituted "St. Callaway" for "St. Lalluwy" in the inscription. Nevertheless, *Ora Pro Me*—"pray for me"—has since become the motto of the LaGrange Callaways.

By the early 1600s, as English settlements began dotting the North American coast, the records of Hampshire—located between Wiltshire and London and still close to Devon—are rife with Calloways. It was likely one or more of these who set forth to England's plantations in the New World, arriving within the first few decades of settlement.

Thirty years after Captain John Smith took charge of an endangered Jamestown and helped save it from ruin, Virginia records note the presence, in 1639, of Edmund Callaway.

At roughly the same time, Oliver Calloway, likely of Puritan stock, made his appearance in Watertown, Massachusetts. Still, things remain sketchy for the rest of the century.

The murky records at last begin to clear and coalesce with the advent of Thomas Caloway, who was—perhaps—born in Bedford County, Virginia, in 1712. From this Thomas came a branch of Callaways who spread to North Carolina, Georgia, Kentucky, and beyond. One of the most famous of the Kentucky line was Richard Callaway, compatriot (and sometime opponent) of Daniel Boone, who along with Boone marked the Wilderness Road through the Cumberland Gap into Kentucky. It was Callaway's daughters, Elizabeth and Frances, whom a mixed Cherokee/Shawnee war party captured along with Boone's daughter Jemima in 1776. The teenagers had been floating in a dugout on the Kentucky River so that Jemima could soak her foot, which she had recently injured, when the war party abducted them. A few days later a white party led by Boone and including Richard Callaway, along with his nephew Flanders Callaway, rescued the girls in a dramatic shootout that was to become one of the most famous episodes of Boone's life. It was so famous, in fact, that it became the basis for the plot of James Fenimore Cooper's novel *The Last of the Mohicans*, which was perhaps the first true "Western" ever written. The year after the rescue, Boone and Callaway blood were united when Flanders Callaway married Jemima.

While the early members of Thomas Callaway's line were adherents of the Church of England—Thomas himself served as an Episcopal vestryman—eventually the North

The Capture of the Calloway Girls and Jemima Boone by the Indians attributed to Karl Bodmer, 1852.

Carolina and Georgia branches became ardent Baptists. According to one report of the 1920s, Thomas Callaway's line produced no fewer than thirty-one Baptist preachers named Callaway, and as many more whose mothers were Callaways. This family took its religion seriously. In fact, young Fuller Callaway's father Abner, uncle Brantley, and grandfather Enoch were all Baptist ministers.

Enoch Callaway, grandson of Thomas Callaway, son of Revolutionary War veteran John Callaway, and grandfather of Fuller Callaway, was born in 1792 in Wilkes County, Georgia, where his father had taken up residence a year after the British surrender at Yorktown. In 1808 he joined the Sardis Baptist Church and was baptized by Jesse Mercer, the prominent Baptist minister and later founder of Mercer University. Fifteen years later, Enoch himself became a minister and eventually was one of Mercer's successors at Sardis Church, serving as pastor there for more than three decades; as a member of the

Silver teaspoon inscribed "Callaway" made out of silver coins circa 1855 for Abner Reeves Callaway.

Posthumous portrait of Abner Reeves Callaway (1832-1893), painted by Adah Mendenhall Awtrey in 1924.

Abner married Sarah Jane Howard in 1852. This portrait of Sarah Jane (1835-1878) was painted by Adah Mendenhall Awtrey.

Executive Committee of the Georgia Baptist Convention, he helped to supervise Mercer's new college. His son, Abner Reeves Callaway, born in 1832, was named for Enoch's father-in-law Abner Reeves.

Abner, like his father before him, was born in Wilkes County. Enoch had inherited more than a thousand acres of land from his father, and Abner no doubt put in much of his childhood helping his parents farm it. In 1850, however, eighteen-year-old Abner followed Enoch into the pulpit, delivering his first sermon in his father's church.

Except that he didn't. He'd planned to, but as the old saying goes, men make plans and God laughs. Today the joke was to be on young Abner.

As church was about to begin and the would-be preacher stood ready, he caught sight of two young ladies making their way down the aisle. One of them, a certain Miss Sarah Jane Howard, had the same impact on Abner that the angel Gabriel had on Zechariah, the father

of John the Baptist. In other words, Sarah, whom Abner later coincidentally described as "the most beautiful angel," literally struck him speechless. Utterly smitten, Abner forgot what he had planned to preach and helplessly turned to Enoch, who had to fill in for his son.

This inauspicious beginning kept Abner out of the pulpit for another two years. But he put the delay to good use; by the time he managed to find his preacher's voice in 1852, the blooming young Sarah had consented to become his bride. When he finally did preach his first sermon, six people stepped up to be baptized, and Abner realized he'd found his calling as well as a wife. He was ordained the following year.

The Callaways were hardy folk, and undoubtedly hard working. In those early years, Abner was not merely preacher but teacher as well; in 1860 he founded the Hyperion High School, a boarding school just outside Greenville, Georgia. Even as the storm clouds of war gathered and darkened, his prosperity grew.

The secret was cotton, of course. Grown throughout the South, milled and spun in New England as well as the states of the mid-Atlantic, the crop was ubiquitous. In the 1850s it counted for well over half of America's export earnings. Tobacco was valuable in Virginia, as was hemp in Missouri and the burgeoning wheat of the old Northwest. But cotton was special. It enriched the entire nation, including people who neither grew it nor dealt in it. Cotton profits trickled down throughout the society and made the whole system work.

It was certain that Abner and his family remained active in farming, and likely that some of the farming involved cotton. The census of 1860 shows that he had assets totaling around $30,000, a sum equivalent to more than half a million dollars in modern terms even by the most conservative estimates. And during the terrible war years from 1861 to 1865, Abner's business acumen really showed itself. In the final months of the conflict he had the foresight and luck to be able to invest his remaining, failing Confederate dollars in cotton, which he sold to cotton-starved Northern textile concerns. This enabled him to buy up some land in Troup County, where the fusion of LaGrange,

cotton, and a mercantile spirit was to remake not only the town, but the Callaways.

~

All through the years of storm clouds, war, and aftermath, the Callaway family was growing. The first child of Sarah and Abner, Enoch Callaway, arrived in the summer of 1853, followed eventually by eight others, including two who died in infancy. The last of them, Fuller Earle Callaway, was born on July 15, 1870, in LaGrange where Abner was serving as Professor of Natural Science and Belles Lettres at Southern Female College. This, too, was a harbinger of the family's future; Fuller would show a great interest in education, although sometimes in unconventional and even startling ways. The Callaways prized learning even when they had scant opportunity to gain it; while fate would deny Fuller much formal schooling, he would find other ways.

By 1873, that fate was very nearly sealed. The Reconstruction-era South was impoverished. By the war's end, 90 percent of Southern banks had collapsed, a third of its cattle and other farm animals had disappeared, and its commodity output had fallen by half. The victorious Union had destroyed

Abner Reeves Callaway bought this farm in Long Cane in 1867. Abner Callaway had a larger home in LaGrange. His son, Fuller, often walked from there to his house in Long Cane. This photograph is from the 1890s after the property was purchased by the Hudson family.

Cotton bales arriving at the LaGrange town square in 1874.

Southern productivity, and in the following years it did little to help financially needy Southerners, either black or white. Even cotton prices were barely a third of what they had been before the war came. In economic terms, the former Confederacy was a wasteland. Shortly after Fuller Callaway's birth, by some accounts, Abner was only making $500 a year—less than $7000 in modern terms—with which to support his wife and half dozen children.

As if this weren't bad enough, the hammer blows of the Panic of 1873 soon fell on the whole nation's economy, touching off a major depression that would last for the rest of the decade. Before it ended, a quarter of the nation's 300-odd railroads would fold, 18,000 businesses and banks would fail, and unemployment rates would peak at 14 percent. Fuller, it seems, had picked the wrong time to be born.

Even so, life in the Callaway family seemed to go on cheerfully. As an adult, Fuller loved a good story, and he became famous as a teller of tales, though sometimes (as Huckleberry Finn remarked of Mark Twain) stretching the truth a bit. (Fuller's son and namesake, Fuller E. Callaway Jr., a valuable source of tales about his father's life, stretched things still more, compounding the problem.) This can make it hard to separate fact from fiction, but at the same time it tells us a lot about Fuller's character as an entertaining, extroverted conversationalist.

As Fuller later told it, his mother always had roasted peanuts and parched or popped corn, and cookies too, in the pantry for her children and their neighborhood friends. The Baptist preacher's home, as everyone called it, always had an open door for guests, especially at mealtime, and as an adult, Fuller, too, would adopt this habit. But there was one time when the young Fuller was not very happy about a guest, one Mr. Gosey. A tenant on one of Abner's farms, Gosey was at dinner one day when Sarah produced a sponge cake for dessert. As Fuller looked on, Gosey helped himself to the whole thing. Naturally this meant no sponge cake for Fuller, but rather than showing disappointment, he laughed out loud at the guest's manners, much as Scout Finch would later be aghast when Walter Cunningham poured syrup all over his food.

But Abner didn't need a Calpurnia to keep his children in line. "Fuller," he said sternly, "what are you laughing at, sir?"

Fuller immediately knew he was in trouble, but he was already a quick thinker. His chair faced the door to the kitchen, and that door was open. "You ought to have seen our old cat jump on the red hot stove!" he exclaimed.

Abner glanced into the kitchen. "I don't see any cat."

Fuller was ready for him. "Why," he replied, "she jumped off quicker than she jumped on!" In the meantime, Mr. Gosey had replaced the sponge cake, so Fuller got a piece after all. Even Abner had to laugh when he later learned the whole story.

Although Fuller could be inventive, he was also good at learning from others. He often hung around the elderly retired businessmen who spent their days sitting in front of the Troup County courthouse. One of Fuller's earliest life lessons came from these encounters.

One story that the adult Fuller loved to tell was of the agitated farmer who once approached the courthouse group. "I have lost a fine cow, and can't find her anywhere," he told the men. "I will give five dollars to whoever finds her and brings her to me!"

A young boy named Bill, by accounts not very bright, overheard this offer, and a few minutes later, after some thought, he trotted off. Soon he returned, leading a cow.

"Hey, mister," he said, "is this your cow?"

Yes," responded the relieved farmer, "but where did you find her?"

"I just set down and thought, if I was a cow, whar would I go?" the boy told him. "I thought of a green patch of grass growing by the roadside, and I said, 'that's whar I would be if I was a cow.' I went, and she was there. Give me my five dollars!"

The episode made quite an impression on Fuller. "Bill, the half-wit, wanted this five dol-

Fuller E. Callaway as a five-year-old boy.

lars worse than he wanted anything else in the world," he would tell his audience after relating the story. "This helped him to think and work hard—which is what brings success."

In fact, this way of learning was to become one of Fuller's most important means of educating himself as he grew older. In 1878, with the death of his mother and the continuation of the national depression, his formal schooling largely came to an end. His father was busy raising the children on his own, and times were hard. School was a luxury that the Callaways couldn't afford, even though they valued it highly.

Even so, Fuller was no conventional student. "I had but two weeks' schooling in grammar," he later confessed. "At the end of this period my teacher offered this counsel of desperation. 'Get your pappy to take you out in the smoke-house, make a good fire, strip off your clothes, pile the books around you, and you may possibly get some grammar in through your pores. You will never get any in through your head.'"

Now, as young Fuller walked into La-Grange with his nickel, he had two choices. He could use his nickel to treat himself to some luxury, such as candy, to take his mind off the hardships of his young life—or he could become a producer instead of a consumer, choosing the role of asset rather than liability. And despite the brains and work ethic of the Callaway clan, only he could make this decision.

The old family tales mention that even before this moment, Fuller had talked about being a salesman, about owning a store. According to these tales, Fuller had even run a small shop of his own at home, a crate on which he displayed all of his wares: bent nails, bits of glass, rocks of various hues, and other such bric-a-brac. His mother was his best customer, bartering with biscuits and slices of ham in exchange for his goods. Maybe things fascinated him because things were scarce in postwar Georgia. Maybe that's where he first got the idea of value.

Now he had some real money. And the way he decided to use it was completely in character, both with his salesman persona of earlier times and with the adult he was to become.

He entered a store, say the tales, and took a good look around. Most of the goods were too costly for him: a bar of soap was beyond him, and a pair of suspenders would have wiped him out several times over. But, providentially, one item stood out: thread. He could buy three whole spools of it for a nickel.

"Life is just like a ball of yarn," Fuller Callaway would say many years later. "You begin winding, and it's mighty hard to get it in shape at first. It runs crooked, and knots up. If you keep on winding, however, you find you have a start that seems as if it might be a ball some day. Then, as you wind, it gets bigger and bigger, and uses up the yarn faster and faster. Soon it is not as much trouble as it was at first. Then it starts to run so smoothly you hardly know you are winding, and you've got your ball." When he said that, perhaps he was thinking specifically about his first textile purchase, the thread that he would follow into the world of sales, of retail and wholesale, and ultimately to an industry that, in 1878, was barely imagined in the South.

Before Fuller E. Callaway was done winding, he and the men like him would create, phoenix-like, a new South. The New South. And for him it would begin as it ended: with thread.

~

Very early on, perhaps that same day, Callaway learned a basic concept of classical economics: labor is the source of value. A spool of thread that sold in the store for one and two-thirds cents was worth five cents when a twenty-mile walk was added to it. Soon he'd sold his entire stock to his neighbors and plowed all of his profits into more, his fifteen cents going for nine spools of thread. Before long he was branching out into needles and scissors.

Other things were changing as well during those years. In the summer of 1879, the recently widowed Abner remarried. His new wife was Mary Wilbourne Ely, whose brother Robert was Georgia's attorney general. In fact, the wedding took place in Atlanta, in the governor's mansion, with Governor Alfred H. Colquitt himself giving away the bride.

There was no undue haste involved here. A family, especially a large one, needed both a father and mother, and as not only a preacher but a teacher, Abner needed a wife who could help him out with his duties. Fuller and Mary got along well, but times were still lean, and a year later more children began to arrive with the birth of Fuller's half brother Ely. Two others eventually followed.

(Facing page) This 1891 photo depicts Fuller with five of his brothers. Seated left to right are Harry Y., Howard R., and Dr. Enoch Callaway. Standing left to right are Pope F., Fuller E., and Ely R. Callaway.

Today, with the modern notion of adolescence as well as college requirements, children are a liability for two decades and more. In the nineteenth-century South, they had to become assets sooner than that. Fuller had sensed this, and it had fueled his own nascent career as a peddler. "In a house where there were so many children," he figured, "one would not be missed." In fact, he sometimes made sure he was missed. When Abner wanted to hold a family meeting, he would call out the names of all of the Callaway children, beginning with Enoch, the oldest. When Fuller heard the litany start, he would take off running, so that by the time Abner got to his name, he was safely out of earshot. This tactic gave him a certain freedom of action in his business ventures.

He used this freedom to add to his territory. As he grew, he ventured farther and farther afield, sometimes all the way to Alabama. Over the months and years, people got to know him. From the first, he was an extrovert, and always just as willing to help out people in need of it as he was to make a sale. By the time he was twelve, he was a already a fixture in west Georgia.

It was around 1880 when Fuller made another key decision: like so many of his recent forebears, he became a Baptist. Joining the First Baptist Church of LaGrange, where he would remain a member until his death nearly a half century later, he soon learned the importance of community and giving back to it. In time he would become one of the congregation's biggest contributors, and often an anonymous one. But in 1880 that was still in the future. For now, Fuller was still laying the groundwork for his later successes. By 1882 things were taking shape. After four years of peddling, he'd amassed a small fortune for a twelve-year-old Georgia boy, somewhere between fifty and sixty dollars. At that point he began looking around for some kind of investment, and he found one: a farm.

Selling was key to the economy, but producing was even more basic, and in the 1880s agricultural goods were still America's most valuable products. William Jennings Bryan, whom Fuller would later come to know and respect, captured this idea the following decade in one of the most famous speeches in the nation's history. "Burn down your cities and leave our farms, and your cities will spring up again as if by magic," he declared during his presidential campaign in 1896. "But destroy our farms, and the grass will grow in the streets of every city in the country." Living in an overwhelmingly agricultural region and having helped with family farming his whole life, Fuller was almost predestined to try his hand at working his own farm.

Two of the people who knew the adult Fuller best, his wife Ida and his son Fuller Jr., told slightly different versions of the farming adventure. Ida stated that Fuller worked one of Abner's farms for a year; Fuller Jr. reported that the young entrepreneur leased a farm and worked it for two years, spending his $60 to buy a plow, a mule, and a wagon. By the latter's account, the youngster doubled his investment during the first year, taking in $120. Ida Tarbell, who presumably got the story directly from Fuller Sr., wrote that he leased the farm and that his first cotton crop made $36.34. He also learned exactly how demanding the farmer's life is. Farming, Fuller later declared, was "a good way to make a poor living, or a poor way to make a good living." At the near-subsistence levels of impoverished regions, it was hardly a living at all. The experience gave him a great understanding of, and sympathy for, hardworking farmers, and he would keep these things in mind throughout his career.

One day, when Fuller was fourteen and presumably into his second year of farming, someone offered him a half a dollar to take a calf into LaGrange. Five times the money he'd cleared in his first sale of thread! Three times his daily profit margin during his first year of farming, if his son's figures are right. Fuller gladly accepted the offer.

He found he had to work for it. The calf, being a calf, showed contempt for roads and straight lines, meandering into the underbrush, ditches, and fields all the way while wearing out Fuller. But the pair finally made it, with the boy wearily coaxing the calf up a LaGrange street—and, as luck would have it, past the residence of his older brother Enoch, who was now a town doctor.

Enoch's new wife, Fanny, saw the bedraggled young farmer-turned-cattle-driver approaching, and she invited him to stop and have a drink of well water. She took a liking to him, and that evening she had a talk with her husband. "Your brother Fuller passed here today," she told Enoch. "I talked with him and I was very much impressed." Fuller's visit, in fact, had given her an idea. "When you go out at night on calls and leave me here alone, I'm frightened," she confessed. "Why don't we ask father Callaway to give him to us? He can get a job and we can give him some opportunities, and I'll have somebody here with me at night when you go out on calls."

Enoch liked the idea. "Well," he pondered, "we'll drive out Sunday and see what father says."

When Sunday arrived, Fanny and Enoch visited Abner and asked what he thought of the plan.

"Why, sure, Enoch," Abner responded. "You can have him if you can find him."

And that was how Fuller Callaway ended his life as a farmer and came to LaGrange.

~

Ida Tarbell, the great social crusader, once observed that Callaway was "literally as self-made a man as can be easily found." And given his early experiences, she continued, "[b]y the time he was thirteen years old, he was a capitalist." When one of his brothers, possibly Enoch, asked him,

Fuller E. Callaway learned the general store trade while working for Edwin R. Bradfield from 1884 to 1888. Bradfield's store was located at the northeast corner of the square.

"Fuller, what are you going to make of yourself?" the youngster was surprised.

"Make of myself?" he replied. "Why, I am made!" With that, he produced his bankbook and showed his brother the money that he'd earned. "Look at that!" he crowed, pleased with himself.

Nevertheless, now that Fuller was back in LaGrange, he would need to find a new enterprise, especially since he would have to pay room and board to Enoch and Fanny. Returning to the sales field seemed a logical move. So he secured a position at the Bradfield Clothing Company, the town's largest store, serving as a delivery boy. It was to prove quite an experience.

In fact, something soon happened to Fuller at Bradfield's that he later described as "the turning point in my life." It was an event so small as to seem barely worth noting, but to Callaway it seemed huge. It was nothing but a routine delivery—to a black family.

Slavery had been gone for nearly twenty years, but the lines between the races were still strong throughout the country. And Fuller objected to having to deliver to blacks. At first glance this appears to be simple racism, but for Fuller it was something else altogether. He had been his own boss for too long; this was the first time he'd worked for anyone except family members and his own customers. He found being a paid worker chafing. He, like nearly all

other whites of that era, believed that African Americans in postwar America were a separate, and lower class, so when he was told to make this delivery, he seized on it as a pretext, returning home early.

Enoch was surprised when Fuller arrived. "What's the matter?" he asked.

Here was the moment for which Fuller had planned. "I quit," he declared. "They gave me a package to deliver to a Negro house." Nothing more, he probably figured, needed saying. He imagined that Enoch would agree with him that such work was too demeaning for a Callaway to consider. "It was a deliberate scheme of mine," the adult Fuller explained years later. "I was calculating to make a move which would enable me to loaf the rest of my life." Enoch would be his meal ticket. That was the plan, anyway. But it didn't work out quite that way.

"Well, you won't eat tonight," Enoch answered, "and you won't sleep here if you're too proud to deliver a package to a Negro. That's honest work. You go back up there and get your job and deliver the package."

The indications are that Fuller was surprised, perhaps shocked. He'd gotten too full of himself, and Enoch, quite rightly, had slapped him down hard. "That fixed it for me," he told Ida Tarbell. "I was at the store by daylight the next morning." The turning point had arrived. "It signified whether I was to remain an independent, self-respecting individual or become a deliberate idler."

It was an interesting choice of words. Fuller—at least the older Fuller, and likely the young Fuller too—thought of himself, correctly, as independent even at age fourteen or so. He'd already proven by then that he had both the brains and the energy to be a financial success. What he learned from Enoch that day was that he had to keep using them. He could never rest on his current or past achievements. He had to keep moving forward, working and being productive. He also learned that money was a great equalizer. Thomas S. Bradfield, his employer, didn't mind who bought his goods, as long as they paid him. This alone was an important lesson for Fuller.

He learned other things from Bradfield as well. The merchant was quite a salesman. For decades, people—Fuller included—remembered how he never let things go to waste. On one occasion he had a single unmatched lady's glove. A young woman arrived to buy her trousseau, and Bradfield sold her the lone item. "You always carr[y] them anyway," he told the soon-to-be bride. "Nobody [will] know whether [you have] one or two." Bradfield got rid of the glove, and his customer probably got a bargain price; it was a good exchange all around. The lesson wasn't lost on young Fuller.

In fact, he was a very quick study. Eventually advancing from delivery boy to salesman, taking pages from Bradfield's book and combining them with his own gregarious nature and native ability, before long he was outselling everyone in the store, including Bradfield himself. By the time he was eighteen, he was worth $500. A wage-earner would have to make $10,000 today to equal such value.

~

Fuller continued to work at Bradfield's for about four years, learning all the while. By then he had gone as far as the job could take him. He had plans, and by the time he was nearing the age of eighteen, he had not only the drive but the skill to carry them out.

Unlike some youngsters who take time to decide on their direction, Fuller never gave a sign of wavering. From the moment he had bought his first spools of thread—perhaps before—he'd been a salesman. That was what he would be as an adult. His post-Bradfield plans weren't different from his earlier dreams. But they were bigger. For as he was approaching adulthood, Fuller set out to own his own store. And that first store would help to change the nature of sales in America.

(Facing page) Studio photograph of young Fuller Callaway by the well-known photographer J. L. Schaub.

FULLER CALLAWAY AND IDA JANE CASON WERE
MARRIED ON APRIL 28, 1891.

·2·

THE PROPRIETOR

By the time he was nearing adulthood, Fuller Callaway had already passed through a variety of business experiences. He had been a traveling salesman for nearly half his young life, he had worked a farm on his own for a year or two, and he'd served as a town-dwelling store clerk. In his personal life he'd cemented family relationships, particularly with his brother Enoch and sister-in-law Fanny, after going his own way much of the time as a child.

All of these experiences provided a foundation for Fuller as he became a young man. As an adult he would continue to travel in search of business opportunities and work in LaGrange stores. Even his farming experiences were not over just yet. More important, although he himself would no longer work in the fields of a farm, he would grow to a new awareness of the Southern farmer's needs and importance to the South's economy. In short, the roles Fuller played as an adult would be more elaborate, more mature versions of those he had already filled as a youth. And his family attachments also would continue to grow . . . but not until he'd seen to some other things first.

While continuing to work at Bradfield's store, Callaway apparently kept his hand in other enterprises as well. One of them, briefly at least, was a return to farming.

In the fall of 1887, Abner Callaway conveyed more than 1,100 acres of farmland near Cuthbert, Georgia, to his sons Fuller and Pope. The conveyance was in essence a gift, with no other consideration being listed but the stock phrase "love and affection." The twin facts of Abner's ownership of the farm and his gift of it to two of his sons strengthens the picture of the elder Callaway as an erstwhile member of the planter class, though perhaps land-poor in the wake of the war. Cuthbert was 100 miles from LaGrange, and much farther from Memphis, Tennessee, where Pope lived at the time. Abner almost certainly intended the farm to be an asset and not a way of life for his sons, especially since he noted its likely value, $3,500, in the deed itself. And that was exactly how Pope and Fuller treated it.

Before long the two young men—Pope was about five years older than Fuller—traveled by horse and buggy to Cuthbert, where they sold the farmland to one A. J. Moye for $3,000. However much Fuller had made working for Bradfield's, his share of the sale amounted to quite a windfall. Soon he began to make excellent use of it.

By the time he was seventeen or eighteen years old, Fuller Callaway not only had money; he had a firm understanding of basic economic, financial, and legal principles, which was even more valuable than the money itself, especially in an enterprising and energetic young man. One early example is his relationship with the local bank.

According to Ida Tarbell, who heard it directly from Callaway, the young entrepreneur had a bank account as early as his thirteenth year, when he flourished his bankbook before his brother and declared himself "made." It was also apparently around this time when he attempted to cash his first check, drawn on his own account, for twenty cents in order to buy a copy book.

When Fuller presented his check, there was some trouble. "Why, my boy," the banker told him, "we are not accustomed to accepting checks for less than a dollar."

"But I don't want a dollar," replied Fuller. "My copy book is only 20 cents. I am afraid if I had 80 cents more I might spend it."

This made quite an impression on the banker, according to Callaway and Tarbell. "You may cash a check for 20 cents or one cent at this bank any time you want to," the banker reputedly answered. Even though after this, the story goes, the bank never gave Callaway trouble about cashing checks, other banking run-ins followed.

When he was around eighteen, Callaway was ready for a larger venture than that of a mere copy book, and to get it off the ground he needed a line of credit amounting to $1,000. But A. D. Abraham, of the LaGrange Banking and Trust Company, was leery of the request.

"Why, Fuller," Abraham said, reluctant to run afoul of the town doctor's brother, "I'd be delighted to lend you the money, but . . . I have a strong, fast policy that I don't lend money to a minor, and you are not of age."

But Callaway had prepared for this. From his pocket he pulled a certified copy of a joint resolution of the Georgia General Assembly legally emancipating him—in effect conferring majority status on him, as if he were already twenty-one.

"Well, Fuller," Abraham responded, "I know if you lived you'd pay me, but I'm not in the life insurance business, and I just can't lend you the money."

Fuller now pulled out another document. This one was a $1,000 life insurance policy on himself, with Abraham named as the beneficiary.

With that, Abraham gave up. "All right, Fuller." He began to make out a note.

"Wait a minute, Mr. Abraham," Fuller interjected. "I don't want to sign a note. . . . I may not need that money."

"What do you mean?" Abraham shot back. "I thought you wanted the money."

"I want credit," Fuller explained. "I want you to guarantee my overdraft up to $1,000 and charge me interest on the average overdraft." It was a canny request. It meant that Fuller would be paying less interest and that Abraham would consequently be making less money.

"Why you young whippersnapper," exclaimed Abraham, "that's the English banking system. Where did you ever hear of that?"

"I never heard of it," said Fuller. "I just don't want to pay you interest on money I'm not using."

"All right," said Abraham again, no doubt with a great deal of resignation. "Your overdraft is good for $1,000."

The story is a good one, but some of its details—in particular the matter of Callaway's emancipation—are suspect. No such joint resolution or private law relating to Callaway's early majority appears in the Georgia session laws, at least where it normally should be. Then there was the sale of the Cuthbert farm, which also took place around this same time.

In April 1892, with his twenty-first birthday behind him, Callaway formally ratified his earlier sale of the farm and noted that at the time of the sale he had made out a bond to buyer A. J. Moye promising to ratify the sale upon reaching legal adulthood. Upon this ratification Moye was to return the bond to Callaway, which he presumably did.

Perhaps the legislature passed the resolution—if it existed—between Fuller's sale of the farm and his exchange with banker Abraham. But if so, one wonders why he did not go ahead and promptly ratify the sale of the farm immediately instead of waiting three more years to recover the bond from Moye.

But particulars aside, the point is that Callaway, by his late teen years, was already showing an aptitude for the principles of finance, and he was about to put it to work in earnest. He was busy preparing to open his own store. In July 1888, at the age of eighteen, he did it.

Through his negotiations with Abraham and the sale of his farm, Fuller Callaway had enough capital to begin his new enterprise. His next tasks were to find a location, and then to stock it.

The first goal was simple, but as usual he showed sound judgment in achieving it. He rented a space on LaGrange's courthouse square, where traffic was likely to be heavy, from L. M. Park at the rate of twenty dollars per month. The space was a big one; with twenty feet of front footage and eighty feet of depth, in fact, it was almost too big, at least at first. But Callaway's plans, too, were big, and the width of the space was probably what appealed to him.

The caption reads: The LaGrange Banking and Trust Company was the first business to issue credit to Mr. Callaway.

His next task was to decide on his stock. With the limited amount of funds and leverage available to him, the only type of money-making venture he could think up was a dime store, or more accurately and as he was to call it, a five-and-ten-cent store. He later explained that this approach would allow him to "pay cash, sell for cash, and keep up quite a stock of goods in fives and tens, on five hundred dollars."

This brief statement tells us a great deal about Callaway's early days as a store owner, and indeed about the business philosophy he favored throughout his adult life. Cash transactions, or at least a conservative use of lending and borrowing, were among his core business principles. A good stock with strong customer appeal and a consequent fast turnover was another, especially when it came to his retail career. And the figure of $500 is also significant, for all sources (this statement of Callaway's not the least of them) seem to suggest that it represented the total cash available to him at this juncture. In light of the Cuthbert farm sale, which presumably netted Fuller and Pope $3,000, as well as savings from his job at Bradfield's, the amount seems low. It is even possible that his arrangement with Abraham came some time after he first opened his store. But whatever the explanation, $500 seems to have been his ready capital.

Fuller E. Callaway's Mammoth Department Stores on the town square. Fuller is left of center wearing a white jacket. Note the tinware hanging in front of the store.

Having already spent some of his money to rent his storefront, Callaway now came to the big question: what should he buy with the rest of it?

He found the answer in Atlanta. Traveling to the capital, he made his way to the Charles A. Conklin Manufacturing Company, a tinware maker that had been in business since Reconstruction. Conklin, an immigrant tinsmith, had a large stock of pans that he was having a hard time selling. As Callaway approached, he saw tin pans of every size piled here and there. He also saw an opportunity.

Callaway found Conklin and explained his circumstances to the tinsmith. "I want to be fair with you," he told Conklin, emphasizing that he would need generous credit terms in order to reach a deal. Callaway's gregarious salesman's personality, which would serve him so well throughout his life, finally won Conklin over, and the manufacturer sold him a carload of tinware on ninety days' credit.

It was a major deal for both men. "To give you an idea of what a big businessman I was at the time," an elderly Charles Conklin reminisced near the end of his life, "I didn't have a back door to my place. . . . I had to load [Callaway's] order out on the sidewalk for the dray to pick it up. . . . All my friends stopped by and asked where I was moving."

Callaway shipped the tinware back to La-Grange and placed it in his storefront. But even as large as the shipment was, it didn't come close to filling the store. So Callaway curtained off the back half of the space, making it appear full. And then, with his stock in place, the time had come for Callaway's Famous Mammoth Five-and-Ten Cent Store to open its doors.

Of course, it wasn't famous just yet. Callaway later claimed that for every $5,000 he made, he dropped a word from the store's name. Eventually this process ended with a store simply named Callaway's, but for now, with no sales, he needed as long a name as he could get. It was a cheap form of advertising.

This emphasis on advertising was to be a main element of Callaway's business approach. Of his initial cash outlay of five hundred dollars, he spent all of it—with the exception of sixty dollars, which went to three months' store rent—on advertisements of various sorts. It was essential for him to get his name out to a public that currently gave its business to his established rivals. Before long he'd engaged in all sorts of methods, ranging from newspaper ads to posters or broadsides he nailed to trees and

than mere advertising; the pressure was on. Callaway had bought in volume so as to be able to sell cheaply, but given his terms with Conklin, he also had to sell fast. He had a greater amount and variety of tinware, at lower prices, than anyone else in town, and he let people know it. His goal was to turn over his entire stock as quickly as possible, and within a few weeks he'd done it, finishing off his campaign with his first grand closing sale.

The young businessman had succeeded as a store owner on his first try. He paid off the tinware company with time to spare. And

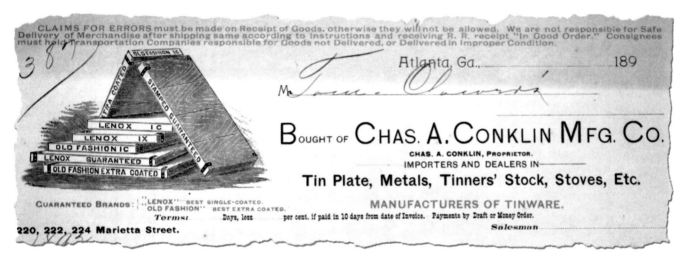

Fuller ordered large lots of tinware from the Charles A. Conklin Manufacturing Company in Atlanta so he could sell them at a discount to his customers.

poles all over the county to pamphlets that he spread around town, and even to discount coupons. Callaway believed, or at any rate soon came to believe, that advertising was extremely valuable even though it was also extremely expensive. But he was good at coming up with ways of advertising for free when he could. One example of this was the store's elaborate name. Another was his grand opening.

"The greatest free advertising in the world is a grand opening or grand closing," Callaway once told one of his sons. "If I had had a lot of capital, I would just have had one in my life, but since I didn't, I used to have one every month." Of course this tactic involved more

Fuller Callaway and Charles Conklin both died wealthy men.

～

Up to this point, Callaway had neither studied nor traveled much. On the other hand, he had been in a mercantile environment and talking with merchants for some years now. Whatever the explanation, by chance or design, he'd devised a business model that included some of the most important innovations of the country's greatest salesmen. Rowland Macy, Alexander Turney Stewart, John Wanamaker, and others had spent the previous generation revolutionizing retail sales

Advertisement promoting Callaway's Department Store in an 1895 edition of *The Graphic* newspaper.

in the large Northern cities. Now, with some modifications and refinements, Callaway pioneered their system in the small-town South.

The retailer of the 1800s had operated a general store. The only specialized retailers were in fields which required some highly technical knowledge, such as jewelry and pharmaceuticals (or physic, as it was then known). But by midcentury, specialization had come into fashion.

The machines of the Industrial Revolution could turn out goods at much faster rates than could the craftsmen of old, and new transportation networks, especially the railroads, could move those goods farther, faster, and cheaper than ever before. This meant that the main limits on commerce shifted from production to distribution, and as the rail system grew explosively, even this problem lessened, at least for the larger cities

and towns. The store owner of the late nineteenth century was able to supply more goods, in greater variety, than those of earlier generations. Variety was so great, in fact, that owners had to choose their stock carefully. The natural result of this was specialization in a single line of goods, such as tinware. Specialization, in turn, meant that the retailer could buy in large quantity, and thus at a discount that reflected economies of scale and allowed him to cut his prices, passing the savings on to his customers. This was precisely the model Fuller Callaway followed as he began his career as a store owner.

In this high-volume world, the retailer needed a fast turnover, since his sales margin was low. A mass demand for his goods was one of the things that made the new system work. This, too, was something Callaway understood. Long after his first load of tinware had left his store, he still used strategies geared to turning over his stock at a fast pace. And the key to it all was advertising.

Fuller Callaway clearly understood the value of advertising from the moment he decided to spend nearly all of his cash on it when he first opened his five-and-dime store. He chanced to open that store when an advertising revolution was about to begin. Advertising as an industry did not yet exist, but it was on the verge of creation. "Without imagination, no wants," Katherine Fisher, a pioneer in the ad industry, declared in 1899. "Without wants, no demand to have them supplied." In other words, as the would-be seller envisioned things, good advertising captured the imagination, which created the demand for the product.

Callaway took an approach to advertising that was suited to a smaller community. Like the new wave of modern advertisers, who drew heavily on the visual arts, he spent a lot of his money on posters and flyers. But he used other methods as well. For his grand openings and closings, he would hire people to stand along the street, equipping each of them with a tin pan and iron rod for banging, to get the attention of passersby. And he didn't limit this sort of showmanship to opening and closings. On Saturdays, when a lot of county dwellers were in town, he would sometimes put up a greased pole outside his store with something valuable at the top, such as a pair of shoes. He would also set up a table on the sidewalk with a selection of overalls. Since the country farmers were well-dressed for their trip into town, they would naturally buy the overalls in order to try their chances at climbing the pole.

When the crowds weren't already in town, Callaway had no problem enticing them to show up. He once enlisted the help of a well-known town slacker who obligingly ran an ad in the newspaper. "Wanted," the ad read, "A white mule named Maude, about 15 to 16 hands, weight about 1,000 lbs., that I would enjoy plowing. Will pay $200.00 cash. If you have a mule that meets this description, meet me in front of Callaway's Store Saturday."

On the appointed day, people started arriving at the store with white mules named Maude. Callaway's man would then ask each mule's owner about the animal's height and weight, agreeing that it fit nearly every specification the ad mentioned—except one. To each claimant, the slacker would finally state, "I just don't believe I would enjoy plowing that mule." But by then, of course, the crowds would be at Callaway's door.

Callaway always had an eye open for the chance opportunity, and advertisement was no exception. On one occasion a traveling merry-go-round had arrived in Newnan, where its owners' hoped for business had been rained out. The owners ended up lacking money enough to move on. Callaway heard about their predicament and went to Newnan.

"I'll pay freight on the merry-go-round from Newnan to LaGrange and pay freight from LaGrange to the next place to get you started again," he told the owners. "But the two weeks you are in LaGrange, nobody rides on that merry-go-round except who I say."

"O.K.," answered one of the owners, and that was that.

Callaway had the merry-go-round set up in the courthouse square near his five-and-dime. Then he began handing out tickets in his store, one ticket for each dollar a customer spent.

In short, Fuller Callaway's style of advertising was an extension of his own personality—gregarious, playful, but with a serious purpose. There were other sides to Callaway too, and these also found expression in how he did business.

Specialization, as new mass-buying markets developed, meant that the seller needed high-volume sales and high turnover. To ensure these things, he had to sell at low margins, making only a small profit on each item he sold. This in turn required him either to buy at especially low prices or sell at low prices. Callaway, exactly in the manner of earlier innovators such as Rowland Macy, did both.

As for buying, Callaway's first purchases of tinware, towels, and such in job lots had been Macy's early New York practice, and Macy also had emphasized (even to his customers) the need for high turnover. Macy cited in his own advertisements the link between his high-volume purchases and his low sales prices. Callaway did this as well, at least partly. "Our terms are strictly cash," reads one of his early ads. "Our prices are strictly low." To prove it, Callaway, as had Macy, took the step of listing in the rest of the ad the actual prices of particular goods—a measure almost unheard of in Macy's time and still rare in Callaway's.

These ads reveal still more about innovations in the retail world that Callaway both shrewdly understood and enthusiastically adopted. One such innovation was his insistence on cash payment.

Fuller Callaway had an abhorrence of personal debt, and he was strict about his business debts. He showed a corresponding reluctance to extend credit to his retail customers, especially in his early years, probably for a number of reasons.

First, as astute as Callaway was, he probably realized that in his era a huge number of retail concerns—as many as half or even two-thirds—closed within three years of opening, and many of these business failures were due to customer credit problems. This was a danger that Callaway would naturally have tried to avoid. But more than that, it was a likely concern for his customers, or to put it more abstractly, the community. Time after time in his career, Callaway not only gave a great deal back to LaGrange, Troup County, and west Georgia, but he also showed a great interest in teaching his employees and fellow citizens how to fish, investing in programs that would help them make more of themselves. His requirement of cash transactions, or at least very short-term credit of less than two weeks, was in retrospect one of the earliest examples of this interest in the community. He was a maverick in refusing to sell on credit; not many businesses were cash only prior to the end of the First World War. The credit restrictions might sting, but the sting was lessened by Callaway's discount prices, and the long-term benefits of avoiding the

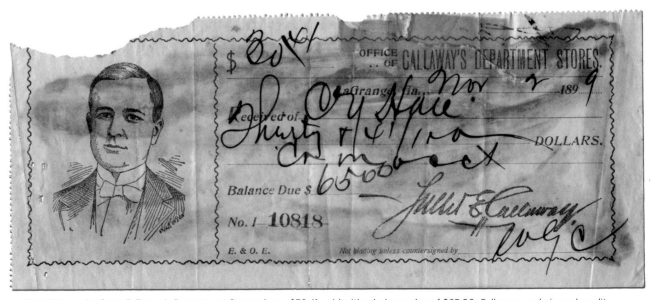

This 1899 receipt from Callaway's Department Stores shows $30.41 paid with a balance due of $65.00. Callaway rarely issued credit, but apparently trusted this customer to make payment in full.

Fuller Callaway established his first store in 1888 on West Court Square in LaGrange. This picture includes store workers gathered around Fuller's half brother Ely Callaway, who managed the store.

credit trap were great for a town whose citizens needed to save every penny they could.

But even this was not all. The set prices that Callaway dared to quote in his ads show yet another innovation: the one-price system.

Before the modern consumer age, the word "bargain" found much more use as a verb than as a noun. It described the haggling process between buyer and seller. The reason for bargaining lay in the fact that goods weren't standardized until the industrial age, and in cash-poor regions, bartering rather than selling for money was common. Even when cash was involved, there was more equality between buyer and seller. A sale was a highly personalized thing, and often a seller would fix his final prices based on the buyer's perceived ability to pay.

But that began changing with the arrival

of mass-produced goods sold on low margin. The great immigrant merchant Alexander Turney Stewart, founder of the biggest stores in mid-nineteenth-century America, pioneered a new system in his new country shortly before Callaway's birth, a system of standardized prices; now Callaway brought it to rural Georgia. As time passed, moreover, and Callaway's store grew and he hired assistants, he ran into the same problem that Stewart and other successful proprietors before him had faced: he couldn't be everywhere at the same time. Fuller Callaway had an extraordinary talent for selling that few employees would be likely to match. In order to continue to have input into sales concluded by others, then, he had to standardize prices and take away his employees' discretion.

By actually labeling a product with a nonnegotiable price, Callaway helped his store grow, because it let him rely on an inexperienced (and thus a relatively low-paid) staff. Even if he'd been able to find someone who had a talent for sales that equaled his own, that talent would have come at a high salary. Setting fixed prices let him hire more people, allowing his profits to trickle down through the community. It was a pattern that Callaway would follow over and over again in his lifetime, to LaGrange's great benefit.

The one-price system, as it was known, at first often involved the use of a special code on the price tag to remind a storekeeper of his own set price, rather than listing the actual price in a way that the customer could read. Such a code, for instance, might print letters on the tag, with each letter having a number value. An example of one common code was

V A N D E R B I L T
1 2 3 4 5 6 7 8 9 0

A price tag bearing the code BE, for instance, would tell the seller that the price was seventy-five cents. Other words commonly used for the code were "make profit," "Caleb Smith," and "Chelmsford." Callaway, too, used such a code to tell his employees how much the item had cost him: his was "Sunday Girl." He also used some special codes. A tag with the letters PM, for example, signified that whoever sold the attached item would earn a premium for the sale. It was Callaway's way of making sure that his stock, including slower-moving items, turned over quickly. But in addition to codes, Callaway also listed the selling price openly on the tag, so that the customer could see it. He was the first to do so in LaGrange; his listing of prices in his newspaper ads was merely an extension of this policy.

This one refinement shows how Callaway's policies were all part of an integrated system. Purchases of job

lots at special sales allowed him to set low prices and avoid credit trouble, using the one-price system to streamline the sales process. This streamlining helped ensure the high turnover he needed to achieve the profits that allowed him to buy at low prices and hire salesmen who would raise the sales volume—and thus profits—still further. The whole system was a smoothly oiled machine and a recipe for success.

~

Having sold all of his tinware, Callaway set out to repeat the pattern that had worked so well. This time he found his way to the North Carolina mill of James William Cannon, an up-and-coming textile maker. In 1898 the Cannon Manufacturing Company began milling the first towels anywhere in the South, but according to Callaway's son, Cannon sold Fuller a carload of cloth suitable for

Cash Register made by National Cash Register Company for Fuller E. Callaway.

towels well before then. Cannon, like Conklin before him, was having sales trouble, which made Callaway's offer attractive. The young shop owner bought the cloth in rolls just as they'd come off the loom, uncut and un-hemmed, which saved Cannon a good bit of trouble and Callaway a good bit of money. Shipping the cloth to LaGrange, Callaway then cut the rolls into towels himself. String-ing wires across his store, he hung up all the newly cut towels rather than folding and stacking them, making the store seem as if it were bursting with stock.

Again he began advertising; Again he put on a grand-opening spectacle. And again the system worked out. According to an old say-ing, if someone does something twice in the South, it becomes a tradition. So Callaway kept up the pattern, and after another repeti-tion or two, he had peoples' attention. County residents and customers from nearby commu-nities were soon traveling to LaGrange to see what Callaway's latest purchase had been. His success was beginning to build on itself.

But there was always a risk, and one of his buy-and-sell cycles nearly had a very bad end-ing. The main danger in Callaway's system of specialization and bulk purchases was that with every cycle he was putting all of his eggs into one basket, betting all his credit as well as his capital that he'd be able to find enough buyers. A miscalculation in even a single cycle would wipe him out. After a half dozen profitable cycles, his number came up, and as so often happens in business, it was due to something unforeseeable: a hard freeze late in the spring.

It was May, and summer with its promise of ripe, sweet fruit was barely a month away.

The large elephants atop Mr. Callaway's retail store attracted attention and drew customers.

Callaway knew that ripe fruit meant preserving and canning all over the South, so he bought a huge load of fruit jars on two months' credit.

Then came the disaster. On May 25, La-Grange experienced one of the latest freezes in its history. Icicles were hanging from roofs. The freeze spelled the doom of every berry and peach in Troup County. Callaway's jars were suddenly worthless.

Obviously the desperate merchant had to do something. He ended up traveling to America's rising business capital, New York City. Having convinced the railroad to give him a free pass based on his earlier carload shipments, he arrived in the metropolis with no fixed plan but with his usual eye for opportunity.

This was almost certainly Callaway's first trip to New York and, just as likely, his first journey outside the South. Perhaps it was even the first time he'd left Georgia. He was to become quite familiar with New York, and eventually he would be a prosperous world traveler, but for now he was just one poor young seller—and perhaps buyer—among many.

Avoiding the streetcars, which cost money, Callaway eventually found himself walking through a cheap manufacturing district. As he walked, a sign caught his eye: black pepper manufacturer. Obviously nothing was wrong with the actual fruit jars; they could still hold something, such as black pepper. But how did one *manufacture* black pepper? Intrigued, Callaway entered the basement of the indicated building, only to find quite an odd setup.

A man was busy grinding up coconut hulls, to which he was adding not black pepper but cayenne—just enough to make the concoction taste hot. No peppercorns were involved. Perhaps the mixture was black, though, which might have been enough to justify the name in an age before heavy regulation of advertising. But the public was smarter than that; nobody was buying the product. Of course, this was a story Callaway

had heard more than once, from people such as Charles A. Conklin and James William Cannon. The lack of sales meant that the price was right, so he bought a carload of the stuff and shipped it down to LaGrange.

In order to get the best rates from the railroad, Callaway listed the shipment as fertilizer on the bill of lading. This bothered him not at all; ground-up coconut hulls, he reasoned, would probably make excellent fertilizer. And if the product failed to sell, he probably thought, it likely *would* end up being used as fertilizer.

But how to market it to his customers? That was a bigger problem, for Callaway did have qualms about calling it black pepper. Filling all of his fruit jars with the concoction, he settled on calling it by the curious name of "half p pepper." Since there were three Ps in *pepper*, he thought, and there was so little cayenne in the mixture, a sharp reduction in the number of Ps would be just about right. Then he set out his fruit jars inside his store with the price of a dime per quart jar.

Somehow he sold the strange product. In fact, the jars sold so well, and he had so much of the "pepper," that he got hold of a wagon and traveled the country stores, buying out their stocks of useless fruit jars at wholesalers' prices. This let him sell the rest of the "pepper" even more cheaply. Ultimately he ran through all of the stuff, but his wholesale fruit jar purchases were too lucrative to abandon. Traveling to north Georgia, he found a supply of cooking soda and snatched up a carload, pouring it into a fresh batch of quart jars. Business was booming.

Although Callaway's fruit-jar venture had a happy ending, he'd had a close call. No doubt he now realized, even if he hadn't before, the danger of sinking all of his resources into a single product. Perhaps, too, his trip to New York had opened his eyes to the epochal change in retailing that the Industrial Revolution had spawned. It would

The lobby of the Prince George Hotel, where Fuller Callaway often stayed during his early business trips to New York City.

have been natural for the La-Grange salesman to take in Alexander Turney Stewart's legendary Marble Palace and the lavish window displays of Macy's on Fourteenth Street. Even long afterward, Woolworth's held a special fascination for him. "I always went to Woolworth's store on Sixth Avenue to see what Woolworth had," an older, established Callaway once said. The phenomenon must have been fascinating to a man who was a born salesman. The large retailers had moved beyond specialization and even beyond the cramped world of the general store. They had in fact created something new to the world of sales: the modern spectacle known as the department store.

Such a store appealed to Callaway in at least two ways, probably three, and possibly more. First, diversification of stock would be a good safeguard against the danger of another hard freeze, so to speak. Second, the greater regularity of a continuously operating business, rather than the taxing cycle of openings and closings, was appealing now that he was building up respectable capital. The third thing was probably the glamour of the inherent advertisement that was built into the department store with its dazzling array of goods, its architecture and appointments, and the eye appeal of its windows. Such things wouldn't be lost on Callaway.

Before long he took the plunge. Business continued to boom, and he was soon hiring people to help. By the end of the decade he had fourteen employees.

While from the beginning Callaway bought and sold in regional markets, and eventually national ones, sometimes his products were literally homegrown, or at least county-grown. On one occasion he advertised for interested persons to pick blackberries on

halves. Blackberries grew wild, so many poorer members of the community, mostly black, went out with buckets and brought the berries to Callaway's store. Callaway got half of the berries and bought the other half from the pickers, perhaps with store credit instead of a cash outlay. It went much more smoothly than had his first venture into the world of fruit with his mass purchase of quart jars.

But for the most part Callaway shipped his goods in from considerable distances, and being his own principal buyer, he traveled a great deal. As his staff grew he found travel easier. But one aspect of running a department store bothered him. Because he no longer bought such huge lots of goods, as he had in the beginning with his specialty store, he no longer got the lowest prices on the things he bought.

So in the end he found a way to get the prices he wanted. Modern industry, combined with the railroad, had brought forth the modern hotel and the age of the traveling salesman, and his counterpart, the corporate buyer. Whenever Callaway went to New York in those years, he would usually stay at places such as the Prince George Hotel, or as he called it "the wagon yard," probably because of all of the other commercial agents who stayed there. This throng of potential buyers gave him an idea. When calling on wholesalers, rather than buying the relatively small quantities of goods he planned to sell in his own store, he would purchase an option on job lots of products—just large enough to get him the best prices. In the evening, after several such deals, he would return to his lodgings. Taking a chair on the sidewalk, or perhaps in the lobby, he would either join or start up a conversation with others who were in town to buy, drawing on his native ability to tell stories and relate to nearly anyone. Then, at some point, he would get down to business. "By the way," he might ask, "anybody need any sheets?" Often several people showed an interest. He would then sell them parts of his optioned job lot, at prices higher than he would pay with the option but still lower than the other merchants would pay for small orders. He'd keep up the work until he'd disposed of all the goods he'd optioned, except for the amounts he wanted for his own LaGrange store. The next morning he would return to the wholesalers and exercise all of the options, giving the sellers the shipping addresses he'd collected the evening before. He had, in effect, become a jobber in order to get the best prices for his retail concern.

From there it was a short and logical step to the full-scale wholesale business. Being based in LaGrange, Callaway decided that his natural customers would be retailers in nearby towns. So he began to approach them. He found that

Cast-iron seal stamp embosser from the Fuller E. Callaway Company, which operated Callaway's wholesale outlets. The decorative top features a lion's head.

most were set in their ways when it came to how they bought goods. "Callaway's all right enough, and the goods are all right," he once overheard from a retailer, "but I just don't care to do business with that small a man."

The obvious way around this objection was for Callaway to become a visibly larger concern, and while he was at it, to show that he knew his trade. So with his LaGrange department store well-established, he began opening other stores in nearby communities, going head-to-head with the men who thought him too small.

For his openings, he dusted off and delved into his old bag of advertising tricks, adding some new ones as well. One of the best was a hot-air balloon ascension, which really got people's attention. And as he opened more stores—a second, a third, then a fourth—he found it easier to buy at wholesale rates for his own retail trade, thus undercutting his competitors.

In the face of the competition that Callaway presented, and the undeniable fact that his was a big operation, the established retailers gave up and started approaching him for their wholesale requirements. Eventually Callaway closed his non-LaGrange stores, having made his point clearly, while at the same time expanding the wholesale side of his business. Before he was done, he was supplying buyers in thirty-six states.

All of this meant expansion of staff, and it was during these years that Callaway formed some of the most important friendships and business relationships of his life. But foremost among them was a young lady named Ida Jane Cason.

The daughter of Alexander Toombs Cason and the former Miss Olivia Pratt Jewell, Ida was not from LaGrange. She'd traveled there from the tiny community named for her mother's family on the eastern

Fuller's future wife, Ida Jane Cason, was from Jewell, Georgia.

Portrait of Ida Jane Cason while she was attending Southern Female College.

side of the state: Jewell was not far from the rail line between Atlanta and Augusta, closer to the latter than the former. A teenager, two years younger than Fuller, Ida had come to LaGrange to attend Southern Female College, where Abner Callaway had once taught.

The college, with an enrollment of about two hundred women from nearly a dozen states, was one of five Baptist institutions of higher learning to be found in Georgia at the time, all of them except Mercer University being schools for women. Southern, founded in the 1840s, was particularly well thought of, described by one scholar around the time of Ida's attendance as "first among many, and second to few schools for the higher education of females in the Southern states." Even Fuller had gone there briefly, for the school had a co-educational "primary department" in addition to the women's college-level curriculum. What was more, a cousin of Fuller's happened to be Ida's roommate. It was this cousin who introduced the two of them at a college function.

Though still a young man at not quite age twenty, Fuller was undoubtedly taking on his adult personality and appearance. At 5'10", he tended to be considerably overweight in maturity, though at this stage, if that was already the case, he no doubt carried it well and with great energy. His hair was dark brown, his voice somewhat deep and resonant. His striking blue eyes revealed energy, enthusiasm, and good humor. He made quite an impression on Ida, and Ida certainly made one on him.

As time passed, the romance bloomed. Fuller and Ida both likely attended the same Baptist church—perhaps Ida was even the Sunday Girl who inspired the code for Fuller's pricing system—and Ida likely shopped at Fuller's store. Fuller also made use of his younger half brother Ely, who like Fuller before him, was taking classes at Southern, to carry notes to Ida on campus. Sometimes, instead of notes, he sent bananas, which were still an exotic treat in west Georgia.

For her part, Ida loved reading a publication in which Fuller had a hand, a newspaper published by a group of LaGrange youths. Its name was the "Buzz Saw" because, as Ida explained, it "ripped folks up the back going and coming. . . . No one could have any secrets while the 'Buzz Saw' flourished. It was no respecter of persons." One can't imagine Fuller Callaway writing maliciously about townspeople—he appears not to have had a malicious bone in his body—and at any rate such writing would have been bad for his business. More likely it was probably an organ for good-natured mischief, and indications are it focused on campus life, particularly the doings of the editors' college girlfriends. Certainly the ladies of Southern, Ida included, were always eagerly waiting to see what the next issue held, especially since the contents always irked the school's professors.

By 1891 Ida had consented to wed Fuller, who by now was heavily into running his store. His work, in fact, led to a bit of premarital

Southern Female College, LaGrange, Ga.

Fuller Callaway met Ida Jane Cason while she was attending Southern Female College.

drama. Ida, quite naturally, wanted the wedding to take place in Jewell, nearly two hundred miles from LaGrange. But Fuller objected. "You're already here," he commented, "so let's just get married here." The problem, as he saw it, was that a Jewell wedding would mean an absence of at least a few days from the store.

But Ida was adamant, so Fuller gave in—to a point. "All right," he said. "I'll marry in Jewell, Georgia under one condition and that is that we marry at half past eleven in a morning—not tomorrow morning," he clarified, "but a morning."

"That's a crazy time to get married," Ida observed. But in the end she agreed to the condition.

Fuller had chosen the time with great care. Train schedules had become very regular by the 1890s, and Fuller now put that fact to good use. He planned to close his store on the evening of April 27, 1891, the eve of the wedding. He would then travel by rail to Atlanta and from there catch the train to Augusta. Leaving the train at Sparta, he could then take a hack up to Jewell. If the schedules held, he'd arrive at the church at 11:15 on April 28.

But that was just half the equation. If the service went quickly, Fuller calculated, he and his new bride could then get to the train station in nearby Warrenton in time to catch the Atlanta-bound train, spending their wedding night in the capital and catching the early train back to LaGrange. Fuller could then promptly reopen his store, having had to close it for only a single day.

The schedule did work, and everything came off as planned. But even that wasn't the end of Fuller's plans. As the train pulled into Atlanta on the couple's wedding night, Fuller brought up the question of lodging. "We don't want to start out wrong," he observed. "We don't want to go to a hotel tonight and waste money."

It wasn't a very romantic thing for him to say, but Ida heard him out. "Now I've got a brother who lives here in Atlanta"—his brother Howard Callaway—"and he has a perfectly good home and we'll just spend the night with him." Almost incredibly, Ida agreed.

And even more was to come. After supper, Fuller and Howard began talking business. Eleven o'clock arrived and the conversation showed no signs of slowing. At that point Howard's wife, Lula, seeing the writing on the wall, spoke up. "Ida," she told the new bride, "I know you are tired, so don't you want to come on up and get some rest?" So as the men continued to talk, Ida went upstairs, spending her wedding night with her new sister-in-law.

Lula woke Ida at four o'clock the next morning, and the women found their husbands still in front of the fire talking, having never made it to bed. The newlyweds caught the 5 a.m. train for LaGrange, and upon their arrival, Fuller and Ida took a carriage from the station. Fuller had it drive him straight to the store, where he alighted and sent it on to the house with the luggage and Ida. The new bride next saw Callaway around midnight, after a usual day at the store. And so began her married life. "Thirty-seven years later," Ida wrote of the wedding day, "we both still felt it was the best day's work we ever did."

The statement was accurate, given the devotion that Fuller and Ida had for each other. But it was also remarkable, especially since that day was typical of many to come. Fuller gave his business priority, or at the very least put it on a par with his marriage. Decades later, one of his sons noted "two amazing things" about the marriage. "One was how father put business first and the second was how mother put up with it."

Fuller was clearly what a later age would term a workaholic. During his early adult years, he regularly worked sixteen-hour days and usually got home around midnight. In fact, one of the anecdotes Callaway sometimes told had a basis in his own work habits. It concerned Willie, a black night watchman at LaGrange's first electrical plant, although sometimes the details changed from telling to telling. After several years with no incidents, the watchman was injured on the job and sued the mill. At the trial, the mill's attorney questioned him. "Now, Willie, tell the truth about this matter. Isn't it true that you just dropped off to sleep and were awakened by the noise of something wrong, so put your hand in the wrong place?"

"Well, boss," answered Willie, at least as Callaway put it, "it might've been that I dropped off to sleep just a little . . . but that ain't no wonder," he explained, "because I work for that heartless corporation twenty-five hours a day."

"That couldn't be," interjected the lawyer, pouncing on the exaggeration, "because there are only twenty-four hours in a day."

"Yes sir, boss," replied Willie, "but I get up an hour *before* day." The same was true of Fuller Callaway, even though he worked for himself.

Of course, Callaway loved eating almost as much as he loved working. Fruit was a favorite of his, and he would often start the day with an entire soup bowl of peaches or fresh berries, followed by a whole cantaloupe. But for well over a decade that would be his last daily meal at home. He would stay at the store through lunch as well as supper; Ida got used to sending hot meals to her husband there. It was a lifestyle that clearly reflected her husband's favorite saying:

Late to bed, early to rise,
work like hell and economize.

The newlyweds' living arrangements also followed the saying, showing frugality from the beginning. For the first several months of their marriage, they stayed in Fuller's old lodgings, that is, with Enoch and Fanny Callaway. After that they moved in with another couple, Mr. and Mrs. Warren Seay, living in what was commonly known as the Huntley Place, on the corner of Broad and North Greenwood Streets, partly because Ida did not like to be alone during Fuller's long hours at work. The two couples hit it off so well that when they changed accommodations they stayed together, moving one block up Broad Street to the corner of North Lewis Street. The arrangement later survived yet another move, again of a single block, this time up North Lewis to the corner of Haralson Street, when the couples bought what was then called the Owens lot, the present site of the First Presbyterian Church. Eventually, with both men's businesses doing well and more room being needed, the Seays sold out to the Callaways and moved into a house of their own.

Even so, Fuller was still mindful about not spending too much on housing and other living costs, even as his success and wealth grew. While all of the Callaway homes thus far had been downtown, Ida still wanted to keep up

Fuller (far right), Ida (far left), and their elder son Cason (sitting on a fence post) pose for a photograph in front of their Haralson Street home. The extensive plantings suggest an early interest in gardening. The man next to Fuller is his brother, Pope Callaway.

with the Joneses, although the Joneses were apparently outspending their budget, so she asked Fuller one day about the possibility of buying a carriage and horses.

"That reminds me of a good story I once heard about another couple who were on the way up," Fuller remarked. According to the story, he claimed, a wife had similarly gone to her husband about transportation. "Dear, most every one of our friends has a family carriage and pair," Fuller quoted the wife as saying. "Don't you think we're able to have that convenience?"

The husband thought about it for a few moments. "Yes, dear . . .," he responded. He paused, and then concluded, "Let's *stay* able."

Ida apparently got the point, dropping the subject. But Fuller got the point too, and not long after the conversation he went to Atlanta to see his brother Howard, telling him what had happened.

"Of course Ida was right," Howard

declared. "I'll bet you're better able to than any of your friends to support a carriage and pair." Howard then located an excellent carriage and a single fine horse for his little brother. Fuller no doubt saw it as an excellent investment—in his marriage.

And Fuller did see the arrangement through the filter of his business life and experience. His love for Ida notwithstanding, in many ways he saw his marriage in economic terms. Once, just after returning from a trip to New York, he was at work in his office when Ida arrived in the carriage and invited him for a ride. "Awfully sorry, Ida," Fuller called from the door of his office. "I can't leave just now. See you tonight." Then back to work he went.

The exchange naturally bothered his wife, and she said so at dinner. "Fuller," she told him, "I was disappointed about what happened this afternoon and don't quite understand it. I'll bet if I had been Aunt Anna

Priddy"—an elderly, wealthy businesswoman who had often had dealings with Callaway— "you would have at least taken time enough to go out to the carriage and speak to me."

"You're perfectly right, Ida," Fuller conceded. "You see, she's a customer, and you— you're my partner."

But if this was true, then in business terms at least, Ida was the junior partner. Early in the couple's married life, Fuller, as the only one with income, gave Ida a weekly allowance of $6.25 to cover household expenses. But early in the arrangement, just after a move to new quarters, when he returned home Saturday evening, he found Ida sitting and crying. "What's the matter?" he asked.

It was about the allowance. She had gone over budget, spending an entire dollar more than she had.

Fuller didn't want to fight about money, but he decided that if he simply gave Ida the dollar, she would have no incentive to stay within budget in the many weeks to come. He could foresee the deficits growing each week. At some point there would indeed be a fight, and it would be over more than a dollar.

"Honey, that's nothing to cry about," he said. "You started with nothing, and look at the money you had to spend for soap powders to clean the place up and get started. You won't have that every week. You had unusual organization expenses. In addition to that," he continued, speaking in the vein of a business partner, "you started with no inventory and now you have an inventory. You've got a little flour in the sack; you've got a little pepper in the box, and you don't need to worry. You aren't going to have any trouble from now on."

All this was preparation for how Fuller planned to deal with the problem. "I'll tell you what I'll do," he said, getting to the heart of the matter. "You have to amortize those things over a period of time. You can't stand your whole organizational expenses in one week.

I'll lend you a dollar and you can pay me back by the week."

The approach worked. Fuller tendered the dollar, Ida stopped crying, and she made weekly ten-cent payments for the next two and a half months. According to Ida, it was the last conversation the couple ever had about money.

Perhaps she should have said that it was the last unpleasant, or potentially confrontational, conversation about money, for other monetary discussions did happen from time to time. Ida learned a useful lesson, and thereafter she managed to make her allowance last the whole week. At first this meant that she sometimes ended the week with nothing but salt and pepper remaining, but there is no evidence that Fuller ever complained about what she did or didn't put on the table, or about any other aspect of how she ran her house. Over time the allowance increased, and Ida began managing to save a bit here and there. Whenever she accumulated fifty dollars, Fuller would match the funds with fifty more, and then the couple would use the money to buy stock. "It was always a 'gala day' when I could turn over the fifty to him," Ida reminisced happily in her later years. Money conversations thus took place, but they seemed to have been good ones.

The idea of Fuller as the senior partner may rankle modern readers, but we should remember that nineteenth-century marriages weren't the same as early twenty-first century ones. Even well into the 1800s, when women married, their separate existence in the eyes of the law simply ceased. Legally, as the common law saying went, when a couple wed they became one—and the husband was the one. In 1890s Georgia this was no longer strictly true, but much of that mind-set remained. Viewed in this light, the marriage of Fuller and Ida wasn't unusual. The only remarkable thing was that Fuller was a workaholic who saw his marriage as a component of his work life, and probably not the most important component at that.

~

Despite this somewhat unorthodox approach to marriage, Fuller was devoted to Ida. One of the stories that shows this most clearly involves the couple's first anniversary. When Fuller got home from the store, near midnight as usual, he found Ida waiting for him. "What's the matter?" he asked.

"I'm sitting up waiting for you," Ida said. "It's our anniversary," she reminded him. "We've been married a year today."

Fuller took the hint and sat down with her next to the fire, and the couple talked for a while. "We've been married a year today," Ida repeated, "and neither one of us has told the other one a single fault or a single thing that the other could do to improve himself." Obviously she was working up to something. "I think once a year we ought to have a moss scraping," she finally said.

"All right," replied Fuller. "It's your idea, so you scrape first."

"Well, there's just one thing I would change about you," Ida admitted. "I just wish you wouldn't chew quite so much tobacco."

"All right, what else?"

"That's all; nothing else. Now you scrape."

"Darling," Fuller told her, "I wouldn't change a hair on your head."

It was the last moss scraping the couple ever had.

~

Another important point is that while Fuller enjoined Ida to be frugal, he imposed that frugality on himself as well. In that respect the two were equals, with no double standard. Working hard to live within his means, Fuller was concerned that he and Ida as a couple never overextend. This was true of their living quarters as well as their board. Despite the early changes of household, the pair apparently never went into the red. Fuller referred to West Haralson Street, where they lived after the Seays moved on, as "Cash Street," because, as he explained, "No one would give credit to the people who lived on it," but also apparently to emphasize the need to stay on a cash basis and avoid the credit trap. He had bought the house there for $1,200, and he and Ida continued to live there for years after they could have moved to what he termed "Mortgage Avenue." And even after the Seays moved out, he and Ida did not live alone.

For one thing, there were the visitors—frequent ones. Fuller genuinely liked people. One can imagine him, and not Will Rogers, as the originator of the saying about never having met a man he didn't like. And he would usually invite people he met to visit. On the occasions when he came home to lunch, which became more common as he grew more established, he often brought people with him with little or no notice to Ida. It bothered her not at all. She would simply duck into the kitchen to tell the cook—once she had one—"Put some more water in the soup." The couple enjoyed having people around. On business trips Fuller would often issue open invitations for people to drop in on him; as a result, salesmen and other businessmen would frequently call without warning, always finding a warm welcome and a hot meal. The Callaway home was always a beehive of activity.

And those were just the visitors. In 1893 Callaway's father Abner died, but Fuller and Ida produced their firstborn the following year, maintaining the equilibrium. In a time-honored tradition, since the new arrival bore his father's surname, his given names reflected his mother's line; his parents named him Cason Jewell. And Cason was soon surrounded by aunts, uncles, and cousins, some of whom moved in with the family just as Fuller had moved in with Enoch and Fanny.

Over time, in fact, more than a dozen relatives lived with Fuller and Ida, often going to work in one of Fuller's concerns and learning what had become the family business.

And with Fuller, there was little distinction between "family" and "business," as his marriage to Ida had quickly revealed. The street ran both ways, as shown by his relationship with his half brother Ely.

A decade or so younger than Fuller, Ely was the first child born to Abner and his second wife, Mary. He would become a prime example of a hardworking Callaway who learned the family operation from the bottom up. When Fuller first hired him, the boy was around ten; the proprietor put him to work running errands and minding the cash. Other than hiring Ely, Fuller showed the boy no favoritism and expected him to behave himself.

One night, though, Ely acted up. A delicacy that Fuller sold on Saturday was fresh oysters, which of course had practically no shelf life. So when Saturday evening arrived, if any oysters remained, he and his staff would take them into the back of the store, mix them with milk, and turn them into oyster stew. All of the men would then sit around in the back visiting and telling stories—and likely talking more than a little business, since it was Fuller Callaway's operation—while eating oyster stew along with crackers from the barrel.

All of them, that is, except Ely. One Saturday night shortly after hiring the boy, Fuller summoned everyone else to the back and then addressed his younger brother. "Ely, you stay up here in front while we go back and eat oyster stew," he directed. "Then when we get through, you can come back there."

Frustrated, Ely minded the store while the sounds of the party drifted up from the back. Hearing the talking, joking, and laughter, he began to feel sorry for himself. By the time Fuller came up front, Ely was in a dark mood.

"All right, Ely," Fuller said cheerfully, "you can go back and get your stew now."

"Brother Fuller, I don't want any stew," Ely declared sullenly.

"What's the matter? Do you feel sick?"

"No," Ely told him. "If I can't eat with you all, I just won't eat any stew."

Fuller didn't like Ely's tone, so without fanfare he picked the boy up by the seat of his pants, carried him to the back, and dunked his head into the stew. "You want any stew, Ely?" he asked.

"No sir, brother Fuller," sputtered Ely. "I don't want any stew."

Fuller dunked him again. "You want any stew, Ely?"

Again Ely said no, so Fuller dunked him a third time. "You want any stew, Ely?"

Ely gave in. "I thank you for some stew, brother Fuller," he gasped.

~

Ely, like many adolescents, did need other occasional adjustments. One day when he was ducking out a lot from his post at the cashier's cage to shoot marbles behind the store with some of his friends, Fuller noticed and challenged him. Ely claimed that he had been leaving the cage to go to the bathroom, but Fuller knew better. So he went to the hardware department and came back to the cage with a large pot. He put it into the cage and chained it in place. "Now you won't have to go in the backyard."

In time, though, Ely ripened into a responsible and capable worker who showed proper deference to his employer. In fact, he even showed too much deference, and Fuller had to teach him a different sort of lesson. Shortly after Fuller had promoted him to the position of credit manager, one of the salesmen reported to Ely that a particular customer wanted to charge a bag of feed. Ely had his doubts about the man and went into Fuller's office to report on the problem. Sitting at his desk, Fuller listened to Ely, then stood up and smiled. "Who is the credit manager of Callaway Department Stores?" he asked. Then he sat back down and resumed his own work.

Ely made the decision, and he always remembered the moment as a valuable experience.

Of course, Fuller didn't limit his employees to family. Another youngster he hired in the early- or mid-1890s was J. A. "Ab" Perry. Like Ely, Perry served in many different roles, and he soon became indispensable to Fuller. In fact, he was probably one of the people eating oyster stew with Fuller the night Ely got his dunking. Early on, Perry became the manager of the store's book department; later he became Fuller's personal secretary, as well as serving as secretary for several Callaway companies. He also grew to be a very close friend and so much a part of the Callaways' life that Fuller would sometimes absentmindedly call Ida "Ab."

Later in the 1890s Callaway made the acquaintance of another man who was to become part of the close-knit inner circle of the Callaway operation. Hatton Lovejoy, from the town of White Plains (not too far from Jewell), was fresh out of the University of Georgia with engineering and law degrees under his belt when he met Fuller Callaway in 1897. The young attorney had come to LaGrange to practice with his brother-in-law, Frank Harwell; some connection with Ida is not out of the question, given the small age difference between the two as well as their nearby hometowns. Lovejoy was a slightly built young man and no natural athlete, but he had played football as well as baseball in college with a resolve that was one of his strongest characteristics. (Day after day, the story went, the scrawny youth showed up for football practice despite the constant roughing up he endured, until his sheer grit won him his teammates' acceptance.) This trait impressed Callaway, who also liked Lovejoy's intelligence

Fuller hired his younger half brother Ely Callaway (1880–1956) to work in his department store. Ely would go on to become a very successful businessman later in life.

and his capacity for hard work and willingness to do it. In these regards, the two men were kindred spirits. From the late 1890s on, Callaway entered into few projects without turning to Lovejoy as an attorney or an advisor. In fact, the younger man—though he was not that much younger—became much like a son to Callaway.

And Lovejoy had a lot of work to do for Callaway. By the late 1890s, the proprietor's interests were diversifying, as were those of LaGrange. Just as Callaway had, the town was reaching out into the larger world in search of business opportunities. Callaway, though still quite young, was already making a name for himself in the community, so he

John Albert "Ab" Perry (1877–1965) was Fuller's right-hand man, and served as his personal secretary for many years.

naturally began to play a bigger role in town and county affairs. By around the turn of the century he was serving on the LaGrange board of trade, an early version of the chamber of commerce; this, according to one account, was how he had gotten to know Hatton Lovejoy. His department store was doing quite well; he'd even retained the Famous Mammoth Store, which he and Ida referred to simply as the "Famous," as a sort of bargain basement concern. His wholesale business, meanwhile, had made him known in commercial circles in dozens of states. The Atlanta & West Point Railroad, which ran through LaGrange, connected Troup County to the rest of the nation. And as Callaway and

LaGrange reached out to that nation, so, too, did America notice LaGrange.

During this age of the department store boom, Callaway was becoming a local and even a regional legend in sales. In fact, when he was only twenty-five, he was nearly recruited to Atlanta based on his reputation. A group of investors wanted to build a major department store in the 100 block of Peachtree Street, the eventual site of the Piedmont Hotel and later the current Equitable Building, and they wanted Callaway to run it for them. They prevailed on him to travel to the capital, where they made him a staggering offer. "We'll build the building," they told him. "We've got the land and we'll build the building. You get the architect and draw it up like you want it, and we'll furnish the money."

But that was just the beginning. "We'll give you an option on 49% of the stock," the investors continued, "and we will pay you twenty-five thousand dollars a year salary, and you come to Atlanta and build this store and operate it for us."

If Horatio Alger had been writing this story, this would have been the great rags-to-riches moment. The salary alone in that day and age was almost princely equivalent to well over a half million dollars annually by 2010 figures—and this for a twenty-five-year-old. And given the success of the proposed store, a likely result with Fuller in charge, the value of the stock option might well have dwarfed the salary. It was a phenomenal offer.

Callaway turned it down.

The reason he gave was simple. "I had rather be a big frog in a little pond," he explained, "than a little frog in a big pond." The statement is an interesting mix of self-effacement and self-recognition. Callaway wasn't selling himself short; on the contrary, he had grand plans, and the Atlanta job would have been too confining. Rather than turning his back on success, he was going after it on his own terms.

The turning point in Callaway's life, as he saw it, had been some years earlier, when Enoch had threatened to throw him out of the house if he quit his job rather than deliver goods to a black family. But the turning point for LaGrange may have been when Callaway said "no" to the Atlanta investors. It meant that the west Georgia town would be the beneficiary of, and even perhaps have a claim on, Callaway's resources: his vision, his energy, and eventually his wealth. Whether or not Callaway realized this when he turned down the Atlanta department store offer isn't certain. But in retrospect it was one of the most important decisions a LaGrangian ever made.

This decision came at around the same time that another big event took place in LaGrange. In April 1895, a group of Pennsylvania businessmen and their wives visited the town. The visit was rather mysterious; the newspaper suggested that the Pennsylvanians were on a scouting mission for some Northern industry. LaGrange went out of its way to accommodate and entertain the guests, lodging some of them in citizens' homes and even arranging a reception and concert by Southern Female College students. This attention from Northern investors was exactly the sort of thing LaGrange businessmen had been hoping for.

Five months later came the payoff. The newspaper announced that a new textile mill was to be built in town. There is no definite link between this project and the Pennsylvanians' visit the previous spring, but given the timing, and the press's announcement that secret planning had been underway for a while, some sort of connection seems likely.

At any rate, the proposed mill sounded impressive. A group of New England manufacturers, the story went, were retooling their mill to produce a new product, and they wanted to relocate their existing equipment, ostensibly in good condition, to another facility. Given LaGrange's proximity to cotton

Fuller met Hatton Lovejoy in the late 1890s and they became close business associates. Fuller rarely entered a business venture without Lovejoy's legal counsel and advice. Lovejoy (right) is pictured here with Hubert Quillian.

fields and its location on the main rail line between Atlanta and New Orleans, it seemed a good place for the new operation, so the New Englanders set things in motion. The complete plans detailed a three-story building more than four hundred feet long and one hundred feet wide, to be situated on land that had already been donated by the town. This Dixie Mills project, while apparently Northern in origin, was chartered by a combination of local residents and men from New Hampshire, simultaneously with the newspaper announcement. Now that the incorporators had a parcel of land and architectural drawings, the main thing they were looking for was local investment capital.

Dixie Cotton Mills, La Grange, Ga.
Photo by Schaub.

The Dixie Mill was Callaway's first foray into the textile business.

The townspeople did not disappoint them. Industry seemed the wave of the future, and a new mill meant workers coming to LaGrange from the country, complete with their requirements for food, clothing, and shelter. It also meant money flowing into the town from the mill's customers. Dixie Mills was, in short, a potential engine that could power the town's economic growth—in many different ways. And Fuller Callaway, with his eye for opportunity, was there.

Although not officially affiliated with the mill, he invested ten thousand dollars, all of his ready capital. According to his son Fuller Jr., he was making money so quickly from his other concerns by this time that his businesses couldn't absorb all of it. Dixie Mills seemed to be the perfect home for it. The five-figure sum must have made Callaway one of the mill's largest nonaffiliated investors.

Because of the solid community backing, the project moved ahead quickly. A year after the first public announcement, in the fall of 1896, Dixie Mills opened its doors. But then the trouble began.

Almost from its genesis, the mill needed more money than the owners and investors had planned for. The biggest problem was that of production costs; the owners found that they simply couldn't compete with their rivals. By now the New England mill owners who had sold the equipment to Dixie were nowhere to be found. After making the sale, they'd taken the money and left.

Gradually the truth became plain. The story of the Northern mill's retooling, the sources agree, was apparently fabrication. The equipment the New Englanders had sold to Dixie Mills was both obsolescent and worn out. In short, Dixie was a white elephant.

When Callaway awoke to the fact that he was about to lose his money, he decided to act. According to one account, Dixie's treasurer came to him and asked for his help. This story has Callaway refusing official involvement but working as a stockholder to try to salvage the mill. Another version states that it was Callaway who took the initiative. In this version he obtained a list of Dixie stockholders and then wrote a letter to each one of them, turning his salesman's powers on full. In this letter he declared that Dixie Mills was, in his son's words, "on the rocks" and about to collapse. He didn't know if it could be saved, but he did propose that if the shareholders give him their proxies, he would assume control of the operation and see what he could do. Since by now the name of Callaway was starting to be associated with the Nelson—or perhaps the Midas—touch, he gained the support of enough of the shareholders to give him control of more than fifty percent of the voting stock.

It was a start, but the road would remain long and hard. Ida recorded that Fuller tossed and turned at night, and that he got his first gray hairs from the ordeal. Still he threw himself into the project. Wielding the power of the shares he owned or controlled, he called a stockholders' meeting, electing himself (in the second version of the story) Dixie's president, vice president, secretary, and treasurer. Then the new executive fired the deadwood. Next he traveled to New England, which was still the heart of America's textile industry and the region with the most experience and best machinery. Using his skill at buying and selling that he had been honing for years in his retail and wholesale trades, he bought modern equipment for Dixie at the best prices he could and shipped it down to LaGrange.

Of course the building itself was new. That was something, anyway. So when Callaway arrived on-site to oversee the new machinery's installation and observed the old, useless equipment being brought down in the new elevator, he had a better idea. "That stuff isn't worth wearing out the elevator," Ab Perry heard him call out. "Throw it out the window." The junk was soon flying out of the mill's large second- and third-floor windows. Later, after the crisis had passed, townspeople would laugh when remembering the image of the equipment that they had once prized crashing onto the ground in order to save wear and tear on the mill's one good piece of machinery.

Because of the new equipment, Dixie was now at least a marginally competitive mill—or it could be, if Callaway could find buyers. But it was also handicapped by the large costs of the unanticipated new capital assets. To handle the first problem, Callaway went to New York, which by now was becoming familiar ground for him. There he got to know Jim Lane, Coit Johnson, and O. A. Barnard. These three men were the leading partners of J. H. Lane and Company, one of New York's largest cotton merchandising firms. Callaway and the men made a deal whereby the company agreed to sell Dixie Mills products. It was a major step toward recovery.

But there was little to be done about the second problem. Callaway's purchase of the new equipment clearly had been essential, but it still had to be paid for. Because of that purchase, Dixie survived as an independent company for another twenty years, at which point it was bought out by the Wellington Sears Company, but it would never be very profitable. Long before the Wellington Sears acquisition, however, Callaway sold his interest in Dixie. Within two years of saving the mill, in fact, seeing that it would never be a moneymaker, he liquidated his stock at about the same price he'd paid for it, advising others to get out as well.

Callaway and LaGrange had survived the ordeal relatively unscathed. In fact, as Ida noted, Callaway gained not only gray hairs from the episode but valuable experience with the textile industry as well. "That's when I learned to run a cotton mill," he later declared. "I cut my eyeteeth getting that mill in better condition."

That hard-earned wisdom was important. Callaway might have washed his hands of Dixie Mills, but the episode had opened doors for him. His involvement in textiles, as it turned out, was only just beginning.

FULLER EARLE CALLAWAY

·3·

COTTON

In 1874, four years after the death of Robert E. Lee and the birth of Fuller E. Callaway, a young journalist penned an editorial in the *Atlanta Herald* on what he called the "New South." It was essentially a response to Northerners' fears that the South was a dangerous place for Northern investments. The journalist, Henry W. Grady, took issue with those claims, and he would keep doing so for the rest of his brief life. By the time he died in 1889 he'd become America's most visible apostle of the New South, respected on both sides of the Mason-Dixon line.

For Grady, the Old South—the South of slavery and secession—had literally been a losing proposition. Its heavy focus on agriculture had helped doom the Confederacy's military chances against a fast-industrializing North. Grady knew that all too well: his father, not coincidentally a successful merchant of the sort that Callaway was soon to become, had been killed at Petersburg while serving as an officer under Lee. But the loss to the South wasn't just military. By putting all of its eggs into the agricultural basket, Grady argued, the South had enslaved itself to the North.

Grady, along with many other Southerners, wanted and planned to change this.

Impoverished, having lost the underpinnings of its economic system with the coming of the Thirteenth Amendment, the South had to turn to industry, Grady believed. It was the only way Southerners might become residents of something more than an economic colony of the North, gaining self-sufficiency and ultimately wealth.

There was no reason, Grady and others maintained, why the South couldn't keep its money at home by building southern factories to process raw southern materials. Iron foundries should be built near iron deposits; lumber mills should arise in the forests. And, of course—and this was key to the New South—the textile mills should come to the region that, even in the wake of the disastrous war, had a national monopoly on one of the world's most valuable crops: cotton.

The creation of the Dixie Cotton Mill in 1895, for all of the excitement in La-Grange that surrounded it, actually wasn't a revolutionary occurrence. Textile mills were springing up, it seemed, all over the southern Piedmont, the center of cotton production. Even Troup County had a history of

Henry W. Grady (1850–1889) coined the term "New South" in an 1874 editorial. He advocated industrial development as a solution to the South's postwar economic troubles.

and finished goods back south to the consumers when everything could be done at home in the South? As early as 1866, in fact, one New South proponent gave the movement a slogan when he declared that "the spindles and looms must be brought to the cotton fields." By 1880 it was happening.

And the South wanted everyone to know about it. In 1881 Atlanta hosted the International Cotton Exposition, the first of many such events in the South. The Atlanta exposition gave a huge boost to the Southern mills. It hosted more than a thousand exhibits, and nearly four thousand people a day came through its doors for the two and a half months it was open. One of the exposition's highlights came when workers picked some cotton within sight of the exhibitors and those attending, and by the end of the day turned it into a suit that Alfred H. Colquitt, Georgia's governor and a former Confederate general officer, proudly donned.

The exhibition was a time and a place for brainstorming and cross-pollination with an eye to improving production. When it ended, its buildings were promptly converted into a mill that went on to operate for

textile production that was nearly a half century old by the time the Dixie plant opened its doors. In 1847 a Scotsman by the name of James Robertson constructed a woolen mill there, and a year later a local grist mill converted itself into a cotton mill. As recently as the mid-1880s a group of investors, Fuller's brother Enoch among them, had built another mill in LaGrange.

Textile mills had big advantages over most other industries. Cotton was more widely grown than tobacco, and unlike sawmills and mines, a textile mill could economically go anywhere there was power, either water or steam. Textile mills were cheaper to build than iron foundries, and work in them was both simpler and easier. Grady and others stressed the higher profit margins of manufacturing relative to farming, comparing profits in Northern factories to those of Southern farmers. Why, he and others asked, should Southerners pay to ship raw fiber north

Governor Alfred Colquitt speaking at the 1881 International Cotton Exposition in Atlanta. The exposition promoted textile and business development across the region. Colquitt hosted the marriage of Abner Reeves Callaway and Mary Wilbourne Ely at the Governor's Mansion in 1879.

It is likely that Fuller attended the 1895 Cotton States and International Exposition held in Atlanta. The exposition promoted the business resources of the region and was designed to promote international trade.

nearly a century. During what was left of the 1800s, Louisville, New Orleans, and Nashville hosted other and sometimes even grander expositions, and Atlanta twice repeated her performance, culminating in 1895 with the Cotton States and International Exposition, complete with a march composed for the event by John Philip Sousa and a major address on race relations by Booker T. Washington. There was no way that anyone in nearby LaGrange could have missed coverage of such a major event, especially an up-and-coming businessman like young Fuller E. Callaway.

To build a successful mill, several things were required. Labor was probably the easiest problem to solve. A huge proportion of the southern population relied on subsistence farming, so these farmers could become mill operatives (as they were called) without much disruption to either the economy or the food supply. The textile industry didn't require highly skilled labor, so training workers was easy and cheap. Confederate army veterans who had commanded men on the battlefields had some idea how to manage numbers of

workers. The lack of strong unions in the early years of the boom made the labor supply easy to deal with. As cotton prices went down and poor white farmers wrestled with poverty, grew disenchanted with country life, and faced competition from newly freed blacks, the pool of potential mill workers grew fast.

Capital was another matter entirely. The South was poor, to a degree hard for Americans to appreciate today. In 1870, of the sixteen hundred national banks in existence, the South had only a hundred. By the early 1880s, New England's banking capital was nearly $170 million; the entire South had only $8 million. Even as late as 1900, the states of the Southeast had only 5 percent of the nation's banks, savings and loan companies, and life insurance firms. In fact, the South was not only poor, it wasn't even a part of the national capital market that would have boosted money supplies and made borrowing easier.

As a result, mill capitalization tended to be based on local subscription; promoters would usually appeal to the community to buy shares in the mill company in order to raise money for construction. This meant not only that the capital came from the South but that it came from a broad-based segment of local citizens. This in turn tended to make a cotton mill a cooperative enterprise in a way that it wouldn't have been if a Northern firm had simply built a mill and then hired local workers. Of course Northern textile concerns sometimes did exactly that, or else bought shares in a Southern venture, but that was the exception, not the rule. Nearly every study has found that most of the money—and according to some of them, the overwhelming majority of it—came from the South.

Then there was the question of management, the final building block of the textile mill. Just as the South had few skilled workers at the mill era's outset, it had few people who knew anything about industrial management. There were, of course, lawyers, teachers, preachers, doctors, the odd banker, and merchants; these men were relatively educated and often civic-minded, and some of them could spare a bit for investment in mill shares. In fact, they were key to the mills' capitalization. But they also provided, in the absence of experienced mill people, a pool from which managers might be drawn. As community leaders already, they were naturally the ones to whom citizens looked not only to set a mill up but to run it. "If Belton got a mill, Williamston would want one," explained one of these self-made textile managers in 1916. "The townspeople would go to their leading citizen. It made no difference what a man was; so long as he was the leading citizen he had to become a mill president."

The most important civic leader in the process was usually the local merchant. The reasons why are obvious; merchants knew the local economy and depended on it, and if anyone in the community had ties to the national commodities and credit markets, it was he. Merchants were also a good bet not only when it came to building the mills but running them too. They specialized in buying

and selling, and that was perhaps the most important aspect of mill management.

Selling could be especially tricky, since the textile business largely sold its wares through Northern commission firms, which matched buyers to sellers and thus moved the mills' products. The problem was that these commission houses might well look to their own interests instead of the mills'. Commission firms might value selling the goods quickly instead of being patient and waiting for a higher price. They might even do things that were unscrupulous or illegal, such as dumping a mill's goods on the market to drive down prices, thus letting the firm speculate in the textile market, or simpler still, underreporting profits. The textile business was no place for the neophyte. To look out for itself, then, a Southern mill needed a manager who was no stranger to a dog-eat-dog world such as this. The Southerners who best fit the description were merchants.

And in all of Georgia, there was probably no better merchant in the late 1890s than Fuller E. Callaway.

≈

"It was like measles in the South in those days," Callaway once told Ida Tarbell in his attempt to explain cotton mill fever. "Every town wanted to build a cotton mill. We caught it at LaGrange. We did not have much of anything, but we got up a cotton mill."

The Dixie Mill, however, was not the one Callaway was talking about. That venture had been a near disaster, and even after Callaway helped turn it around, it never became the moneymaker that the community had envisioned. Callaway was referring instead to a milestone of much greater importance: the Unity Cotton Mill, in which he played a crucial role from the beginning.

During his struggle to save the Dixie concern, Callaway made a good many business contacts in Northern textile circles. Among the most important of these were Jim Lane, Coit Johnson, and O. A. Barnard, the main partners at J. H. Lane and Company, the New York commission house with which Callaway had established a relationship during the Dixie adventure. These men had been in a good position to see how Callaway went about the job of salvaging Dixie, and what they saw impressed them. In 1898 or 1899 Barnard came to LaGrange to tell Callaway so.

By this time Callaway had turned most of his attention back to his stores and his wholesale business, which was where Barnard found him. "Fuller," he told the young merchant, "we've had a meeting of our partners and we have decided that you're the most natural born cotton man we've ever seen." Based on this, he continued, "It is utterly foolish for you to get out of the cotton mill business." The Lane Company, he stated, was ready to front a sizable amount of money for the inauguration of a new mill in LaGrange if Callaway could raise the balance needed from the local citizens to build the mill.

This was one of those moments that Callaway must have had in mind when he tried to describe to Tarbell what cotton mill fever had been like. On the one hand, the Dixie experiment hadn't gone well; on the other, Callaway had learned a lot from it. J. H. Lane, moreover, was offering money rather than trying to get some up front as Dixie's Northern organizers had done with their sale of outmoded equipment. By now, too, Callaway probably had taken Lane's measure and knew it to be a firm of repute. The effects of the depression of 1894 could still be felt in Troup County; LaGrange needed an infusion of capital and another solid money-producing business. And new imperial possibilities

were opening up as well at that very moment. In 1898 America fought and beat Spain at sea and in Cuba, gaining control of Puerto Rico and concessions in Cuba as well as turning the Philippines into a springboard, it was thought, for U.S. companies seeking East Asian markets. Chances for overseas commercial expansion seemed to be on the rise. All of these factors, and probably others, likely occurred to Callaway. "Well," he said to Barnard after thinking about it, "we will see what we can do."

Callaway evidently continued to think and make plans. Often during this time he would go for Sunday afternoon walks with Ida and their son, Cason. They would stroll along just outside of town, in an area that would come to be called Southwest LaGrange, across a cow pasture that lay next to a pond known as Carey's Pool. But Ida should have known, after nearly a decade, that the workaholic she'd married could never completely take his mind off of his labors. During one of these outings he was unusually pensive and quiet, and she asked him if he felt ill.

"No," Callaway answered, and then he proceeded to tell her what he was thinking.

Unity Cotton Mill opened in 1901 and was formed mostly with local capital. The main investors were John M. Barnard, Fuller E. Callaway, George E. Dallis, Joseph E. Dunson, and Cornelius V. Truitt.

Cornelius V. "Neal" Truitt (1861–1942) invested in numerous textile ventures with Fuller.

"Some other businessmen and I are going to build a cotton mill here some day, if we can buy this land." In fact, Callaway already had an option on the property.

In October 1899 he successfully made the purchase, buying a lot of nearly a hundred acres with his own funds. It was the first major step toward making the new mill a reality. He'd picked out the spot carefully, selecting it for two major reasons. The first was its good water supply, which the mill would need in order to run a steam engine. The second was its proximity to the railroad, which was the artery through which the mill would pump out its finished product to national and international markets.

The following spring saw the next big step toward the mill's establishment. During the winter of 1900, Callaway was at work, making plans with other businessmen; in May they applied for a charter, which was granted that same month. Unity Cotton Mills was now a reality, on paper at least. The next step was to raise capital.

Some of the money was relatively easy to get, since the mill's promoters quickly made

big investments. Callaway put in the $10,000 he had managed to retrieve from his Dixie adventure, and J. H. Lane's partners personally put up $25,000 each. The sons-in-law of the banker A. D. Abraham, Cornelius V. "Neal" Truitt and Joseph E. Dunson, each also subscribed that amount, as did James G. Truitt, Neal's brother. Still other major investors, as had Callaway, put in $10,000 apiece. All of this raised Unity's capitalization to well over $100,000, but more was needed.

This, of course, was one of the areas in which Callaway shone. He was, after all, a salesman. "Fuller Callaway could start a subscription to dig an oil well on the town square," laughingly exclaimed one of his many friends, "and everyone he smiled at and asked for a subscription would subscribe to it!" It was certainly true when it came to selling Unity stock. Callaway worked hard to convince everyone he could think of to buy shares in the venture, even if $100 was all an investor could manage. He came up with other ideas too. As the first Unity board meetings took place in the spring and summer of 1900, Callaway and the other promoters tactfully awarded directorships in the company to induce some investors to increase their subscriptions. Callaway, as Unity's treasurer, was instrumental in persuading some of the mill's suppliers to take shares in lieu of cash payments for goods or services. One of the biggest success stories was that of a lumber supplier from south Georgia who furnished $10,000 worth of lumber and took the whole purchase price in stock. That wood was for prospective mill workers' houses. When the time came to arrange for the construction of the actual mill, Callaway and the other board members convinced a local contractor to take 5 percent of the cost in shares. Even the railroad agreed to put in $1,000 of its own money and, what was more, to install side tracks to the mill free of charge. Callaway arranged similar deals with others, thus managing to build the new mill for a smaller cash outlay than would have been possible otherwise.

All in all, the fund-raising went well, and it was undoubtedly one of the keys to the company's later success. It went so well, in fact, that the initial capital stock, originally set at $100,000, was quickly raised to an allowable maximum of $500,000. In the end the actual capitalization came not to the round sum of a quarter million but instead to $250,700. When Callaway's son Fuller Jr. once asked why the company had settled on such an odd figure, his father gave a straightforward answer: "I couldn't find anybody else who would put $100 into it."

In time the new factory was completed. Six-year-old Cason Callaway had the honor of blowing the factory whistle for the first time—a sign not only of the great interest that his father took in the project but his importance to it, and his continuing involvement in it as well. Fuller Callaway wasn't Unity's president; he was instead secretary, treasurer, and director. But from the first he seemed to take the lead in running the company, and in running it just the way he wished.

Perhaps his first major operation concerned the particular textile that Unity would produce. The Southern mills, being relatively new in the field and having less experienced managers, were generally more competitive with coarser grades of cloth that were easier to turn out. The finer goods they left, for the time being, to New England. It was likely for this reason, at least partly, that Callaway decided to first produce cotton duck. Better known to nontradesmen as canvas, duck is a coarse,

heavy cloth suitable for tents, tarpaulins, sails, and other uses in which strength and water resistance are important. Given the introduction of cotton into tire manufacturing in the 1890s and afterward, duck also had a potential future in the cycling and nascent automobile industries. But there was one major problem, in the form of the Cotton Duck Trust.

Railroads had allowed Callaway not only to travel far in search of business opportunities but also to sell to large geographical markets. The same was true of other merchants and manufacturers. Because of the railroads and the growth of industrial capital, as businesses grew, they encountered distant competitors who would have remained unknown to them if not for trains. One way of dealing with this competition was to join forces with the competitors, reaching agreements on which company sold where, and for what price.

An even bolder step was an actual merger of sorts, famously known as the trust. Its classic form was fairly straightforward. A group of trustees would acquire the stock of several

This bow tie was made with the first cotton processed at Unity Cotton Mill. It was presented to Mr. Callaway by Roy Dallis.

The fabric for the sails of the schooner *Thomas W. Lawson* was produced at Unity Mill. Launched in 1902, the steel-hulled, seven-masted ship carried over 46,000 square feet of sail.

competing companies from the firms' stockholders in exchange for bonds or trust certificates. The trustees thus gained legal control of the companies and could coordinate them so as to produce minimum competition and maximum prices. If a trust succeeded in acquiring—or destroying—its remaining competition and creating a monopoly, it could dictate the terms of sale to anyone who wanted to buy its products.

In August 1899, while plans for Unity were still underway, the *New York Times* announced the formation of the Cotton Duck Trust. Based in Baltimore, acquiring more than a dozen duck mills stretching from Alabama to Connecticut in less than a month, and capitalized at nearly $25 million—a hundred times the capitalization of Unity—the new trust from the outset accounted for the manufacture of 90 percent of the nation's duck. Even as the paper made the announcement, duck jobbers and retailers around the country scrambled to buy supplies of the fabric for fear that the new trust would soon raise duck prices.

The partners at J. H. Lane were as aware of this development as anyone else. It was no problem for Unity, they thought, since the

plan was for it to produce yarn, not duck. But then Callaway traveled to New York to meet with the Lane people while the factory was under construction. "I think we ought to make it a duck mill," he told them. Coming from the man they'd sought out to build a profitable new factory, the idea was enough to terrify them. "What do you mean?" one of the Lane partners asked, probably after a moment or two of shocked silence. "You know the duck trust has it absolutely sewn up. We couldn't sell a pound of duck."

"I know it," affirmed Callaway, but it didn't matter to him. "I think it's better if we start out with the roughest competition we can have. Let's make it a duck mill; I'd like to bust the duck trust."

"All right," they answered with resignation, "go ahead if that's what you want to do." If this account is accurate, Lane and the others must have had a massive amount of confidence in Callaway.

Somehow he made it work. The duck trust, as it turned out, didn't immediately raise prices, relying instead on the savings from combined operations to turn a profit. This fact, together with Callaway's prodigious selling abilities, was enough to allow Unity to succeed. According to Callaway's son Fuller Jr., Unity made its highest percent return on investment in its first year that it ever made.

With the mill showing an early profit, the question soon arose of what to do with the money. Here, too, Callaway's voice was highly important. After all, he was the mill's treasurer. He'd always been frugal in his personal life and in his own business dealings; now, as a corporate officer, he adopted the same approach. It was probably natural for people to

Unity Cotton Mill representatives were very proud when the first cloth was shipped from the mill on January 5, 1901. Left to right: Orin A. Barnard, C.V. Truitt, George W. Murphy, Fuller E. Callaway, Francis Walker, and James H. Lane.

want to see a quick return on their investments, and, in fact, a few Unity directors, when they learned of the profit, started arguing that the company should declare a dividend. By some accounts, there was even pressure from some quarters to pay out all of the profits, which would have left Unity cash-strapped.

The very idea was anathema to Callaway, not just because of his frugal nature, but because he knew the business world. "Son," he once told Fuller Callaway Jr., "paying dividends is the exact same value to the corporation as if you stuffed the money in a rat hole." Depreciation of equipment and the certain eventual cost of replacement; fluctuating markets and seasonal variations in capital; the possibility of another major depression like the one of the mid-1890s, still a recent memory in 1901—all of these were powerful arguments in favor of a conservative approach to Unity's finances. There was also probably a lingering aftertaste of what had happened with the Dixie Mills, which the promoters had likely intended from the start as a get-rich-quick scheme designed to take advantage of Troup County citizens. Callaway didn't want anyone to get rich quick if it meant killing the goose and foregoing a future of golden eggs.

The trick for Callaway was to convince other directors to see things his way. That was where his personality came into play; he could get along with nearly everyone, and sell nearly anything, including his own ideas. During a heated discussion on the dividend issue, Callaway managed to calm things down. "By all means, friends," he exclaimed, "let's work together first to catch the rabbit before we begin quarreling among ourselves over how to divide it." His plea worked; the directors agreed to a modest dividend policy.

On the other hand, Callaway was never afraid to pass up a good opportunity when he saw it. One example was his entry into the commercial paper market.

Commercial paper was a relatively new financial development. It was essentially a means of procuring short-term loans that had developed in the North during its war against the South. A company would sell its paper in a manner similar to bonds. But unlike most bonds and long-term promissory notes, commercial paper matured quickly, usually somewhere between a month and a year. It was often sold by an established business whose income fluctuated with the seasons. It was a way of evening out the natural feast-or-famine cycle of things. If an industry was predictably flush with money at certain times of the year and stretched thin at other times—for instance, during the season of harvest of perishable foods, when it had to buy huge quantities for preserving or canning—it could sell commercial paper for short-term cash and then buy it back a few weeks or months later at low interest rates.

Before the turn of the century, the seat of the commercial paper market lay in New York

Fuller Callaway working at his rolltop desk. He was notorious for working long hours.

and New England. But the market was gradually spreading, and Callaway wanted some of the action. Cotton, of course, wasn't as perishable as some other goods, but it still grew on a seasonal schedule. By selling commercial paper, Callaway figured, Unity could gain great flexibility in its money supply.

At first, companies usually sold their paper among their officers' own contacts and other acquaintances. By 1900, though, this was changing, and commercial paper brokers had come into being, many of them, predictably, in New York. Callaway managed to attract the attention of one of the biggest and most successful, Elkan Naumburg. A patron of the arts, the Bavarian-born financier had founded E. Naumburg and Company in 1893, which quickly grew into a firm rivaled only by Goldman-Sachs. Naumburg took a liking to Callaway, and it is possible that the New Yorker's appreciation of the arts—especially

music—rubbed off on Callaway and spurred his own efforts to improve civic life in La-Grange in the following decades. In the commercial paper realm, the friendship certainly paid off. Naumburg carefully sold Unity's first twenty-five thousand dollars worth of paper to New York buyers, and Callaway made sure to repay the money by the maturity date. After that, Unity paper had a good reputation in America's financial capital, and Callaway had gained the monetary flexibility he'd been craving. This gave him the leverage to expand Unity's operations as he saw fit, without the painstaking hunt for investors that had been needed when the mill was first established.

But securing money was only part of the story, as was its careful spending. Callaway also needed to know exactly what Unity had, and to guard against mistakes, and worse. So from the outset he made audits a priority. Early in Unity's history, he got the directors' approval for the use of an outside auditing agency. These specialists—being specialists—were a good value, and since Callaway established a system to let them drop in at the mill without warning and with unlimited access to all records, any potential wrongdoers would be deterred from cooking the books or making off with ready cash.

Before long Callaway added another level of security, winning the appointment of a permanent audit committee of three directors who would carefully review all audit reports and then make suggestions to the entire board as to how to safeguard assets and spend Unity's money in ways that made the mill competitive with other textile concerns. Two men in particular who served on this committee were Callaway's competent attorney and friend, Hatton Lovejoy, and Roy Dallis, another of his most capable lieutenants.

All of these conservative financial policies that Callaway enforced paid off quite

quickly for the company itself—so much so, in fact, that Callaway soon took steps to expand operations. The original Unity mill, large enough for its time, was dwarfed by later expansions, and as demand for Unity products rose, the managers added equipment to the mill in order to boost output. But soon they hit a limit.

Unity's power plant was a single Corliss steam engine. The industry standard in mill applications for a half century, the Corliss design was actually more energy efficient than a water-powered mill system. It was what allowed mills to be located in places without a flowing river or stream. It was powerful, but it was also very large.

Under Callaway's guidance, Unity's output ramped up so quickly that soon it was consuming nearly all the power that the monster engine produced. In a sense this was a good problem to have, but there was no way the mill building could hold another one of

Fuller Callaway (front center) with Roy Dallis, Hatton Lovejoy, and others at Coney Island, New York.

Mill villages were scattered across LaGrange. This is a 1951 view of the village near Unity Spinning Mill.

the engines. So Callaway put Roy Dallis on the job of figuring out how to overcome the new limitation.

After investigating the situation, Dallis came up with several stopgaps. Chief among them were water purification and the use of higher-grade coal to make the existing engine run more cleanly. Dallis also oversaw a thorough descaling of the boiler and tubing, as well as the hiring of better-trained firemen—steam engine operators—and tighter maintenance schedules. This maximized the engine's power output while at the same time reducing the chances of one of the more interesting aspects of steam engine operation: a boiler explosion. Still, the writing was on the wall. At some point, to increase output, Unity's owners would either have to agree to a major expansion, or it would have to open another mill.

Although Unity's shareholders weren't ready to take either of those steps, Fuller Callaway was, and when he saw an opportunity to expand, he seized it. A group of Atlanta investors had chartered a mill of their own in

Conyers, Georgia, in 1901, and set about organizing it in 1902. By now Callaway was well-known in Atlanta, and because of his efforts at Dixie and Unity, his name was spreading in textile circles. In 1902 the owners of the new Milstead Mill, as it was known, asked Callaway to serve as their agent. Callaway accepted the offer.

One of Fuller Callaway's defining traits was that he liked—even demanded—to be in charge. This was likely due, not only to his ambition and energy, but because for the first half of his life, beginning with his early sales of thread, he was his own boss. He had been good at that arrangement and had gotten used to it. He would probably have chafed at having to follow the lead of someone with less vision and drive. Even generations after his death, LaGrange residents would speak of three ways to do things around town: the right way, the wrong way, and the Callaway.

With Milstead, what Callaway wanted to do was essentially establish a common selling pool with Unity. While the two mills weren't officially related, he would nevertheless work to sell their output in tandem, thus catching the eye of any buyer who needed more than Unity alone could supply. One of the keys to this strategy, of course, was to turn Milstead, like Unity, into a duck mill.

As Milstead's agent, however, he lacked the power to pursue his vision for the Conyers mill. Others were in charge of the major decisions. A lot of those decisions, he believed, were leading to problems with mill operations. Responsibility without authority irked Callaway, and before long he said so to the mill's owners. He was prepared to quit, or at least he said so as a bargaining ploy. He probably meant it. The result, though, was likely just what he wanted. In 1903 the owners named him as Milstead's new president.

Callaway immediately started taking the sort of steps that had worked at Dixie and Unity. He selected a new management team and promptly switched production from yarn to duck. It wasn't always an easy road; as had happened at Dixie, he had to undo a good many things and solve a number of problems. One recurring headache was the mill's power train. The thing that Ida remembered most clearly about the Milstead adventure was the number of times that Callaway would announce, just before she put dinner on the table, "I'm sorry, I will have to disappoint you. I have to go to Milstead Mill; the shaft has broken again." But eventually the road became smoother and Milstead began doing well. In fact, Callaway and his friends began purchasing stock in the company, and eventually they gained a controlling interest.

It was Callaway's involvement with the Milstead Mill that was the occasion of—or at least

Callaway became the agent for Milstead Mill in Milstead (now Conyers), Georgia, in 1902.

Milstead Mill weaving room employees in 1912.

the pretext for—one of the most important events in his business life and in the life of Unity Mills. The occasion had probably been a long time coming, and afterward nothing in La-Grange would be the same. It involved the relationship between Callaway and Joe Dunson, another leading citizen of LaGrange.

Joseph Eugene Dunson was born into a prominent Troup County family on June 9, 1865, at the war's very end. His relatives had been involved in many LaGrange concerns, including the near disaster of Dixie Mills, and they elected to stay with the Dixie operation after Callaway salvaged it and cashed out. In many ways Dunson's life and career mirrored Fuller Callaway's. Although he attended school while young Fuller traveled the county as a salesman, Dunson, too, became a salesman and bookkeeper with a supply house in LaGrange at roughly the same time Callaway moved into town. Later Dunson, like Callaway, set up his own firm, the farm supply business of J. E. Dunson and Brothers. In 1886 Joe Dunson married Mary Lee "Mamie" Abraham, the daughter of the banker A. D. Abraham who had first grudgingly bankrolled Callaway, and in 1892 he took over the presidency of the bank from his father-in-law. Beginning in 1888

he served as a town councilman, and along with Callaway he was a Unity incorporator. Like Callaway, he was young, highly involved with the community, and above all ambitious.

The story of what happened around 1904 is a confusing one, with several accounts existing. According to some, friction between Dunson and Callaway began at least as early as Callaway's decision to be conservative about declaring dividends. The size of J. H. Lane's commission was another potential issue. While Dunson apparently objected to the

Joseph E. Dunson (1865–1916) founded the Dunson Mill Company in 1910. He was an early investor in Unity Mill, but later he and Fuller Callaway became staunch competitors.

commission, Callaway believed that given Unity's market niche, a selling agent was a necessity. Other, perhaps more biased, accounts charge that Dunson was unhappy because Callaway refused to hire Dunson family members to leadership positions at Unity, or even that Dunson and others objected to Callaway's one hundred dollar monthly salary.

Whatever the reason, the showdown came at a Unity directors' meeting in August 1904. At this meeting a resolution was proposed, apparently at Dunson's instigation, to the effect that no Unity officer could serve as an officer of another company. The resolution passed by a single vote, necessitating Callaway's replacement as secretary and treasurer given his Milstead connection. In his place as treasurer, the directors installed Tom Thornton, a longtime Dunson ally.

As Callaway was finishing up his entry of the minutes into the record book, one of the directors approached him to express his regrets. Callaway, thinking out loud, replied that he wasn't worried about his own prospects, but that he was indeed concerned that Unity would have trouble repaying its loans.

Other accounts go further. According to them, as news of Callaway's dismissal got out, banks in Atlanta notified Thornton that they would no longer make loans to Unity. Banks in New York called their existing loans, the Lane Company cancelled its contract with Unity, and twenty of the mill's biggest customers wired to announce that they would no longer buy Unity products.

According to his son, the man who made sure that word of the ouster spread so quickly was none other than Callaway himself. He figured that the goodwill Unity enjoyed was largely because of his own involvement with the mill. If the accounts are accurate, he figured correctly. Within a day the directors held a special meeting in which they rescinded the

Dunson Mill was originally built in 1910 and expanded in 1923 to become one of the largest mills in the state. Dunson competed with the mills operated by Mr. Callaway.

resolution in question, unanimously reelected Callaway as secretary and treasurer, and passed another resolution stating that the episode was due not to any question about Callaway's integrity or ability but instead to an honest difference of opinion "which has now been satisfactorily adjusted."

Things were back to normal—for the time being. But the episode had shown Callaway several things. On the positive side, it had confirmed to him that he was the linchpin of Unity. On the other hand, despite the resources he obviously now commanded, he was still an employee, a salaried officer subject to dismissal at the whim of others. From nearly his first day as a Bradfield delivery boy, having a boss had never sat well with him. Finally, the animosity between him and Joe Dunson—a director for whom he technically worked—had at last become plain. From then on, his son claimed, he was in open competition with Dunson and his associates, including the Truitt and Abraham families.

Based on these circumstances, Callaway quickly determined that his current position as a virtual Dunson employee was unacceptable, and that he must change his relationship to Unity. Once he accomplished that, he would have a free hand in running the mill. The first thing for him to do, then, was to

Supervisors and managers from numeorus Callaway textile enterprises pose for a photo with Fuller (center rear on his horse).

consolidate his position at Unity so that no one could ever fire him again. To achieve this objective, he went to Atlanta attorney Preston Arkwright.

It is a mark of Callaway's sophisticated understanding of corporate structure that he sought out Arkwright. A lawyer by training, Arkwright in recent years had been making a prominent name for himself as a businessman. A few months younger than Callaway, Arkwright shared his vision and drive, which had led him into the utilities industry.

Just before the turn of the century, Henry M. Atkinson and Joel Hurt had waged a war to control Atlanta's electric, streetcar, and steam heat businesses. In 1902 Atkinson, who controlled the Georgia Electric Light Company, won the war by buying out Hurt. He then hired Arkwright to charter a new corporation—essentially a trust—that would consolidate all of Atkinson's various interests. The new corporation, at first called the Georgia Railway and Electric Company, would later become known simply as the Georgia Power Company, and Atkinson immediately put Arkwright in charge of it. When the attorney brought some papers into Atkinson's office for his signature, Atkinson said, "Sign them yourself," and kept on working.

"I'm sorry, Mr. Atkinson," replied Arkwright, "but they must be signed by the president of the company."

"That's all right. You sign them," repeated Atkinson. "You're the president now." Arkwright would remain at the helm of the business until his death in 1946.

The year after its creation, the new company gained control of still another business: the Atlanta Gas Light Company, which traced its origins all the way back to 1856. Although technically a separate concern from Arkwright's company, Arkwright was in effective control of it as well. Thus by 1904 Arkwright, both as lawyer and corporate officer, was well-versed in building and running modern corporate structures. In short, he had exactly the skills Callaway needed.

Having been involved in both the electricity and gas businesses, Arkwright had gained some familiarity with a device known as a holding company. It was a relatively new idea in 1904, though a simple one. At its heart was one corporation's ownership of another corporation's stock—enough stock either to control the second corporation outright or at least influence its governance. Although the law had traditionally looked down on the ownership of shares in one corporation by another, since 1888 states had begun relaxing their restraints on the practice. In Georgia it was apparently allowed by 1900, at least under certain conditions.

The modern trusts quickly found uses for holding companies as the ideal means to

combine ownership, management, and finances of multiple corporations. All that was needed was for a holding company to buy up the stock of whatever firms its owners wished to combine. Holding companies were also particularly useful for public utilities. Unlike most other industries, in which monopolies could hurt the consumer, the benefits of a unified electrical, gas, or telephone infrastructure made a monopoly more efficient and acceptable, provided it was subject to public regulation. What was more, this allowed the industry to focus all of its technical expertise on a single network. In fact, Arkwright had bought the Atlanta Gas Light Company from the nation's first utilities holding company, the United Gas Improvement Company, via a stock swap. This stock swap, along with the holding company idea, was undoubtedly at the forefront of Arkwright's mind as he advised Callaway on the issue of how to achieve undisputed control of the Unity Mill.

During the meeting with Arkwright, Callaway explained what he wanted: a way to gain control of Unity Mill for himself and prevent any future ousters. "This thing can't happen anymore," he said in regard to the directors' revolt. "Now I don't know what can be done, and I don't own but $10,000 worth of stock," he informed Arkwright, "but we've got to do something. What can I do?"

How about a holding company?" Arkwright suggested.

"What's that?"

Arkwright told him. In fact, what Arkwright suggested was not only a holding company, but one with an element of business trust and even a hint of stock swapping thrown in. He explained what he had in mind.

Callaway was fast to catch on. "All right," he answered, "we'll give it a try."

Returning to LaGrange, Callaway gave Hatton Lovejoy the task of setting up the new corporation Arkwright had outlined. Callaway directed that the new corporation be called Calumet, after the so-called peace pipe used by many North American tribes. Explaining the choice of name, he stated that all he wanted was peace. But perhaps it meant more to him than he said. The calumet was wrongly called the peace pipe, for it was used not merely in peace but in war as well. Fr. Jacques Marquette, the famous Jesuit explorer, gave one of the earliest descriptions of the Indian people's pipe to Europeans. "There is nothing more mysterious or more respected among them," he wrote. "It seems to be the god of peace and of war, the arbiter of life and of death. . . . There is a calumet for peace, and one for war, which are distinguished solely by the color of the feathers with which they are adorned; red is a sign of war. They also use it to put an end to their disputes, to strengthen their alliances, and to speak to strangers." This more rounded description seems to fit Callaway's outlook on the Unity affair far better than an improper concept of the calumet as a mere peace pipe. If the resolution to the Unity problem were to be peace, it was clearly to be a peace born of strength—Callaway's strength—and his silencing of the opposition.

Early corporate charters often cited exhaustive lists of activities that the corporations in question were permitted to undertake, since the law originally took a strict line toward corporations and refused to let them act beyond what their charters specifically allowed. Calumet's charter was no different, listing such typically minute details as the power to dig wells and sell horses. Buried so far down in this list as to be unobtrusive was the authority to own and vote stock in other corporations—the key power that was the essence of a holding company. Nobody in LaGrange noticed, even during the public advertisement stage. That was exactly the way Callaway wanted it.

As soon as Calumet was established, Callaway exchanged his stock in Unity for stock in Calumet, making him—for the time being—the new company's only stockholder. He immediately held a stockholders' meeting and approved a resolution naming himself as the permanent proxy for all stock in other companies that Calumet owned or acquired in the future. Then the real work began.

In the following days, Callaway approached everyone to whom he'd sold Unity stock a few years earlier. Working hard to keep his campaign a secret from the Dunson faction, he persuaded those he approached to exchange their Unity stock for shares in Calumet. Given his recognized business abilities and the decades of goodwill he'd amassed by now, he met with great success. The J. H. Lane people, of course, went along readily. The big question mark was Jim Truitt.

Truitt was risky. His younger brother

James G. Truitt (1849–1923) was a charter member of Unity Mill and a business associate of Fuller's for many years.

Neal was a Unity incorporator and was also married to Nonnie Holt Abraham, and Nonnie's sister, Mary Lee, was the wife of Joe Dunson. But Callaway had to approach Jim Truitt, since he held so much Unity stock. Nevertheless, the secret apparently held, and just as important, Truitt agreed to trade in his Unity stock. This was the clincher, for it was this deal that gave Calumet ownership of more than 50 percent of Unity stock. Callaway held the proxy for all of it.

At the next Unity shareholder's meeting, Joe Dunson—Unity's official president—told Callaway, as Unity's secretary, to call the roll of shareholders. Callaway began doing so. Very quickly he came to the name of Calumet Company, on record as holding 1,471 shares of Unity.

Dunson interrupted the roll call. "Who in the hell is Calumet Company?"

It was the moment Callaway had been waiting for. "That's me!" he replied.

This was when the Callaway-Dunson feud truly began. Callaway promptly removed Dunson as president, and then he put

Dunson and everyone in his faction off of the board of directors. Before long Callaway was in unassailable control of Unity. From then on, until the deaths of Dunson and Callaway, the town was polarized, the two factions in a constant war with each other. The feud was so powerful that whenever a new family moved to LaGrange, both Dunson and Callaway representatives would call on the recent arrivals, the same way that members of various churches would. That Callaway was a Baptist and Dunson a Methodist made the parallel even more fitting. Nevertheless, the feud was highly personal between the two men, passing with their deaths, and later generations would recall little of it.

While the Calumet maneuver was the start of the Dunson-Callaway feud, it was by no means the end of Callaway's careful use of the holding company principle. By now Unity was beginning to build up enough cash reserves to permit an expansion, and the following years saw plenty of it. Callaway managed it carefully. Each new mill was also a new corporation, and Callaway used a variation of a system called pyramiding* to control it. When the first new mill was chartered, Callaway made sure that Unity held 51 percent of its stock, giving him control of it. When the next new mill was built, the two existing mills together took 51 percent of that stock, and so forth. This meant, of course, that by his control of Calumet—and through Calumet, his control of Unity—Callaway gained control of each new mill in succession. In this manner he came to dominate a virtual empire of mills, although he personally owned only a few thousand dollars of stock in any one corporation, with Calumet at the top of the pyramid and the mill corporations forming the broad base. The system worked magnificently. Even Neal Truitt switched sides and backed Callaway, and Callaway ultimately rewarded him with

the presidency of Unity. The key to Callaway's control lay in the fact that he was the permanent proxy of those 1,471 shares of Unity stock he owned. And Callaway securely locked away those Unity certificates, always voting them but never touching them until the day he died.

During the following decade, Callaway's mill empire grew quickly. First came Elm City Mills, a project that was underway even as Callaway was putting together Calumet. In October 1905 an organizational meeting took place in LaGrange's Masonic Hall. The potential investors decided that, in light of Unity's success, the town was capable of supporting another mill, and they also chose to capitalize it at a quarter of a million dollars. Some suggested that the new enterprise be named Harmony Mills, which would have been a natural complement to the name Unity, but the name Elm City ultimately prevailed. The mill was chartered just over a month later, with Callaway's name standing at the top of an imposing list of investors, including both Jim and Neal Truitt as well as several Bradfields and Dallises.

Elm City Cotton Mill was incorporated in 1905 and produced cotton duck. The name was derived from LaGrange's nickname, "the city of elms and roses."

---

* Not to be confused with a pyramid scheme, or Ponzi scheme.

Unity had been so successful that this time the promoters had no trouble raising the money. Just a few days after obtaining the charter, in fact, they found that the new mill had been oversubscribed. The initial capital stock was thus adjusted upward to more than $315,000.

Not long afterward came an expansion of the actual Unity corporation. In 1909 Callaway supervised the opening of Unity Spinning Mills, an operation that—unlike the original mill—concentrated on various twines, cords, and yarns rather than woven cloth. Callaway had already opened both a warehouse and an electric ginnery since funding Calumet, and Troup County's textile industry continued to grow. Unity Spinning, however, was a special victory for Callaway, being funded entirely from Unity profits. Callaway's early fights not to declare dividends, which had resulted in his dismissal and caused him to force out the Dunsons, had finally come to fruition.

All of this expansion, as well as the struggle for control of Unity, revealed that the migration of the textile industry from New England to the South was still underway and gaining more ground. In fact, even as Calumet was still in the process of formation, Callaway was working on his most ambitious mill project yet: an entirely new town, dedicated entirely to textiles.

By 1906 a new railroad was being built through west Georgia: the Atlanta, Birmingham & Atlantic, in which Fuller Callaway had a major interest.* Sensing that this rail line might be the key to a new textile operation, he traveled by horse and buggy thirty-five miles out into the country, to a spot in southern Meriwether County near a likely junction point for the new railroad. Selecting a plot of 1,029 acres, he convinced its owner to sell him the land. At the end of 1906 Callaway chartered still another corporation, the Chalybeate Development Company, as a

device to oversee the development of a mill-based community there. Chalybeate Springs, located a few miles east of the likely rail junction, had been named for its mineral waters—which possessed some of the highest iron content in the country—and in the 1880s a resort had been established there to take advantage of those springs. Perhaps the new corporation's name risked revealing too much about the location Callaway was thinking of developing, but at any rate, in July 1907 he renamed it the Manchester Development Company, after the city in England whose textile business had grown in connection with one of the world's first commercial railroads.

By 1908 when the new line finally reached Birmingham, running to Montezuma, Georgia, through the point that Callaway had foreseen with a line branching off from there to Atlanta, things seemed ripe for the new undertaking. By October, having gained many subscriptions for the new Manchester Cotton Mills, Callaway joined with J. H. Lane Company, Roy Dallis, the Truitts, and Milstead's vice president, Allen F. Johnson, to organize the new firm and the town to go with it—which would also be known as Manchester. On January 8, 1909, the new mill was formally chartered, with Callaway as a director. In this case he also served as the new mill's president, unlike most of the other mill operations with which he was associated; he usually preferred the post of treasurer.

Acting as an agent for the new mill and as head of his own Manchester Development Company, Callaway now promptly bought—and sold—much of the latter company's 1,029 acres for mill use at twenty-five dollars per acre. This was a sizable amount for a mill, but from the beginning the plan was to found not just a mill, he explained in an early report to Manchester shareholders, but a community complete with "plenty of room for the mill

---

* The story of the railroad appears in Chapter 4.

Dunson Mill, one of the largest mills in LaGrange, opened in 1910. Joseph, Walker, Edgar and Sanford Dunson Jr. were all investors.

plant and operatives' cottages, as well as a liberal surplus." This approach, he continued, would allow the mill to give its workers "free pasturage for their cows, and, if practicable, recreation and play grounds. Incidentally, this surplus lands [*sic*] will come in most advantageously in case of extensions or additions in the future." And given Unity's recent expansion, Callaway was clearly contemplating similar growth in Manchester. He further planned for this by having the development company divide two hundred acres into building lots, which it sold to potential residents at seventy-five dollars per acre.

Expansion came almost immediately, as Callaway sensed opportunities arising in the market. Initially capitalized in early 1909 at $263,000—roughly the same as the original Unity mill—Manchester was reported by Callaway less than a year later to have a half million dollars in capital, twice that of any

other mill in which he was involved, except for Elm City Mills, which had $300,000. And Manchester wasn't even on line yet. The new mill's physical plant, far advanced by the end of the year, also reflected the difference, boasting nearly 21,000 spindles, roughly twice the number of any of Callaway's other mills, and 472 looms, a number that far eclipsed that of the other plants. The original Unity mill, for instance, had only 132 looms. Callaway was investing heavily in this new venture, with others following his lead.

But this heavy investment created a near crisis. During Manchester's construction, narrow fabrics had boomed in popularity, so Callaway had bought a large number of looms geared to narrow fabric production. But before the factory wheels began turning, the market suddenly changed, and narrow fabrics were out.

The LaGrange Reporter

PUBLISHED WEEKLY. · ESTABLISHED 1842.

LAGRANGE, GEORGIA FRIDAY SEPTEMBER 13, 1912 NUMB[...]

[...]NDABLE ACTION OF [...]TON-FREEMAN AGENCY

[...]eraple Loss Protects Athens [...]olicyholders, Although Under [...] Obligations to do so.

[...]in this issue of [...]notice from the [...]man Insurance [...]Athens Mutual [...]hens, Ga., had [...]remarkable an- [...]at this agency [...]d at their own [...]for their pa- [...]licies in the [...]immediate pro- [...]ny fire loss by [...]ese risks to be [...]of the largest [...]ible companies [...]h policy hold- [...]and receive a [...]on which the [...]fully paid by [...]eman Agency, [...]the contract

LaGrange College Opens Today.

Prospects Bright for the Biggest Year in History of College. Students Will Be Enrolled and Classified Today, To- morrow and Monday. Changes in Faculty.

The Methodist College will open this morning at 10:15 o'clock with devotional exercises and addresses at the college auditorium, to which the public is invited, and the outlook for the school year is the brightest in the history of the school. Several new teachers have been added to the faculty. The new teachers are: Mis[...]

MILLS HOLD ANNUAL MEETINGS REPORTS MOST GRATIFYING.

The Two Unity Mills and Elm City Mill of LaGrange, and Manchester Cotton Mills of Manchester, Georgia, All Hold Meetings on Wedneseay.

Wednesday, Sept. 11th was a day of meeting at the general offices, being the occasion of the annual meeting of the stock- holders and directors of the Unity Cotton Mills, Unity Spin- ning Mills, Elm City Cotton Mills and Manchester Cotton Mills.

The reports of the officers were highly gratifying to the stockholders, showing substan- tial surpluses over the divi- dends and the amounts which are taken from each year's earn- ings into the Renewal Accounts in accordance with the sound policy of these well managed

been substantially decreased and both plants showed highly sat- isfactory earnings. All of the old officers and di- rectors were re-elected with the addition of Mr. J. Carroll Payne, the prominent attorney and cap- italist of Atlanta, to the directo- rate of the Unity Cotton Mills. The officers and directors of the several mills are as follows:

Unity Cotton Mills.

C. V. Truitt, president and general manager; S. H. Truitt, vice-president; Fuller E. Calla- way, treasurer; J. A. Perry, sec- retary. The directors are the above [...]lowing: J. C. Tra[...]

NOW RAILROAD FOR LAGRA[...] WITHIN THE NEXT Y[...]

Chief Engineer Flournoy of Colum[...] City Confering with Officials of Chamber of Commerce.

S. F. C. Opened Yesterday Morning

Outlook For College For Coming Year Very Bright—Dormitory Is Taxed To Its Utmost To Accommodate Students.

With the prospects of an at- tendance that will tax the ca- pacity of the new dormitory even more than during the last year, the Southern Female Col- lege opens its doors for the pre- liminary exercises of its seven- tieth session today. Every room in [...]

That LaGrange is [...] new railroad line [...] next year is a strong [...]ity at this time on [...]the fact that a rece[...] porated line with on[...] directors at Columbu[...] its engineer, Josiah[...] through this section t[...] a proposed route. W[...] are two other routes[...] neer states that there [...]tage to be found in [...] proposed routes and th[...] which would bring [...]line through LaGrang[...] mind very feasible. [...] line be built LaGran[...]ceived assurances of st[...]acter as to its proba[...] construction and [...]

The September 13, 1912 *LaGrange Daily Reporter* featured a story highlighting the profitability of Fuller's numerous textile enterprises.

The question for Callaway was what to do about it. The new company had invested a great deal of money on the narrow looms, but if it used them in churning out narrow fabrics, it might throw good money after bad. Callaway decided that the solution was to spend more money on capital assets. "We have a tremen- dous investment at Manchester," he pointed out to O. A. Barnard at J. H. Lane, "and should begin operating the plant at the earliest possible moment." But not with narrow looms, Call- away decided. "It might pay us," he declared, "to buy some additional wide looms and store these narrow looms in our warehouse."

Callaway thus borrowed $100,000 to procure new wide looms and stored the nar- row ones. His successful track record and his by-now considerable experience in finance made it relatively easy for him to raise the money quickly, and the goodwill he had amassed among suppliers helped him procure fast delivery of the looms. By the summer of 1910 the new mill went into production, and the crisis was averted.

By September 1911, even with the broad loom hiccup, the new mill had earned 8 percent for its investors; Callaway in- formed shareholders of this figure while trumpeting the firm's advantages. "We have the best mill plant that can be built," he de- clared, "equipped with the latest machinery for economical production of high-class goods." He also reminded them that the company's president, vice president, and treasurer were serving in their posts without drawing salaries. Pointing out that 8 percent net profit was acceptable for a new opera- tion, Callaway nevertheless stated that the mill's directors, no doubt at his urging, had decided against declaring a dividend. This time there was no serious complaint.

The first decade of the twentieth cen- tury saw Callaway's transformation from a mer- chant with some slight experience in textiles to a major force in the regional economy. By the century's second decade, most of the mills in

In 1913 Callaway (far right) traveled to Dayton, Ohio, promoting the mills. He was accompanied by several mill superintendents: (left to right) W. H. Turner, Ira B. Grimes, Oscar D. Grimes, and S. Y. Austin.

Callaway's growing empire had been established, and Callaway himself was a recognized, undisputed leader in the textile industry.

By 1910 Joe Dunson played an instrumental role in building his own textile operation, the Dunson Mills, managed at first by his friend Tom Thornton. None of the mill's organizers were in the Callaway group. It played an important public and civic role, like the Callaway mills, and Dunson himself, like Callaway, wore many hats in town and oversaw many businesses. By the time Manchester was underway, Dunson was owner of a large amount of Troup County farmland; president of J. E. Dunson and Brothers Company, a farm supply business; and treasurer of the Troup Fertilizer Company. He had long since succeeded to the

presidency of his father-in-law's LaGrange Banking & Trust Company. He also had a record of public service, holding, among other posts, seats on LaGrange's City Council and Board of Education. By the time of his death in 1916 he was being mentioned as a likely governor of Georgia.

But for all that, in the field of textiles, Callaway had long since eclipsed Dunson. Nevertheless, Callaway had faced several hard battles in his efforts to develop LaGrange in addition to his struggle for control of Unity. And of those, none—not even his battle with Joe Dunson—had been tougher or longer than his war with the greatest economic and financial engine America had ever produced up until that time: the nation's corporate railroad empire.

A GROUP OF LAGRANGE BUSINESS LEADERS GATHERED ON THE REAR OF A DEPARTING
TRAIN TO PROMOTE BUSINESS INVESTMENT IN THE COMMUNITY.
FULLER IS STANDING THIRD FROM THE RIGHT.

· 4 ·

BUILDING A MODERN LaGRANGE

The railroad is at heart a simple concept. It involves the pairing of two components: a steam engine or some other power source that produces great speed, and a set of smooth, low-friction tracks, which allow energy efficiency. By the time these two things were combined in the early nineteenth century, both technologies were quite old. Their marriage took place when it did because of the Napoleonic Wars. Europe's armies made heavy use of the horse, and war drove up the price of fodder, so businessmen began to look for a cheaper power source. Between 1800 and the Battle of Waterloo, English inventors developed a number of small-scale steam locomotives.

After the end of the war, inventors and investors picked up the pace. In 1830 came the inauguration of the Liverpool and Manchester Railway. Connecting a port to a major manufacturing city—the likely namesake of Manchester, Georgia, for obvious reasons—the railway offered regularly scheduled steam-powered freight and passenger service between the two. In these respects it ranks as the first true modern railroad. It is significant for the Callaway story, moreover, that the most important commodity this rail line

hauled was raw American cotton.

The impact of the railroad on American life is almost impossible to overstate. Many of the changes apply to Callaway with particular force, given his role as merchant and textile giant.

For one thing, there was industrial development, especially in the coal and iron industries. Coal is bulky, and iron ore is heavy. The railroad soon proved not only a fine way to haul them, but a major consumer of both. In 1900, for instance, mining products accounted for fully half of American railroad freight tonnage. As coal and iron combined to form a major rail network, railroads helped unleash steam power in industries across the American continent. Cities such as Birmingham, Alabama, in fact, came into being and grew into a major industrial centers because of the symbioses among coal, iron, and the railroad.

The greater availability of steam engines in industry, which the railroads enabled, unleashed a power far greater than that of animal muscles or even water. The resulting productivity led to higher incomes and standards of living. Bad harvests in a particular region no longer meant starvation for the people who

This Atlanta & West Point Railroad station served LaGrange from the end of the Civil War until 1910.

lived there. Industrial cities began flourishing, as urban dwellers could now buy fresh milk, fruit, and vegetables brought to town by rail from distant farms and pastures. This meant improved health for factory workers, and thus still greater productivity.

As for freight, the factories' products flowed out over the country both quickly and in large amounts. The speed and reliability of the railroad, and the lower transportation costs it permitted, meant that merchants such as Callaway no longer needed to keep a large inventory on hand. This freed up money they would have otherwise kept tied up in their goods, making it available for investment. Because of the railroads, Callaway could make huge purchases, transport everything to La-Grange at once, liquidate everything fast, and then repeat the cycle quickly. This strategy, and his near-meteoric rise from traveling salesman to specialty and then department store merchant and finally to wholesaler (with sales over a large geographical area), would have been impossible without railways.

The railroad also had a nationalizing influence in ways besides the economy, uniting the different regions of the country socially and culturally as never before. By the early twentieth century, Pullman sleeping cars hosted fifty thousand people nightly, and Callaway was often one of them. Because of this mobility, the gene pool itself was affected: people routinely now began marrying spouses who lived

well beyond the boundaries of their local communities. It is quite possible that Fuller Callaway and Ida Jane Cason would never have met if rail lines hadn't connected Jewell and LaGrange—and if their son's account is to be believed, even if they had met, they might not have married anyway if the railroads hadn't allowed them to wed in Jewell with Fuller missing only a single day's work.

Everyone wanted in, of course. In 1910, twenty-three hundred different companies owned America's tracks, which at the time amounted to nearly a quarter of a million miles, 40 percent of the world's total. And that doesn't count the thousands of railroads that had gone extinct by then, either through failure or acquisition by rivals.

Railroads were relatively inexpensive to run, and their rates were certainly low, but their initial capital costs were extremely high. This led to cutthroat practices, and investors could just as easily lose their shirts as become millionaires. Between 1847 and 1905, for instance, fully a dozen railroads were either planned for rural Troup County or actually built there, though most of them failed quickly and long ago.

The problem was that rail transportation was so cheap that such competition was easy, assuming funds could be raised to build a road in the first place. It cost very little more to ship goods six hundred miles than it did to move them only three hundred miles, so railroads had many options when building or acquiring tracks from point A to point B. That made competition for business between points A and B fierce if several roads offered service between those two places, which happened quite often. As a result, the rates between two such competitive points—for instance, New York and Chicago—tended to be very low, as each company tried to lure business away from competitors.

To balance out such low rates, then, railroads charged more—often a lot more—at

Large steam engines, such as this one, traveling through Troup County about 1906 were critical to the success of the growing textile business in LaGrange.

the stops in between the competitive points, at villages and smaller towns served only by a single railroad. In those towns, where the railroad in effect had a monopoly, it could charge what it wished. As a result, it was common for freight traveling a short distance to one of those stops to have a much higher shipping cost than the same kind of freight traveling a longer distance to a competitive point on the same set of rails—even perhaps in the same car. This was the notorious short-haul/long-haul distinction.

Farmers complained, and businessmen from the noncompetitive points—people such as Callaway in LaGrange—joined in as well. In response, many states began passing laws aimed at regulating railroads and their rates. At first the courts upheld these new Granger Laws, as they came to be known, but a major setback came with the *Wabash* case of 1886, in which a railroad challenged Illinois's attempt to ban the short-haul/long-haul discrepancy. The federal Supreme Court struck down the Illinois law, ruling that since the railroad traveled across state lines, this was a matter of interstate commerce, which was a matter for federal, and not state, regulation.

This was enough to goad Congress, the very next year, into passing the Interstate Commerce Act and creating the Interstate Commerce Commission, the first permanent federal regulatory agency. The act mandated fair railroad rates; the

Callaway's size 7⅜ derby was made by John B. Stetson. Callaway purchased the hat in New York.

Atlantic and West Point Ry. Passenger Depot,
Showing Southern Express Co., La Grange, Ga.

In 1911 a new Atlanta & West Point depot was constructed in LaGrange.

commission had the power to hear complaints from shippers about those rates, and to require rate adjustments.

This was a tall order. Short-haul/long-haul discrepancies and other monopolistic practices were the norm all across America. In the South there was even a formal structure known as the Southern Basing Point System, a formula that calculated rates depending on a town's distance from the nearest competitive point. If a merchant, for instance, wished to ship goods from New Orleans to LaGrange on the Louisville & Nashville Railroad and its subsidiary, the Atlanta & West Point Railroad, the system would charge him the price between the two base points of New Orleans and Atlanta, and then add to this charge the cost of shipment from Atlanta back to LaGrange. This was the bottom line the customer would have to pay even though the goods were put off the Atlanta-bound train when it first got to LaGrange.

One result of this was that shipping costs from New Orleans to LaGrange were significantly higher than the costs from New Orleans to Atlanta—a classic short-haul/long-haul discrepancy. Another result was that towns even farther from New Orleans than LaGrange would pay less than LaGrange, since they were closer to Atlanta. Hogansville customers, for instance, paid the same New Orleans-to-Atlanta rates that LaGrange customers did, but since Hogansville was closer than LaGrange to

Atlanta, they had a lower additional cost to tack on to this base charge. Even to the west of LaGrange the story was the same, since Opelika was also a base point. This put La-Grange farther from a base point than any other stop between Atlanta and Opelika, which meant that its rates were the highest of any town on this stretch of railroad.

This state of things irked Fuller Callaway. Even as a young merchant he had background enough to realize that his attempts to compete with other businesses beyond LaGrange would be handicapped by the shipping rates that he, but not others, had to pay. In 1895, as he began seriously contemplating the idea of opening up a wholesale operation, he decided to use the new regulations to take on the Atlanta & West Point Railroad, the line that ran through LaGrange, along with its powerful parent company, the Louisville & Nashville.

It was to be one of the longest and most fateful battles of his life.

It isn't surprising, that as a merchant, Callaway knew the importance of railroads. What is revealing is that, even in his mid-twenties, he was both aware of the new wave of railroad regulation and prepared to work this new system to his own advantage.

He began with the Georgia Railroad Commission. Created in 1879, and later evolving into today's Public Service Commission, the agency was initially charged with overseeing the railroad industry within Georgia. Callaway lodged a complaint with the commission against the Atlanta & West Point, appearing before the commissioners in June 1895. But that same day he learned the limits of the commission's power, running into exactly the same problem that had first spawned the ICC. The commissioners advised him that since the Atlanta & West Point was part of an interstate system, they had no authority to regulate it. This was, in fact, the stock answer they gave to a lot of complainants. And as part of the stock answer, they suggested that Callaway look to the ICC for relief.

He wasted no time doing so. Two days after appearing before the Georgia Railroad Commission, Callaway had secured a letter of reference from Francis Marion Longley to ICC commissioner Judson C. Clements. Longley was perhaps LaGrange's biggest political gun; since the end of the war he had seemingly served in nearly every important public position. At one point or another he'd been town councilman, county commissioner, mayor, superior court judge, and state legislator, as well as having been involved in the Unity mill. In his letter, Longley spoke of Callaway as "one of our most enterprising merchants . . . a young man of fine character, qualifications and business habits." Longley assured Clements that Callaway "would not present this matter but for which seems to me a clear violation of the U.S. Statutes."

Barely a week after the referral, Callaway was back in Atlanta, meeting with Clements. In this he was lucky. Clements, a fellow Georgian and a Confederate veteran, had studied law and then gone to Congress in the 1880s, where he had helped pass the Interstate Commerce Act before being named to the ICC. He very much wanted his commission to gain some real power so as to be able to regulate the railroads effectively, and he was thus naturally quite interested in Callaway's cause. After meeting with Callaway, he agreed to help the merchant draw up a complaint against the Atlanta & West Point, which Callaway then submitted to the commission.

Under the Interstate Commerce Act, Callaway had several grounds for his action. A complainant could argue, for instance, that a railroad's rates were inherently unreasonable or unjust, and he could also argue that a railroad was treating some customers preferentially even though other customers

Judson Clements, Chairman of the ICC and a fellow Georgian, directly oversaw Fuller's complaints about the unfair rates the Atlanta & West Point Railroad charged.

were in "substantially similar circumstances." Likewise, he could argue that a railroad was treating a customer or a locality with "undue or unreasonable preference or advantage" or "undue or unreasonable prejudice or disadvantage." Finally there was a provision that spoke exactly to Callaway's problem: it forbade railroads from charging customers more for short hauls than long ones "under substantially similar circumstances." Taking full advantage of Clements's help, Callaway challenged the Atlanta & West Point's rates to LaGrange on all of these grounds.

The railroad was slow to respond to the complaint, and, in fact, it missed the legal deadline for filing an answer. George C. Smith, president of the Atlanta & West Point, claimed as an explanation that the complexity of coordinating efforts between the Atlanta & West Point and its parent, the Louisville & Nashville, had delayed the reply. In retrospect the delay reflects a cavalier, almost a contemptuous, attitude that railroads seemed to have against the ICC, as later events would substantiate. Callaway was understanding at first, but as the weeks turned into months, he grew impatient. "Will you please appoint a day for the hearing of my case?" he finally wrote in aggravation to the commissioners in October 1896, more than a year after filing his initial complaint. "In June they asked for 60 days more time—they have had 90 days time."

That message seemed to get the ball rolling. About a month later, on November 9, the ICC convened a hearing in Atlanta that Callaway attended. Acting without an attorney, he was also the sole witness on his side of the case. And his testimony was to the point. "The rates that I complain of are admitted by the railroad," he told Clements, the commissioner conducting the hearing. "They will haul stuff from New Orleans through LaGrange to Hogansville, Newnan, Palmetto and Fairburn to Atlanta for less rates than to LaGrange." In fact, he continued, "[t]hey can haul stuff from New Orleans to Atlanta and ship back to Hogansville cheaper than I can get it to LaGrange, much less my shipping it to Hogansville."

By now Callaway had inaugurated his wholesale business, having given up his strategy of waiting for the ICC's ruling. This fact was of interest to Clements. "Are there any other wholesale houses there besides yours?" he asked Callaway.

"Not strictly wholesale," Callaway answered. "They would be there if we could get the rate but we cannot compete up there, strictly wholesale." This answer may be one of the early indications that Callaway was interested not merely in his own business prospects but in growing the town of La-Grange as a whole.

Callaway next faced a cross-examination from Ed Baxter, the Nashville attorney who was the chief lawyer for the Louisville & Nashville. Nearing age sixty, Baxter was an accomplished litigator. Although he was a Tennessee native, he was well acquainted with Georgia and its rail system, having served in both Atlanta and Macon as a Confederate artillery officer. Nevertheless, Callaway handled the questioning well.

"What kind of goods do you buy in New Orleans?" Baxter began.

"Sugar, molasses, and rice."

"Do you know about what is the tonnage of goods that you buy in New Orleans?"

"No, I do not know," replied Callaway. "It is not so very great on account of the rates being so high," he added pointedly. "We would like to buy more . . . that is what is the matter."

Callaway had already noted the lower rates to Hogansville, and now Baxter focused on this. "Would there be any difficulty in your using these rates to Hogansville and these other points which you think have a preference over you, and then supply your customers from there?"

Callaway had an easy answer for this one. "I could not afford to have a storage warehouse at each place." For the same reason, he added, he couldn't use the depots in those towns, which also charged for storage.

Baxter then turned to the fact that the Macon and Birmingham Railroad also ran to LaGrange, asking why Callaway simply didn't use that railroad instead since he thought the Atlanta & West Point rates too high. Callaway explained that for some reason Southern Railway, which operated the Macon line, would not accept shipments in Atlanta that were bound through Macon for LaGrange. "The Southern Road will not talk to me about whether they should compete with the West Point Road at LaGrange." In his words was a subtle suggestion—nothing so strong as an accusation—that the Southern had an arrangement with the Atlanta & West Point not to compete for LaGrange traffic, no doubt in exchange for concessions to Southern elsewhere.

In contrast to Callaway, the railroad—which had already filed masses of tables, statistics, and arguments—put on a great deal of testimony. Its basic argument was that "the rates from New Orleans to Atlanta are fixed by the competition between markets . . . and are just and reasonable." In simpler terms, the railroad argued that the competition that it faced from other railroads in Atlanta forced it to have low rates there or else lose business, and that it thus had to make up for these low rates in the rates it charged towns down the line—towns that had rail service at all only because they were on the route to Atlanta. "The reason that Fairburn, Palmetto, Newnan and Hogansville have lower rates than La-Grange," continued the railroad, "is due alone to the fact that they are nearer to Atlanta, and not to any favoritism or discrimination."

Despite all of the testimony and filings—or perhaps because of them—another long delay followed the December hearing. Two months later Callaway wrote Clements to ask when he might expect a decision, only to be told that the railroad had yet to file its final arguments. More time passed. In December 1897, thirteen months after the hearing, Callaway sent still another letter to Clements. "Is there any likelihood of a decision being rendered in my case against the A & WP R R Co., et al, that was heard in Atlanta, Ga., last November a year ago?" he half-demanded, his irritation obvious. "I want to open a WHOLESALE GROCERY STORE here as soon as a decision is rendered."

Perhaps that was the message that got the ball rolling. At any rate, the ICC announced its decision just two weeks later, on the last day of the year, and its ruling, if long in coming, was all that Callaway could have hoped. In a longish opinion, the commission ruled completely in his favor, finding that the railroads' rates violated three different sections of the Interstate Commerce Act. Among other things, the commission noted that "the local charge of the Atlanta & West Point back from Atlanta to LaGrange is unreasonable and unjust and unduly prejudicial to complainant and others doing business at LaGrange." These were words drawn from the statute, intended to show that the railroad had violated it. But the commission went further, stating flatly that LaGrange's location, "71 miles southwesterly of Atlanta, and that much nearer to New Orleans," made the railroad's claim that its rates were reasonable "seem almost absurd."

To remedy the situation, that same day the commission entered a "cease and desist" order in which it commanded the railroad to stop charging LaGrange traffic from New Orleans higher rates than traffic bound for points between LaGrange and Atlanta. The order also contained an interesting provision in which the commission recommended its own rate schedule, advising the railroad to adopt it.

If things had stopped at that point, then the situation would have been ideal for Callaway. But the commission's decision and order were merely, as Winston Churchill might have put it, the end of the beginning.

~

Six weeks after handing down its decision, the ICC sent a curious letter to Callaway. "Since the issuance of the order in your case," it read, "the Commission has not been notified of any change in the rates affected. Kindly state whether you are informed of any action taken or contemplated by the companies in the direction of compliance with the order, and what, if any, steps you have taken in the matter." Obviously the ICC wanted Callaway to do the investigative work himself.

Callaway needed no prompting. "I wrote to Mr. Geo. C. Smith about one month ago asking him if he would put in the rates as per the decision of the Commission," he informed

Judge Harry T. Toulmin of the United States District Court for the Southern District of Alabama ruled in favor of Fuller Callaway, but was later overturned.

the ICC, "and he never replied to my letter. I wired him today, and he answered '*that he would not talk on the question now.*'"

That wasn't all. Not only was he paying the same rates as before, declared Callaway; "In fact we have been paying slightly higher rates."

If the railroad's slow responses prior to and during the proceedings before the commission suggested that it was being obstructionist, this casual ignoring of a legal order seems to confirm the idea. Callaway certainly thought so, at least, asking the ICC what he should do. "I have no idea the Railroads will do the 'right thing' unless they are made to do so," he declared.

One of the weaknesses of the ICC was that it lacked the power to enforce its own orders, and the railroads knew it. But the commission could—and, in fact, was technically required to—bring an action in federal court to enforce its orders when necessary. In July 1898 this is exactly what the ICC did

with Callaway's case, filing a petition in the United States Circuit Court for the Southern District of Alabama. After describing what had happened before the commission, the petition charged that the defendants had "wholly disregarded and set at naught" the commission's order, "and have willfully and knowingly violated and disobeyed the same." On these grounds, the commission asked the court to issue an injunction to prevent the railroads' continued violation of the order.

No doubt to Callaway's chagrin, another long delay now ensued. Not until a year and a half later—in December 1899—did the court rule on the case. But at least it, too, sided with Callaway. Judge Harry T. Toulmin largely agreed with the ICC's findings of fact, concluding, as the ICC had, that the railroads had violated sections one, three, and four of the Interstate Commerce Act. He differed with the ICC on a point or two, but he noted that the law was clear: he had to defer to the commissioners unless their findings of fact were clearly erroneous, and they weren't. As a result, he readily issued the injunction that Callaway wanted.

Once again, if things had stopped there, Callaway would have won. But now it was the railroad that took things further, appealing Toulmin's decision to the federal Circuit Court of Appeals in New Orleans. Another year and a half elapsed, and during this time Callaway still had to keep paying the same high rates, for the court had suspended the injunction pending the case's outcome. In May 1901, with a short, dismissive opinion, the appellate court threw the case out, refusing to enforce the ICC's order.

Callaway had just run into a problem that was the bane of nearly everyone who had turned to the courts to enforce ICC orders. The problem, in a nutshell, was that the commission and the courts tended to read the Interstate Commerce Act differently—and since the commission had to rely on the courts to enforce its decrees, the courts' interpretation prevailed. But Callaway had no choice. Despite his victories before the commission and in the trial court, the railroads had yet to lower their rates. So he took the next step, appealing this latest court ruling to the United States Supreme Court.

It was nearly an exercise in futility. From the commission's founding down to 1905, sixteen ICC cases went to the Supreme Court, and in every case but one, the ICC lost. The key difference of opinion was that the courts, unlike the ICC, saw the existence of competition in major cities such as Atlanta as a justification for high short-haul charges. Ed Baxter, the Louisville & Nashville's attorney, knew this quite well; he'd argued and won two of the key cases in which the Supreme Court had set forth this rule. He knew, therefore, that once Callaway took his case to the federal courts, the odds would be against the LaGrangian. But again, Callaway didn't have any choice.

In May 1903, nearly eight years after Callaway first took his complaint to the Georgia Railroad Commission, the Supreme Court ruled against him. The decision had the effect of sending the case back before the ICC, but it also tied the commissioners' hands, since they now had to accept the competition that the railroad faced in Atlanta as a legitimate factor in setting the rates to LaGrange. It would be hard, if not impossible, for Callaway to win under those terms.

Ida Callaway reported that her husband was "very much exercised" over the whole issue of freight rates, and even though he didn't let the delay in the litigation stop him from opening his wholesale concern, he wasn't prepared to let go of the matter. Although he was no lawyer, as bright as he was he had to know that he wasn't likely to win in the federal courts. So once the Supreme Court ruled against him, he shifted his attention away from the ICC action and focused instead on a major new project: the construction of a new railroad from LaGrange to Atlanta.

In the spring of 1905, he became part of a committee to secure rights of way for a new line through town. On April 18 a group of Boston and Atlanta investors chartered the Atlanta, Birmingham & Atlantic Railroad, with plans to extend it between these two fast-growing cities and Brunswick on the Georgia coast. A month earlier Callaway, along with Hatton Lovejoy, Roy Dallis, J. G. Truitt, E. B. Clarke, and even Joe Dunson, had met with some of the railroad's future officers and had gotten them to agree to run the new line straight through LaGrange.

It was a major victory for Callaway and for all of Troup County. Not only would the new railroad force the Atlanta & West Point to make its rates competitive; it would allow Callaway to bypass the latter altogether if he so chose. The same went for every other businessman in LaGrange who ever shipped goods in or out—including, of course, the textile mills. As one of Callaway's friends noted, "This is the date of the new birth of LaGrange."

Callaway's storage box for the Atlanta, Birmingham & Atlantic Railroad paperwork was inscribed with the initials A.B + A R.R. Com. Callaway played an important role in making sure the newly chartered Atlanta, Birmingham & Atlantic Railroad ran through LaGrange starting in 1905.

Trained as a lawyer, Robert Hatton Lovejoy (1877–1964) worked closely with Fuller for over thirty years. The courtroom at the University of Georgia School of Law is named in his honor.

Almost from the beginning of the railroad era in the mid-1800s, state governments had often given railroad companies the power of eminent domain, the power to take private property (in exchange for compensation to the owner) in order to secure rights-of-way for tracks. Georgia was no exception. Within Georgia, in fact, railroads could go so far as to condemn property belonging to other rail companies, as long as the property in question wasn't already in actual use for railroad purposes. This point was at the heart of the next round between Callaway and the Atlanta & West Point.

In June 1905, barely six weeks after the chartering of the Atlanta, Birmingham & Atlantic, the Atlanta & West Point petitioned the Fulton County Superior Court for an injunction against the new company. The Atlanta, Birmingham & Atlantic had informed the Atlanta & West Point that it intended to take some of its land in downtown LaGrange, near the intersection of Morgan and Depot Streets and the Atlanta & West Point depot, and the Atlanta & West Point wanted to prevent that.

The Atlanta & West Point, at the time, wasn't actually using the land in question, and so arguably, under Georgia law, the property was ripe for condemnation. But the Atlanta & West Point did have a card to play. Due to its increasing business volume, it claimed in the petition, it was in the process of splitting itself into two divisions. One would oversee the line from LaGrange to Atlanta, while the other would manage the route from LaGrange to Opelika. Since LaGrange just happened to be the junction between the two new divisions, stated the Atlanta & West Point, it planned to build an expanded depot on the land that the Atlanta, Birmingham & Atlantic wanted. This meant that the new company couldn't condemn the property.

The Superior Court didn't buy into the argument. Concluding that in reality the

Of course the railroads were noisy and dangerous, and steam engines in particular produced large amounts of black, soot-filled smoke. A few holdouts disliked the idea of another railroad in town, and one of them reportedly claimed it would ruin LaGrange. James Fannin, an elderly civic leader, replied with words that might well have come from Callaway. "Yes, I've observed how railroads have ruined New York, Philadelphia, and Baltimore," he quipped, referring to booming northern centers of commerce and industry, "and I'd like to see our city ruined in the same manner."

But the Atlanta & West Point wasn't ready to stop fighting yet. Within a matter of months, the next battle began.

Atlanta & West Point wouldn't be needing the land any time soon, the court flatly refused to enjoin the condemnation. Things had turned once again in Callaway's favor, but as it had in the ICC case when Callaway won at the trial level, the Atlanta & West Point appealed, this time to the Georgia Supreme Court.

Now that Callaway had both the initiative and the law on his side, the Atlanta & West Point, insultingly slow to respond to the ICC and the courts in the past, moved quickly. The Supreme Court heard arguments in the case within just a few months of the Superior Court ruling, in October 1905 to be exact, and issued its own decision barely a month after that. Again Callaway and the new company won. The court refused to second-guess the trial judge's findings of fact to the effect that the Atlanta & West Point wasn't about to start building a new depot. "Under such circumstances," the Supreme Court declared, "the future needs of the company must yield to the present lawful needs of the new company seeking a right of way through the city of LaGrange."

But the Atlanta & West Point still didn't give up trying to block the construction of its would-be competitor. At a century's remove, in light of its glacial responses to Callaway during the ICC litigation, the speed with which it acted in these new cases, once it was losing ground, is amusing, although at the time Callaway would probably have described it in very different terms. Within a month of the Supreme Court's decision, the railroad company filed a new case against the Atlanta, Birmingham & Atlantic, again in Fulton County Superior Court, asking for another injunction.

This time it argued that the new railroad had simply taken Atlanta & West Point property without paying for it or even trying to condemn it. The property in question now was a strip of land running down Morgan Street near Depot Street. The Atlanta & West Point's claim that it owned this land—

effectively, that it owned Morgan Street itself—was based on deeds that it could trace back to the early 1850s. This particular stretch of Morgan Street hadn't even existed then; the city didn't extend the street that far until the 1890s, and by then the railroad had been using the land for decades.

The Atlanta, Birmingham & Atlantic and the Callaway team fought back. Roy Dallis, in particular, along with more than a dozen other longtime residents of LaGrange, offered affidavits to the effect that the new rail line would be good for LaGrange's economy as well as for the value of the property adjacent to the new tracks. While this argument reveals one of the group's main goals in building the new line—economic development—it had no legal significance, and the court excluded it. But Dallis also pointed out that the new Morgan Street had now been in place for more than ten years, and never in that time had the Atlanta & West Point objected to it. Only now, he observed, was the railroad speaking up. The inference that he clearly wanted the court to draw was that the Atlanta & West Point wasn't concerned about public use of its property; instead it wanted to monopolize rail transportation to and from LaGrange.

Dallis made his point. The Atlanta & West Point lost again, at least for the most part. The court refused to grant this new injunction just as it had in the first case, but it did find that the Atlanta & West Point had proved its ownership of the land—although LaGrange had gained a right-of-way over it in the form of Morgan Street. Atlanta & West Point appealed this case, too, to the state Supreme Court, continuing to act with its newfound haste.

In May 1906 the Supreme Court largely agreed with the trial court. There were secondary issues involved; the Atlanta & West Point prevailed on some of them, and the Atlanta, Birmingham & Atlantic won on others. But in the last part of the opinion, the court reached the big question.

The justices, for the most part, agreed with the Atlanta, Birmingham & Atlantic. Echoing the trial court, they concluded that the Atlanta & West Point *did* own the land in question, but that the city just as clearly had gained a right-of-way across it. Since any member of the public could use that right-of-way as long as he didn't interfere with others' use of it, the Atlanta, Birmingham & Atlantic could run a track down Morgan Street without paying the Atlanta & West Point or even getting its permission—if the track and the trains that ran on it would not interfere with other public use of the street.

Here, though, the court dealt a blow to the new railroad. Locomotives were large and hazardous, noted the court. "On account of the ponderous and unwieldy nature of the machinery necessary to be employed over this railroad," it concluded, the Atlanta, Birmingham & Atlantic "could not observe the ordinary rules of the road. Its use of the street would be dangerous and inconsistent with that of pedestrians or the general public according to the various modes of travel. Its whole tendency would be to exclude others." This, in turn, meant that the Atlanta, Birmingham & Atlantic couldn't run its tracks down Morgan Street after all.

It was a setback, but only a minor one. Indeed, since both cases could have been avoided if the two companies had only been willing to negotiate, the fact that the cases were filed and litigated all the way to the state Supreme Court so quickly, shows the cutthroat competition between them. A small shifting of the route so that it was no longer on Morgan Street itself would fix things, and that could be done by a simple condemnation of a nearby strip of Atlanta & West Point land. In fact, to guard against a possible loss in the Supreme Court, the Atlanta, Birmingham & Atlantic was already taking steps three months before the court's ruling to do just that.

Callaway's case before the ICC was still technically open, and from time to time since his loss in the federal Supreme Court there was a bit of activity. But postponements continued in that case, often because Callaway himself now wanted them. His attention was now on the Atlanta, Birmingham & Atlantic instead of the ICC case. In August 1906, Judson Clements wrote Callaway to update him on the case. Two months previously, Congress had passed the Hepburn Act, a law that had finally given the ICC some teeth. Under the new act the commission could clearly determine the reasonableness of shipping rates, and what was more, its orders were now legally binding without a need to resort to the courts for enforcement. If the Hepburn Act had been in force in 1895, Callaway's case probably would have turned out differently.

It wasn't too late, though. That was why Clements was now writing Callaway. The thing to do, Clements advised, was to dismiss the old complaint and file a new one under the Hepburn Act provisions.

But now that victory before the ICC seemed likely, Callaway demurred. Possibly this was due in part to his exasperation with the long fruitless battle, but it was also certainly due to something else that was happening. "For special and particular reasons, we would much prefer not to have the cases now pending dismissed," he told Clements. "Writer is not at liberty to go into details, but will say that there is a prospect of our getting what we want by an amicable adjustment, and if the cases now pending were to be dismissed at this time, such action might have a disastrous effect upon the negotiations." Clearly Callaway was no longer interested in the ICC action per se; he simply wanted to use it as pressure to get his way on another front of the battle.

The negotiations—perhaps the term "amicable" was a relative one in light of the bitter legal fights of the past decade—must have been a delicious turn of events for Callaway. On March 27 Hatton Lovejoy, acting as an attorney for the Atlanta, Birmingham & Atlantic,

Callaway played a critical role in getting the Atlanta, Birmingham & Atlantic Railroad routed through LaGrange to provide competition for the Atlanta & West Point. This photo depicts Engine 1517 on the maiden trip of the A.B. & A. through Atlanta. The men include railroad officials and members of the Atlanta Chamber of Commerce celebrating the completion of the line through Atlanta.

contacted the Atlanta & West Point with some new information. "You are hereby notified," Lovejoy's communication read stiffly, "that the Atlanta, Birmingham & Atlantic Company . . . having failed to agree with you upon a price mutually satisfactory for the estate, privileges and user hereinafter named, proposes to acquire title by condemnation in accordance with the laws of Georgia." The estate in question was a long, narrow strip of Atlanta & West Point land running down the west side of Morgan Street just north of Depot Street, 267 feet long and about 25 feet wide—just wide enough for a set of railroad tracks. What Lovejoy didn't say was obvious: the condemnation was going to happen. The amount to be paid for the land was the only matter at issue. And if the railroad again went to court to try to

block the condemnation, Callaway could always go after it again under the Hepburn Act, and this time he would likely win.

To decide on the price, Lovejoy continued, each railroad would name an assessor, and together these two would select a third. Lovejoy went on, probably with a feeling of payback for the long years of delay, to inform the Atlanta & West Point that the Atlanta, Birmingham & Atlantic had already picked its assessor. His name, Lovejoy wrote in the blank space contained in the form, was Fuller E. Callaway.

In June 1906, less than a month after the final Georgia Supreme Court decision, Callaway and the other assessors announced that the price for the land would be $625—no doubt a pittance compared to shipping rates, attorney's fees, and litigation costs that the parties had paid out since 1895. By mid-July the deed was filed, and construction of the new railroad proceeded, and was completed within a few years. In late 1907, with the battle now clearly decided, Callaway agreed to dismiss the original complaint that he'd filed with the ICC more than twelve years earlier. The fight had been long, costly, and ugly, but Callaway in the end had won it.

~

Besides railroad development and reduced freight rates, Callaway took major steps in other areas designed to modernize LaGrange's economic structure. Except for the railroads and the textile mills themselves, perhaps the most important area was banking.

The defeat of the Confederacy wrecked not only the Southern economy generally but its banking system in particular. By 1865, nearly every bank in the South had closed its doors. In 1860, Georgia and South Carolina between them boasted forty-nine state-chartered banks; in 1865, only four of them were left. Even in 1880 the North still had three times the number of banks per capita as the South.

The economic and financial collapse was bad enough, but Northern developments made it even worse. In 1863 and 1864 the Congress passed the National Bank Acts. The laws set up a process for chartering banks under the authority of the national government. To qualify for a national charter, a bank had to deposit government bonds with the comptroller of the currency, a federal officer in Washington. Prior to 1900 the amount could be as high as $200,000— more than $5,000,000 in modern purchasing power. (A bank could gain a state charter, on the other hand, for as little as $5,000.) In exchange for this deposit, the national bank would be issued national currency. This arrangement gave national banks great stability in a way somewhat similar to today's FDIC. If a national bank failed, the federal treasury would honor the currency it had issued because of the bonds the bank had deposited with the government, a circumstance that decreased the danger of a run on the bank in the first place.

All of this was well and good for the North. But even years after the war, the South faced huge obstacles to joining this system; among other things, impoverished Southern communities simply couldn't afford it. As a result, in 1870 the nation had more than sixteen hundred national banks, which among themselves held roughly half of all bank deposits, but only sixty-nine of them were in the former Confederacy. Lacking the wherewithal to charter national banks, Southerners instead had to rely on state-chartered banks, which, being poorly capitalized, had less lending power, were more prone to failure, and were subject to a 10 percent federal tax on their bank notes.

The situation in LaGrange was typical during this period. Prior to 1900 only four chartered banks appear in the town's history, with fewer than a half dozen others in West Point and Hogansville. Most of these banks failed quickly, and some of them apparently existed only on paper, never making it into actual operation. The only relatively major bank of the entire nineteenth century was the LaGrange Banking and Trust Company, chartered by A. D. Abraham and others in 1871 and lasting until the Great Depression of the 1930s. In 1883 the First National Bank of LaGrange opened its doors, but it only managed to survive as a national bank until 1890, presumably due to undercapitalization. Afterward it became a state bank, which also fell victim to the Great Depression. Due to its low capital, it was of no help in financing the town's new textile ventures of the late 1800s.

This weakness in banking makes the emergence of the Dixie and Unity mills all the more impressive, since without a vigorous bank LaGrange, like most of the South, was locked out of Northern capital markets, which could have

Fuller Callaway helped charter the LaGrange National Bank. In 1917 it moved into this new building at the corner of Main and Broome Streets. Callaway maintained his office at this location.

funded industrial and commercial development. It was all part of a long, vicious cycle. Small, poor southern farms and impoverished citizens meant that there was little spare money. Tight money supplies, and the fact that nearly everyone was a farmer subject to the same risks, such as drought and boll weevils, meant high interest rates on loans. This impeded the development of banks that could have tapped Northern money, which could have allowed the South to invigorate its economy and break out of the cycle. The results are apparent in Callaway's agonizing attempts to raise capital for Unity Mills among private subscribers, sometimes in blocks as small as one hundred dollars. Without his gift of salesmanship, it might have proved impossible. The extremely tight money supplies probably do much to explain his

extreme desire to spend very carefully, both in his personal and professional lives.

But with the coming of the new century, many things were changing. The mills were beginning to bring a new prosperity to the town, which meant that more capital was available. By now, too, Callaway was in his thirties, and he had doubtless learned even more about both the importance and the techniques of finance through his experiences with the mills and other businesses. Then there was the new Atlanta, Birmingham & Atlantic Railroad. It is by no means a simple coincidence that in May 1905—less than a month after the chartering of the new road—Callaway, the Truitts, and other key citizens chartered the LaGrange National Bank with $150,000 startup capital, three times the minimum amount legally required for a town of LaGrange's size. The new bank had Callaway as its president and Neal Truitt as vice president.

Opening its doors in June, the new bank was soon closely involved with financing the new railroad, including supplying its local payroll. The bank also emphasized customer service in an attempt to gain broad-based support. Although its official hours ran from 8am until 3pm, officers and employees worked to accommodate customers' reasonable needs any time between 7am and nightfall.

The date of the bank's founding, along with its aggressive effort to gain and serve customers, is more than coincidental in another way. The fact that Joseph E. Dunson was now president of the new bank's long-established rival, the La-Grange Banking and Trust Company, and at the beginning opposed the creation of a new competitor, may well have contributed to the bad blood between the Dunson and Callaway factions that caused trouble at the Unity Mill around this same time.

A year and a half later, as part of the attempt to expand his customer base, Callaway took part in organizing a second financial institution, the LaGrange Savings Bank, which did business out of the same building as the LaGrange National Bank. Unlike LaGrange National, though, this was a state bank, which required lower capitalization. Through a typical Fuller Callaway advertising campaign—advertising then being a rarity among banks—it encouraged customers to establish savings accounts, and, in fact, it didn't even offer checking accounts. And as a state bank it could do one thing that national banks couldn't do until 1913: it could make loans on real estate, allowing prospective homeowners, many of whom were mill operatives, to buy their own houses, financing the purchase through the mortgage process. The combined, closely coordinated resources and abilities of the two banks, then, created a local financial powerhouse.

All this, in turn, spurred still other developments. As the number of homes grew, so did the demand for electricity. The earliest electric plant in the area was the one at Dunson's LaGrange Mills, which by the early 1900s was fast becoming inadequate as a power source. Since the Georgia Power Company didn't extend service to town until 1911, LaGrange had to deal with the problem itself for a time. Many citizens, Callaway included, supported the idea of a city-owned power plant, but Dunson and LaGrange Mill stockholders naturally objected to the potential competition. But, partly through Callaway's efforts, a local election approved the new plant's construction.

Of more immediate financial concern to Callaway was the task of protecting the new bank's real estate investments. The obvious answer, of course, was to require all the new homeowner-mortgagors to carry insurance. Callaway thus took part in setting up the new LaGrange Insurance Agency.

Taking still another step, not only in ensuring LaGrange's increasing assets, but also in drawing new business, in 1906 Callaway also helped establish the Security Warehouse Company, the centerpiece of which was a large, modern warehouse. It was the first completely modern one in LaGrange, equipped with brick interior partitions, automatic fire doors, and an automatic sprinkler system. These modern safety measures meant that insurance rates were so low on the property that the company itself provided insurance to its customers free of charge. The warehouse thus became a major drawing point for cotton merchants, and as more and more of the crop found its way to LaGrange, Callaway and others proceeded to build a new electrically powered gin. Success continued to breed more success.

As the Calumet Company spawned more new mills, Callaway took part in expanding banking as well, not only in Manchester but also in Franklin and in the Alabama towns of Wadley and Standing Rock. By now he'd developed a keen appreciation for insurance, likely because of his recent involvement with it, and he made sure that each bank with which he was affiliated was insured against theft. On one occasion, at least, this insistence quite literally paid off. The Bank of Heard County in Franklin fell victim to a burglary that cleaned out all of its cash. To deal with the crisis, Callaway immediately sent replacement funds under guard; once the immediate problem had passed, the insurance policy covered the entire loss.

Burglary wasn't the only threat. LaGrange was booming by now, but it wasn't so flush that an economic downturn couldn't cause major damage. The South, after all, still had much fewer resources than other parts of the nation. One of the greatest early tests of the new commercial and industrial center's finances came with the national Panic of 1907.

This was the third national economic crisis to have happened in Callaway's lifetime, and the second financial meltdown within fifteen years. Like the Panics of 1873 and 1893, it involved the railroads. In the case of the 1907 panic, some people claimed that one of its chief causes was the 1906 passage of the Hepburn Act, the same law that would have given Callaway a second chance to beat the Atlanta & West Point in an ICC hearing, although he turned down the chance when he condemned the road's land instead. Railroads had continued to expand throughout 1906, as they had been doing for decades, sinking even more money than usual into growing their infrastructure. But the Hepburn Act scared potential railroad investors. Now that the ICC had some teeth, passenger and freight rates might go down, making railroads worse investments. So when railroads sought out Wall Street capital to finance their newest wave of expansion, they found nothing but closed doors.

In October 1907, with money supplies tight given the railroad's capital investments and similar reasons, a speculator tried and failed to corner the copper market. The failure destroyed the value of the United Copper Company. This in turn wrecked banks associated with the company, and a domino-like chain of bank failures began. What had begun in part as a railroad issue turned into a banking crisis, thus striking two of Callaway's most important projects outside the textile industry itself.

The dominos continued to fall largely because there was no central banking system. A central bank could have shored up any member bank that found itself in trouble, shifting resources from healthy banks to endangered ones. In fact the Panic of 1907 was one of the reasons for the creation of the centralized Federal Reserve System six years later. But that was of no help in 1907. In the absence of a centralized system, each bank was on its own. If customers came to believe, rightly or wrongly, that a bank was in debt to United Copper—or was in debt to a bank that was in debt to United Copper, and so on—a run on that bank would begin, creating a self-fulfilling prophecy that would quickly drive the bank into insolvency, even if it had been completely healthy before the start of the run on its resources.

But if there were no central bank, there was still one potential solution: the clearinghouse.

Clearinghouses are institutions created by banks to settle accounts among themselves. When a customer of one bank cashes a check drawn on an account at another bank, the clearinghouse is where the two banks sort out the debt created between them. A clearinghouse, of course, involves far more than one check and two banks; it is the central location for settling the multitude of transactions that take place every day, balancing the sheets of every bank in the community against each other.

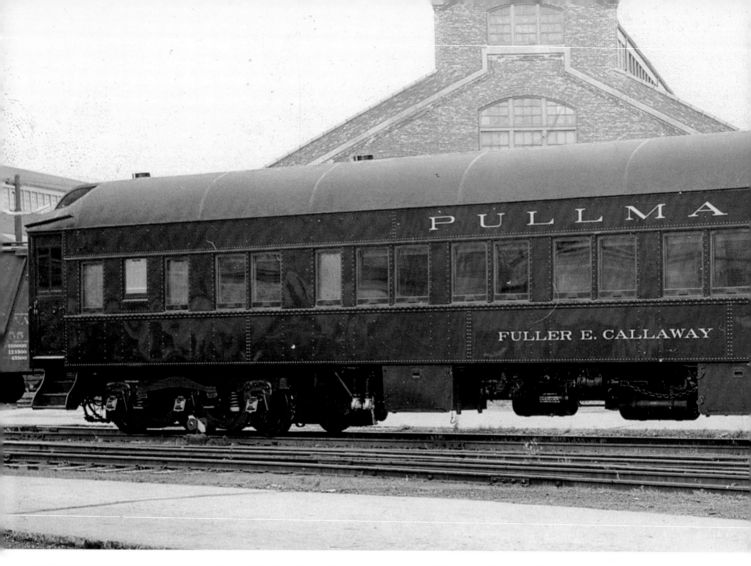

In 1939, a Pullman car was named in memory of Fuller E. Callaway. The car regularly passed through LaGrange as it traveled between New York and New Orleans

This central device was a key to stopping the panic, or at least to stopping its spread to places such as Troup County. If a sound bank was facing a run that could kill it, then the clearinghouse—in effect, all of the other banks in the region—could lend money to the targeted bank, enabling it to cover all of its clamoring customers' withdrawals and still stay in business. In the event—now unlikely—that the bank failed anyway, the other banks would share in the loss, which they could absorb more easily since there were several of them. The clearinghouse, then, was the central organization that let the banking community limit or end the panic by pooling its resources.

Clearinghouses had done this in economic panics as far back as 1857. But beginning with the dreadful Panic of 1893, they went a step

further, borrowing money directly from the public to increase their money supply and gain still more stability. In exchange for this money they issued loan certificates to their lenders. In 1907 clearinghouses all over the country repeated this tactic to ward off financial crisis in the face of the disastrous copper scheme.

As the panic swept through the nation, clearinghouses in Atlanta, Columbus, and Macon began issuing loan certificates to the public. But Callaway hated the idea of doing so. The certificates, he decided, being printed hastily to deal with the emergency, were too easy to counterfeit. There was even a danger that if he accepted loan certificates from a depositor that had been issued elsewhere, he could end up holding the bag if they were forgeries. So instead of issuing his own loan certificates, he managed to secure engraved,

hard-to-counterfeit currency from Washington, using the LaGrange National Bank's own stock as collateral. He also set an important policy designed to make sure that his banks didn't get stuck with someone else's bad paper. When customers deposited loan certificates with him, he had the paper rushed to Atlanta depositories before the end of business that day. This helped guarantee that the LaGrange banks had nothing but sound currency, and plenty of it, both on deposit and in circulation.

Because of these and other conservative steps Callaway took in safeguarding the assets of the many businesses in which he now had a hand, LaGrange continued to flourish and grow. The economic base prospered so much, in fact, that in 1917 the LaGrange National Bank constructed a large new building at the corner of Main and Broome Streets—the same

building that remains there to this day, although later the bank successfully merged into the venerable C&S institution. Some people thought that the bank shouldn't move so far away from its old headquarters on the courthouse square—an entire city block—but Callaway knew what he was doing. When the new building was finished, he moved his own center of operations to the top floor.

From his new office, Callaway could look out over the city that he had taken such a large part in building. Below were his stores, the new warehouse, and the mill to the southwest. And just a block to the east, of course, on Morgan Street, were the shining tracks of the Atlanta, Birmingham & Atlantic Railroad, which now connected LaGrange to the larger world, helping to usher in his city's new age of prosperity.

IDA AND FULLER WERE MOST PROUD OF THEIR TWO SONS
CASON (LEFT) AND FULLER JR. (RIGHT).

·5·

THE MIDDLE YEARS:
FAMILY AND TRAVEL

Everything about Fuller Callaway suggests at first glance that he was acquainted only with work, but this isn't quite the whole story. Callaway enjoyed his life greatly, and his wife and family, both immediate and extended, were important parts of that life. Ida Callaway was speaking for Fuller as well as herself when she titled a chapter of her memoirs "Nine of Our Happiest Days," and all nine days were about the family they had made together.

The first of these days, chronologically, marked the birth of the couple's elder child. In September 1893 Fuller's father Abner passed on, but just over a year later, on November 6, 1894, another Callaway arrived to help fill the empty place. Since he quite naturally bore Fuller's surname, the couple honored Ida's family in choosing his given names, a common approach of the time. The son thus took the name of Cason Jewell Callaway.

Ida was thrilled to be a mother, taking a dim view of what she called the emancipated woman, what we would think of as the feminists of the early twentieth century. The woman who sought a career rather than a traditional role, Ida proclaimed, "is 'emancipated' from the dearest things of this world," motherhood being the main one.

Home and family life, she wrote, were "worth more than the highest office any woman could attain."

But Fuller, too, took an interest in Cason's upbringing, seeking out Enoch, his physician brother, when the boy was ailing, and pampering the youngster during fits of colic. He and Ida also had plans for Cason, putting them into effect early on. When Cason was just a few years old, Fuller began exposing him to public events. When he was almost four, Ida took him with her to a meeting of the Woman's Missionary Society. At this particular meeting, the group was choosing a new leader. "We will now vote for president of the society," announced the chairwoman at one point. In response, Cason stood up and raised his hand. "I vote

Cason as a young boy with his mother, Ida.

The Barracks,
Bingham Military School,
Asheville, N. C.

Cason attended the Bingham School in Asheville, North Carolina.

for McKinley!" he sang out, naming the country's current Republican chief executive. This provoked some ribbing for his father, who was a supporter of McKinley's two-time Democratic opponent, William Jennings Bryan.

Around this same time Cason first showed that he had inherited his father's taste for sales. Sinclair Cason, daughter of Ida's brother Edward, was visiting the Callaways for the summer, and the family had decided to get rid of her old clothes. Among them was a hat, which Cason set about trying to sell to an elderly black woman. When Fuller came home for supper, he came across Cason sitting on the steps, lost in thought. He was so quiet that Fuller asked him if he were sick.

"No, father," said Cason. "I'm just trying to think up a way to get that old woman to buy that hat!" Eventually he succeeded, which Fuller probably found quite encouraging.

Cason would indeed have a promising future in the mills. In fact, Fuller let him blow the whistle that announced the Unity plant's official opening when the boy was only six years old. But Cason was almost too eager to become a merchant. When he was around twelve, he set up a store of his own, but only a pretend one. Nevertheless, he got hold of some of Fuller's business stationery and used it for his own "firm's" correspondence. A wholesaler received one of Cason's business letters and hopped a train to LaGrange right away, only to

be met by Fuller as well as Cason, the former upset and the latter embarrassed.

Soon, however, a maturing Cason began preparing for his career in earnest. As he grew older he held various summer jobs. One summer, in emulation of Fuller, he worked on a farm, delivering his produce to customers in the same way his father had traveled with wares and delivered goods for Bradfield's. During other summers he operated lunch stands—real businesses this time—where he sold Coca-Cola and fried fish sandwiches, and during Christmas he sold fireworks.

His major preparation, though, was mill work. During his adolescent summers, Cason rotated through every mill department, becoming closely acquainted with the Callaway operation from the ground up. As did most mill operatives, he found the work long and demanding. Arising at four in the morning, he would cook his own breakfast, walk to the mill, and put in a twelve-hour day, usually pausing only to eat his lunch on the mill steps. At five o'clock he would return home, where Fuller would reward him with four hours of free time. But Cason was usually so tired that he would be in bed well before nine.

The work was hard, and in addition Cason developed a persistent cough for a time. Ida, no doubt thinking of the dreaded condition of byssinosis or "brown lung" that plagued textile workers, worried that the cotton lint in the mill would be bad for her son, but the exercise apparently had the opposite effect. "The cotton mill seem[s] to have cured this cough," Fuller observed. The moral of the story, he declared, was "Put all boys who have coughs to work in a cotton mill!"

In his midteens Cason enrolled in the Bingham School of Asheville, North Carolina. A boys' boarding school with a military dimension, the Bingham institution was a spin-off of the prestigious Bingham Academy in the heart of the state. The particular draw for the Callaways was that it was known for its strong business curriculum, among other things. The student body was drawn from throughout the South and even the North, which would allow Cason to make contacts that would serve him well in a business career. It provided a rigorous education that would be an important foundation for his later successes.

Even in much of his personal correspondence with the now far-off Cason, Fuller sometimes sounded as if he were instructing an apprentice in financial affairs and business tactics. "I am glad that you passed your examinations so creditably," he wrote his son, choosing a revealing adverb, "and made full sophomore in all of your studies. 'Well begun is half done.'" When the Christmas holidays approached, the father suggested that the son plan ahead financially for his journey home. "I suspect that you had better buy a round-trip ticket when you get ready to come," Fuller observed, "as it may be that you can save something on your fare coming and going by doing so."

But Fuller would never have let finance blind him to Cason's welfare and comfort. He freely offered any money the youngster needed for the trip, and he also suggested that Cason rent a sleeping berth on the New Orleans–bound section of the train beginning at Washington, even though he wouldn't board until it reached the Carolinas. The extra expense would mean that Cason could sleep all the way home; if he saved money by getting a berth on the Atlanta-bound cars, he would be awakened an hour or two earlier, as the train was approaching Atlanta, rather than being able to sleep all the way to LaGrange.

Fuller even took some time out of his own busy schedule to spend a few days with Cason that autumn prior to the holidays.

Arranging to rendezvous with Ida in Asheville when he returned from a business trip to New York, he made plans to stay in the mountain town for an entire week. He likely did a lot of business while in North Carolina, but at least the family was together again.

It is even possible that Fuller used this occasion to further Cason's education in the textile and mercantile concerns. One certainty is that in his subsequent letters to Cason, Fuller sometimes reported offhandedly on how his businesses were doing. "The high cotton is not so bad in the mills as it might be," he mentioned in one such letter, "as we have a very good stock of cotton bought before the advance." He placed this intelligence matter-of-factly between noting that his cold was improving and congratulating Cason on Bingham's recent sports victory over the rival Mooney school.

For his part, Cason found this sort of apprenticeship natural, and he apparently needed no prodding to work hard or to prepare himself for a career of his own in the mills. He treated his education at Bingham seriously,

The family gathered in the boxwood garden at Hills and Dales, which Fuller purchased in 1912. Cason was twelve years older than Fuller, Jr.

doing well on his exams and taking on many roles of leadership. By the third year at the school he earned a promotion to adjutant, served as editor of the school's annual, and became secretary of the college YMCA. (In connection with this last, Ida named as one of the Callaways' nine happiest days the occasion when Cason joined the Baptist church, likely while in LaGrange, as his younger brother would also do in time. "It did our souls good to have our children journey on the same road with us," she wrote.)

Cason also knew when it was time to move on. When he had learned all he could at Bingham, he traveled to the University of Virginia, one of the premiere colleges of the South, where he focused on specialized courses, which he believed would prepare him for a textile career, rather than working through the standard liberal arts curriculum. But even this wasn't enough for him. After exhausting Virginia's offerings in the field, he enrolled in a course of study at Eastman Business College in Poughkeepsie, New York. Eastman was a prestigious school that drew a lot of Southerners to its student ranks, many of them prominent ones, such as North Carolina's James B. Duke. Unlike most other business schools of the day, Eastman focused on the practice, and not merely the theory, of running a business, with exercises that emulated real-world operations.

During his summers, Cason continued to work in the LaGrange mills. Some of the particularly unpleasant tasks he encountered there, in fact, may have been planned especially for him by his father, so that Cason could learn how to handle adversity.

All the hard work paid off. Finishing his schooling and moving into the mills full-time, Cason was named a director of Unity a few weeks after his twenty-second birthday.

As Cason assumed his first role of leadership, his younger brother, Fuller E. Callaway Jr. was still enjoying life as a child. More than twelve years separated the two; Fuller Jr. was

Young Fuller Jr. sitting in the garden at Hills and Dales with Ephram Fitzpatrick.

not born until January 1, 1907. But despite the age difference, the youths' early lives were quite similar. When Fuller Jr. was very young, Ida even often sang them to sleep together, and this, like other events, became an occasion for their father to imprint them with his views. One night, as Ida was singing a song to them called "Bye Bye," her husband interrupted. "Ida," he called out from an adjacent room, "sing 'sell, sell' to them instead of 'buy, buy!'"

As it had with Cason, the lesson took with Fuller Jr. About the same time Cason became a Unity director, when young Fuller was six, Callaway headed into town one morning without saying good-bye to the boy. The youngster quickly climbed over the fence and ran up the street after him. "Father," he exclaimed, "don't you ever go off without kissing me good-bye any more; have you got any loose change about you?"

Young Fuller's financial canniness increased with age. Once while the family was deep-sea fishing in Miami, Fuller Sr. made

Fuller Jr. landed this sailfish on a fishing excursion in Florida when he was a young boy.

an expansive promise. "If anyone catches a sail fish today," he proclaimed, "I will have it mounted." To his surprise, his namesake caught one, and when the party returned to shore, the taxidermist quoted a mounting price of one hundred dollars.

"It costs so much, son, to have it mounted," Callaway hinted, "do you think it will be worth it?"

"Well, father," young Fuller answered slyly, "if you want to sell out your promise for a hundred dollars, it's all right with me!" Callaway opted to go ahead and pay for the mounting.

As he grew older, Fuller Jr. continued to walk the same paths Cason had before him, manning Coca-Cola stands in the summers and selling fireworks in December. Like Cason he farmed for one summer, learning— as his father the erstwhile farmer put it— "which end of the mule kicked, and which end of the bee stung."

The two sons' educations even over-

lapped, although not entirely. Instead of Bingham and Virginia, young Fuller attended Georgia Tech, then known as the Georgia School of Technology, but then he moved on, as had Cason, to the Eastman Business College. (The apprenticeship and business school route was fast becoming traditional for Callaways; the boys' uncle Ely, in addition to working in the Callaway stores, had attended the business department at Valparaiso.) Interspersed with the younger son's formal education was the same apprenticeship in the mills his father had arranged for Cason, doubtless including similar unpleasant experiences. His first job there, in fact, was one of the dirtiest, that of a coal stoker in the Elm City plant's basement furnace room.

While Cason was drawn to the managerial side of things, Fuller Jr. gravitated more towards the mechanical side, at least at first. Thus he was a natural fit for Georgia Tech. The school was an integral part of the New South.

It had been founded by the state in 1885 at the urging of two prominent Macon residents, Nathaniel Edwin Harris and John Fletcher Hanson, both of them Confederate veterans who knew that the South had lost the war largely because of its technological and industrial weakness. Hanson, like Fuller Callaway, was a textile man, the founder of the Bibb Manufacturing Company. He knew that the South needed mechanical engineers if it were to become an industrial region. In seeking to found the school that would provide them, he drew Henry Grady's enthusiastic support.

In its early years, Georgia Tech shared an important trait with Eastman: its educational approach was heavily practical and shoplike rather than theoretical. This explains the appeal it held for young Fuller. His education there, culminating with a degree in textile engineering in 1926, helped foster a strong relationship with the school, not just for him but for the entire Callaway family. The connection was furthered significantly by the fact that Marion L. Brittain, Tech's new president during Fuller's time at the school, was a cousin of the Callaway family through Wilkes County connections. Fuller Jr.'s matriculation at Tech marked the beginning of a long relationship between the family and the school.

Young Fuller and Cason were by

no means the only additional members of the Callaway household. During their marriage, Fuller and Ida took in between fifteen and twenty family members, many of them nieces and nephews, for lengths of time ranging anywhere from one to five years. The nieces and nephews often came to LaGrange to attend college, or to learn what was now thought of as the Callaway family business—the stores rather than the mills. But older relatives stayed too. Ida's parents moved in with the young couple not long after the 1891 wedding; LaGrange was growing, while Jewell

would eventually become an almost-vanished community. Fuller and Ida also took in widowed siblings and even siblings-in-law. In 1923, following the death of Howard Callaway's wife the previous year, the couple invited Howard to live with them. When Ida's brother died, his widow also came to live with the Callaways.

And of course there were nonrelative guests, many of whom came to town for business with the stores or the mills. Callaway was likely to bring them home at any time. The constant comings and goings and the uniformly high traffic sometimes made the house seem more like a hotel lobby than a home, but nobody seemed to mind. As more people came to stay, Callaway simply

Fuller Jr. was particularly proud of this catch. circa 1920.

FULLER EARLE CALLAWAY, JR., Φ Δ Θ
"Casey"
LaGrange, Georgia
Special Textile Engineering

" 'Tis not a lip, or eye, we beauty call,
But the joint force and full result of all."

Casey is too intent on learning in a hurry what we
offer in the Textile Department. We fully expected to
enjoy his company for years, but probably he thinks
more of carrying on the work of his family. It seems
that Casey's greatest delight is chasing grizzly bears of
a dark night in the garden at his home with the Atlanta society girls.
Honor Roll (1).

Fuller graduated from Georgia Tech in 1926. According to his feature in *The Blue Print*, he was a member of the Phi Delta Theta fraternity and his nickname was "Casey."

added more rooms, including, of course, bathrooms. The house, he half joked, was the only one in town with three bathrooms on the first floor—the joke being that it was a one-floor house.

One of the most notable and long-term residents, was an older brother of Fuller's. Pope Francis Callaway—one genealogy states that his name was Francis Pope Callaway, but he was known to the community simply as Pope F. Callaway—was Fuller's senior by five years, the seventh child of Abner and Sarah. Described by his nephew, Fuller Jr., as "a character," Pope was nevertheless a true Callaway. He and his brother Fuller shared many traits. Like Fuller after him, Pope became a businessman, learning a lot about the mercantile world and traveling throughout the South, particularly to Atlanta and later to Memphis.

But there were differences, too. Unlike Fuller, Pope was a life-long bachelor. Without a wife's stabilizing influence, his youthful wild streak wasn't quick to die off. By the time he was around thirty, he'd made an interesting life for himself in Memphis as a fiddler in an orchestra. Memphis had experienced a disastrous series of yellow fever epidemics in the 1870s, which caused a huge population decline as residents died or fled the city in droves. In the following decades, rural citizens throughout the South—Pope among them—gravitated to the recovering city in search of opportunities, and a thriving musical community

formed. Unfortunately, other forces were drawn to Memphis as well, making it a rather wild place, in a way that fed Pope's own wildness. This made for a bad combination. Even in LaGrange, Fuller heard that Pope had grown to like his liquor too much. While the details are vague, one gets the general idea that Pope had stopped being a businessman and had fallen into a lifestyle that was bad for both himself and the Callaway name. Since by this time Abner was gone, it was Fuller who decided to take action.

In 1897 he traveled to Memphis. Finding Pope, he presented his older brother with something that was second nature to both of them: a written contract. The terms of the deal Fuller proposed were both straightforward and strict. Pope would return to LaGrange and, like so many other Callaways, move in with Fuller and Ida. The couple would provide room and board—three full meals a day—as well as a monthly allowance for him. In return, Pope would undertake never to play the fiddle or drink within the borders of Troup County. Pope agreed to the bargain.

Ida Cason Callaway's father Alexander Toombs Cason (1845–1918) lived at Hills and Dales from 1916 until his death in 1918.

Olivia P. Jewell Cason (1849–1921), Ida's mother, lived at Hills and Dales from 1916 until she passed away in 1921.

The deal worked out well. Indications are that while the adjustment was rough on the household at first, especially for Pope and the proper, churchgoing Ida, Pope took the contract seriously. Ida, in fact, while supporting Fuller's decision to rescue his brother, found the first days and weeks trying as Pope weaned himself from his pleasures.

On the whole, though, the turnaround was remarkable. In a fairly short while, Pope managed to abandon his old ways entirely, or almost entirely. Once a year, apparently, he would go on a trip with a few friends and indulge himself, but never in Troup County, in keeping with the terms of the contract. Meanwhile, Pope's old business skills soon reasserted themselves, and as Fuller did with his other relatives, he put Pope to work.

Rather than the mills, Pope focused most of his energies on Fuller's stores, although later, in 1911, he did also become a director of Unity. He concentrated first on the buying lists, eventually becoming the stores' principal buyer. He also took an interest in supervising the salesmen, coordinating their efforts for maximum efficiency and earning their respect. In one way in particular he confirmed himself

Ida Cason Callaway with her son Cason at Hills and Dales. Cason is in his navy uniform. circa 1917.

as Fuller's brother—in his appreciation for publicity. He liked to take out huge advertisements in the newspapers, many of them offering deals for a limited time only, thus imparting a sense of urgency to customers, which drew them to the stores.

Another way in which Pope resembled Fuller was in his liking for bulk purchases and rapid turnover. This made him a natural for the wholesale market, and thus in time he became head of the Fuller E. Callaway Company, which specialized in wholesale dry goods.

Pope did, however, have a slightly different outlook on money than Fuller did. Even in their youth Pope had been freer both in spending his money on nonessentials and in borrowing it too. In fact, Pope began borrowing money from Fuller when the latter was only nine years old, almost always in nickels, dimes, and quarters. Ten years into this cycle, when Fuller and Ida were about

Members of the family and friends pose for a portrait in the garden. Left to right: Ephram Fitzpatrick, Alexander Toombs Cason, Ida Cason Callaway, Olivia Jewell Cason, Fuller Callaway Jr., Cason Callaway (back), Fuller Callaway, Unknown, and Pope F. Callaway.

Pope Francis Callaway (1865–1923), Fuller's older brother.

Pope, still a bachelor, was approaching fifty and well set in his ways. According to young Fuller, Pope would sometimes go for a few days without speaking. But still the two were friends. One of the youngster's interests was the magical new technology of radio, and Pope was happy to finance the hobby. With the money the youngster got from his uncle, he built a radio shack in the yard and installed the best equipment in it. By 1920 he was a licensed amateur radio operator with the call sign 4MJ. In the early years of the 1920s he even became one of the first people in the area to receive the broadcast of KDKA in Pittsburgh, the nation's first commercial radio station, six hundred miles away.

By then, Pope and Ida had long overcome the early days of friction between them and had become devoted to each other. Pope was undoubtedly aware of what he'd put Ida through in the beginning as he'd struggled to break his addiction, and of the graceful way in which she handled it and had taken care of him. And later, when he once became seriously ill, it was Ida who nursed him through the illness. By the time Fuller Jr. came along, Pope fondly referred to Ida as "Sis I." Pope would go on to become the manager of Hills and Dales and the garden that Ida loved.

After 1917, when he retired from his position in the Callaway stores, Pope also started managing the Callaway farmlands near Hills and Dales, developing orchards of Elberta peaches and large purple plums. He was so successful that the family couldn't possibly use all the fruit the orchards produced, so he sent out the farmhands and even the workers at Hills and Dales to try to peddle the excess. But the hands, unlike Pope, made terrible salesmen. "Dammitall, Pope," Fuller finally burst out in frustration, "we've no setup for peddling! Ida needs her men helpers and you need yours. There's no telling how much it cost us to raise the fruit, but plenty, I'm sure; so the only way we can come out whole on it is to

to get married, Fuller called in the markers. He sent Pope an itemized bill of every loan Fuller had made him since the very first nickel. "Here's the bill," the letter supposedly read, "and if convenient I would appreciate your paying me." Pope, who had a job by then, came through with the money, and Fuller used it to buy his wedding suit.

Even after his return to LaGrange, Pope remained freer with money, but often in a more calculated way than before. Like Fuller—indeed, at Fuller's behest—he made business investments. Whenever Fuller started a new concern, he would prevail on Pope to buy shares in it. But Pope went beyond that, investing, and sometimes speculating, in other stocks, and also in real estate. Speculating was something Fuller almost never did, but Pope was his own man in this regard, and on the whole his investments paid off.

In terms of personality, Pope could sometimes be a bit odd, or so it seemed to Fuller Jr. By the time the boy got to know his uncle, give it to our friends." It was the only way to avoid waste, so that was what Pope did, to everyone's delight.

In all, Pope lived with Fuller and Ida for twenty-six years, from 1897 on. He enjoyed generally good health until almost the last day of his life, and he remained true to the contract until his death. Most of his investments, including his speculations, had paid off, leaving him a wealthy man, and he left his entire fortune to the person he most credited for turning his life around: his sister-in-law, Ida.

≈

On the two occasions when Fuller Callaway did speculate, things went badly.

Two times, he claimed; he speculated only two times, once on meat and once on cotton. He didn't talk much about either episode, but he was willing to say repeatedly, as a warning to others, that he lost a lot of money.

The meat speculation is the better known one, and the less typical, since bulk cotton at least was more directly connected to Fuller's line of work, and sometimes he had to make educated guesses about its outlook and when to buy. When the price of pork side meat was bottoming out on the Chicago exchange—or so it seemed to him—Callaway bought in. Shortly thereafter he made one of his business trips to New York. He spent a hot day floating around Canal Street, buying up bargains for his department store. He concentrated on purchases that he figured on the fly would net him profits of twenty-five to fifty dollars. Then, buying a newspaper before catching a streetcar back to his hotel, he saw that the price of side meat had kept on dropping. In one day he'd lost hundreds of dollars, his Canal Street bargains not even coming close to offsetting the loss.

Things kept going badly even after he got back to LaGrange. One night, in an unhappy coincidence, Ida served pork for supper, apparently unaware of Fuller's recent investment. Fuller said nothing at dinner, but that night in bed he tossed and turned. Normally he slept like a log, so it was at this point that Ida apparently began to suspect that something was wrong.

"Fuller," she finally asked, "are you worrying about anything?"

Even now he couldn't help showing some levity, though it may have been lost on Ida. "All that side meat I ate for supper is disagreeing with me!" he exclaimed. Then he grew serious.

"Ida, I'm going to tell you something," he continued. "I hate to worry you, but I will tell you anyway. I bought some side meat and it's gone down, and I am losing our hard-earned money."

If Fuller was apprehensive that Ida would be mad, she quickly took care of that. "Oh, I'm so relieved," she answered. "I was afraid that you were worrying over something that couldn't be remedied. You're young, strong, and smart; just take your loss cheerfully, and go ahead."

Then, according to her account, she told him a story to lift his spirits. "You remind me of your friend you tell about so often." The man had lost money on cotton, and his wife found out. One night, as a rooster was crowing outside the window, the husband, too, was restless, and his wife asked him why.

"That old rooster crows so loud it has gotten me nervous," he answered.

"Maybe he's been buying cotton, and it's gone down," responded the wife, not unsympathetically.

The story worked. Fuller had a good laugh and, unburdened, went to sleep.

Since Fuller's other speculation involved a loss on cotton, one wonders if the story Ida claims to have told him that night was actually about the two of them on that other occasion rather than the friend it was ostensibly about. At any rate, the two bad deals were apparently enough to cure Fuller of speculation forever.

While he didn't talk much about the

Fuller and Ida sitting together. They appear to be watching some type of event.

specifics of his own failures, Fuller didn't at all mind sharing the sentiments he formed because of them. One story he developed was that of the hog and the trough. A hog, he was fond of pointing out, was greedy. It would put both front feet in its trough in order to eat more, and sometimes it would even put in one of its hind feet as well. When that happened, though, it would tip the trough over, losing everything through greed.

"The hardest trial a young man is called upon to stand," he said later in life, "is a little quick prosperity. Lots of folks climb so high they can't stand it and get dizzy and fall." He was clearly thinking about himself, at least in part. "You feel the whole world is going your way, and you whoop and holler and plunge in and get everything you want. Right there you want to take that left hind leg of yours out of the trough—quick!"

Another anecdote he told was about cotton. "A dry May makes successful cotton," he observed. It forced the plant to develop a

strong, deep taproot that made it hardy, while a wet May would pamper it too much. "Most of us don't want a dry May," he noted, "but we need it to stand the drought of August."

Even when it came to specific advice, and not merely general outlook, Callaway's statements reflected the two times he'd burned himself. When an acquaintance asked his opinion on current cotton prices, Callaway stated his belief that it was a bear market, going on to issue a warning. "Personally, if I were going to speculate at this time"—small chance of *that*—"I would not get too nervous and buy too quickly, as I would prefer to get left and neither make nor lose money than to buy too soon and sweat over the mistake."

Indeed, the lessons he learned from speculating stayed with him for the rest of his life. "No set of rules can be laid down for the safe guidance of investors," he once wrote formally, "because after all, it is an individual proposition, both as to the plan which is best for a particular person and as to the form of the investment. . . . This much can be said, however: BEFORE YOU INVEST, INVESTIGATE."

While he didn't try to prescribe rules for others, though, Callaway developed some for himself, and these, too, he shared at least with his friends. "Never fall in love with anything until it is yours," he once told young Fuller. "And never fall out with it until you've sold it. Never fall in love with it until it is yours and you won't pay too much for it. Never fall out with it until you've sold it and you'll get a good price for it. Most people do just the opposite."

Another one of his rules was, if anything, even simpler, and this one he got from his own father Abner. "Don't ever do what the crowd does," he explained, since "the crowd is always wrong." As usual he gave a graphic illustration. "If you are on a boat and all the crowd runs over to one side of the boat, you get on the other side of the boat. Then if it turns over, your side will be on top. When everybody is selling, buy. When everybody is buying, sell."

According to his son, that rule enabled Callaway, near the end of his life, to predict the stock market crash of 1929, as well as the bursting of the Florida land bubble in 1925 and 1926. "The Lord is good to people," he told his son after the Florida collapse. "He always gives them a warning before anything happens. The Florida burst was a warning of the stock crash that's coming."

Callaway uttered this prophecy during a bull market when, as he might have put it, everyone was dashing to the same side of the boat. "When the stock goes down 50 percent," he warned young Fuller, "it is just going to be started down. It's going down 60 percent, 70 percent, 80 percent—lots of it is going down 90 percent. . . . When it crashes, the handle is just going to break off the jug, all in one piece, and it's coming."

"When is it coming, father?"

Stock market panics, recessions, and depressions actually occur with some regularity in American history, usually every two or three decades, but Callaway's prediction was especially accurate. "It's coming in October 1928, 1929, or 1930," he answered. "I can't tell which of the three years because other things can change it in the meantime, but it's coming; get ready. It's going to crash wide open."

Taking the advice, Fuller Jr. and Cason, in the words of the former, "sold everything we had except the mills, wives, and children." During the October 1929 mill directors' meeting, Fuller Jr. discovered that the mills still held fifty shares of stock in an electric company. He immediately got up and walked out of the meeting, made a phone call, and sold the stock, fearful that the market would drop before the meeting ended. He made it with a week to spare. At the end of the month, when the crash occurred, that particular stock dropped by well over 90 percent.

While Fuller Sr. may have learned the hard way to capitalize on the market due to his failed speculations, he continued to make money for himself and his concerns by hard work rather than gambling. One would think that by avoiding speculation he avoided a lot of unnecessary worry. Indeed, this was one of his prescriptions for both a successful business and personal peace of mind. "I never did believe worry helped work," he once declared. "Worry is a hindrance to work. The work that pays is joyful work. For twenty years I worked sixteen hours a day and loved every minute of it. I did my best work after supper. And three minutes after I hit the bed I was asleep. It doesn't pay to worry over anything."

Yet Callaway did worry, at least over details. Aside from his natural energy, his driven nature, and his use of humor and storytelling to connect with others, this was in fact, one of the main ingredients in his recipe for success. A related one was his prodigious memory. Hatton Lovejoy made note of Callaway's "all-embracing mind . . . a remarkable mind" with a remarkable ability to remember things. Fuller Jr. claimed that it was an "absolutely photographic memory," frequently testing him on it by asking the details of an ancient sale or what the price of cotton had been on a particular day some years previously. Callaway always gave the right answers.

Nevertheless, the elder Callaway worried over details, apparently never fully trusting that memory. He was almost fetishistic about keeping an orderly desk and taking systematic notes about nearly everything. Each morning his desk always contained a neat stack of "to do" items that he would work through methodically. Before he had much money, he got into the habit of making notes on old envelopes. Whenever a thought occurred to him, he would jot it down on an envelope immediately. Later, when money became less of an issue, he kept using envelopes, but he did begin using new ones. As he accomplished whatever tasks he'd set for himself, he would carefully cross the item off his list.

When arriving at the office each morning, Callaway would pull his envelopes from his coat pocket and hand them to his office boy. The assistant would transcribe the notes that Callaway hadn't yet crossed out onto fresh envelopes via typewriter, rubber band the new envelopes, and return them to his employer. Callaway would also use the notes as a basis for memoranda that he dictated for inclusion in the most important file in his office, the follow-up file. This system greatly reduced the chance that anything would slip through the cracks.

Many of these notes doubtless held the details Callaway needed when preparing to make a sale or enter some negotiation or transaction. Among his family and close associates, his system was famous. When making plans for a sales trip, he would almost obsessively collect every fact he could find that he believed was relevant to the potential sale. Calling in his department heads as well as others he thought could be helpful, or getting in touch with them by telephone, he would probe them for any intelligence that might relate to the subject of the upcoming journey. He then used this intelligence to formulate his entire sales strategy—not just the broad outlines but every detail.

Then came the rehearsal. Using his memory for detail, he would summon up every account he had in the region to which he was bound, and every transaction for each one of the accounts. While he was doing this, his employees would leave him alone so he could concentrate.

The rehearsal continued during the trip. The night before a conference, Callaway would lie on his hotel bed and play out statements and counterstatements. If he foresaw that an argument was available to defeat a statement of his, he would formulate a better statement, as if he were playing a chess game. This meant that by the time of the conference, he was as ready as possible for any argument he might come up against.

In addition to rehearsal, another one of Callaway's late-night activities was general study. "He studied two hours, not read, studied, two hours every night," noted Fuller Jr. The distinction is important: Callaway read carefully, on nearly every subject, heavily annotating the books. He came from a family that valued education. His brother Enoch was a physician; their father had taught in college. The postwar depression and his own youthful ways had robbed Fuller of his own chance of formal schooling, so as an adult he made up for the loss. But even in his self-education, he always retained a bias towards the practical. Much like Sherlock Holmes, he cautioned his sons not to fill up their minds with classical learning, such as Latin or Greek, for fear that it might leave too little room in their brains for more directly useful subjects. Their choices of schools and curricula show that they took the advice seriously. Yet Callaway himself was knowledgeable in many areas besides those clearly related to his businesses. He often quoted poetry to his family and friends, and when Fuller Jr. was a student at Tech, he discovered that his father could perform advanced mathematical equations in his head, without using a slide rule.

One of the things Callaway focused on was psychology, but it was a practical psychology rather than a subject to be learned from his books. "In everything you do," he once said, "try to work with nature; get nature to work with you, human nature. . . . [Y]ou increase your efforts a thousand-fold . . . if you have human nature working with you." He applied this rule in many ways, such as dangling premiums in front of his salesmen, premiums on remainder goods that he didn't want to sit around gathering dust for months or even years. He also figured—by all accounts correctly—that if he banned newly hired salesmen from selling to established customers, it would prevent the new hires from inadvertently mishandling existing customers while at the same time making them more aggressive in their hunt for new business.

Another exercise in psychology (at least he claimed it as one) was a certain mannerism in his way of talking. At pauses, and at the ends of sentences, he would almost invariably, according to Fuller Jr., interject a "huh"—Ida described it as a "huh huh." When someone asked him a question, he would usually reply with that same "Huh?" thus making the questioner repeat himself. Fuller Jr. once asked him why he did that.

"It gives me twice as long to think up an answer," the elder Callaway explained. Perhaps it was true, or maybe it was just another of his tales, intended to make light of the affectation.

His ability to handle people, especially customers, by joking, telling stories, and otherwise putting them at ease, was a major weapon. But he also knew how to be straightforward, even blunt, when unpleasant matters had to be discussed. This fact about Callaway has often been overlooked, perhaps because he only rarely did so. Normally, according to Hatton Lovejoy, he chose not to speak ill of people and simply ignored any enemy he happened to make. When it came to his employees, he preferred using carrots to sticks, not only praising workers directly but bragging on them to others. On occasion, though, the stick came out, although only when it was called for. Lovejoy also noted that Callaway could be strong in his criticism. But only once, he stated, did he hear Callaway criticize an employee severely in a way Lovejoy thought unfair, and indications are that he told Callaway so. At any rate, Callaway thought better of what he'd done, called the man back in, and apologized to him. The proof of overall fair treatment, Lovejoy maintained, was that few employees ever left the Callaway businesses.

Callaway could also forcefully defend his business interests when dealing with other firms, even (perhaps especially) those with whom his organization had long-running relationships, such as the J. H. Lane outfit. In late 1909, for instance, while working feverishly to get the Manchester plant online, Callaway found himself facing several roadblocks in addition to the problem of its outmoded narrow looms. Roy Dallis, his right-hand man, was seriously ill; the railroad was being slow about installing crucial side tracks to the mill; a subcontractor in charge of pouring concrete at the plant was on strike; and some of the people at Lane, worried that Callaway wouldn't be able to deliver some promised goods on schedule, were breathing down his neck. Finally Callaway spoke up.

"For some weeks past," he wrote O. A. Barnard at Lane,

a number of your letters have reflected a disposition to nag and find some feature to criticize in nearly everything that has been done. Now, I do not claim perfection, and know that I have many faults and frequently make mistakes, as is the case with all who accomplish anything, but I do not believe that anyone can honestly question my zeal and interest, and I think it must be conceded that the average results are on the whole not so bad.

In view of our mutuality of interest, I feel that we should always be candid, and I should like to know just what it is that has caused you to adopt this spirit and attitude toward me of late.

At the same time, he also wrote a letter to Coit Johnson at Lane that illustrates both his generosity of spirit and his pointed irritation. "Your kindly expressions with regard to the success of our efforts at the financing end here are appreciated," he noted in a very different tone from the one he'd used with Barnard. "It is gratifying to know that *you* have not succumbed to the recent epidemic of criticism."

Apparently the Manchester delays weren't the main things bothering Barnard. Rather, he blamed Callaway for negotiating with a particular customer directly rather than going through the proper channels at Lane.

Callaway replied with a reasoned but firm defense of his actions. "You, of course, are exactly right . . . that as a general rule, correspondence with customers should be conducted through your office," he conceded. "Like all good rules, however, there are occasional instances when an exception seems advisable in accomplishing the results desired by all, and I must ask that you trust to my discretion in such instances." In this instance, he continued, a business acquaintance had

offered to help him move some difficult merchandise, and Callaway had taken him up on it. Dallis, because of his illness, had forgotten to send Barnard copies of the correspondence; that was all.

The closing lines of the letter exemplify Callaway's ability to combine the conciliatory with the firm.

It is unnecessary to assure you that there was no disposition to overlook you in the matter, but that, as is sometimes the case, my zeal for promoting the results we are all striving for led me to overlook the ethics of the case.

I am sure that you will understand this situation and approve, since the desired end was accomplished.

The approach worked. Barnard left Coit Johnson to smooth things over with Callaway, who also wrote placatingly to him once the grievances had been aired and settled.

I appreciate your kind letter … more than I can tell you and assure you that your feelings and action are fully understood and taken in the kindest spirit.

I guess all of us have been under considerable strain for the past several months, and such a condition is naturally not conducive to equanimity always. I think we understand each other, however, and that while some unimportant differences may arise occasionally, as happens in the best of regulated families, I feel sure that we will not allow anything of this kind to lead us into forgetfulness of the splendid results that have been and may be accomplished through cooperation [and] team work.

By now Callaway had achieved great success, standing at the head of large, complex, and growing concerns, feeling both the pressures of responsibility and the advantages of financial power. If, on the one hand, he felt the stress of making sure things went right, and

Fuller with a cane in the historic Ferrell Gardens.

because of that responsibility he decided he had to be stern on occasion, on the other hand, he was also finally reaping the benefits of his decades of work.

For one thing, he'd begun shopping at Brooks Brothers. He never cared much for fashion; his style of dress was simple, usually a plain-cut dark business suit. When he began patronizing Brooks Brothers, that basic preference didn't change; almost certainly he shifted to the upscale store because of the quality and durability of the suits and not as a fashion statement. He certainly didn't do so out of flamboyance or profligacy. He preferred the Ivy League–style sack suit that the store had pioneered at the close of the 1800s. While he was invariably neatly dressed, he had few clothes at any one time, and he was apt to let his collar or his one or two ties fray before he did anything about them, usually at Ida's and the boys' insistence. When at Brooks Brothers he would buy a single suit and wear

it out of the store, leaving his old one behind. His hat was a darkish gray, worn at a jaunty angle, and as with his other clothes, he rarely replaced it with a new one. Fuller Jr. claimed that later, when his father traveled to Europe, he took nothing but an extra shirt, a few collars and pairs of socks, some handkerchiefs, and a supply of cigars. Lovejoy said flatly that this couldn't be so, that Callaway was too neat for such behavior; but according to young Fuller, his father would buy extra clothes at his destination if he needed them.

The one extra costume piece Callaway allowed himself, even as a young man, was a cane or walking stick. He would always carry it, usually hanging over his arm—he didn't need it to walk, especially when he was younger—and he would often use it to point and gesture.

The only truly unkempt thing about him was his pockets. His whole style of dress was, ultimately, utilitarian, designed to be useful and to present him to customers as a respectable businessman, but when it came to his pockets, utility was everything. His basic equipment for doing business—pencil, notebook, and watch, along with a plug of tobacco, a knife for cutting it, and of course his envelopes with their copious notes—were always, without exception, in his pockets when they weren't in his hands. And there were other things in his pockets as well, which could make him look (and even seem) like a peddler, which of course he'd once been and in a greatly magnified way still was. The two Fullers could be walking on a Sunday afternoon, and if the youngster offhandedly said "I wish I had a banana," suddenly his father would produce one from a pocket.

And he never emptied the pockets, even at night when he took off the suit, folding the pants and putting them on the seat of a chair and hanging the coat over the back. His reasons, like his purpose in everything, were practical. "The average man will lose a month out of his life taking things out of his pockets and putting them back in," he once explained. "If I had to take all the things out of my pockets at night and put them in another suit . . . I never could have done what I did."

He gave the same reason for his paucity of ties: "The average man loses a month of his life deciding which necktie to put on." To keep them from accumulating, he disposed of them at Brooks Brothers the same way he got rid of old suits; when he bought a new tie he gave the old one to a salesman and wore the new one out the door.

As Callaway moved up the sartorial ladder, he also changed his accommodations to match. Having started out at New York's Prince George Hotel, he stayed in better inns during his trips as his business stature grew,

undoubtedly because of the higher caliber of potential customers he could find there. Ultimately he settled on the Waldorf-Astoria; as he put it, "I changed over from the wagon yard to the Waldorf." Wherever he stayed, though, he always charmed the maids into giving him fast laundry service (important, given his small wardrobe), but he grew especially friendly with the Waldorf staff, with whom he became a great favorite.

The improvement in lodgings wasn't limited to hotels. In 1909, after nearly two decades in the house on "Cash Street"—West Haralson Street—the Callaways decided that the time had finally come to move. This was a major sign of success, and one of the keys to that success, as he once pointed out in an interview, had been frugal Cash Street living.

One day I met a man on the street and said "Callaway, I hear you made a million in cotton. I congratulate you."

"Well," I said, "it may be true I made a million in cotton. But I want to tell you why I made it. It was because my wife was willing and happy to live seventeen years on Cash Street when we could afford to live on Mortgage Avenue."

Now, with two sons, Pope, and more family and visitors than ever before, the Callaways figured that they needed, and could afford, a bit more leeway. Just before Christmas 1909, Callaway contacted the *LaGrange Reporter*. "Gentlemen," he wrote briefly, "please insert the following advertisement in your next issue: 'FOR SALE: My residence, corner Haralson and Lewis Street. Can give possession latter part of January.'" In fact, the move wasn't complete until February 23, 1910. At last Fuller and Ida had come to well-to-do Broad Street, which Callaway termed Mortgage Avenue, but they had come there strictly on a cash

This silver-handled walking stick was given to Fuller on June 15, 1916, by Robert Morrison Miller to commemorate the completion of Hills and Dales.

Fuller and Ida lived on Broad Street in LaGrange in a house locally known as "Buckingham Palace." They moved from here to Hills and Dales in 1916.

basis. "The Roper place," as Callaway identified it during the purchase, was a house with an expansive two-acre lot on Broad, owned by Margaret Swanson Roper, daughter of a large LaGrange family, and her husband, Joel Charles Roper. While the street was only a block south of Haralson, the move signified (as if by now any such sign were needed) that Callaway had arrived. In fact, he was now, just shy of age forty, in the prime of his life and career.

But the climb had cost him, in terms of mental stress, as is suggested by his exchange with Lane, and in his physical health as well. His usual joking manner had grown somewhat muted by then, and his physicians were seeing a physical decline. He and the family had begun taking vacations to Miami, usually for a few weeks in the winter, and these trips would soon become a regular feature of Callaway life. But as early as 1907, with Callaway still in his mid-to-late thirties, his doctors told him that he needed a longer rest. So that year he decided to take a long vacation.

Word soon got out about the journey. Oddly enough, Callaway planned to go by himself, with even Ida remaining behind. Still, the prospect of his taking some time off came as a relief to his family and friends, who arranged a banquet for him as a *bon voyage*. His associates even planned a special surprise gift: a loving cup, to be bestowed upon Callaway at the banquet. Ida knew about the cup, and with great difficulty managed to keep the news to herself until the night of the dinner.

Finally came the day of the banquet. The cup was initially hidden under a pyramid of flowers. When it was revealed, Callaway read the lengthy inscription:

To Fuller E. Callaway
From his friends and business associates

An expression of their
appreciation of loyal friendship
and
able and efficient labor
in all of their personal and business
relations—and in recognition of his
resourceful, interesting and successful
efforts for the advancement of the
City of LaGrange.

For once Callaway was at a loss for words, choking up, and then he pulled himself together. "I did not know you all thought so much of me," he told his friends. "I believe I won't go on the trip after all!" But they were firm with him. "Yes, sir, you have to go—and take your much needed rest!" one of them answered. And that is what he did in the end.

Fuller treasured his gold pocket knife and carried it almost everywhere he went.

Callaway had never traveled to Europe, so he elected to go there, perhaps in emulation of an earlier age's Grand Tour of the Continent, but more likely because of business opportunities. Technically this was a rest trip, but Callaway was constitutionally incapable of leaving his business behind. For that reason, too, he chose to embark from New York, which at any rate was a hub of Europe-bound shipping. While there he could check in with Lane and his other contacts.

From the first the journey seemed to restore Callaway's spirits, as it would his health, at least to some degree. The account he gave of the journey was itself heavily salted with levity and perhaps the usual exaggerations. When he got to New York, having already looked up departure schedules, he went to the steamship office and, feigning ignorance, asked the agent which was the best ship departing on the following day. The agent asked where he was bound; Callaway replied that he didn't care. This no doubt surprised the agent, who informed his customer that a ship was bound for Europe the next day.

That was the ship Callaway had planned to take all along, and he next asked for good but cheap accommodations. Since he was so offhanded about his destination, the agent had to be sure to offer him a good deal, and he suggested a cabin with three berths, provided that Callaway wanted to take a chance that no one else would claim a berth. On this

small matter Callaway was willing to gamble, telling the agent that chance was his middle name and taking the deal. This time the chance paid off; he got the whole cabin to himself. Once again his meticulous preparation, together with the fact that he had more information than the other party thought he did, worked in his favor.

The crossing invigorated him, as evidenced by the fact that it inspired a typical Callaway story. He spun an embellished tale of a husband and wife making the crossing with their young son. The couple suffered badly from seasickness, although their son did not; in fact, he made a huge nuisance of himself, running and jumping around the deck while the stricken couple looked on helplessly. Finally the woman turned to her husband. "You must speak to Willie!" she implored him.

Quite green around the gills, he turned in his son's direction. "Hello, Willie!" he said feebly.

Callaway's levity continued as the ship arrived in Europe. Going down the gangway, he made a loud announcement to everyone around him. "There is an animal over here," he warned, "who puts his front foot on one's chest, and, with his whiskers in one's face, tickles him to death!"

He got the response he hoped for when one man asked apprehensively, "What's the name of that animal?"

"A calliope," Callaway answered.

A few moments later a weird foghorn boomed out. "That's the calliope roaring now!" whispered Callaway to his target, who, gratifyingly, nearly fell off the gangway in fright.

Although he'd found the salt air of the crossing restorative, Callaway simply couldn't leave business alone. One of his regular practices during this first tour of Europe was frequenting the street markets in the various cities he visited, trying to discover whether such a thing would work in LaGrange. Dressed in his dark suit, although

Fuller Callaway's match box cover engraved with FEC.

lacking the appropriate collar, he claimed to be mistaken frequently for a priest while on the Continent. He often tried, but apparently failed, to give a coin to the lame; they would shake their heads in refusal while calling him "Father" in their native tongues.

He didn't stop his research with the street markets. He also made several contacts among manufacturers, visiting factories and taking note of how they were run. This was to become the pattern for all of his future visits to the Old World; his trips there, even vacations, were to be working ones.

In London, Callaway got himself invited to a Masonic meeting, where he enlisted the help of an accomplice. His assistant introduced him to various men, stating their names loudly and then whispering their occupations to Callaway. Near the end of the meeting, Callaway announced that he could tell people's vocations simply by looking at them. To prove it he selected one of the three men to whom his partner in crime had introduced him.

"That man is shrewd, loves to argue and give advice," he said.

An excited murmur arose. "That's right, he's a barrister!"

Callaway picked out the next mark. "This man imparts information, trains and disciplines young people."

"Yes," the crowd exclaimed, "he is a teacher!"

Callaway moved on to the third and last man his friend had told him about. "He is a merchant," he declared. "He buys and sells at a profit."

"Extraordinary," hummed the audience, "extraordinary!" Others pressed forward. "Tell about me," several of them called out. "What am I?" Callaway, out of information, looked at his watch and announced that he had to leave immediately to catch his train.

Reading Callaway's account of his journey, one would think that it consisted of nothing but business research interspersed with mild

practical jokes. With his connection to the La-Grange National Bank, Callaway had access to uncut sheets of ten-dollar national bank notes, which he would sign as he needed them, thus using each as a sort of traveler's check. The likeness of the recently assassinated William McKinley was on the notes he took with him to Europe, and Callaway bore a fairly strong resemblance to him, as well as to William Jennings Bryan; all three were hefty and round-faced. Once while in Switzerland after being shaved by a barber, Callaway produced a sheet of money, tore off a note, signed it with a flourish, and presented it to the barber.

"Is this good money?" asked the barber dubiously, put off by the strange ritual.

"Sure," Callaway replied breezily, pointing to the image of McKinley. "Don't you see my picture, and didn't you see me sign my name?"

It worked. The barber ran excitedly out into the street. "Everybody," he cried, "come see the man who makes all the money in America!"

Between all the jokes and the visits with manufacturers, Callaway returned both reinvigorated and full of new business ideas. "It is simply wonderful how I have improved," he told Ida when he got back. "I feel better than I have for years, and hope to establish this condition for good."

It didn't happen. Callaway had simply burned the candle at both ends for too much of his life to recuperate fully, especially as he was now passing from youth to middle age. By 1909, the year of his disagreement with Lane, signs of stress were returning. Once again his family told him that he had to take a break.

By this time Callaway had learned the valuable lesson that he could combine a vacation with a business trip, as he had in Europe. In 1909, with his efforts to get the Manchester operation running, he didn't feel as if he could be away from LaGrange for too long. So this time he decided to see something of his own country and take a trip to the West.

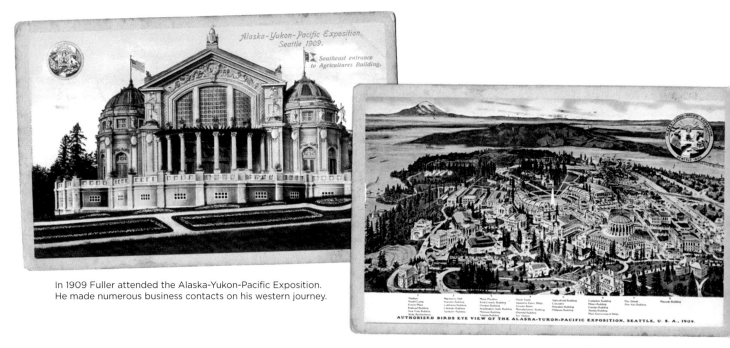

In 1909 Fuller attended the Alaska-Yukon-Pacific Exposition. He made numerous business contacts on his western journey.

While he was interested in general sightseeing on this trip, he made specific plans to visit two places in particular. The first was Yellowstone Park. The second, a business-related one, was Seattle's Alaska-Yukon-Pacific Exposition, slated to open in June 1909.

Since its founding in 1871 as the first national park, Yellowstone had become quite a tourist attraction, and by 1909 it drew visitors by horse, rail, and automobile. In late July, Callaway arrived there in the company of two friends, Ida apparently remained in LaGrange, as she had in 1907. The huge park, with its lake, canyon, geysers, and wildlife, would have been plenty to occupy him. Still, he didn't neglect to check in frequently by telegraph with his office, keeping himself up-to-date about the progress in Manchester as well as with more routine matters.

As for the Seattle event, Callaway no doubt saw it as a means of educating himself about potential markets and making business contacts. The Alaska-Yukon-Pacific Exposition was designed to highlight the commercial opportunities of the Pacific Northwest and the Asia trade, much as the southern expositions of the previous decades had endeavored to showcase the cotton states. America had taken the Philippines and Hawaii a decade earlier, just as the Klondike gold rush hit its peak in the Yukon and focused world attention on the region.

More recently, Japan had come into its own as a world power, signified by its crushing defeat of Russia's fleet at Tsushima and attested to by its exhibition in Seattle, complete with warships. A contemporary described the exposition as belonging "away down the list in point of size but away up the list in point of beauty." In the distance Mount Rainier provided an impressive focal point for the layout of the exposition's grounds, beckoning investors and businessmen as a gateway to Pacific and Asian commerce. Millions of visitors attended it from June to October. Callaway would likely have found it a valuable experience.

While Callaway always maintained that his "vacation" travels invariably left him fully restored and feeling better than he had in years, in truth his health was never the best after he turned forty. This fact came home to him in a frightening way a year and a half after his western travels. In January 1911 he was in New York on a routine business trip. Ida had observed that when setting out on his journey north he was already quite run down from overwork. Then after his arrival in New York, her husband wrote her that he had a cold—perhaps the flu (or the grippe as it was often called in those days, even by Americans). He assured her that he would be all right before long.

He was wrong. Soon Ab Perry telephoned Ida to tell her that he'd gotten a cable from a friend in New York. The cable stated that Fuller was very ill and that Ida should go to him right away.

Ida caught the first northbound train, collecting Cason from Asheville on the way, and found her husband at the Waldorf, very ill indeed. Doctors had diagnosed the condition as facial erysipelas, a strep-based infection of the deep epidermis that produced a hard red rash. Perhaps Fuller had been right about having a cold; it was quite possible the disease had begun with a strep infection in his nasal passages. But things were now far more severe. Without antibiotic treatment, erysipelas can travel through the lymphatic system and even produce septic shock and ultimately death, as it did in England's Queen Anne, Charles Lamb, John Dryden, and John Stuart Mill. And in 1911 there were no antibiotics.

For many long days, Fuller Callaway lay in the Waldorf, fevered and delirious. Ida was afraid he would be sent to a hospital; the age when hospitals were deadly places was still in the recent past. But he remained at the Waldorf, ministered to by his family, doctors, associates from Lane, and the highly attentive hotel staff from the manager on down. Once, when Cason tried to tip a bellboy, the employee refused, saying that he was in and out of the room so often that he didn't expect a gratuity every time. Nurses constantly attended Callaway, who believed they were stenographers. He later told Ida that he believed he'd bought the recently deceased Mark Twain's unfinished book and was dictating its ending to the nurses.

The delirium remained, ominously, even after Callaway's fever broke, and the doctor recommended that Ida consult a brain specialist. She asked him to bring in the best one in New York.

By the time the specialist arrived, things seemed to be looking up. He asked Callaway

what time it was; Callaway retrieved his pocket watch from his vest, which hung on the bedpost. "This watch has stopped," he answered quite logically. The doctor then asked him to add series of numbers, and the patient did so correctly every time. Finally the specialist turned to Ida. "Mr. Callaway's mind is all right," he told her, to her huge relief. "When the toxic poison has gone out of his system, his reasoning will be as clear as it ever was. The only request I have to make is that you have him come around to my office after his recovery. A man as smart as Mr. Callaway is when he is delirious must be sure enough interesting to talk to when he is well!"

But Callaway wasn't out of the woods yet. As he himself later reminded Ida, math presented no problems for him, apparently even when he was delirious. The questions the doctor had put to him, he noted, were "like

When Callaway visited New York, he was a regular at the Waldorf-Astoria Hotel.

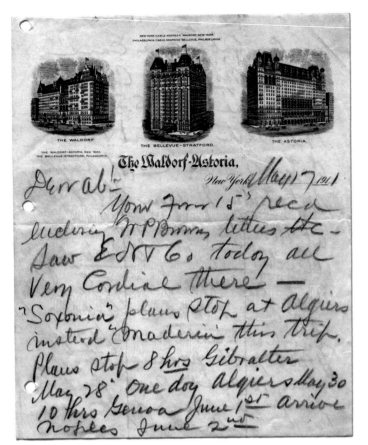

A 1911 letter from Callaway to Ab Perry from the Waldorf-Astoria. The letter was written just prior to Callaway's Mediterranean trip and mentions correspondence with W. P. Brown, a prominent cotton broker.

putting old 'Brer Rabbit in the briar patch!'" Even when he grew well enough to make the long trip home to LaGrange, he was still dealing with the toxic effects of the erysipelas. In February the couple went to St. Petersburg, Florida, accompanied by Howard Callaway, who was willing to abandon his own business for as long as needed in order to make sure his brother recovered.

In Florida Fuller developed jaundice, suffering a relapse so severe that Ida and Howard feared for his life. The group returned to La-Grange, although his wife and brother weren't sure that Fuller would survive long enough to arrive. But he did, and by the time they got home, he was even somewhat better. Before long Fuller headed to Tate Springs, Tennessee, in hopes that the waters there would reduce his blood toxicity.

By May, once again back in LaGrange, Callaway was clearly so far from a complete recovery that his doctors prescribed another long journey to convalesce. Fuller agreed.

Unknown to the doctors, Callaway had an ulterior motive. In the last several years, he had developed an interest in cotton waste, the raw material that a textile mill threw away. He'd been studying it since at least 1904. On the one hand, it was natural to want to make a mill highly efficient, so that it produced as little waste as possible; in 1911 as much as 20 percent of a bale of cotton ended up as waste. On the other hand, there was an entire industry dedicated to using cotton waste to produce useful goods, such as cotton balls and other products that don't require a high tensile strength. While America had a number of cotton waste plants, the heart of the industry lay in Europe, particularly Germany. Callaway wanted to go there and see the operation for himself.

In mid-May 1911, then, he set out on his second voyage to Europe, bound from Boston for the Mediterranean on the Cunard liner *Saxonia*. Keeping Ida, Ab Perry, and others informed via a stream of postcards and letters, he assured them that his health was quickly returning. "It is simply wonderful how I have improved every day at sea," he wrote from the Mediterranean. "Am greatly improved already, and thank you for the books sent from Brentano's,"* he wrote to Perry from Gibraltar. From there he made his way to Algiers, Genoa, Naples, Rome, Florence, and Milan, lingering for an extra several days at his Italian stops.

From Milan he continued to reassure Perry. "I have met a great many nice people, both tourists and natives," he noted, "and have improved in strength beyond my hopes, and if I can hold this improvement and continue to gain, will come home stronger in every way than for years."

His sense of humor attested to the truth of his statements. As a result of the erysipelas, his hair had turned gray and begun to fall out. During his time in Switzerland he targeted another hapless barber. This one

* A bookseller with branches in New York and Paris.

wanted to know why Callaway's hair was falling out so rapidly.

"Why," Fuller replied in all innocence, "doesn't everyone over here have his hair turn gray and fall out in the winter, and new suits of hair the natural color come back every spring?" The barber thought that to be the most amazing thing he'd ever heard about America. Later, with new brown hair, Callaway wanted to go back and tell the barber that he'd been pulling his leg, but he never got around to it.

A major part of the trip, of course, involved Germany as well as the Austro-Hungarian Empire, with Callaway stopping at Munich, Innsbruck, and Vienna. In Znaim, Austria (now Znojmo in the Czech Republic), aided by a letter of introduction from former Georgia governor Hoke Smith, Callaway got to tour "a beautiful waste mill," clearly a highlight of the journey. Then it was on to Scandinavia, where he traveled among the Norwegian fjords. From there he steamed to Newcastle and spent some time in the famed English mill districts of Manchester and Lancashire, no doubt engaging himself heavily in research for his own enterprises.

Callaway sent this postcard from the Rock of Gibraltar to Ab Perry in LaGrange in 1911. On the postcard he proclaimed, "Am greatly improved already."

At last, in mid-July, he embarked for New York on the White Star liner *Celtic*. Ida was waiting for him there, and the couple then spent a week or two in Atlantic City. From there it was back to LaGrange, where the Callaways arrived in mid-August.

Callaway's return, both to town and to health, was a major news item, and he gave a detailed report of his travels to the LaGrange and Atlanta papers. "I'm glad to get back to 'dear old Georgia' once again, and particularly LaGrange," he said.

I have seen many of the wonders of Europe, but I am content to come back to my native state and view the wonders of the Southland and the progress which is being made in my home state and city. I just talked plain "Georgia" over there, and did not attempt to fool them into thinking that I could speak any other language than English; consequently I got along famously. I just let the other fellow try to talk English to me, and did not try to put on any "language" airs.

Although his tour had been a long and detailed one, its emphasis had been on recuperation rather than work, perhaps more so than any of his other travels, and there were many places it hadn't taken him. For certain reasons he wanted to see some particular places quite badly. Thus it was that two years later he prepared for a third trip to the Old World.

During his 1911 European tour Callaway sent this card featuring the Christopher Columbus Monument in Genoa, Italy.

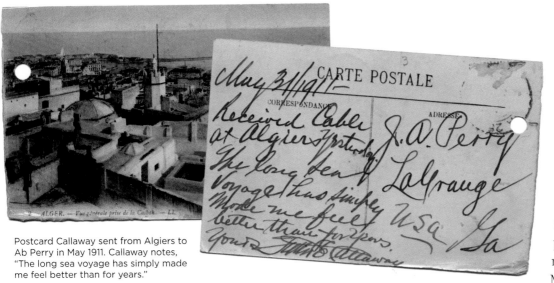

Postcard Callaway sent from Algiers to Ab Perry in May 1911. Callaway notes, "The long sea voyage has simply made me feel better than for years."

During his illness, Callaway had been attended by a male nurse who had once served under Horatio Herbert Kitchener, in 1911 a British viscount and recently named a field marshal. The nurse evidently told his charge stories of his time with Lord Kitchener; Callaway, fascinated, decided that he wanted to meet the famous soldier for himself.

Kitchener stands as one of the great imperial names of the Victorian and Edwardian eras. Born in 1850 he saw lengthy service in southern Africa during the Second Boer War and in India as commander-in-chief of British forces, he is nevertheless most famously identified with Egypt and the Sudan. In 1911 he was, by any standard, one of the empire's most towering figures.

In 1869 the Suez Canal opened, instantly turning Africa into an island and cutting the distance between England and India by more than four thousand miles, nearly halving travel time. The opening of Suez, together with the near-simultaneous completion of the American transcontinental railway that Callaway had recently taken to the West, meant that the world in 1869 suddenly became a vastly smaller place. It is no coincidence that Jules Verne published his famous novel *Around the World in Eighty Days* only four years later.

During the great age of imperial competition, Suez was a natural target for the other great powers of Europe, especially since much of Africa and the Middle East were still up for grabs, including Egypt. For decades it had been under the nominal control of the Ottoman Empire, but in the early nineteenth century Mohammed Ali and his successors won *de facto* autonomy from the Turks. Years of international intrigue followed as Britain, France, and the Ottomans jockeyed for influence in the region.

By 1881 England had become heavily involved in Egypt, and protection of the canal was a major reason. This in turn required Britain to control Egypt; since Egypt depended on the Nile, this in turn meant that Britain needed to control the river all the way to its mysterious, undiscovered sources. This spawned the famous explorations of men such as Sir Richard Burton, David Livingstone, and Samuel Baker. But in the final decades of the nineteenth century came the Mahdist War in the Sudan. This prototype uprising of Muslim populations against their western overlords that would occur so often in the twentieth and twenty-first centuries threatened the entire British program. The most severe blow fell at Khartoum, Sudan's capital, where the White Nile and the Blue Nile merged; here British Major General Charles "Chinese" Gordon was killed in 1885 while trying to defend the city.

After the fall of Khartoum, the Mahdists reigned supreme in Sudan for a decade. But by 1896, reports of Mahdist savagery moved the British to take action again. It fell to Kitchener to make the assault.

He was no stranger to Egypt, having fought there since the fall of Khartoum. By 1896 he was commander of the Anglo-Egyptian army, a small, modern force that was equipped with the best weaponry that Europe had to offer. A young Winston Churchill, one of Kitchener's junior officers, later wrote his first book about the campaign. In 1898 Kitchener took the battle to the enemy's heart, marching his force to Omdurman, a city directly across the Nile from Khartoum. There, on September 2, he avenged Gordon's death by winning a lopsided battle that gave Britain an undisputed control of both Egypt and the Sudan that would last until the 1950s. Churchill called it "the most signal triumph ever gained by the arms of science over barbarians. Within the space of five hours," he wrote, "the strongest and best-armed savage army yet arrayed against a modern European Power had been destroyed and dispersed, with hardly any difficulty, comparatively small risk, and insignificant loss to the victors." In fact, Kitchener had inflicted roughly 25,000 combat casualties, nearly half of them deaths, at the cost of only 48 of his own men killed and fewer than 500 wounded.

In the wake of this victory, Kitchener soon became known as Kitchener of Khartoum, being granted a barony of that name in 1898. The following year he was sent to the Cape Colony with strong reinforcements to fight the Boers; here he personally signed Breaker Morant's death warrant. In 1902 he became commander-in-chief of the Indian Army, serving in that post until 1909.

In 1911, the year of Callaway's illness, he was appointed British Agent and Consul-General of Egypt and Sudan—the *de facto* ruler of the entire region. This was where Kitchener was in 1913 when Callaway decided to go there and meet him in person.

The journey wasn't entirely about Kitchener. By the beginning of 1913, Callaway's pattern of overwork and exhaustion had again repeated itself, and he was in need of another rest. This time, instead of focusing on Europe, he chose the Middle East as his destination

The renowned Shepheard's Hotel in Cairo was Callaway's base of operations while he was in Egypt.

because of two attractions it held: Kitchener and the Holy Land. His friends were relieved, since one thing the region didn't have much of was a textile industry that could distract Callaway from his rest. They should have reflected further. Egypt was known for its cotton. In fact, cotton was Egypt's major cash crop, having become a major product in the early 1860s, when the American cotton supply dried up as a result of the war.

At the end of January, Callaway steamed out of New York on the *Caronia*, one of Cunard's largest steamers. Over the next two weeks he stopped briefly at Funchal, Gibraltar, Algiers, Monaco, and Naples, keeping in regular contact with home via cable. On February 17 he arrived in Alexandria, and soon he was on a train bound for Cairo. There he checked into Shepheard's Hotel.

Built in 1841, Shepheard's was one of the great hotels of the empire, ranking alongside the Raffles in Singapore and Watson's in Bombay. "When once the Englishman has removed himself 400 yards from Shepheard's Hotel," wrote Harriet Martineau as early as 1846, "he begins to feel that he is really in the East. Within that circle . . . he is still in Great Britain." Shepheard's registry held a host of famous names: Henry Morton Stanley, whose name is forever linked with that of David Livingstone; Winston Churchill; and America's own Theodore Roosevelt. It had served as a

CUNARD LINE

MEDITERRANEAN ~ EGYPTIAN ~ ADRIATIC CRUISES

In 1913 Fuller left New York via the Cunard Line's *Caronia* en route to the Mediterranean and Egypt.

military headquarters during the Crimean and Boer Wars as well as during the Sepoy Mutiny, and it would serve in that capacity again in the Great War, when T. E. Lawrence would add his name to the register. But Callaway was mainly interested in the most famous name on the list as of 1913: that of Lord Kitchener himself.

A national figure in his own right by now, and making Shepheard's his own base of operations for the duration of his stay in the East, Callaway was armed with various letters of introduction. But given Kitchener's eminent status, he doubted that even these credentials would be good for more than a handshake. What Callaway really wanted was a chance to get to know Kitchener. The fascination seems a bit odd; the stories his nurse told him of the imperial hero must really have piqued his interest.

By all accounts, Callaway decided to introduce himself through Kitchener's social secretary. According to Ida, her husband donned a fez—the local uniform for Egypt's British overlords—arrived at Kitchener's headquarters in a carriage, marched into the building, and sent in his calling card. When the secretary emerged to fend him off, Callaway switched on his charm and dazzled the man into admitting him to Kitchener's inner sanctum.

Young Fuller gives a more elaborate, almost certainly embellished, version of the same story—one in which his father's interest seems an outright obsession. According to this account, Callaway stalked his prey the way a hunter might stalk a tiger in Burma. Casing the immediate neighborhood of Kitchener's headquarters, he located a small restaurant nearby and observed that it was frequented by members of Kitchener's staff. Callaway went in and ordered a cup of coffee, likely served in the usual eastern style—"blacker than hell and sweeter than love," as the expression goes, and rich with finely ground beans—and began to chat up the establishment's owner. All the while he watched the comings and goings of the English officials.

He hung around the restaurant for a couple of days, continuing his observations and asking the owner about various patrons. In someone lacking his reputation and stature, the behavior would certainly have been alarming. Finally his gaze settled on a frequent visitor to the establishment. "Who's that?" he asked the proprietor.

"That's the loafer," the owner replied. "He's Kitchener's social secretary; he don't have a thing to do because Kitchener don't do any society."

That was the opening Callaway had been looking for. He got up, walked into Kitchener's headquarters, and asked specifically to see the social secretary, sending in his card.

The gambit worked. The secretary invited

him in and Callaway started to charm him. After a fifteen-minute conversation, he made his crucial play. "Well," he said casually, "I've got an engagement and I've got to go."

The secretary took the bait. "Just a minute, Mr. Callaway," he said. "If Lord Kitchener isn't busy, I'd like for him to meet you."

"Well now," Callaway answered, "I don't know but I guess I could be a half hour late for my appointment."

Exactly what the secretary told Kitchener is anyone's guess, but young Fuller was sure he knew. "There's a man out here from Georgia, the most interesting man I've ever talked to," he had the secretary say. "I told him I wanted him to meet you and he said he could spare half an hour, and if it's all right . . ."

"Bring him in."

And so it was that Callaway got to meet Lord Kitchener, British Agent and *de facto* ruler of Egypt. Upon entering Kitchener's office he beheld a tall, strongly built man with a stern face and an elaborate, rather Germanic mustache. Later the famous Uncle Sam "I want you" World War I recruiting poster was based on a 1914 British poster that featured Kitchener's well-known countenance. But the sternness was mostly appearance; Callaway found that Kitchener, as had been suggested by the restaurateur, was almost painfully shy, and the sternness was softened once he smiled.

The two men hit it off, probably thanks in part to Callaway's charm as well as the traits the two men shared: ambition, memory, and a capacity for hard work. Young Fuller further maintained that the two men talked for the rest of the day and that Kitchener then had Callaway ride home with him, and Fuller Jr. speculated that Callaway even stayed in Kitchener's home as his guest for a time.

One thing is certain: cotton was a major subject of the men's conversations. Egypt was by now a major cotton producer, and Kitchener took a serious interest in the industry. But in Egypt, as in the American South, the cotton crop was under attack from the weevil. A particularly nasty variant in Egypt was the pink boll worm, which would grow into a major problem in the next few years, especially in light of the needs of war production. Kitchener told Callaway of the problem: the pink boll worm ate all of the cotton before the crop had a chance to mature.

"Why don't you grow an early maturing cotton that flowers before the pink worm can get in its work?" Callaway asked.

"We grow a cotton now that matures in one hundred ten days," Kitchener told him. But that was still too long. The worm would strike at about a hundred days' growth.

"You can cut twenty-five percent off that time," declared Callaway.

"My plant biologists tell me the thing cannot be done."

"Well," Callaway said, "there is a variety at home a friend of mine developed . . . that I figure will mature here in 90 days." That would be enough to beat the worm. George Truitt had worked hard to produce what was described as "a prolific, medium-early, big-boll cotton." In 1911 Truitt seed was used throughout the South; now Callaway wanted to see how it would fare in Egypt. "Call your secretary," he suggested.

While traveling in Egypt, Fuller met Field Marshal Horatio Herbert Kitchener, First Earl Kitchener. The two shared an interest in improving cotton production. This medallion was struck to commemorate Lord Kitchener's death in 1916.

The secretary came in, and Callaway dictated a cable to Ab Perry, asking him to expedite five pounds of Truitt early-maturing seed to Kitchener. "I figure it will mature in 90 days," he repeated. "Plant it and try it."

Before Callaway took his leave, Kitchener provided him with a priceless memento: his personal calling card, engraved "Field Marshal Viscount Kitchener of Khartoum—United Service Club." It would not only remain one of Callaway's most prized possessions, but also serve as an almost magical talisman during his further travels in the East. On it Kitchener had written "To introduce Mr. Callaway, of Georgia."

Those words were an "open sesame," as both Ida and Cason put it, to anywhere in the empire that Callaway wished to go, and he took full advantage of them. Steaming up the Nile on a three-week journey, he toured the Aswan Dam—one of the age's great engineering marvels—as well as Luxor and, of course, Khartoum, where he spent two days taking in the scenes of Gordon's death and Kitchener's triumph. Upon his return to Cairo and Shepheard's, he then prepared to set out on the next stage of his journey, a tour of the Holy Land.

As a Missionary Baptist, Callaway was no doubt fascinated by his sojourn in Palestine, which took him to Bethlehem, Jericho, the River Jordan, the Dead Sea, and naturally Jerusalem. He wrote Ida of his visits to such key sites as the Holy Sepulchre and the tomb of Joseph of Arimathea. He acquired, among other things, two playful gifts for her: a small work of clay pottery and an icon of Christ's baptism painted on a flat rock, probably from the bed of the Jordan.

At the end of March, Callaway returned again to Shepheard's for a few days, and then set out for a brief stop in Europe. At Naples he boarded the Cunard steamer *Saxonia*, on which he'd traveled in 1911, and ten days later he arrived in New York, where Ida was waiting for him. He presented her with his

two gifts and told her that the pot was a type known as Eve's tear jar; a Palestinian widow, he explained, was required to cry the jar full of tears before she could marry again. (Ida didn't record what she thought of that.) As for the icon, it showed Christ standing in the river as St. John the Baptist poured water onto his head. Wickedly, Callaway told his wife that he'd brought home this painting to show her that Christ had not been immersed. To this Ida replied primly, "I was convinced more than ever that I was right" about Christ's immersion, which gave Fuller a good laugh.

Several months later, Callaway was gratified to receive a cable from Kitchener. "Picking your cotton eighty-six days after seed were planted," it read. The Truitt strain had beaten the pink boll worm by a full two weeks.

The 1913 journey was undoubtedly one of the high points of Callaway's life. Indeed, any one of his many adventures in the East, taken by itself, would have made the trip a high point. But best of all had been making Kitchener's acquaintance. And though Callaway couldn't know it in 1913, his path was to cross Kitchener's again, at a key moment for both of them.

~

Less time than usual had passed when Callaway again set out for the Old World. Scarcely a year went by before he was preparing to depart for Europe in the company of his brother Howard as well as Sam Y. Austin, manager of the Unity mill. This time it was Howard who needed a rest. While Fuller's health was of some concern, for him this trip was mainly for business. He was getting more interested every day in the possibilities the cotton waste industry promised. His earlier visit to the waste plant in Znaim had been tantalizing, and he now wanted to carry out a thorough survey of the industry with Austin's help. Clearly, a new Callaway mill was in the offing.

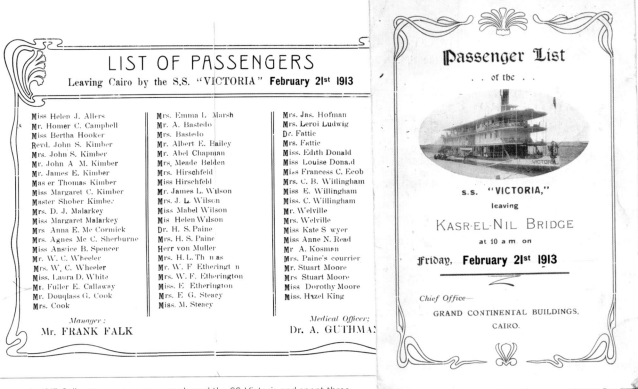

LIST OF PASSENGERS
Leaving Cairo by the S.S. "VICTORIA" February 21st 1913

Miss Helen J. Allers	Mrs. Emma L. Marsh	Mrs. Jas. Hofman
Mr. Homer C. Campbell	Mr. A. Bastedo	Mrs. Leroi Ludwig
Miss Bertha Hooker	Mrs. Bastedo	Dr. Fattie
Revd. John S. Kimber	Mr. Albert E. Bailey	Mrs. Fattie
Mrs. John S. Kimber	Mr. Abel Chapman	Miss. Edith Donald
Mr. John A. M. Kimber	Mrs. Meade Belden	Miss Louise Dona.d
Mr. James E. Kimber	Mrs. Hirschfeld	Miss Francess C. Ecob
Master Thomas Kimber	Miss Hirschfeld	Mrs. C. B. Willingham
Miss Margaret C. Kimber	Mr. James L. Wilson	Miss E. Willingham
Master Shober Kimber	Mrs. J. L. Wilson	Miss. C. Willingham
Mrs. D. J. Malarkey	Miss Mabel Wilson	Mr. Welville
Miss Margaret Malarkey	Mis Helen Wilson	Mrs. Welville
Mrs Anna E. Mc Cormick	Dr. H. S. Paine	Miss Kate S wyer
Mrs. Agnes Mc C. Sherburne	Mrs. H. S. Paine	Miss Anne N. Read
Miss Anstice B. Spencer	Herr von Muller	Mr A. Kosman
Mr. W. C. Wheeler	Mrs. H. L. Th n as	Mrs. Paine's courrier
Mrs. W. C. Wheeler	Mr. W. F Etheringt n	Mr. Stuart Moore
Miss. Laura D. White	Mrs. W. F. Etherington	Mrs Stuart Moore
Mr. Fuller E. Callaway	Miss. E Etherington	Miss Dorothy Moore
Mr. Douglass G. Cook	Mrs. E G. Steacy	Miss. Hazel King
Mrs. Cook	Miss. M. Steacy	

Manager:
Mr. FRANK FALK

Medical Officer:
Dr. A. GUTHMA

Passenger List
. . of the . .

s.s. "VICTORIA,"
leaving
KASR-EL-NIL BRIDGE
at 10 a m. on
Friday, February 21st 1913

Chief Office—
GRAND CONTINENTAL BUILDINGS,
CAIRO.

In 1913 Callaway was a passenger aboard the SS *Victoria* and spent three weeks exploring the Nile.

Fuller did his homework for the trip carefully, planning to spend a lot of time in the cotton waste centers of Europe and corresponding with R. G. Dun and Company, the forebear of Dun and Bradstreet, to identify the major players in the field. He would give some attention to England's mill districts, but the focal point of the journey would be in Germany.

In May 1914, the trio set out for Europe. Although neither Callaway nor anyone else could possibly know it, this timing, combined with his particular interest, would make their journey one of the most fateful of his life.

Throughout June and July, Fuller traveled the breadth of western Europe. The three men often went their separate ways, with Austin doing his own research and Howard spending a great deal of time in Karlsbad, then an Austrian city, with its health-giving spas. Fuller, too, passed some time in Karlsbad, with a local doctor prescribing light meals designed to help him avoid his habit of overeating the wrong foods. But he devoted most of his time to making business contacts,

touring factories, and taking notes. Karlsbad would have been a good place to make contacts, but he also went to the cotton waste centers themselves. In London he contacted shipping agents; in Manchester he made the acquaintance of dyeing machine manufacturers and yarn agents. He also contacted engineers and export merchants while in Manchester, revealing his interest not only in making, but in shipping, cotton waste products. At some point the two brothers met John H. Callaway, a distant cousin, who resided in London.

Fuller traveled to Belgium and France as well, getting in touch with various agents there. But July found him in Germany, where he flitted among Karlsbad, Stuttgart, Frankfurt, Cologne, Hamburg, and Berlin. His timing couldn't have been much worse.

On June 28, Serbian nationalist Gavrilo Princip, part of a group that wanted to see the creation of a national Serbian state, assassinated Archduke Franz Ferdinand, the heir to the Austro-Hungarian throne. This was a major event in Austro-Hungarian politics.

While traveling in Europe, Callaway sought the healing properties of the famous hot springs at Karlsbad, some eighty miles west of Prague. He collected these stamps while there.

But because of a chain of diplomatic and technological developments, it also caused an international crisis, a crisis that Europe had unwittingly been setting up for decades. The competition for world empire that apparently interested Callaway, to judge from his fascination with Kitchener and his pilgrimage to Khartoum; the weakness of the Ottoman Empire, the "sick man of Europe," which had let Britain get its foot in the door of Egypt; the rise of Germany as one of the world's great industrial powers, the very reason why Callaway was there in the first place, and its naval challenge to Britain; the rise of ethnic nationalism, particularly pan-Slavism—all of these had helped spawn high levels of military preparedness and a competing series of mutual defense treaties throughout Europe.

Callaway, too, would have understood the role of the railroad in the overall picture. Rail networks had become crucial not just in commerce, but in the mobilization and deployment of armies. To take full advantage of the railroads, though, each country in Europe had to work out mobilization schedules and rail timetables, almost to the minute, months in advance. This meant three things of great importance to the sometimes widely separated Fuller, Howard, and Sam Austin. First, it meant that once an emperor, king, or prime minister ordered his army to mobilize, the process couldn't be stopped without wrecking that army's intricate mobilization schedule, thus opening up his country to a disastrous defeat by an enemy. In other words, once a country started to mobilize—which would undoubtedly spur its enemies to do likewise—the process took on a life of its own. It couldn't be stopped. This slavery to the railroad was something Callaway himself had experienced, although in a different context. Second, it meant that once one country began to mobilize, even if it hadn't declared war, its enemies had to do the same or risk being

caught defenseless. This compounded the domino effect.

Finally, and most important to the Callaway group, it meant that if mobilization happened, civilian traffic would be severely disrupted, if not stopped outright, all over Europe. And in the summer of 1914, this is exactly what happened.

Franz Ferdinand's assassination turned out to be the initial domino that activated the whole deadly system. Supported by Germany, Austria, whose leaders decided that the right time had come, made demands for satisfaction that Serbia couldn't tolerate. The July Crisis, as it was called, became acute during the final days of the month, and the mobilizations began.

Despite his travels in Germany, the crisis caught Callaway in England, where he was relatively safe. Sam Austin, on the other hand, was in Belgium, directly in the crosshairs of a German invasion of France. And Howard, as usual, was at the Karlsbad spas, squarely within Austrian territory. The group had planned to meet in Germany and set out from Hamburg for America on the German liner *Imperator* on the last day of July. That was just a few days too late. On July 28, Austria-Hungary declared war on Serbia, triggering an immediate Russian mobilization. By the July 31, Germany and Russia began to draw their swords against each other, and the Hamburg-American Line announced that the *Imperator* wouldn't sail. The following day, Germany declared war on both Russia and Russia's ally France. Four days later came the German invasion of Belgium, and with it the true arrival of the bloody twentieth century. "The lamps are going out all over Europe," Sir Edward Grey, the British foreign minister, is said to have remarked while watching lamplighters at work from his office window that evening. "We shall not see them lit again in our lifetime."

Britain, with the most powerful fleet in the world, sat astride Germany's access to the North Atlantic, and for the time being English seaborne communications with America were unfettered. So as of August 1, the island nation seemed the best hope for the travelers. This presented Howard with the greatest challenge of the three men. Although he was a neutral, the borders were closing, the trains were almost completely at the service of the military, and paper money was worthless. Somehow he got out, walking across the border. Erstwhile *Imperator* passengers, Howard among them, then rode a cramped train with no food to Flushing in the Netherlands; from there Howard managed to get passage for England, which hadn't yet declared war. Austin got out of Belgium shortly before Germany marched in, making his way, like Howard, across the channel to England.

The three travelers reunited in London, safely out of the war zone, but their money was still worthless and their way home uncertain. Even American dollars were no good in England at that moment. Americans stuck there, even rich ones, might as well have been paupers.

As fate would have it, Monday, August 3, was a bank holiday in England, a public holiday when hordes of people made for the seashore, war or no war. On Saturday, August 1, all of these beachgoers began exchanging five-pound English banknotes for lower-denominations, more useful gold sovereigns. In light of the international crisis, this scared some of the smaller banks into refusing to swap paper for gold. Overnight, English banknotes became useless.

Luckily for Callaway, this was exactly the sort of problem that he excelled at handling, and perhaps even enjoyed solving. The gold sovereigns still held their value; it was the paper that was no good. So Callaway simply had to find a way to convert paper into sovereigns.

His first step was to go to the bank and, drawing upon his letter of credit, get one thousand pounds in twenty-pound notes. Then he found a waiting cab. (With paper worthless, many cabs were idle.) He managed to convince the driver that he was a good credit risk. Taking the cab to the nearest post office, he presented a twenty-pound note to the clerk. "Give me five £4 money orders," he said, "payable to Fuller E. Callaway." Having received the money orders, he moved to the next line and repeated the purchase with another twenty-pound note. Forty-eight purchases later—one is amazed that nobody stepped in to stop what he was doing, especially given the climate—he'd converted the one thousand pounds worth of notes entirely into 250 four-pound money orders.

Next he returned to his cab, which he'd held at the post office. "Take me to all the branch post offices in London," he instructed the driver, who by now was doubtless intrigued. He spent the day going from post office to post office. At each one he would cash a single money order, receiving four gold sovereigns. By nightfall he had a thousand of them, more than enough for passage on an America-bound steamer for Howard, Sam Austin, and himself, and he headed back to their lodgings.

The three men were staying at the Hotel Cecil, a large, grand hotel that boasted eight hundred rooms and was known as a focal point of American society in England. Even so, there was a shortage of rooms, staff, and food, given the turmoil that had struck in the war's first hours.

Walking into the lobby, which was crowded with his hungry and effectively impoverished countrymen, Callaway stood up on a chair. "A meeting is being called in the ballroom of all Americans, immediately!" he announced loudly. Once they had all moved into the opulent ballroom, he shared with them his technique of converting paper to

Fuller (standing to the left of the parasol) enjoying a tour of Cologne, Germany. He was accompanied on this trip by S.Y. Austin and Howard R. Callaway.

gold. "Now don't tell anybody but Americans," he warned them, "and make them keep it quiet." He knew that his trick wouldn't last long, even if the gold supply did. "You all get out in the morning and get all the gold you want." That is just what they did. And as he'd predicted, the government soon put a stop to it, extending the bank holiday by fiat for two more days and using the time to print and issue ten- and twenty-shilling notes in order to stop the golden hemorrhage. In later years when he told this story, Callaway liked to joke that he had "forced the British Empire to issue two new forms of currency."

Not everyone managed to get gold before the government stepped in. Callaway often ran across hungry Americans, sometimes whole families of them, on the street outside the Cecil. When he did, he would hand his countryman a sovereign along with his card. He did this as many as a hundred times. Nevertheless, he made sure to hold back enough to be able to afford passage to America for his own party.

He still faced a problem, though, in finding berths on a ship, even though he could pay for them. But his good luck held. Kitchener, having been created Earl Kitchener of Khartoum and Broome just a month earlier, happened to be in England on leave when war broke out, and if a story of young Fuller's is to be believed, Callaway knew it. Although the Foreign Office had ordered everyone on leave back to his post when the crisis became acute, Prime Minister H. H. Asquith personally instructed Kitchener to remain in England, probably to place him at the head of the War Office. On August 3 and 4, Kitchener was waiting in limbo for further orders, unable to leave for Egypt and not yet part of the government. That is almost certainly the only occasion that month when he would have had the chance to see Callaway. The Georgian may have caught up with the earl at 17 Belgrave Square, the home of Kitchener's good friend Pandeli Ralli, which served Kitchener as a sort of London headquarters and where he was waiting for developments during much of August 4.

According to young Fuller, his father raised a question with Kitchener that was on everyone's mind at the moment. "How long do you think the war will last?" he asked. "Three months?" He may have been remembering the Franco-Prussian War of 1870–71, when the hostilities hadn't lasted much longer than that, or perhaps the Spanish-American War of 1898, in which hostilities began in late April and ended in mid-August.

Kitchener had other ideas. "Make it a year and you'll be closer." (This tallies with the fact that the following day—August 5—having indeed been named secretary of state for war, he astonished the entire cabinet with his prediction that the war would last for three years; nearly everyone else there, like Callaway, believed that the war would be over by Christmas.) "You go back to Georgia," he told Callaway, "and build another mill. We will need every yard of goods we can get."

Callaway filed the conversation away. It was an important one, but before he could act on it, he still had to make it back to America.

Here, too, his acquaintance with Kitchener helped. At the steamship office, he flourished the field marshal's card, which—as it had in the Middle East—worked its powerful magic. It allowed him to book passage for himself, Howard, and Sam Austin on each of the first twelve ships scheduled to depart for America. The first eleven didn't sail. The twelfth was an American steamer, the SS *Philadelphia*.

She was a smallish liner, by no means one of the elite passenger ships, dating from the 1890s, when she'd served initially as a troop ship in the Spanish-American War. The only berths she had available were in steerage, but that was good enough.

On August 5, the Callaway group got to Southampton and made its way aboard. The ship was overflowing with passengers, and from the dock hundreds of Americans not lucky enough to get berths waved their farewells as the liner moved away from the

One of Fuller Callaway's luggage tags from the journey aboard the SS *Philadelphia* in August 1914.

dock. The three travelers had made it. But a difficult crossing still lay before them.

As the *Philadelphia* plowed slowly through the Solent and into the English Channel, Callaway still had a few sovereigns left. He gave some of them to a man who minded the gate between steerage and first class. That allowed the three of them to pass the gate, but there simply weren't berths enough for everyone. Even empty seats were nonexistent; the ship, normally rigged for about 450 passengers, had more than 1,000 aboard on this journey.

"Well," said Fuller, taking stock, "we'll just hang on the rail and wait until mealtime." The wait wasn't long. With so many passengers, the crew was running itself ragged and serving several times as many meals as usual, although the food was poor and meager. When the next seating came, some would-be diners vacated a sofa. The three Georgians immediately occupied it, and at least one of them stayed on it all the way to New York, lying down when necessary to hold places for the other two.

The crossing was rough on everyone. A group of French warships forced the *Philadelphia* to heave to until she could establish her identity as a neutral. Women were given dibs on the cabins, with as many as sixteen crowding into each, where they took turns sleeping in the berths. Members of the crew gave up their own berths for the passengers' use. Money was still no good, even for the number of wealthy Americans aboard. A committee formed to deal with problems as they arose, instituting a system of IOUs to serve as currency. Callaway became known as a good Samaritan, doing what he could to see to the needs of both the passengers and the crew. Among other things, he took up a collection for the badly overworked cooks.

On the night of August 12, the long ordeal came to an end, as the *Philadelphia* steamed into New York Harbor with her band playing "The Star Spangled Banner," and the passengers, as well as spectators on shore, singing along. The Statue of Liberty had doubtless never looked so fine to Callaway, or to anyone else aboard.

It had been one of the great adventures of Fuller Callaway's life, not least because of his reacquaintance with Lord Kitchener. But the adventure had ended; now, with the lamps going out in Europe, others beckoned. So, on disembarking, he put the voyage behind him and turned at once to business. Recalling what Kitchener had told him, he went straight to Elkan Naumburg's office. He told the financier the story of all that had happened on the trip, probably including both its original purpose as well as his conversation with Kitchener. Naumburg was fascinated, just as Callaway had intended him to be.

Then Callaway struck. "How's my credit?" he asked, slapping Naumburg on the back.

Having heard the traveler's story, Naumburg knew exactly what Callaway was asking, and why. "I'll lend you a million dollars," he said.

"I'll take it."

Callaway had carefully considered Kitchener's opinion, which ran counter to that of most others; thus, at that moment, the Georgian was one of a relatively few people in the world who believed that the war would be long and costly, gobbling up supplies at a rate that no previous war had ever done. He was prepared to stake a massive amount of cash and goodwill on Kitchener's prediction.

He was right to do it. The Great War would be every bit as demanding as Callaway and Kitchener foresaw, and more. It would see the Callaway organization open new mills, expand its operations, and grow rich. And Callaway himself, at the pinnacle of that organization, would in consequence emerge as an international figure.

THE CLASSICALLY INSPIRED EAST PORTICO OF THE CALLAWAY HOME
SHORTLY AFTER CONSTRUCTION WAS COMPLETED IN 1916.

· 6 ·

HILLS AND DALES

By the outbreak of the Great War in 1914, Fuller Callaway was approaching the height of his prestige, influence, and wealth. He had long since established himself as a top local and regional merchant; since the turn of the century he had become a household name in west Georgia through his connections in everything from railroads to insurance and banking. In the textile world he was achieving national prominence. Among the textile men themselves, he'd already achieved it. The war would bring him, as a textile producer, to the attention of national and world political leaders.

Although Callaway sometimes took bold chances in business—as long as he believed that they didn't amount to speculations—in his personal life he had always tended to frugality. By his fortieth year, the combination was paying off. While the personal frugality would remain a trait of his until his death, by the second decade of the new century he was beginning to allow himself more leeway. It was never unprincipled, though. If someone were to question him about a private expenditure, even one that might seem indulgent, Callaway would doubtless be able to give a number of solid reasons why his action actually made good financial sense.

By far the best example of this new trend lay in where the Callaways chose to live. When Fuller and Ida moved from West Haralson Street to Broad Street in early 1910, it was a clear sign that Callaway believed the change was not merely permissible but necessary. The amount of business he did at home and the demands of his extended family both justified and even compelled the purchase.

Given these facts, together with his rapidly growing wealth and influence, it is not too surprising that within a short time of the move to Broad Street, Callaway began planning to relocate his family again. When the war broke out, those plans were well underway for one of the most iconic of Callaway institutions: the grand home that today is called Hills and Dales.

A house usually tells people something about the social and economic status of the family who lives in it. Hills and Dales certainly reflected Ida and Fuller's status; indeed, it was one of the first, and probably most impressive, such signs they gave. The very fact that they did so, after decades of more modest living, is what tells us that Fuller was at last

Sarah Coleman Ferrell (1817-1903) created Ferrell Gardens between 1841 and 1903.

perhaps feeling a measure of financial security, even though he had objectively achieved it some years earlier.

Fine houses often have fine gardens to go with them, and Hills and Dales, from the beginning a very fine house, was no exception. But in one way it was definitely exceptional. Rather than the gardens being designed for and built around the house, as is usual, Callaway had his house designed and built for the garden. This garden, nearly seventy years old by the time Callaway acquired it and at least as fine as the house he built, is where the story of Hills and Dales truly begins.

Sarah Coleman Ferrell, the woman who created the garden, was born in Jones County, Georgia, in 1817. Jones County was a part of the frontier at the time, the lands to the west belonging to the Creek Nation until a few years later. But by the time Sarah was old enough for school, she would receive some of the best education Georgia had to offer its young women at a succession of good schools. First she attended Clinton Academy in her own county, a school that had an excellent statewide reputation. She then moved on to Sparta, living with relatives and most likely attending the Female Academy there. One of this school's major areas of study was botany, which

would have been a required course for Sarah. Afterward, when she was old enough to attend a boarding school, she became a student at the Scottsborough Female Institute near the state capital of Milledgeville. Scottsborough put a heavy emphasis on aesthetics, such as drawing, painting, music, and even wax flowers, but there were also more rigorous subjects, such as mathematics, science, Latin, and even Greek. History, especially that of the classical world, would also have been required.

During Sarah's time in school, western Georgia opened up for white settlement, and in 1831 her father bought two land lots a mile from the center of the raw new town of LaGrange. A year later, the family, including Sarah, relocated there, and she resumed her Latin studies at the new Troup County

Sarah Ferrell with her husband, Blount Coleman Ferrell (1816-1908).

Horse-and-carriage travel was common along the dirt roads in Troup County during the 1870s and 1880s. A horse-drawn carriage pauses on the north side of Ferrell Gardens, circa 1890. The house of Blount and Sarah Ferrell is on the crest of the hill in the background.

Academy. There, at the age of fifteen, she met and fell in love with a double first cousin of hers, Blount Ferrell, who taught at the school. The teenagers married in 1835 when she was eighteen and he a year older, and then they moved to the territory of Florida to live with Blount's parents while they established themselves, Sarah's new husband becoming a lawyer.

The financial Panic of 1837 hit the rough, young Florida territory hard, so around 1840, with business drying up, Blount and Sarah returned to Troup County. In 1841 Sarah's father gave the young couple eighty acres from the original parcels he had bought a decade earlier. Thus, in Sarah's twenty-fourth year, things fell into place for what was to come.

The elaborate garden Sarah cultivated on the couples' new land is often described as originating in 1841, in or near gardens begun by her mother ten years earlier. In truth, according to Sarah herself, she inaugurated her work on the garden the following year. Another oft-told story is that Sarah had a frail, delicate constitution and that she was only expected to live a short life. The story goes on to say that illness motivated her to spend time outdoors, working on her garden for her health's sake. But, in fact, Sarah lived into her eighties. What is more, in an interview she gave in her seventy-first year, she made no mention of illness as a motivation for her garden work. Actually, the garden seemed to spring from two fundamental things in her background that had nothing to do with health.

The first element was the frontier. Sarah was born on it and lived either on it or near it for the first quarter century of her life, following it from Jones County to Troup County and then to Florida and back. She thus saw, at first hand, the process of wilderness changing into civilization, of forests and countryside becoming pastures, fields, and towns. At the same time, through her education, she was exposed to gentility and high culture drawn from both the classical and modern worlds, things rare on the frontier and absent beyond it. Thus she developed a deep understanding of cultivation in its broad sense, the idea and practice of taking the roughness of nature and refining it.

The second thing Sarah Ferrell drew on was at least as fundamental as her frontier experience: her deep Christian faith, which

The home of Blount and Sarah Ferrell about 1880.

she apparently discovered quite early, largely through the influence of one of her teachers. And, quite clearly, one of the aspects of Christianity that had the greatest impact on her was the book of Genesis, specifically the creation accounts.

The stories of how God created and brought order to the world naturally complemented Sarah's own observations during the settling of western Georgia as well as Florida. In the first chapter of Genesis, God commanded Adam and Eve to exercise dominion over the earth and to subdue it. For Sarah this wasn't an abstraction. For her first twenty-five years and more, it was a hard fact that she daily witnessed being fulfilled. And, of course, the ultimate symbol of this dominion in Genesis was a garden.

It was thus only natural, and perhaps even inevitable, that as Blount and Sarah Ferrell at last settled down on their own land, Sarah would give expression to her life experiences and her Christian faith in a garden of her own, a plot of carefully cultivated ground that had

been wilderness just a decade or two before. Beginning in 1842, and for her remaining sixty-one years, this is exactly what she did.

Despite the setbacks of the Panic of 1837, the Ferrell clan apparently had considerable resources, for the house that Blount and Sarah occupied was no mere dogtrot cabin. Instead it was a one-and-a-half-story Gothic Revival frame house, complete with a brick foundation, gables, bay windows, and on the western side a portico supported by pillars. The couple's house stood on a hilltop, where the Callaway house now stands. Below the peak of the hill, the land had apparently already been shaped into terraces and evidently used for farming before Blount and Sarah settled there. For this reason they named their new estate "The Terraces." The arrangement also gave Sarah ideas about how to create her garden.

Sarah's exact system of designing and planning is uncertain, although she definitely carried out her work in stages over a course of years, and the terracing was key to her design.

Parterres of boxwood surround a decorative urn on the first terrace of Ferrell Gardens.

Most likely she began with the uppermost terrace, the one closest to the house, and then over time worked downward from there. The project took a great deal, not only of time, but of labor and money. By the late 1880s the Ferrells had expended thirty thousand dollars on it—hundreds of thousands of dollars in modern terms.

As Sarah continued to develop her garden over the years, she gave each terrace its own dimensions, and to a degree each terrace had its own theme as well as a particular name: the Upper Terrace, Sentinel Avenue, Bower Avenue, Labyrinth Avenue, Magnolia Avenue, and the Valley. But a few defining elements would be common throughout the garden.

One of the most important of these was Sarah's use of boxwood. The plant had long been a staple of ornamental gardens and, significantly, is mentioned in the book of Isaiah. The art of topiary, of using boxwood and similar plants to create living sculptures, stretches back at least to the time of Pliny the Younger and the Roman Empire. More recently it had been used at George Washington's Mount Vernon estate. Sarah's use of boxwood topiary anticipated by a few years a great renaissance of the practice in England. Today most of the boxwood at Hills and Dales are short, but there is a clue that at one time at least one type of boxwood was rather taller. The story is told that a section of boxwood was designed—as one of the terrace names suggests—as a labyrinth, which was a great favorite with visiting children, and beyond which was a summerhouse. According to legend, Pope Callaway, while manager of the estate, once got hopelessly lost in the labyrinth. The only way to get him out—which indicates the walls were too high to step over—was to cut through the boxwood that imprisoned him. As a result, the labyrinth was removed.

While the boxwood were important, an even more fundamental unifying element—the most crucial and unique of them all—was the nature of the symbols that Sarah created. She clearly linked her strong Christian faith with her gardening. "I would pray that my employment in Heaven," she once told a friend, "would be 'to tend and water from the ambrosial fount the flowers that never would in other climates grow.'" But Sarah went further, much further, than seeing a connection of her gardening to Eden and to heaven. She wanted other people to see it, too. So she wove Christian symbolism into the boxwoods themselves, the garden's very fabric, making it one of a relatively few examples of topiary based on Christian symbols. Some of the symbols that she incorporated into the garden are obvious, while others are buried quite deeply, as if to invite contemplation and discovery of the invisible reality behind common appearances.

One of the best examples of the garden's veiled symbols lies on the fifth terrace, Magnolia Avenue, next to the public entrance. A huge array of dwarf boxwood, only a few inches tall, spells out the word "GOD" in massive letters. Today the word is plainly visible from the air, and perhaps even from space. Placed at the entrance, God is quite literally "in the beginning" of the garden, just as he is in Genesis. But in the nineteenth century, few visitors noticed what the dwarf boxwood said. Those who did discover it, though, likely gained a deeper understanding

Inspired by the book of Genesis, Sarah planted boxwood to form the word "GOD" at the entrance to her garden.

and appreciation not only of the garden but— Sarah undoubtedly hoped—also of the role of God in the world.

The heaviest concentration of symbols was in a square terrace located to the west of the others, fittingly known as the Church. Measuring 135 feet by 135 feet, the Church recalls the square inner room of the temple of King Solomon, in contrast to the elongated shapes of the other terraces. Within the Church was a long boxwood symbol of a harp (or perhaps a lyre), an instrument often played in the Old Testament to praise God. In earlier years Sarah deliberately obscured the harp's shape by planting flowers among the boxwood, a system that she also used to hide the massive "GOD" topiary at the garden's entrance. Also present in the Church was a circular flower bed, which Ida Callaway much later identified as a collection plate.

The square terrace also contains many boxwood sculptures more readily recognizable as furnishings in a more contemporary conventional church. These include a life-sized organ, mourners' benches, chairs, and, in one corner, a pulpit. But one feature has raised questions even among those familiar with Sarah's symbology: an apparent sculpture of a waterway.

In 1932 a writer for the magazine *House Beautiful* declared that this sculpture is a cascade pattern reminiscent of actual water cascades at Italy's Villa Torlonia in Frascati and Villa Lante near Viterbo—the latter also possessing elaborate topiary. On the strength of this declaration, the author claimed that an Italian gardener must have helped Sarah with the Church at some point—a conclusion that, while not obviously wrong, nevertheless rests on a couple of big inferential leaps. Adding to the mystery is that the sculpture possibly has a mirror-image twin facing it, although the

Cindy Cameron poses next to the lyre in the church garden. Cindy was the daughter of Charlie and Janet Cameron, who worked for the Callaways.

"God is Love" Planted in Boxwood

Hills and Dales, LaGrange, Ga.   68777

This color postcard features Sarah Ferrell's motto "God Is Love."

original shape of the latter sculpture is now lost.

The Ferrells did have Irish servants, and the Church did once apparently contain a boxwood symbol of a cloverleaf. A connection between the sculpture, the servants, and Saint Patrick's use of the shamrock to explain the three-in-one nature of the Trinity is too enticing to resist. But the existence of the itinerant Italian gardener is a somewhat greater stretch. Certainly water is of great importance in Christian thought, and it is easy to imagine many ways in which Sarah could have incorporated water symbols into the Church, whether or not the inspirations came from the Italian villas. Among them are the waters over which the spirit of God moved in the opening verses of Genesis, the river flowing through Eden, the parting of the Red Sea (especially likely if the second sculpture, standing apart from the first, did in fact mirror it), the River Jordan, or the waters of baptism.

In other spots in the garden there is no need for speculation. On the Upper Terrace, right outside the Ferrells' house, are two sets of semicircular beds. Shaped like outstretched, welcoming arms, similar to the colonnades of Saint Peter's Square (yet another reason to reflect on the possible input of the Irish servants or the existence of the Italian), one pair of beds spells out two clearly discernible phrases in boxwood. One reads "God is Love"; the other, accompanied by a square and compass, says *fiat justicia*—let justice be done. The latter, of course, was inspired by Sarah's husband Blount Ferrell, a lawyer, judge, and Freemason.

This pairing provides another key to understanding the garden's symbolism, for Blount, while apparently believing strongly in the Masonic concepts of a deity and

morality, was not a church member. Yet some of the symbols that Sarah devised can be seen in both Masonic and Christian terms representing the couple's oneness. Sarah would have found this approach relatively simple because of Freemasonry's heavy use of Old Testament themes, holding its origins to lie in the construction of Solomon's temple.

The best example of this fusion appears on Sentinel Avenue, the second-highest terrace. On its eastern section, Sarah planted three boxwood sculptures: a cross, a butterfly, and a circle. In Freemasonry, a butterfly is representative of the human soul, undergoing metamorphosis and enlightenment as it progresses from birth to resurrection. The circle, used in masonry to verify the angle of squares, represents eternity for Freemasonry. Even the cross, though largely shorn of its Christian message by Freemasonry, is similar to the Masonic square and compass symbol in that it can indicate the cardinal points and determine the correctness of angles.

While this symbolism of the cross is somewhat speculative among Masons, there is no uncertainty about how Sarah understood her cross and its neighboring symbols. When Fuller Callaway was a boy, he spent long hours in the garden, and Sarah once explained the

Sarah Ferrell with her great-granddaughters, Mary B. Ridley and Sarah F. Ridley. The photograph was taken by R. W. Childress in 1894.

significance of the three sculptures to him. "The cross, the instrument of our redemption by Jesus Christ, to be taken up daily and borne by the one who would be the Lord's disciple," she told the youngster, "the circle, a symbol of the complete or well-rounded life; the butterfly, a symbol of life to which there is no end." On another occasion she put it in slightly different words, "If we bear our cross bravely," she said, "our lives will be perfect as the circle, and some day we will have wings."

The labyrinth that once existed in the garden might also have been a shared symbol. Originating in the ancient world, the labyrinth was incorporated into cathedral floors in medieval times and served as the basis for turf mazes—patterns of grass—near churches and monasteries. In Sarah's own nineteenth century, there was speculation that these labyrinths had represented a pilgrimage to the holy city of Jerusalem for medieval penitents. But to Blount the structure could have been not a labyrinth but a

simple maze, designed not to enlighten but to confuse, as it apparently confused Pope Callaway, representing to the Masonic mind all of life's anxieties.

Even the layout of the garden was something on which both Christian and Mason could agree. Being oriented in an east-and-west direction, like early churches, its arrangement acknowledges the rising of the sun as the coming of Christ, as well as the Masonic seeking of enlightenment and knowledge.

Other topiaries are scattered throughout the garden, some of them of obscure meaning. On Magnolia Avenue is a group of small boxwood representing a cluster of grapes, complete with vines and leaves, perhaps recalling the Old Testament story of the spies who returned from Canaan bearing huge bunches of grapes, or perhaps to serve as a reminder of the source of the wine drunk at the wedding at Cana and at the Last Supper. Also on Magnolia Avenue are boxwood sculptures of a locket and chain, perhaps a commemoration of an important event or a tribute to Sarah's youngest son, who died of fever during the Civil War.

For all the importance of the boxwood, there is yet another facet to Sarah's plan: the nature of the trees and other vegetation she planted throughout the garden. The Bible mentions a variety of plants, many of which the Hebrews and early Christians put to some sacred use. Among these are myrtle, fir, and pine trees; the oil tree, which Sarah interpreted to be a type of wild or Russian olive tree, and the linden, which she took to be the tiel tree mentioned in Isaiah; the cypress, from which Noah built his ark; bay trees; and roses. All of these are prominent in the Old Testament. Plants important in both Old and New Testaments include the olive, which grew in groves on the Mount of Olives and which may well have grown in Gethsemane, and the palm, the source of the fronds that people cast down before Christ as he entered

Bunch of Grapes Planted in Boxwood

Hills and Dales, LaGrange, Ga. 68779

Color postcard showing Sarah Ferrell's planting of grapes, a concept inspired by a story in the book of Numbers.

Jerusalem in triumph. Sarah included each of these plants in her garden. A great many of them are mentioned in the book of Isaiah, which the leading scholar of the gardens believes was the inspiration for all of Sarah's work at "The Terraces."

Two biblical trees of particular importance to Sarah were the cedar and the shittah, or shittim, trees, both of which, again, are mentioned together in Isaiah. "I will plant in the wilderness the cedar, the shittah tree, and the myrtle, and the oil tree," reads the key verse. "I will set in the desert the fir tree, [and] the pine, and the box tree together." Although Troup County was no longer wilderness when Sarah began her garden, echoes of the frontier still remained, further suggesting that in creating her garden, she was reenacting key biblical moments. In addition to placing cedars throughout the garden, she lined her driveways with them. She also received a cedar of Lebanon from a friend, which grew into an immense tree with two trunks, still very much in evidence late in Ida Callaway's life. Also, around 1879, Sarah received what she believed to be a small shittim tree, of the type

from which the Ark of the Covenant was constructed, and planted it on the western side of the Upper Terrace, or as Ida much later described it, "on the front of the house." By Ida's day it had grown to sixty feet tall.

Sarah also made considerable use of plants not mentioned in the Bible, although here, too, she likely had a biblical notion in mind. The theme of the plants not thus mentioned was that they came from all over the world, reflecting the Christian commission to spread the gospel to all peoples. Some sources grandly claim that Sarah had managed to collect a tree from every country on earth; more likely, the group included trees

This stereoscope card shows Sarah Ferrell and several family members in "The Valley" of Ferrell Gardens.
Photo by M. G. Greene circa 1879.

Townspeople enjoy a stroll in Ferrell Gardens. A close-up from a stereoscope image taken by M. G. Greene in about 1879.

from every inhabited continent. Researchers have without doubt identified numbers of trees from each of the continents of North America, South America and the tropics, Europe, Africa, and Asia.

Sarah likewise saw her garden as a means for more than one type of missionary activity, and this, in fact, is how her path came to cross Fuller Callaway's. Because her Christian faith was so essential to her character, Sarah was generous in many different ways. She bought and made clothes for the poor and often sent flowers from her garden to the sick. And, of course, she shared the garden itself with the community, for its Christian message and symbolism would have been pointless without people to experience and reflect on it. A boxwood-lined path leads from present-day Vernon Road to the eastern side of Magnolia Avenue, giving the public access to the garden through a gate that always remained open. Many members of the community were regular visitors, and they often had their favorite spots, one of the best-loved being Bower Avenue, so

called because of the bowers at the ends of one section of terrace. Eustace W. Speer, a Methodist minister, wrote many of his sermons there. But the bowers were also favorites with young courting couples, a fact that gave Bower Avenue its more famous name of Lovers' Lane. According to local stories, a great many couples became engaged there.

Indeed, the heavy public traffic even became a nuisance, at least for Blount and perhaps for Sarah too. The issue wasn't with people's use of the garden, but of their abuse of it. In 1870 Blount took the step of putting a notice about the problem in the newspaper to ask parents to control their children. "My garden is thronged with small chaps," he complained, "half grown boys and girls, racing and romping over the yard without regard to walks or beds—injuring the shrubbery, breaking the iron seats, and frequently disturbing the quiet of the family by their noisy and boisterous conduct."

Despite the rather pointed message, the problem continued. The difficulty of maintaining the garden in light of such abuse, together with Blount's and Sarah's advancing age, were likely the motivations for Blount's offer in 1890 to sell the garden to LaGrange for use as a parade ground, park, and cemetery. But the deal never went through, and people kept treating the grounds poorly. Three

Ladies on the stone steps at Ferrell Gardens.

years later Blount again expressed his displeasure through the newspaper, entreating parents "to keep their half-grown children . . . out of my wife's flower-garden on Sundays. . . . [I]t will save my wife the worry of an intolerable nuisance." People still didn't get the message, so three months later he stated with obvious irritation that visitors who behaved in such a manner "mar its beauty and pilfer its treasures." It is worth noting that most of these announcements came in the late winter; apparently Sarah discovered the severity of the damage as she was preparing the garden for the spring growing season.

But despite these complaints, one visitor, at least, was apparently most welcome: Fuller Callaway.

From the beginning of his life, Fuller, somewhat like Sarah, seemed drawn to flowers. As a mill owner he provided both flowering plants and vegetable plants to his workers free of charge, encouraging mill operatives to plant flowers both indoors and out, awarding prizes to employees who produced the prettiest or most improved plants, gardens, and yards. As a youth he spent a great deal of time in Sarah's garden, where he became a favorite of hers. Perhaps he somehow reminded her of her own deceased son, Palmon Ernest Ferrell. As an adult, Callaway claimed that he loved the garden more than anyone except for the Ferrells themselves.

Once he was older, Callaway also helped Sarah in her charitable work—specifically, her making of clothes for the poor. During one of his visits to the garden as an adult, she told him that she thanked God for him every day; the low prices at his dime store, she explained, meant that she could buy cloth cheaply enough to make two dresses for every one she'd been able to make before he opened the store.

One day around the turn of the century, with Sarah now well into her eighties, Callaway

Sarah Ferrell standing in the garden she created in LaGrange.

was showing some out-of-town customers around the gardens. Sarah was busy planting flowers, and he stopped to chat with her. "I want you to have this garden," she suddenly told him as they conversed. "You are the only one that loves it enough to keep it going." Callaway would remember the conversation.

In 1903 Sarah Coleman Ferrell died at the age of eighty-six. Five years later Blount Ferrell, aged ninety-two, followed her. The couple's only surviving child was almost seventy, and since he was unable to take on the responsibility for the labor-intensive garden, the property rapidly went downhill.

In December 1911 the entire estate was auctioned off. The book value at the time was $20,000. Fuller Callaway bid on it and bought it for $8,150. It was only the second, or possibly the third, time the land had been conveyed since the original settlement of Troup County.

Precisely when the Callaways got the idea of building a new home next to Ferrell Gardens is uncertain. The move from Haralson to Broad Street in early 1910, shortly after Blount's death, suggests (but by no means conclusively) that the possibility of buying the Ferrell estate hadn't occurred to them at that point. Even after Fuller did buy the property two years later, he may not yet have gotten the idea of building a residence there. After taking possession, his first actions related to the garden itself, and perhaps even to farming. He commissioned a study of the garden, and it was apparently around this time that he put Pope in charge of managing the estate, complete with a crew of laborers and a foreman working under him. Fuller also set about acquiring the adjoining parcels of land in order to expand the estate. As he once half-jokingly explained, he had a penchant for "owning all the land that 'jines me." Not until January 1914, fully two years after his initial purchase, did Callaway publicly announce plans to build a new home adjacent to the gardens as well as his hiring of an architectural firm. The agency he chose was, at first glance, something of a surprise, for it consisted of two young men who were early in their careers: Hentz and Reid, of Macon and Atlanta.

This stained-glass window at the First Baptist Church on the Square in LaGrange was given in memory of Sarah Ferrell by her family.

But Neel Reid, the partner responsible for all of the firm's design output, was actually an interesting choice, and in a way a natural one. While only twenty-eight, he was prolific, and while he was still in the first stage of his career, the completion of Hills and Dales would mark his coming to full professional maturity. His success with the project would show that Callaway, after all, had chosen his man wisely. Born in Alabama in 1885, growing up in Macon, and having his main office in Atlanta, Reid was conveniently located near LaGrange, and he was a product of the region. He also had strong Troup County connections, which may have figured into Fuller's selection of the firm. Reid's great-grandfather, Judge Samuel Reid, had been responsible for laying out the streets of LaGrange when the town was founded, and had then gone on to establish a plantation on the edge of the town. His father, John Whitfield Reid, had been born on the plantation.

But though Reid was a product of the southern Piedmont, his education was cosmopolitan, and this, too, influenced his work. After apprenticing in Macon and Atlanta, he traveled to New York with his future partner, Hal Hentz, both of them taking classes for two years at Columbia's School of Architecture. In 1907, the two men traveled to France, where they studied at Paris's École des Beaux-Arts, which boasted one of the world's premiere and oldest architectural programs. Afterward Reid came back to New York to practice his craft for a while, but ultimately he returned to Georgia.

The designs Reid submitted for Hills and Dales reflected his varied background, but the gardens were the most important influence. The terraces, perhaps originally planted with cotton before Sarah—possibly with the help of her semimythical Italian gardener—turned them into something reminiscent of the Renaissance, suggested a fusion of Old South and Tuscan villa. Reid capitalized on the combination, referring to Hills and Dales as "Georgian Italian," and Callaway's acquaintances soon referred to the new home as an Italian villa.

Reinforcing the gardens' suggestiveness was Reid's admiration of the work of Charles A. Platt. Two and a half decades older than Reid, the New York–born Platt was not only an architect, but a landscape designer and artist as well. Having once traveled in Italy, Platt was quite taken with Italian designs, in particular the relationship between a house and its surroundings. Specifically, Platt worked to adapt the concept of the villa to the new American suburban house. "The word 'villa,'" he wrote in 1894, describing what he appreciated about the Italian effect,

is used in the Italian sense implying all the formal parts of the grounds arranged in direct relation to house, the house itself being as much a part of it as the garden or grove. . . . The problem being to take a piece of land and make it habitable, the architect proceeded with the idea that not only was the house to be lived in, but that one still wished to be at home while out of doors; so the garden was designed as another apartment, the terraces and groves still others, where one might walk about and find a place suitable to the hour of day and feeling of the moment, and still be in that sacred portion of the globe dedicated to one's self.

Reid clearly saw how nicely Platt's views accorded with his own vision for connecting the new Callaway house with the existing gardens. In designing the house he looked to some of Platt's own creations for inspiration, especially the Timberline estate in Bryn Mawr, Pennsylvania, as well as Villa Turicum in Lake Forest, Illinois, and Sylvania in Barrytown, New York, in addition to drawing on Old South plantation roots.

Left to right: Hal Hentz (1883–1972) and Neel Reid (1885–1926) in the garden at Hills and Dales.

But the LaGrange of 1914 was neither Italian nor antebellum. This was to be neither a town house nor a country house in the English tradition but a suburban house, built in an age when electricity, telephones, and automobiles were fast becoming standard conveniences and even necessities. While a suburban home was to be, like a country house, a place for the owners to retire from the hustle and bustle of town life, unlike a country house, it also had to remain connected to that life, physically close enough to reach town and the owner's place of employment, and equipped with labor-saving devices that were starting to replace a large staff of servants. Thus Reid, inspired by many ideas but copying none of them outright, set about designing a house that would fit in not only with Ferrell Gardens, and not only with the South, but with the lives of Fuller and Ida Callaway.

Neel Reid with a large urn in Italy during his 1922 European tour.

Reid's early design shows a somewhat squarer building than the finished house turned out to be. A hallway was to have bisected the length of the house, and a rectangular loggia, or open gallery, would complete the eastern side. In a later draft the structure became more rectangular overall, with a one-story western wing that featured a sunroom of an elongated shape that Reid often favored. In this later design a semicircular portico, with two-story Ionic columns, replaced the loggia on the eastern facade, calling to mind an antebellum plantation house and becoming one of Hills and Dales's most recognizable features. In this final design, the loggia became a porte cochere on the north facade, which was of a more relaxed design than the southern and eastern elevations.

The southern facade, together with the eastern portico, was much more symmetrical, formal, and classical. In light of the gardens'

public nature as well as all the business Callaway was likely to transact at his new home, it was a given that Hills and Dales would have a great many visitors, and Reid thus made sure that the house's most imposing countenances faced in the most public directions. This was a standard procedure at a time when suburban estates were meant, among other things, to impress. And while Callaway rarely, if ever, made a point of flaunting his wealth, he didn't try to hide it, either.

Despite his money, though, Callaway never forgot that he'd amassed it through careful spending habits. While he undoubtedly could have put more into Hills and Dales, during the design phase he asked the architects to scale back the scope of the project. One feature that is mentioned as being omitted was a terrace of cut stonework, which would have added considerably to the overall price.

Callaway found other ways to economize as well. One was apparently a suggestion from Reid and Hentz: a flat rate for their services. The architects also located a construction firm in Atlanta willing to do the work for a flat rate as well. This helped Callaway to project, and thus control, overall costs, and at the same time it was acceptable to the other parties. Hills and Dales is often characterized as the biggest commission Reid's firm ever received; certainly it was the largest up to that time. At any rate the deal was acceptable to everyone.

The other cost-saving measure was natural for Callaway: he acted as his own contractor. While the Atlanta firm provided the labor, Callaway procured the materials. One piece of correspondence is typical. In an April 1915 announcement, Callaway solicited bids to supply 200,000 bricks, two carloads of Portland cement, a carload of lime, 400 tons of sand, 25 tons of plaster, 120 tons of concrete stone, and a ton of Keene's cement. In this announcement—also typical of Callaway, given his railroad experience—he gave precise information as to where and how the material

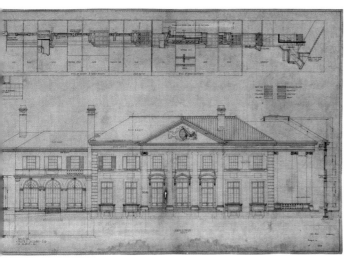

South elevation plan of the Callaway home at Hills and Dales.

was to be delivered, complete with rail-switching charges the sellers would incur, down to the dollar, if they failed to use the Atlanta, Birmingham & Atlantic Railroad.

Despite this careful cost management, the project was a big one, both expensive and time consuming. It was made even more so by the Great War. The United States wouldn't formally enter the conflagration until 1917, but even by early 1915 it had become a major supplier to the Allied Powers, driving prices up tremendously while making materials scarce. Given the project's size, Hentz and Reid took on a third partner, their Columbia classmate Rudolph Adler, thus finalizing the name and membership of their firm. But even with this extra help, things moved more slowly than expected.

Nevertheless, the house met all other expectations. What arose on top of the hill to crown the garden terraces was an edifice of white stucco, trimmed with stone, boasting a red pantile roof. The symmetrical southern facade, seven bays in width and of two stories, was topped with a pediment supported by four Ionic pilasters. Through French doors one stepped directly from the walnut-paneled living hall—the house's largest room—into the garden. On the center of the upper terrace, the architects added a large fountain to further tie in the house and the gardens. Callaway himself, mindful of the connection between the two, commissioned a management plan for the gardens. Pursuant

Detail of south elevation for the Callaway home drawn by Rudolph Adler from the firm of Hentz & Reid in 1915.

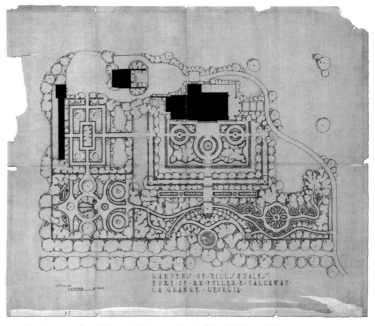

Garden plan for Hills and Dales by Hentz & Reid (circa 1916).

Neel Reid with Fuller and Ida Callaway in 1916 after the construction of Hills and Dales was complete. Pictured left to right: Miss Martha Slaton, Fuller Callaway, Ida Callaway, Mrs. John M. (Sally Grant) Slaton, and Neel Reid.

himself to put up around here and not a damn' one of 'em looks like him!" It sounds exactly like a story that Callaway would have told on himself.

Hentz, Reid, and Adler also designed the various outbuildings in such a way as to complement the overall plan, including a greenhouse, a garage complete with chauffeur's quarters, and a boiler facility that supplied the house with heat. Within the main house, though, things were a bit more eclectic. The coffered ceiling of the dining room, plastered by an artisan, reflected one of the main themes Reid employed, as did the sunroom with its light and airy design and elaborately vaulted ceiling of its own. But the library was more of an English Renaissance design, with paneling that tied it into the walnut-stained birch of the main living room. Across the hall from the library was the much lighter drawing, or music room, differentiated from its neighbors by use of an eighteenth-century French theme.

to this development, the architects added another touch: statues of classical figures placed throughout the gardens. Callaway claimed to have overheard a conversation in the gardens between two LaGrange visitors to the estate some time later regarding these statues.

"What do you think of the place since Fuller's fixed it up?" one of them asked the other, who replied that he saw little difference. "It's a funny thing to me," continued the first, "that he'd buy all those statues of

To work with these various themes, furnishings would need to be chosen carefully. At one point Reid broached the subject by asking if Fuller had acquired furniture yet.

Glass lantern slide of the Callaway home at Hills and Dales.

"Plenty of it," answered Fuller. "Been collecting furniture all my life. Hardly a Saturday night in the last thirty years we haven't gone down to the village store and brought home furniture." According to Ida, when Reid then explained that these items would fail to live up to the new environment, the news came as an unpleasant surprise to Fuller, who was evidently attached to the furniture the couple had bought over the years by scrimping and saving. What they had, he claimed, was "good enough for any place!" But Reid ultimately convinced him, and at last Fuller gave in.

Photo of the Callaways' dining room taken by Thurston Hatcher in 1916. The room was designed by Philip Shutze, who was working for Hentz & Reid.

While Ida generally credits Reid with having a hand in choosing the new furnishings, she also notes that the actual selecting and purchasing took place in New York, with the party consisting of Fuller and herself, along with Ab Perry and Hal Hentz. On this trip Fuller occupied himself with seeing to mill business while the other three made the rounds of furniture and rug sellers. The buyers picked out a large number of items, but before actually making the purchases, they had Fuller come to the stores with them to give final approval of what they'd chosen.

Fuller had obviously been unhappy about the whole furniture issue from the beginning, and apparently his outlook while in New York hadn't changed. One store to which the others took him was run by a young Italian seller, and it was here that they had found some of the best-themed—and most expensive—items. The first piece the owner showed Fuller was an Italian dining room table that, according to Ida, sported a price tag of nine thousand dollars. The other three had fallen hard for the table; Ida bubbled that it was of

"exquisite workmanship." When the seller told Fuller the price, his response was enigmatic. "Why don't you ask eighteen thousand dollars for it?"

The young merchant smiled, no doubt believing that he'd hooked a live one. "Why do that?" he asked.

The answer wasn't what he was expecting. "Because anybody who hasn't got enough sense than to pay nine thousand for it would pay eighteen thousand for it!" Fuller retorted. That wiped the complacent smile from the merchant's face.

Next came a bedroom suite of black-painted mahogany, also quite expensive. "Why paint mahogany black," groused Fuller, "when you can paint pine or oak black, and no one will know the difference?"

Ida had also found a clock of which she was particularly fond, envisioning it on the landing of the new home's elaborate double staircase. The seller picked up on her interest. "That clock was ordered for Daws," he mentioned, dropping the name of a leading business figure, "but he did not take it."

The living room in the Callaway home. A 1916 photograph by Thurston Hatcher.

"Yes," cracked Fuller, recognizing the name, "and Daws is now working in a soap factory, striking 'licks' for himself, instead of having that clock to strike for him!"

And so it went. Fuller managed to find fault with practically everything. Finally Ida challenged her husband, asking if he saw anything at all he'd like to have.

"Why, I want this old iron torture chair, with a hole in the bottom," he exclaimed, "so when our friends come to our costly home, you can chain me in the chair, build a fire under it, and tell them I had nothing to do with furnishing the house, except the suffering!"

Hentz, apparently quite intimidated, took Ida aside. "Mrs. Callaway, what must we do?" he whispered anxiously. "Mr. Callaway does not like the furniture we have selected."

"Why, don't you worry," Ida told him. "I know Fuller like a book. He said all that to hold down our soaring ideas, and to let the merchants know that he himself knew the value of goods, and would not pay an exorbitant price for them."

She was right. While he did reject some of the pieces in favor of less expensive alterna-

tives, Fuller did manage, with his theatrics, to get the sellers to reduce their prices on many of the original selections. In the end, the purchases satisfied everyone, including Fuller, even though he never got his torture chair.

Nevertheless, in the years to come, Fuller publicly continued to maintain an attitude towards his new home's decor that was an interesting blend of self-effacement and "common man." Once, while showing his friend Alfred Pearce Dennis around the place, he pointed to a very old and valuable Italian canvas that hung on one wall. "The thing looks like it came out of a garbage can," he quipped, "but I guess for anybody who likes that kind of a thing that's about the kind of a thing they would like."

Despite all of the hard work and preparation, the completion of the house took somewhat longer than was hoped, more than two years in all. Fuller had wanted to have it ready in time for the celebration of the Callaways' silver wedding anniversary on April 28, 1916, and the evidence suggests that for a time he thought that the deadline might be met. In the end, when it grew clear that the house wouldn't be ready in time, the couple pushed back the event by several weeks. The Callaways wanted to introduce their new home as much as they wanted the anniversary festivities; and, just as important, the number of guests they were planning to invite would require the spaciousness the new abode would offer.

In fact, not even the new villa would accommodate all of the guests as a single

Fuller giving a tour of the garden to a group of friends. circa 1916.

group. Early on, the couple decided to break the celebration into afternoon and evening sessions, inviting guests in shifts, beginning at three o'clock, with a favored hundred or so being invited for both the afternoon and evening. In all, hundreds of invitations were to go out. By the middle of May, Callaway finally nailed down the date: June 15, 1916.

In both LaGrange and Atlanta, and among all who received one of the elaborate, silver-edged invitations, anticipation reigned supreme. One Atlanta friend of Callaway wrote a cheery acceptance letter playing on the estate's new name. "Now, Fuller," he said, "coming down to old Troup County times, I want to suggest that you gather a few goats from the hills and dales and start a barbeque before the sun rises." That way, he noted, all of the Atlanta invitees would have plenty of time to get to LaGrange, feast, and make it back to the capital on the country roads before nightfall without having to make excuses for missing the festivities. "It is not

often," he continued, "that guests dictate to the host the time, the menu, and other instructions, but this is the last silver wedding you will have and every single one of the La-Grange people up here sincerely love you, and I want them all to have a good time never to be forgotten."

At last the day came. It was not only the occasion of the anniversary party, but the Callaways' first day in their new home. The weather was fine; an eight-man orchestra played throughout the afternoon and evening as hundreds of guests came and went. The affair was altogether a success, and people spoke of it for decades afterwards as one of the finest events that LaGrange had ever seen.

In the months and years that followed, Hills and Dales became a Callaway icon. As custodians of the Ferrell gardens, keeping them open to the public as Sarah and Blount had done, Fuller and Ida faced the same dilemmas that had confronted the Ferrells. Ida was initially dismayed that visitors broke off branches from the trees and shrubs, perhaps to try to root them in their own yards, and she found that people would even go so far as to dig up bulbs for the same reason. Children continued to trample through flower beds. On one occasion an obnoxious family, picnicking on the grounds, ignored the trash that they left scattered around them. "This is a hell of a place," the husband ungraciously was heard to declare. "No ice water!"

Finally the Callaways decided to proceed as Blount Ferrell had done—going him one better in fact—and prepared a newspaper announcement.

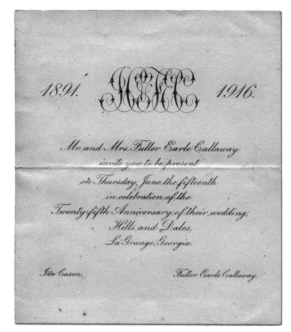

Silver embossed inviation to Fuller and Ida's twenty-fifth anniversary party, which was held at Hills and Dales on June 15, 1916.

It is with profound regret that we find ourselves obliged to withdraw the privilege of general visiting to our grounds and gardens heretofore accorded of the public, but this action is rendered necessary by abuses on the part of some of the visitors.

In future admission will be granted only upon special permit by a member of the family or upon application to the General Offices in the LaGrange National Bank Building. In all cases such permits will be only for quietly passing through and with the agreement that there shall be no pulling of flowers or shrubs, no walking on the beds, nor picnicking on the grounds,

nor damage or destruction in any form. Those who will not comply with these reasonable restrictions are asked not to apply for permits.

But at the last moment, Ida and Fuller decided they couldn't do it. The notice never ran in the paper. Ida, in particular, realized that the garden was for the benefit of others. In the end she was philosophical about all the flowers that visitors picked. "What greater good could my flowers do," she observed, "than brighten the sick room of some suffering one who is not able to buy flowers; or to make a table of humble food seem more palatable; or to lie in the

In 1915 the Callaways traveled to New York with Hal Hentz and Ab Perry to select furnishings for the house. This Italian cassone was purchased from the Aimone Galleries.

This sterling silver tyg (three handled loving cup) was given to Fuller and Ida when they celebrated their twenty-fifth wedding anniversary on June 15, 1916. The entwined script ICFEC represents the union of Ida Cason and Fuller Earle Callaway. The cup was made by Black, Starr & Frost.

Aerial view of Hills and Dales in 1923.

dead, closed hand of a little child?" In this way, too, she followed Sarah's example.

But Ida didn't hesitate to add her own touches to Sarah's garden. In 1921 the Callaways toured a war-shattered Europe, and one of the places they visited was Cornwall. There, in St. Neot Church, Ida beheld the stained-glass Callaway window with the inscription "ora pro me." It reminded her of the circular bed in her garden that bore the Ferrell mottoes of "God Is Love" and "fiat justicia." On her return to Hills and Dales, she was thus inspired to plant mottoes in the matching bed that read "St. Callaway" and "ora pro me."

That was after peace had come—for a time—to a shattered Old World. But by then Hills and Dales, and Ida's husband, had come to world prominence, playing roles not only in the war effort but in restoring prosperity to Europe in the wake of the cataclysm. The silver wedding anniversary celebration five years earlier had certainly been grand. But though Fuller and Ida couldn't have known it at the time, it was only a dress rehearsal for an even grander affair three years afterwards: one that, like Fuller's career, was to have an international impact.

Portrait of Ida Cason Callaway in the garden next to the fountain that was added in 1916. Painting by Malcolm Rae.

1924 PENCIL SKETCH OF FULLER CALLAWAY SR.
BY VANCE LOVEJOY COTTER

·7·

LIFE AS A PUBLIC FIGURE:
LOCAL AND STATE

Fuller Callaway's rise to international fame was mainly a result of his abilities as a businessman. Everything—his leadership in national organizations, his philanthropy, and his role in civic movements—ultimately linked back to his exploits in the world of textile production. But while he was no career politician, he did hold public office for years, and this, too, helped propel him into the limelight. As is the case with most office-holders, he began at the local level.

The journey began on July 5, 1894, when Callaway was sworn in as the newest member of the LaGrange City Council. LaGrange at the time had only a few hundred qualified voters, most of them likely white males. Still Callaway's selection by this group was extraordinary; he was only twenty-three at the time. Immediately he found himself in the company of businessmen and community leaders with whom he'd been dealing as a merchant for the whole of his short adult life: Neal Truitt, T. S. Bradfield, and Roy Dallis, to name a few. (Callaway's great friendship with Dallis was probably greatly strengthened at an early stage by the two men's long council service together.) Elections of mayor and council took place every year or two, and

during the following decade the same people usually either remained there for long periods or rotated on and off the body. Callaway himself would serve most of the next ten years on the council. The one term he didn't, from 1895 to 1897, his brother Enoch was mayor.

Callaway had chosen an interesting time to debut on the council. The Progressive Era was in its infancy, and Callaway managed to get in nearly on the ground floor. Progressivism was a response to the new way of life that modern industry had created. As factories multiplied with great speed in the cities and railroads moved both people and goods throughout the country in ever larger numbers and volume, urban populations grew. The workers who flocked to the cities in search of factory jobs spawned urban problems that civilization had never before seen on such a scale: housing shortages, inadequate food and water supplies, sanitation crises, epidemics, urban crime, and the risk of large-scale fires, among others. Between 1870 and 1880, Chicago doubled in population, raising many urban pressures; in 1871 it experienced a fire that killed two hundred people and destroyed seventeen thousand buildings. In 1878 yellow fever swept

This view depicts the town of LaGrange, including the new Troup County Courthouse erected in 1904. Callaway served on the City Council for ten years starting in 1894.

through New Orleans and Memphis, killing five thousand of the latter town's thirteen thousand inhabitants.

City and state governments were slow to respond to such crises, mainly because there was no precedent for dealing with them; populations and buildings were denser and disease traveled faster than ever before. By the time a young Fuller Callaway was named to the LaGrange City Council, the tide was just starting to turn, as throughout the country reformers turned to science and technology to attempt to solve the problems that had arisen. During Callaway's time on the council, it, too, would act on the Progressive impulse.

Callaway was conscientious about attending council meetings, clearly earning every penny of his lavish salary of thirty dollars per year. With a council consisting of only about a half dozen members, each member usually served on a number of committees, and Callaway was no exception. One on which he almost always found himself was the finance committee, with the chairmanship rotating among him and the other two members from year to year. He also served at various times on other committees, such as the police committee and the light and water committee. But the finance committee was invariably one of his assignments, as it was for Joe Dunson. In 1897 Roy Dallis was elected to the council, and he eventually

joined Callaway and Dunson as a regular on the committee.

During Callaway's tenure on the council, LaGrange began to resemble, for the first time, a modern town. With the southern epidemics still a recent memory, in 1898 the mayor and council enacted public health ordinances to require the vaccination of all citizens. In 1905, doubtless drawing on the input and connections of Dunson and Callaway, the council encouraged mill owners to refuse jobs to people who hadn't been duly vaccinated.

This latter step was an obvious triumph for public health since in any such mill a single diseased operative could quickly infect dozens of fellow workers. But it also benefited the mills directly, using the force of law to help keep the operatives healthy and the mills running. This was a fusion rather than a conflict of interests between Callaway the mill owner and Callaway the councilman and citizen. And it was by no means unique. In 1903 Dunson as councilman asked for and got the city to build a fire station near his textile mill. A loss of one of the LaGrange mills to fire would have badly damaged not only Dunson but also the town's economy.

A more remarkable regulation came in 1900, when Callaway and the others approved an ordinance banning peddling without a license on the streets of LaGrange. This seems odd, given how Callaway had gotten his own start. Similarly in 1905 the city banned the unlicensed operation of merry-go-rounds and more basic carousels known as flying Jennys, again odd in light of Callaway's earlier trick of setting up just such a merry-go-round to drum up business for his store. The best explanation is that these ordinances were part of a string of laws reflecting LaGrange's growing population and need for public order as the mills drew potential employees in from the country. Similar laws banned bicycle riding on sidewalks, prohibited railroad cars from blocking the streets, and forbade both gambling and loitering, all of which the council passed in 1901. Simply put, LaGrange was becoming a city, and old behaviors had to give way to new.

Like any city, LaGrange needed infrastructure. By 1897 the council was already working on developing a waterworks, since a good water supply and sewerage system were indispensable to preventing disease as population density increased. Two years earlier the town had given the American Pipe Manufacturing Company the right to build such a facility, but apparently the company didn't move fast enough, so in 1897 the town canceled the contract. In 1899 the councilmen took the next step, establishing a public waterworks as well as a sewerage system, although the construction of these things sometimes lagged behind their creation on paper. The war on disease was clearly advancing.

Lighting was another matter. The generator at LaGrange Mills was supplying the city with lighting—mainly street lights—by the early 1890s. Electricity, not gas, was clearly the wave of the future when it came to lighting, and by the turn of the century something more than mill-powered lighting was clearly needed. In June 1899 Callaway and Dunson found themselves on a three-man committee to look into the possibility of building a city-owned lighting system, but the process would be a slow one. A few months later the council discussed the possibility of a bond issue to cover the costs of building a lighting plant, but nothing came of it right away, quite possibly because Dunson didn't like the idea.

In 1901 came Dunson's, Callaway's, and Dallis's appointment to the regular lights and water committee. Callaway chaired it, while Dunson chaired the finance committee that year. The great tensions over the Unity Mill hadn't yet arisen between the two men, but they were bound to have differences, and Dallis was no mere Callaway yes-man, sometimes voting with Dunson against Callaway. The stage appeared to be set for a fight over the lighting issue.

In 1904, with these committee lineups the same, the city still hadn't moved forward on an electric light plant. That May, Dunson moved that he, Callaway, and Dallis be named a new committee to investigate how other towns were setting up municipal lighting. Perhaps he thought that the committee—or at any rate, Dallis—would side with him after seeing the problems Dunson perceived with the city involving itself directly in the lighting business.

Dunson also had an ulterior motive for opposing city lighting so consistently and vehemently. In addition to his continued involvement in Dixie and Unity Mills, he was treasurer of LaGrange Mills—the firm that supplied LaGrange power for street lights. This explains a great deal. A month after his

A bird's-eye view of court square taken from the roof of the 1904 courthouse.

Sterling Hall, next to the court square facing Main Street, was an important community and commercial center in LaGrange. It was used for meetings of the LaGrange City Council while Fuller was serving on the council.

push to create the special investigative committee, he voted against the establishment of a city lighting department—the only councilman to do so.

The vote signaled the start of a drama-filled summer. A few weeks after the council approved the city lighting department, in early July it voted to authorize a forty-thousand-dollar bond issue, with twenty-five thousand dollars of the money going to the new electric plant and the rest going to the fire department and to be used for the retirement of general debts. Again Dunson's was the sole dissenting vote. But he hadn't lost yet; the town's citizens would still have to approve the bond issue.

This referendum—a device that enjoyed a lot of popularity among the Progressives— would take place at the end of the summer, in mid-September. A month before that, however, the drama reached its climax. During the first week of August, Dunson arranged to have Callaway fired from his

secretary and treasurer's posts at Unity Mills. A day or two later, after Callaway made the implications of that firing clear— that is, he would take his goodwill and his business connections with him—the board reinstated him. Within forty-eight hours, on August 4, Dunson tendered his resignation from the LaGrange City Council.

"In severing my connection with you," Dunson explained to the council in his letter of resignation,

please permit me to say that since I have been a member of your body that unanimity of purpose and concert of endeavor have almost invariably characterized their every action, and since on the important matter of issuing bonds for the purpose of erecting an electric light plant, my views are not in harmony with those of the other members of the city government, I feel that in justice to you, that you should be unhampered by my opposition in your body, and that I should be free to oppose a measure, that I deem at best inopportune, without subjecting myself to possible criticism. You can readily see that my opposition as Treasurer of the LaGrange Mills, an institution that will naturally be affected, is untenable with my position as a member of the City Council. I take it that the men, with whom I have been officially connected, would perhaps defend me against any suggestion that my personal interest would control my actions as a member of your body, but I can hardly expect everybody to be as kind.

I will say further that I would naturally feel some trepidation in assuming a position contrary to that of all the other members of the Council, for whose general judgement I entertain very great respect, but in this particular matter, the more I consider the question in every phase the more I am convinced that I am right.

With assurance of my personal esteem for each member of the City government, I am

Yours sincerely,
J. E. Dunson

No one has ever remarked on the coincidence of the Dunson-Callaway confrontation with this resignation, but it surely was no accident. Dunson was being no more than truthful about his conflict of interest, which at any rate would have been obvious to the rest of the council, since his role at LaGrange Mills was no secret. Perhaps Dunson even wanted to be free to campaign as a private citizen against the bond issue. But Callaway had opposed him throughout the debate on a city lighting plant, which was taking place at the same time as the dispute over how Callaway was running Unity. It is obvious that the two disagreements reinforced each

Fuller Callaway would have passed by the 1904 Troup County Courthouse and the adjacent Confederate Monument regularly. The Courthouse was lost to a fire in 1936 and the monument was moved to a new site.

other and hastened the breach between the two men. Then, within a month's time, Dunson lost both fights. His defeat at Unity must have been particularly humiliating. Thus Dunson, whose conflict of interest hadn't just suddenly arisen, was doubtless using it now as a way to save face as he withdrew to lick his wounds.

But LaGrange was still a small and interrelated community with many common interests and only a few key leaders. Callaway and Dunson may have been business opponents, but they weren't blood enemies, even in light of Callaway's controversial firing. They could hardly have opened mills and served on committees together for more than a decade and been that. The day after receiving Dunson's letter of resignation, the mayor and council—including Callaway—asked him to reconsider.

Your long and able service, the esteem in which we all hold you, and your recognized capacity for the position you fill as Chairman of the Finance Committee, render us unwilling to have you sever your connection with us. Especially are we unwilling to accept your resignation at this especial time when the City's finances need your ability in their management.

As far as the question of bonding the city for electric lights is concerned, we cannot believe that there would be any unkind criticism of your opposition in that matter, for the Council has now practically finished its connection with it as a body, and the question is now out of their hands and is before the people to be decided.

Assuring you of the high and sincere personal esteem of the Mayor and each member of the Council, and trusting that you can see your way clear to withdraw your resignation, we are

Yours sincerely

A week ensued during which tempers cooled down. Then, on August 11, Dunson agreed to withdraw his resignation. "Gentleman," he wrote most civilly,

I have your letter [of] several days ago in which you request me to withdraw my resignation as a member of the council, and since you state therein that there should be no unkind criticism—& from which I assume that you at least feel that I am at liberty to oppose the bond issue without violating my obligations to the city, I hereby withdraw my resignation.

For your kind expressions in reference to me I am deeply grateful, and trust that my future associations with you will not for any reason cause you to lessen for me the respect that you have so generously expressed in your letter.

Nothing in the record suggests that Callaway carried his Unity quarrel with Dunson over into the City Council. If anything, it shows the opposite. After the unpleasantness of August, the minutes show nothing but business as usual, although Dunson did suffer another defeat when, as was expected, the voters approved the bond issue in September.

When it came to the railroad though, Callaway was happy to use his role as councilman in his battle against his true nemesis, the Atlanta & West Point. In late March 1905, a few weeks before the incorporation of Callaway's Atlanta, Birmingham & Atlantic, the council was already expressing its willingness to grant the new road a right-of-way on Morgan Street—the same stretch of land that the Atlanta & West Point would later sue to protect. The council's action was almost certainly instigated by Callaway, and there is no suggestion in the record that he lacked Dunson's backing. The Atlanta & West Point was clearly a common enemy for most, if not all, of LaGrange's business interests.

By 1905 many people were calling for Callaway to serve his due term as mayor. Among them were a number of voices from the mills. But Callaway wasn't interested. In 1903 Governor Joseph M. Terrell had appointed him assistant commissary general of state troops, with the rank of lieutenant colonel—a post he held for four years. That, together with his council seat, was apparently enough public service on his plate at one time. And 1905 was to be his last year on the council. Both Dunson and Dallis left with him in May,

This unique postcard shows the depots of all three railroad lines serving LaGrange in about 1915. To the left the Macon and Birmingham (M&B), in the center the Atlanta & West Point (A&WP), and to the right the Atlanta, Birmingham & Atlantic Railroad (AB&A). Callaway was instrumental in attracting the AB&A to LaGrange to combat high freight rates.

although Truitt decided to remain. Many things were changing: Consolidated Duck Corporation bought out Dunson's LaGrange Mills, and Callaway and Dallis had their hands full with the new Calumet holding company as well as with the new Elm City Mill, to say nothing of the Atlanta, Birmingham & Atlantic Railroad. But Callaway wasn't through with public office.

≈

During the first decade of the new century, most of Callaway's public activities revolved around LaGrange and Troup County, or (as the decade wore on) Georgia as a whole, but there were a few exceptions. One was his federal case against the railroads, which the Supreme Court decided in May 1903. Another was his appearance as a congressional witness ten months later in March 1904.

The hearing took place before the House of Representatives' Committee on Labor, on which sat Georgia congressman John W. Maddox, who was likely instrumental in arranging Callaway's appearance, as well as William Randolph Hearst, representing New York's Eleventh District. (Callaway made a point of not reading Hearst's newspapers; the puritan in him believed Hearst to be immoral.) The subject was a controversial bill being pushed strongly by Samuel Gompers, the founder and leader of the American Federation of Labor. The provision, known colloquially as the "eight-hour bill," would limit the working day to eight hours for all laborers employed by firms that served as federal government contractors. This would be a near-revolutionary change in an age where the federal government engaged in little regulation of any sort, and in which working hours in many fields were routinely far more than eight hours a day. Since Callaway's mills sold cotton duck—sometimes quite a lot of it—to the federal government, he would have felt the law's bite. On March 23, he was called to give the committee his perspective.

Governor Joseph. M. Terrell from nearby Meriwether County appointed Callaway as the assistant commissary general of state troops in 1903.

This was Callaway's first appearance as a congressional witness, but it wasn't to be his last. This time he was deferential to the congressmen, and while he wasn't afraid to say what he thought, he stayed close to his facts and answered representatives' questions with some specificity.

In his opening statement, Callaway described a dynamic that was to remain true of the South until the twenty-first century: the cheapness of labor as a key ingredient to making the southern states competitive in the national market. "I should not feel justified in taking the valuable time of this committee but for the fact that I come from a section of the country where manufacturing is in its infancy and consequently is extremely sensitive to adverse conditions," he began, "and the effect of a measure so radical and far-reaching as this bill will not only

Samuel Gompers, the founder and leader of the American Federation of Labor, disagreed with Callaway about the merits of the proposed "eight hour bill."

another indispensable component of the southern textile industry.

In answer to a claim that some had made, Callaway next stated that a shorter workweek wouldn't make textile jobs more desirable to potential employees. The real controlling factor, he argued, was whether cotton farming was more lucrative than mill work, and that depended mainly on the price of cotton. "Shorter hours will not induce our people to quit the independent and open-air life of the farm for the mill as long as the price of cotton makes farming remunerative." (This was one of several comments Callaway made in his career to the effect that southerners were essentially forced into manufacturing because they could not make a living by farming—that a mill culture was making a virtue of necessity.) He continued,

The rigor of climate and poverty of soil has drained the New England farm and filled the New England mill. The reverse of these conditions in the South make mill recruiting slow. Our natural advantages are quickly stated. A climate permitting year-round work, cheaper living, and to an appreciable degree only the proximity of the mill to the raw material. Our disadvantages are: Lack of money, high-priced money, unskilled and insufficient labor—an unnatural but unavoidable barrier to immigration.

Apply these provisions of this bill to our labor, and instantly our profits reach the vanishing point. The South is no longer an inviting field for northern capital, and our industries perish. I shall not speak of the political phases of this legislation from the southern standpoint. That it is class legislation. That labor monopoly is as unjust to the consumer as industrial monopoly. I am here as a practical business man, prepared by my actual employment to offer in concrete proof of any proposition I have announced the menace of this legislation to the further prosperity of the two cotton mills I am connected with.

cripple and hinder further progress of our industries but many of them will, I am afraid, be wiped out of existence."

To back up this claim, Callaway noted that manufacturing in the South was based heavily on cotton, and the rougher grades of cotton at that, production that New England had not been interested in keeping. Cheaper goods meant a lower profit margin, making cheap labor a crucial part of the equation. "The South can least of all sections of our country survive arbitrary high-priced labor," he declared. Raise labor costs, he warned the committee, and the southern mills would no longer be competitive, and thus no longer attractive to northern investment, which according to Callaway was

After his opening statement came the questions. "I desire to ask you," Ben F. Caldwell of Illinois began, "how many hours a week or a day your employees work?"

"We work sixty-six hours a week," Callaway answered flatly. He had nothing to hide; sixty-six hours was nothing unusual in the America of 1904.

"Six days of eleven hours each?" asked Caldwell, who was favorable to the bill in question.

"No," elaborated Callaway, "we work five days beginning at 6 o'clock in the morning and work until 12 o'clock. Then we start at 40 minutes after 12 and work until 6, with a short day on Saturday to make up for the extra time during the five days." Again, this was nothing unusual; the idea, let alone the practice, of a two-day weekend was still in its infancy.

William J. Hughes of New Jersey piped up. "I suppose you are aware," he asked Callaway, "that the manufacturers of the North complain bitterly of that fact—that you work sixty-six hours a week?" The comment was revealing. Hughes, who'd as a youngster worked in the silk mills of Paterson, seemed interested not in the welfare of labor but in canceling out the South's competitive advantage over the Northeast, or as it was often termed in the hearings, the East.

"I know that," Callaway answered. "But that is one of our natural resources." This was a major point with the Georgian, an almost Darwinistic view of a marketplace governed by nothing but nature and Adam Smith's invisible hand. Government regulation, he believed, would produce unnatural results, and unjust ones too.

Callaway drove home the equities—and inequities—of government interference with his answers to the next question. "What proportion of your output is taken by the Government?" asked Caldwell. After all, under this bill only the fact that Callaway's mills were government contractors would allow the government to restrict his operatives' hours.

"It varies, according to demand," replied Callaway. "Sometimes it is 25 per cent, sometimes it is 50 per cent. Sometimes it is nothing. It varies according to the demand of the Government for the goods. They buy when they get ready. They do not buy in order to run our mill regularly." His unspoken point was quite clear: even without the bill in question, the government was, or at least could be, arbitrary in its purchases. Most of the risk was on Callaway. That was the way of things. But now the government was talking about adding the burden of regulation to that risk without itself incurring much, if anything, in the way of a downside. The whole thing, as Callaway presented it, was inequitable.

Hughes, a strong supporter of the bill, kept trying to turn the discussion from labor welfare to sectional competition. "You can not get Eastern people or emigrants to work sixty-six hours a week," he huffed. "If there were a factory in my district where they work fifty-five hours per week manufacturing Government duck, you would have quite an advantage over them, would you not?"

"I think so," Callaway readily conceded. "We have a natural advantage in the South because of the long day." There was no point in governments trying to tell the sun when to rise and set, he all but said. He could have gone on to list the natural advantages historically enjoyed by the North, such as cheap energy and good harbors that provided both an influx of emigrant labor and ease of access to world markets, but he'd made his point. Hughes, by comparison, seemed motivated mainly by handicapping the southern competition.

James P. Connor of Iowa seemed intrigued by Callaway's argument of natural benefits. "The Government gets the advantage?" he prompted.

"That reduces the price to the Government," stated Callaway deftly. The South could simply produce the lower grades of textiles more cheaply than could the North, and it passed on the savings to the Government. "The Eastern people have turned it loose, and they say 'This is too cheap,' and they are going on with finer grades."

The committee members began to digress, raising other concerns with the southern labor picture, trying to tar it with several reformist brushes, such as child labor, segregation, and education, thereby making the whole institution seem disreputable. Some of them went after Callaway as if he personified every labor practice they saw as evil. Gompers himself, on hand as both spectator and witness, gave Callaway a particularly hard time on the issue of why the rural South was so inhospitable to unionization. He also asked if there was any movement for maximum hours in the South. "You say there is no agitation for this kind of legislation in Georgia?"

"Not a bit," Callaway replied cheerfully.

"You want them to run twelve hours a day if you say so?" Hughes asked nastily.

"I think it is a pretty good idea to run your own business," shot back Callaway. "We would rather prefer to control our own business."

Gompers kept hammering Callaway on the subject, and Callaway tried to keep his responses both civil and reasonable. "We are against labor laws in the State. We are doing well," he explained. "Industries are growing, and the people are happy and contented." He always enjoyed pointing out that there had never been mass resignations or firings, never any strikes or violence, connected with his mills. "Do not change a good thing until it gets to be a bad thing."

"Then reduce the hours of labor," Gompers suggested.

"No," countered Callaway, "let nature decide it. Nature is the grandest thing in the world, anyhow. I have worked fifteen and six-teen hours a day for the last sixteen years, and I am a pretty fair specimen; and I eat hot bread three times a day, which is against the law up in your country." His audience laughed appreciatively.

In this, one of his first major-league public appearances, Callaway acquitted himself very well indeed. In the face of some frankly hostile opinions and rigorous questioning, he kept his cool and scored several points against the opposition. Thanks in part to his efforts, the bill never did pass; in the end it died in committee, with only Caldwell, Hughes, and Hearst voting to pass it. It was the beginning of an excellent congressional track record for Callaway.

∼

After his retirement from the La-Grange town council, Callaway's next public posting came about largely by coincidence. After more than a generation of conservative state government, the Progressive impulse fairly exploded onto the Georgia political stage in the summer of 1905—during the same month of May that saw Callaway's exit from the council. And that wasn't the only coincidence, or even the most important one. That summer Callaway's decade-long battle against the Atlanta & West Point was entering its final phase as he took part in the chartering of the Atlanta, Birmingham & Atlantic Railroad. His fight in the federal Supreme Court two years earlier, although resulting in defeat, had elevated him to a highly visible position among the Progressives, who saw the railroads as enemies. And in Georgia the most important issue for the Progressives—in fact, the central issue of Georgia Progressivism— was the railroads.

According to leading Progressive politicians, railroad earnings over the previous ten years had doubled even as freight rates remained steady. The Progressives were also fond of claiming that the railroad lobby effectively constituted a third house of the Georgia legislature. The hottest railroad issue was a thing the would-be reformers called port rates, and this was the specific issue that came to a boil in May 1905.

As Atlanta grew into an industrial city, producers there wanted to pay lower freight rates to port cities such as Brunswick and—particularly—Savannah. They argued that lower rates on these routes would make Atlanta businesses more competitive on the national markets, and they also claimed that the railroads were making too much money anyway. In 1902, various Atlanta businesses had formally asked the Georgia Railroad Commission to order railroads to adopt port rates. The case dragged on for three years. At last, on May 10, 1905—two days after Callaway's final council term ended—the commission ruled against the businesses, refusing to impose port rates.

This decision provided the spark to the kindling that Progressives had been laying during the conservative years. Within days the *Atlanta Journal*, a leading Progressive newspaper, called for the commissioners' resignations. By the end of the month it put forward the name of Hoke Smith as a potential "trust-buster" governor.

Fifty years old in 1905, Hoke Smith was a native of North Carolina and a well-known figure in Georgia. In fact, and not coincidentally, he was the publisher of the *Journal*, a position that had helped him become President Grover Cleveland's secretary of the interior from 1893 to 1896, and which he now planned to use to win the governor's chair. But Smith did have genuine Progressive leanings as well. In the 1870s and 1880s he'd been a personal injury lawyer, one of the best in the South, specializing in suing railroads on behalf of employees and passengers. In the late 1890s he'd backed William Jennings Bryan, who like Smith took a dim view of moneyed interests such as railroads. In 1904 and 1905 Smith had battled for port rates, representing the Atlanta Freight Bureau

before the Georgia Railroad Commission. The Railroad Commission's May 1905 ruling likely convinced him that the time had come for the Progressives to take power in Georgia. In early June he announced he was running for governor.

The Progressives were concerned with many issues, among them corporate greed, child labor, public education, and temperance and prohibition movements. But in Georgia the railroad issues eclipsed all others. Quite simply, reformers believed not only that railroads were making too much money at the expense of small businessmen and farmers but that they held too much power over public officials, which frustrated government efforts at regulation. As an example, Smith and others pointed to the impotence of the Railroad Commission. It was a fact to which Fuller Callaway could personally attest; his own war against the Atlanta & West Point had begun in 1895 with an abortive attempt to get the commission to help him. This alone made Callaway a natural, though in 1905 merely a potential, Smith ally. And while Smith almost certainly knew of Callaway's battle against the railroads, he also likely knew Callaway personally from the latter's LaGrange town council days, having represented the city in a waterworks case in 1898. If Smith won the governor's race,

Fuller Callaway used this silver card holder during his many business trips at home and abroad.

Hoke Smith (far right) was Georgia's governor from 1907 to 1909 and again in 1911. Callaway and Smith were allies in the fight to reduce railroad rates. Smith appointed Callaway to the Georgia Railroad Commission.

Callaway had a good chance of becoming part of his administration—likely in some capacity respecting the railroads.

But for Hoke Smith the problem with the Railroad Commission went beyond impotence. One of its three members, Joseph M. Brown, was to Smith's mind an outright railroad partisan. The son of Georgia's Civil War–era governor Joseph E. Brown, "Little Joe" was well-known, well-educated, and well-versed in the knowledge of railroads. In addition he'd worked for the Western & Atlantic for more than twenty years, eventually becoming its traffic manager. He'd voted against port rates while Smith had championed them. Moreover, during Smith's port rate campaign, Brown had written a number of public letters arguing that port rates would do nothing to help the farmers on whose support Smith was relying. Brown also attacked Smith directly, echoing the charges of bias that Smith had leveled at him. Smith

hated railroads, Brown charged, because he made his living suing them.

Whatever Brown's motives, the railroads themselves clearly opposed Smith's campaign for governor. But Smith gave as good as he got, tapping into the same widespread distrust of the railroads that Callaway himself had developed. And one of his main campaign promises was that if he were elected, one of his first acts would be to fire Joe Brown. Smith's platform not only called for port rates, but for drastic changes in the Railroad Commission, a fact that would have a major impact on Callaway. "The geographical situation of Georgia, her extensive seacoast and proximity to deep water navigation, entitle our people to as cheap freight rates as are given to people in neighboring States similarly situated and cheaper than the rates given to States remote from sea-water transportation," Smith's platform declared. It further posited,

It is the duty of the commission to demand of the transportation companies rates based upon our proximity to the ocean. If the commission will not or cannot, under the circumstances, command such rates, then the commissioners should either be removed and others put in their places or a new body should be created with enlarged powers, sufficient to demand and enforce the rights of the people. . . . We call especial attention to the necessity for the reduction of the rates from our sea-ports to and from all interior points. . . . We condemn . . . excessive and discriminating port rates are [sic] unjust and we demand the immediate righting of these wrongs by the Railroad Commission.

Given the political climate, it wasn't much of a contest. Smith's main opponent was Clark Howell, the conservative publisher of the *Atlanta Constitution*. For a year the campaign raged on the stump and in the pages of the two candidates' rival newspapers. The fight was entirely among Democrats, with the party splitting between the reform and conservative factions; there was no Republican Party to speak of in Georgia. Finally the primary election took place in August 1906. The vote was not even close: of about 165,000 votes cast, Smith won nearly 100,000.

Since the primary, and not the general election, effectively decided the race's outcome, there was a long delay between Smith's victory and his inauguration. He did not take the oath of office until June 1907, fully two years after he began his gubernatorial race. But once inaugurated he moved quickly. Coming into office on June 29, he fulfilled one of his main campaign promises less than a month later, firing railroad commissioner Joe Brown on August 21, conveniently waiting until a few days after the legislature's adjournment. This firing would lead to one of the greatest political battles in

Georgia history, one into which Callaway would be drawn.

In fact, Smith didn't even wait until his inauguration to begin his reform efforts. Instead, throughout the spring of 1907, the governor-elect had worked with his supporters in the legislature to draft Progressive laws. The most celebrated, which passed just as he fired Brown, was the Candler-Overstreet Act, which achieved his goal of revamping the Railroad Commission.

Under Candler-Overstreet, the commission became much more powerful, and it was redesigned to reflect more clearly the Progressive and anti-railroad sentiment that was prevalent in the state. In addition to its power over railroads, the commission now gained jurisdiction over docks and wharves, telephone and telegraph companies, and gas and lighting companies. In short, with Candler-Overstreet, the Railroad Commission began its metamorphosis into the modern Public Service Commission, although that name would not come until later.

The new law also enlarged the commission from three to five members, all of whom were to be chosen by statewide election rather than appointed by the governor. But that meant that the commission was now two members short. The law did allow Smith to appoint two new commissioners to fill the empty seats until the next election. And Smith knew whom he wanted. Shortly after the law's passage, and only five days after firing Brown, he announced his choices. One of them was George Hillyer, well-known in Atlanta circles as a former mayor and state judge who had long studied railroad issues. The other was Fuller E. Callaway.

Callaway was a natural for the job, and he was the first man whom Smith picked. In addition to his youth and energy, he was a regular (and major) railroad customer both as a merchant and as a textile man. He had more than a little background in railroad management and rate issues due to his decade-long fight with the Atlanta & West Point and his participation in the creation of the Atlanta, Birmingham & Atlantic. The Atlanta & West Point fight also gave him rock-solid credentials as a critic of the railroads' abuse of power. "Fuller Callaway is one of the really remarkable young men that Georgia has produced within the era," crowed one Atlanta paper.

He carries under a radiant surface of good fellowship and fun one of the clearest heads and one of the soundest judgments that have been given to affairs in Georgia.

He is a business man of extraordinary vigor and success, a worker of easy yet prodigious energy, and a citizen of great popularity. It is doubtful if there is a man of greater and more effective business force in western Georgia. He has been a great power in the campaign which led to railway regulation, and has richly won and merited the recognition which the governor has accorded him in this appointment.

That he will fill it ably, amiably, and yet fearlessly, there is no room for doubt.

Callaway's antler inkwell occupied a prominent spot on his desk. The cap is engraved with the letter C.

Even the *Atlanta Constitution*, with its antipathy to Smith, gave Callaway and Hillyer their due. "Mr. Callaway is a well-known merchant, banker, and cotton mill man of LaGrange, who has made remarkable success in the business world," it commented. "Judge Hillyer is a well-known Atlanta lawyer, now retired. Both are able men, and will undoubtedly give the people good service on the board." In short, from where Smith sat, Callaway seemed the ideal man for the job.

Or almost ideal. In 1907, Callaway had many irons in the fire, even for him. In addition to Calumet, the LaGrange National Bank, and the Atlanta, Birmingham & Atlantic Railroad—all newish concerns—just in recent months he'd established the Security Warehouse Company, the LaGrange Savings Bank, and the Electric Ginnery. By now he was also serving in several statewide organizations, such as the Georgia Immigration Association and the Georgia Industrial Association. The biggest project of 1907 was the Manchester Development Company, which was consuming a great deal of Callaway's energy. The problem, then, was whether he would have enough time to devote to the Railroad Commission. Already he'd refused appeals from LaGrange citizens to run for mayor; the commission, meeting in Atlanta, might prove just as time-consuming.

But Smith really wanted Callaway. Long consultations apparently took place between the two men, during which Callaway almost certainly mentioned his concerns about his other commitments. But Smith likely brought up his idea that the brunt of the work would be carried out by the commission's chairman and its newly hired staff, in the person of commission attorney James K. Hines. Convinced, Callaway finally gave in, although he expressly refused to stay on the commission for any particular length of time.

Just as Smith lost no time in appointing Callaway and Hillyer, the newly revamped commission was quick to meet and organize itself. Smith announced the appointments and personally swore in the new commissioners on the morning of Monday, August 26; at noon that same day the commission met. Its first action was to unanimously elect S. G. McLendon as the new chairman, just as Smith hoped it would. McLendon was also a Smith appointee, having been chosen by the governor to replace the banished Joe Brown. Thus Smith had handpicked three of the five railroad commissioners, and he was putting a lot of both hope and trust in them—particularly McLendon—in his goal of reforming the railroads.

McLendon's inaugural address must have reassured the new governor, but only to an extent. "Four classes of persons are interested in railroads," he declared.

First, the promoter, who issues and sells bonds and stocks; second, the investor, who buys them; third, the people, who pay the freight; and fourth, the manipulator whose clever legerdemain is practiced under the sanction of ill-conceived and ill-executed laws. The first three classes are entitled to the protection of the law. The last is not, for he is the public enemy.

Under his leadership, McLendon continued, the commission would seek to protect the interests of the promoter, the investor, and of course customers, who "must foot all the bills." Interestingly Callaway had claims to being in all three of the legitimate categories McLendon named.

During the meeting, H. Warner Hill, the elderly outgoing acting chairman who would nevertheless remain on the commission, gave an address in which he spoke of both Hillyer and Callaway. "You, sir, Mr. Callaway," he remarked, "your mother and my mother were the warmest of personal friends; you were born within one mile from where I now live,

S. G. McLendon of Thomasville was also appointed to the Georgia Railroad Commission by Governor Hoke Smith. McLendon served as the chairman of the commission throughout Callaway's tenure.

in the good old county of Meriwether, and there is no reason why our personal relations should not be as cordial as they have ever been." This was important to Hill. "From time to time we have asked the legislature to give us increased powers, and the legislature has seen fit to do so," he noted. "I believe that the action of the new commission will be harmonious—that it will be characterized," he said, invoking Georgia's motto, "by wisdom, by justice, and by moderation."

Actually Smith probably didn't fully appreciate these comments. He hadn't run on a policy of moderation, but one of strong Progressive reform. He was less concerned with giving moderate protection to both consumer and railroad than he was with giving great protection to consumers, even at the expense of the railroads. But one thing must have pleased him no end: Callaway's first official statement.

The commission didn't do much actual business that day, other than briefly discussing some of the issues it would be considering in the immediate future. But just as it was about to adjourn for the day, Callaway sprang a surprise.

It was well-known that railroads supplied free travel passes to state legislators and other public figures who were in a position to further the railroads' political agendas. This was a serious problem, and exactly the sort of thing the Progressives wanted to stop. Callaway now suggested that the commission require all railroads in the state to provide it with lists of everyone to whom they gave free passes, along with the reasons for those passes, or as he put it, "who to and what for."

Warner Hill laughed good-naturedly. "You may get them to tell you 'who to,'" he quipped, "but I doubt if you can prevail upon them to state 'what for.'"

"Then we'll find out who they are issued to," Callaway answered, "and I don't doubt that this will result in the cutting off of most of those who are not entitled to them."

McLendon and the others agreed with Callaway's reasoning. If the fact became known that a politician took free travel passes from railroads, he'd be pressured to quit doing so, and his votes on railroad issues would be closely watched.

After a brief discussion, Callaway formally moved that the commission require railroads to furnish it with free-pass lists by mid-October. The commission deferred the vote on the issue until later in the week so that Callaway could carefully draft the final resolution.

The day originally scheduled was Friday, but as things turned out, the commission decided not to wait, going ahead and acting on Callaway's motion the next day. The long meeting began Tuesday morning, with more than a dozen railroad men present to argue against rate reduction. It must have been a tremendously sweet moment for Callaway;

among the supplicants was C. A. Wickersham, the president and general manager of the Atlanta & West Point. The meeting went on for hours, but while the commission didn't impose lower rates that day, neither did it say that it wouldn't do so in the future.

Ironically, the railroads themselves forced the committee's hand on the free-pass issue. In a model of bad timing, Vice President W. A. Winburn of the Central of Georgia tendered a free pass, good for a year, to Chairman McLendon that morning. He apparently sent it in an envelope either by hand or by mail. Unfortunately Winburn was sitting in front of the commissioners when McLendon received it.

Well aware of the public attention that Callaway's motion had focused on the subject, McLendon promptly and publicly returned the pass to Winburn with a courteous letter of his own. "As he was elected a member of the railroad commission on an anti-pass platform," one reporter paraphrased it, McLendon "would be remiss in his place as a public official to accept the same."

The incident likely prompted Callaway to forge ahead that day. He moved the adoption of a rule requiring the railroads to publish their deadhead lists, and the commissioners unanimously agreed. The result was the newly reorganized commission's General Order Number 1, which required all railroads doing business in Georgia to file monthly statements with the commission listing "all free transportation issued during said month, to whom issued, upon what account issued, and between what stations."

This order, the firstfruits of Callaway's time on the commission, was perhaps his most important achievement as a railroad commissioner. It was also certainly one of the most important accomplishments of his entire political life, for it clearly and emphatically established him as belonging to the Progressive camp. Since within a few years a Progressive Democrat with Georgia connections would gain the White House, the deadhead list order would prove to be the key to Callaway's progress to the national political stage.

In the following months, the commission took other important reform steps. In October it made a point of noting that the deadhead list order applied to all Georgia streetcar companies as well as to railroads. This measure would help keep city officials out of the streetcar companies' pockets, just as it would keep the railroads from owning state legislators. "If there are those who do not interpret the order to apply to street railroads," the commissioners stated clearly, "we will issue a special order for their enlightenment."

An even bigger decision came later in 1907, when the commissioners refused to back down on a June order requiring railroads to reduce their passenger rates. The commission even went so far as to order some freight rate reductions. These passenger and freight reductions amounted to some of Hoke Smith's greatest victories, and Callaway was instrumental in achieving them. But the triumph Smith really wanted—the institution of port rates—was another matter entirely, and in the end a frustrating one.

Part of the problem was timing. Two months after Callaway's appointment, the Panic of 1907 burst upon Wall Street and toppled major New York banks, sending shock waves throughout the country. As a banker, Callaway managed to ride out the storm fairly well due to his wise decisions, but there were political effects as well. The causes of the panic had nothing to do with Smith's election; factors ranged from the San Francisco earthquake of 1906 to an abortive attempt by a couple of Wall Street magnates to corner the copper market. Still, many conservatives blamed the Progressives and their campaign for government regulation of business and industry, claiming that such regulations were a damper on the economy that had turned the market bearish. Their biggest

target was Theodore Roosevelt, the young, trust-busting president of the past six years. Smith also was clearly in the Progressive camp, and as the economy dropped, support for him began waning.

Callaway, however, wasn't affected. Apparently people viewed his deadhead list motion not as an economic regulation but as an anticorruption measure. His appointment, an interim one, ran only until the 1908 election, but he never faced serious opposition even in the sudden anti-Progressive climate.

In 1908, Robert H. Buchanan of Decatur announced that he would challenge Callaway for his commission seat, but the following month he failed to qualify. R. H. Jenkins of nearby Hogansville did qualify, however, and he became something of an irritant over the next few weeks.

Hogansville, a few miles northeast of LaGrange in Troup County, was a rival to LaGrange with its lower freight rates. Callaway had often cited it as an example of discriminatory rates during his battle with the Atlanta & West Point. Jenkins's decision to oppose Callaway in the election suggests that Hogansville reciprocated the feelings.

For his part, Callaway didn't treat the election as a high-profile event. Making no announcement of his candidacy, he quietly did the paperwork and paid the qualification fee. One of the two open seats was for a long term, which would expire in 1913; the other seat was for a shorter term that would end in 1911. Callaway chose the short-term seat, letting Hillyer qualify for the long-term position, a choice that showed his ongoing concern for all of his other time commitments.

One of Callaway's favorite anecdotes dates from the 1908 race. A well-known story in Georgia held that one day Callaway was walking down Decatur Street in Atlanta when he bumped into an intoxicated man who refused to get out of his way. Callaway grabbed the man by his lapels, the story went, and shook him. "Do you know who I am?" he barked officiously.

"No," replied the drunk.

"I'm Fuller Callaway from LaGrange!"

"You've got nothing on me," the drunk replied. "I'm full of corn liquor from Alabama!"

Years later, after hearing the story from several of his professors at Georgia Tech, Fuller Jr. asked his father if it was true. "Son," laughed Fuller, "I made up that story and I hired four men and sent them all over the state for three months to tell it when I was running for railroad commissioner." He explained further. In an election for a post like railroad commissioner, he told young Fuller, nobody cared, or even paid attention to, who was running. "When they come to vote," he observed, "if they have ever heard of one of the fellows on the ballot, they'll vote for him. That's the only politicking I did; the only cent I spent politicking—I made up that story and sent men all over the state and I was elected." The story was such a favorite with Fuller Sr. that now and then he would sign letters to family with the name "Fullercorn."

As the all-important Democratic primary approached in June 1908, Jenkins unleashed a strong attack on Callaway, in which he tried to paint the LaGrangian as a railroad man. "What is Mr. Callaway's relation, in a business way, to Harry M. Atkinson, president of the Atlanta, Birmingham & Atlantic Railroad Company?" he asked Callaway in a public letter. He continued,

Is not Mr. Callaway virtually one of the officers of the said railroad company?

Did not Mr. Callaway exert himself and aid in securing the right of way for said railroad through Troup County?

Did not Mr. Callaway and his business associates form a committee to aid the said railroad to obtain its right of way through Troup County and to secure it for the company as cheaply as possible?

Did not Mr. Callaway bend all his great energies in aiding the condemnation proceedings instituted by the said A., B. & A. R. R. Co., to condemn the lands of the people of his county for this railroad corporation? . . .

What consideration did he receive for his work? Is he not so closely aligned with the said railroad corporation that his appointment as a commissioner is virtually the same as appointing any railroad official on the commission? How much stock does he hold in said railroad, either legally or equitably?

Jenkins tried to make Callaway's involvement with the Atlanta, Birmingham & Atlantic sound like a bad thing. Perhaps it was, from Hogansville's perspective, given the LaGrange/Hogansville competition. But Hogansville was not Georgia, and as McLendon had noted in his initial speech as chairman, nothing was wrong with being a railroad promoter or investor. What Jenkins was trying to do in his letter was insinuate that Callaway was a manipulator.

Callaway wisely ignored the letter. Within a week, in a primary election that was one of the most celebrated in Georgia history, he soundly beat Jenkins, 107,229 votes to 40,754, taking more than 72 percent of the popular returns. This was a considerably wider margin than the two gubernatorial candidates, with the victor there winning by only 12,000 votes.

This latter race was by far the biggest news of the election season, for the winner wasn't Hoke Smith. Instead Smith lost to the man he'd ousted from the Railroad Commission the previous year, Joseph M. Brown.

There was no stronger sign than Smith's defeat that Progressivism in Georgia was in trouble. Brown had waged a virulent campaign against Smith for months, advocating an approach to railroad regulation that a later generation would describe as trickle-down economics. At least partly because of the 1907 panic, it was an effective approach.

Callaway established the Manchester Cotton Mill in Manchester, Georgia, in 1909. This entirely new town was named after Manchester, England.

Now, for a year, Georgia would have in Smith a lame-duck Progressive governor.

But Smith didn't care that he was on the way out. In February 1909 he wrote the Railroad Commission, exhorting it to adopt port rates. Soon thereafter, several Atlanta businesses filed petitions requesting port rates as well. The battle promised to be dramatic, and potentially damaging to all public figures involved.

Given all the earlier popular support for Smith, and the fact that he'd handpicked a majority of the commissioners, the commission's failure to deliver on the port-rates issue up until this point seemed remarkable. But the issue was never simple. Callaway's actions in the following months revealed the complexity of the port-rates question. On March 15, 1909, after a year and a half on the Railroad Commission, he abruptly tendered his resignation, to be effective at the end of the month.

Callaway likely had many reasons for his decision, the growing fractiousness over port rates and his heavy (and increasing) private

commitments being the main ones. The Manchester development project was by now in high gear; a notice about the new cotton mill there had appeared in the *Atlanta Constitution* only two days before Callaway's resignation announcement. Callaway had also taken on other duties, some of them at Smith's behest. The previous autumn the governor had named him as a delegate to a cotton congress to be held in New Orleans by the Farmers' Educational and Cooperative Union, and by March, Callaway had come to the executive committee of the Georgia Bankers' Association. Simply put, he was quite busy.

But the press raised other possible reasons for his resignation, and these reasons weren't entirely wrong. The port-rates issue was never as clear-cut as Smith would have it to be. "Take, as an illustration, the rates on cotton," he entreated the commission at one point. "They have been practically the same for many years, yet the cost of handling has been reduced." Callaway, however, had a different perspective. In the first place, port rates would mainly benefit Atlanta, and the whole reason he'd fought the railroads initially was that Atlanta's rates were already good when compared to LaGrange's. The fact was that high freight rates worked like a protective tariff for Georgia, raising prices on goods from out of state and thus making Georgia manufacturers' products more desirable to Georgia buyers. Port rates, on the other hand, would lower prices for Georgia consumers, but (argued Joe Brown and others) would hurt Georgia producers, including textile men such as Callaway, and thus slow Georgia's economic development by making out-of-state goods cheaper and Georgia products less competitive in the local market.

It probably galled Callaway to realize that in this battle he was on the side of the railroads, but realize it he did. Of course he had many business concerns; as a merchant, he would benefit from lower rates, which would help him sell goods out of state more cheaply. But he obviously did the math and came down on the side of the current freight rates. This, more than anything else, confirmed Callaway as a textile magnate rather than a merchant; in fact it may have been a defining moment for him. In any case he marked the occasion by writing a letter that port rate opponents used in their case before the commission.

In this letter Callaway noted that the railroads with which he dealt charged lower rates on cotton goods moving from the South to the North than they did on similar goods traveling in the opposite direction. This directly helped Southern textile men compete with Northern textile firms while simultaneously putting Northern firms at a disadvantage in the South, including Georgia. This policy, Callaway noted, seemed deliberately designed to build up the southern textile industry. He didn't note, although it was obvious, that his own mills were beneficiaries of that policy.

As Callaway had undoubtedly foreseen, acrimony over the port-rates issue grew in the weeks immediately following his resignation. Smith, incensed by his inability to get his own commission to back him, went on the warpath against Chairman McLendon barely a month after Callaway's departure. Callaway might have sensed this coming and decided to resign to avoid unpleasant and unproductive partisan battles. Nevertheless, reporters pressed him to reenter the fray. In late March, with his resignation on record, Callaway was returning home from New York and Boston, having been on an equipment-buying trip for mills in both Manchester and LaGrange. In Washington a correspondent spotted him and tried to get a statement, but Callaway simply refused. "I am a private citizen once more," he told the reporter in his typical good-humored fashion, "and you have it on distinguished authority that they may be reasonably expected not to have anything interesting to say for publication."

But speculation continued. The issue was so big that the press stayed interested in nearly everything that seemed to have anything to do with it. Rumors flew that Callaway's resignation signaled an open breach with Smith.

It wasn't a question of impropriety, at least on Callaway's behalf. The *Atlanta Constitution*, long a critic of both Smith and port rates, simply seemed interested in painting the governor in a bad light by showing that even his supporters and allies were deserting him on the issue. "It is now reported," the paper set forth in May, "that Commissioner Callaway was strongly opposed to the revision of the port rates which is being urged, and that the real reason, or one of the foremost reasons for his resignation was that he did not wish officially to oppose Governor Smith, who appointed him as a member of the commission."

The "interesting gossip" that the editors claimed to have heard produced by Callaway's evidentiary letter to the commission, coupled with the paper's speculations, finally provoked Callaway to break his silence. A few days later, while in Atlanta, he called on the commission in what was apparently an unofficial visit. While there he cheerfully told reporters that his business interests, and not the port rates, were the overriding reason for his departure. That same day he wrote a letter to the *Constitution*, taking issue with what the paper had stated in the earlier article.

"To correct the erroneous impression which might be created by this article," Callaway declared,

I wish to state that I did not resign from the railroad commission for any reason except the one stated in my resignation, namely: that it was impossible to continue to give to the discharge of its duties the amount of time which this important office should receive.

Governor Smith knew of this months before he called the commission's attention to port rates. The letter written by me which was introduced in the hearing before the commission was not an expression on this question, but was merely in answer to an inquiry as to the treatment accorded southern cotton mills in the matter of freight rates.

I wish also to state that there never has been, nor is there now, the slightest friction between Governor Smith and myself. I hold him in high esteem and consider him one of the ablest men of his time.

The strongest evidence for Callaway's veracity is Smith's agreement, by his silence, with Callaway's statements. In contrast, Chairman McLendon, initially one of Smith's men, had clearly parted ways with the governor by the time Callaway left the commission, and Smith made no secret of his displeasure. The situation got worse after that. On June 18, the big vote finally took place. By a three-to-two vote, the commission decided against port rates, with McLendon casting the tie-breaking vote. (The commissioner whom Smith had appointed to fill Callaway's seat, C. Murphy Candler, voted

along with Hillyer in favor of port rates; had Callaway stayed, the outcome would have been the same regardless of how he voted.) The decision brought down Smith's wrath on McLendon. As one of his final actions, the outgoing governor suspended McLendon in much the same way he'd fired Brown at the start of his term, and for the same reasons.

The feud continued after Smith left office, with allegations that McLendon, while serving as chairman, had engaged in unethical transactions of railroad bonds, and counterallegations that Smith had known of the transactions and hadn't cared until McLendon betrayed him. A year and a half later McLendon belatedly tried to drag Callaway into the fray by claiming that Callaway and Smith had been in on a deal with the Atlanta, Birmingham & Atlantic to get low railroad rates at Manchester, although nothing came of the charge. But at no time did Smith publicly go after Callaway, and in August 1910 Callaway made a point of calling on Smith and visibly supporting his bid to regain the governor's seat. "While a friend and cordial admirer of Hoke Smith for his ability, honesty, courage, and usefulness, my interest in him in this matter is chiefly as the defender of principles which as a citizen of Georgia I am deeply interested in seeing prevail," Callaway said in a public statement. "The railroads, the corporations, the vast liquor interests, the men who rode on free passes, and the discomfited politicians laid their heads together to compass his defeat." These arguments had an effect on Georgia's citizens, who returned Smith to office in that year's rematch against Brown.

The fireworks over McLendon showed that Callaway had been right to leave the commission when he did. He had distinguished himself in his brief time there, especially in the eyes of the Progressives, and he'd gotten out before things turned ugly. It was as good a performance as that of any state official during that tumultuous season of Georgia politics, and it was better than most.

During the next few years, Callaway's public presence was somewhat lower than it had been during his time on the railroad commission, but never again would he completely depart the public stage. From time to time the press took note of his private commercial activities. In January 1910 the *Constitution* noted him as an incorporator of the new Bank of Manchester, which he'd chartered the previous December 22 and which went into formal operation on February 1, and the following June the newspaper announced that he'd been elected vice president of the Georgia Industrial Association. Callaway also continued to involve himself in local political topics, such as when he backed a Troup County bond issue in 1910, proposed for the purpose of improving the local roads, or as the campaign slogan put it, "getting Troup County out of the mud." In 1913 he was one of the featured speakers at the Georgia Products Dinner, a promotional event set up by the Atlanta Chamber of Commerce. The areas in which he was held in greatest repute continued to be textiles and railroads, and the papers weren't averse to quoting Callaway on these matters. By this time he was without doubt one of the state's most noteworthy citizens.

During this intermezzo in Callaway's official public service, from 1909 to 1913, William Howard Taft was in the White House. Embracing a Roosevelt-style trust-busting policy, Taft went after business combinations without Theodore Roosevelt's sense of practical restraint, suing nearly twice the number of trusts for Sherman Act violations in his single term as Roosevelt had in two. That wasn't good for cotton prices or for the textile industry. Callaway spoke up on this point, and when he did, people paid attention.

In January 1910, with cotton prices low, Callaway was traveling home from New York in the company of W. P. Brown when the press caught up with the men at the Atlanta train station. Brown was one of the leading

traders of both the New York and New Orleans Cotton Exchanges, and one of the men America listened to most closely in the matter of cotton prices. When pressed for a comment on the bad figures, Brown accommodated them. "You know, so many newspaper men want to treat cotton and its sale flippantly," he charged. "I don't care for that. Cotton is a serious proposition, and should be treated seriously." With that warning, with which Callaway no doubt would have agreed, Brown made his prognostication. "I feel more bullish than ever. This is based purely upon a matter of supply and demand. . . . I don't believe that we have begun to see high prices for cotton yet. I expect to see it sell higher, and in the immediate future, and I would not be surprised to see it sell for 20 cents a pound."

"How about the recent slump in prices?" asked a reporter.

"That was to be expected," Brown answered.

"Was it brought about by manipulation?"

"No," said Brown, "I wouldn't say that. You must remember that I am a member of both exchanges, and want to be very careful how I am quoted. I think the slump was caused by many persons being long, and when they began to unload, the price broke. But it is going up again."

During this discussion, Callaway had wandered off in search of the most recent market reports, and he now came back with distressing news that appeared to contradict Brown's hopeful statement. The prices had dropped, he reported, by fourteen to twenty-nine points.

That got Brown's attention. "What caused that?"

"The fact was bad enough," Callaway told him. "I didn't look at the cause."

It was a rough day for cotton and an embarrassing moment for Brown. He grabbed the papers Callaway offered him, then changed his mind. "No, we'll read them after we get aboard." He pulled out his pocket watch and announced that it was time to leave, and moments later the men were back on the train.

In an ominous portent, this news ran side-by-side with an article that the Taft administration was about to crack down on cotton gambling, a practice that essentially consisted of making side bets on anticipated prices of cotton and other agricultural products. In the following months Taft's attorney general, George Wickersham, went on a campaign against the gambling houses where this betting took place, which were known colloquially as bucket shops. Simultaneously Wickersham went after several leading cotton brokers in court for attempting, he claimed, to corner the cotton market. Among his targets was William P. Brown. Just as Brown had predicted, the price of cotton had shot up; Wickersham believed he knew why, and in April he announced a major investigation.

While high prices were good for cotton producers—assuming that the farmers and not the speculators saw the money—they put textile men in a tight place, forcing them to cut back production and even to lay off some of their operatives. Even so, Callaway was vehemently opposed to Wickersham's charges, and he said so in a rare public statement, blaming short-sellers for the high prices.

It occurs to me that undoubtedly Attorney General Wickersham was unwittingly inspired by bears who have sold what they do not own, thereby depressing the cotton market at the expense of the farmers and demoralizing the market for cotton goods.

A great many mills have bought cotton on the New York Cotton Exchange cheaper than it is selling in the South, and intend demanding the cotton. The bears hope by this attack to scare the mills out of this legitimate trade and further demoralize the cotton and cotton goods markets. In my opinion, this attack will prove a boomerang for the bears, as it only accentuates

William Perry Brown, a native of Mississippi, became an important and very wealthy cotton broker in New Orleans and New York. Brown and Callaway periodically discussed the cotton market. Brown constructed an elaborate mansion in New Orleans in 1904.

the shortness of the last cotton crop and betrays the predicament they are in through having sold something they do not own.

I can not believe that the more responsible members of the New York Cotton Exchange are behind this movement, as it questions the right of mills to buy contracts on the New York Cotton Exchange with the expectation of receiving cotton, thereby denying the exchange's reason for existence.

This was another key point in Callaway's public life. In the past few years he'd shown himself amenable to government regulation of industry—particularly the railroads—but only when it was reasonable, and he'd held an even more conservative attitude toward government regulation of the markets. He stood as neither a doctrinaire conservative nor a wild-eyed radical and thus was an excellent candidate for appointive office in the future.

Governor John M. Slaton, from adjacent Meriwether County, tapped Callaway to serve on the important ad hoc Western & Atlantic Commission. He is pictured with his wife, Sarah Frances Slaton.

At the state level, when the call came, it was—not surprisingly—in relation to railroads. But it did come from a somewhat surprising quarter. In September 1913 Governor John M. Slaton, at one time a Joe Brown supporter, asked Callaway to serve on a special *ad hoc* state commission involving ex-Governor Brown's old company, the Western & Atlantic. Since Callaway was visibly a Hoke Smith man, the request from Slaton, who enjoyed a reputation for high integrity, was a great tribute.

The Western & Atlantic was a major Georgia railroad, owned by the state, and of considerable historic and commercial importance. Running 137 miles between Chattanooga and Atlanta, it was the path down which William T. Sherman had advanced in the terrible summer of 1864. After the war the state leased the road to a private concern, the Western & Atlantic Railroad Company. But by the early twentieth century problems had arisen, culminating in lawsuits by Georgia against the company for breach of contract, which the company decisively won. As a

result of these conflicts, the legislature named a special ten-man commission consisting of legislators and private citizens to look into the company's operation—and perhaps mismanagement—of the railroad.

For Callaway the opportunity was too good to pass up. There were strong suspicions that his old nemesis the Louisville & Nashville was a major silent partner in—perhaps even the parent of—the Western & Atlantic Company. This, coupled with the possibility of getting more favorable freight rates on such an important road by re-leasing it to some other entity, persuaded him to sign on.

For several months the time requirement was intensive. The commission held meetings, sometimes in the Senate chamber, and made at least two excursions up the line all the way to Chattanooga inquiring into everything from the condition of equipment to rights-of-way and encroachments—a Callaway subspecialty. Of particular interest was the rumor of a "syndicate of wealthy Atlanta business men" who wanted to take a stake in the railroad. By October 1913 the rumor was confirmed, with Atlanta officials advocating for a share in the railroad, offering to build a plaza downtown to cover the tracks for several blocks, which would have been a forerunner of Underground Atlanta, although the commission ultimately rejected the proposal.

A particular problem the commission faced was an old story to Callaway. One of the most important issues with which it dealt—or rather with which it tried to deal— was the possibility of re-leasing the railroad. Callaway and the other commissioners wished to explore the terms they could get for leases of thirty, fifty, or even a hundred years. But the Louisville & Nashville, by now revealed as a Western & Atlantic stakeholder and a potential lessee, simply refused to discuss this or any other matter with the commission, apparently claiming that the group lacked authority to speak for the state.

In reply, when the commission filed its final report in July 1914, it was highly critical of how the Western & Atlantic Company had run the state's railroad. The road wasn't yet double-tracked, noted the report, a massive handicap in the expanding economy. Much of the road's property had been badly neglected, and there were encroachments all along the line from Atlanta to Chattanooga. "These matters are of very serious import," the commissioners stated of the encroachments, "and all of them demand the attention of the legislature." Things were so bad, continued the report, that the commissioners recommended that the chairman of Callaway's old outfit, the Georgia Railroad Commission, be given the authority to take charge of the road "with broad duties and powers."

Although Callaway was in Europe on his fateful visit to Germany when his commission filed the report, the evidence shows that he took a very active part in its preparation, including joining in the recommendations for closer state supervision of the road. In the end the legislature went him one better. By late 1915, instead of giving supervisory authority to the chairman of the Georgia Railroad Commission, it created a permanent Western & Atlantic Railroad Commission to supervise, among other things, the re-leasing of the road. The original plan was to have this body consist of five men, including the governor, the chairman of the ad hoc commission on which Callaway had been serving, and Callaway himself. Few if any men in Georgia, after all, could equal his experience in railroad regulation.

Governor Nathaniel E. Harris was quite pleased with both the new law and the proposed members, calling the new body "ideal" in a public statement. "I believe it is as good a commission as could have been obtained in the state of Georgia," he happily declared.

But the legislature and the governor had gotten ahead of themselves. Callaway had been content to serve on the temporary commission. But a long-term position on a permanent body posed the same problems for him that the Georgia Railroad Commission job had six years earlier. There are indications that nobody even checked with him before the announcement of his appointment was made. At any rate, Callaway acted quickly once the news of it came out. Within twenty-four hours he notified Harris that he must decline the appointment. "I regret exceedingly that it will be impossible for me to serve on the commission named by the Legislature to act for the State in re-leasing the Western & Atlantic Railroad," he informed Harris by letter.

I appreciate the honor and would be very glad to serve if I were in a position to do so. But the fact that we are just now at the most vital stage in the construction of a new cotton mill, and my duty to our stockholders and my associates in our enterprise, will render it impossible for me to give proper time and thought to any other responsibilities for the next few years.

In my opinion, the terms of the act of the legislature governing the re-leasing of the road are eminently wise. The legislators are entitled to the appreciation of our people for their action. The other members appointed to the re-leasing commission are peculiarly and well qualified for this service, and this increases my regret that I am unable to serve with them.

Callaway's statement regarding his duty to stockholders, in retrospect, is inadvertently misleading, for by now his commitments were no longer purely private. He was now a national figure, being drawn by fate more and more into major national and international affairs; his private business commitments were not merely an indicator of this fact but a result of it. Two major developments had brought about this state of affairs: the election of a Progressive Democrat as president and the coming of the Great War.

MANY FOREIGN DELEGATES TO THE 1919 WORLD COTTON CONFERENCE, HELD IN NEW ORLEANS, WERE INVITED TO VISIT LAGRANGE AND HILLS AND DALES EN ROUTE TO THE CONFERENCE. FULLER IS JUST TO THE LEFT OF THE AMERICAN FLAG. IDA IS WEARING THE WHITE DRESS.

· 8 ·

LIFE AS A PUBLIC FIGURE: CALLAWAY, THE GREAT WAR, AND THE NATIONAL STAGE

As Callaway was returning to state office in 1913 by accepting a place on the *ad hoc* Western & Atlantic commission, he was also coming to the attention of national leaders. That year saw the inauguration of only the second Democratic president since Reconstruction, and the first with southern connections. Woodrow Wilson wasn't exactly a Southerner; he was more accurately a Southern expatriate. He'd been born in Virginia and raised in the Carolinas and Georgia, but he'd spent most of his adult life in the North. Still his Southern roots were something, and of course the "solid South" was largely responsible for putting him into office. As a result, many of his high-level appointments went to Southerners. Among them were Albert S. Burleson of Texas, who became postmaster general; Josephus Daniels of North Carolina, whom Wilson appointed secretary of the navy; David F. Houston of North Carolina and Missouri, chosen to head the Department of Agriculture; and William Gibbs McAdoo, like Wilson a former Georgian, named by the president to be secretary of the treasury.

It was only natural for Wilson to dispense patronage to southern Progressive Democrats, and it was just as logical for Call-

away, with his qualifications and bona fides, to end up on Wilson's list. In early 1913, while Callaway was in Cairo on his mission to meet Lord Kitchener, he learned that Frank K. Lane, Wilson's choice to be secretary of the interior, had recommended that Wilson nominate him as Indian commissioner. Even here Callaway's railroad experience had been important. Lane, a Californian, had come to know of him while serving on the Interstate Commerce Commission, and Hoke Smith, now a senator from Georgia, had likely mentioned Callaway to Lane as well. "I want a man," Lane had declared, "whose very name will be a notice to the land-grabbers and despoilers of the Red men that they cannot ply their trade."

It was an important post. The Bureau of Indian Affairs and its five thousand employees administered a population of nearly a quarter-million Native Americans and millions of acres of land. As commissioner, Callaway would be only one step below cabinet level, directly responsible to Lane. Still, given his background, Callaway would seem better suited to be secretary of commerce, or perhaps agriculture, or even an ICC seat. But it was all academic. Indian commissioner was a full-time job, unlike his past and current railroad offices, and the same forces that were to make him decline a seat on Georgia's permanent railroad re-leasing commission also convinced him that the federal appointment would require too much of him.

From Cairo he let Lane know of his decision. A month later, back in America and on his way to LaGrange, he stopped over in Washington to speak to Lane personally. "My duty to the stockholders in the various banks, cotton mills, and other corporations which I am directing," he said in a public statement, "is more binding upon me just now than a call to a political office. I deeply appreciate the fact that Secretary Lane thought of me away off in Egypt rather than of the many men in his own state of California to whom he might have offered the place." Callaway acknowledged that he would normally be happy to serve. "I like Mr. Lane and would work a month for him for nothing if that was all that was involved," he declared, "but if I deserted the people who have put their faith in me I wouldn't deserve the place any more than if I should desert my wife and babies." After he retired from his businesses, Callaway concluded, the story would be different.

The Democrats hadn't limited their resurgence to the White House. In 1912 they picked up seats in both the Senate and the House, and by the end of Wilson's first term they had assumed control of both houses for the first time since before the Civil War. From the start they made the most of it. One area of particular interest both to congressional Democrats and to Callaway, in light of recent swings in cotton rates, was the regulation of cotton exchanges.

The exchanges had served a valuable role in getting the southern cotton economy back on its feet in the years since Reconstruction, and Callaway recognized that fact. But the exchanges had also led to a lot of speculation in cotton futures, and that had

led in turn to both mills and growers getting hurt at times over the years. On the other hand, Attorney General George Wickersham's heavy-handed assault on the exchanges a few years earlier had left a sour taste in Callaway's mouth, and in others' too. Now that the Democrats were in power, they began seeking a different regulatory scheme. In April 1914 Callaway was summoned to Washington to give his opinion on the matter to the House Committee on Agriculture.

The hearings involved rather technical testimony on a complex subject, one that involved cotton futures, the grading of cotton fibers, and the prospect of regulatory taxation of the industry. Nevertheless, they had their share of fireworks as well, for Callaway was only one witness among many. In addition to mill owners, representatives of the exchanges were on the list, including Edward K. Cone and E. J. Glenny, the respective presidents of the New York and New Orleans Cotton Exchanges. The exchange people had been fighting government regulation for years; now the Progressives were about to win the battle, and the presidents were carrying on a rearguard action, hoping at least to influence the regulation that was nearly certain to happen.

The main problem, as Callaway and others described it, was that the cotton traders weren't uniform in their definitions and contract terms. As a result, buyers such as Callaway could never be sure what sort of cotton they would get. To make matters worse, the traders wouldn't mark individual bales to show their grade, which meant that buyers had trouble figuring out what they'd actually taken delivery of, since the shipment might consist of many different grades of cotton. Often it would turn out that some, or many, of the bales would be unsuitable for milling.

Callaway was reasonable and a bit folksy in his testimony and tone, obviously much more at ease than he had been in his first congressional hearing a decade before. At one point he retold a version of one of his stories about the farmer who offered a reward of five dollars to anyone who could find his cow. He also emphasized that he was by no means opposed to the exchanges, as long as they played fairly, and he tried to make that clear.

"Do you understand that these cotton men are in any way selfish?" a congressman asked him at one point.

"Oh no, sir," Callaway answered. "I am not criticizing them. I would do the same thing if I was in their place. It is human nature for a man to do what is in his own interest. But," he continued, "let us fix it so it can not be to a man's interest to 'rig' the game and then we will lose our 'riggers.'"

"Do you believe that it would be better to have these conditions that you have enumerated continue to prevail in the cotton exchanges," another congressman broke in, "or to have them discontinued—to have the cotton exchanges abolished?"

"If you are going to let them run like they are running now, " Callaway stated flatly, "I would rather abolish them, because this last fall, when I hedged my cotton, I would have done as well to have bought pork or sold pork and bought butter beans or sold pigs than I would to buy my cotton in New York." This from a man who hated speculating.

Such talk bothered the exchange men who were present. At one point, when Callaway noted that the exchanges used categories of cotton that differed from the government standards, he looked to the president of the New Orleans exchange for confirmation. "Is that not so, Mr. Glenny?" he asked.

"They base on the Government standards," replied Glenny huffily, "and the deliveries are based on the Government standards."

"But you deliver other cotton than the Government standards?" pressed Callaway.

Franklin Knight Lane, secretary of the interior under President Woodrow Wilson, asked Callaway to serve as Indian commissioner, but he declined to focus on business matters. Lane and Callaway would cross paths numerous times during the ensuing years.

"It is within the Government standards of cotton," Glenny insisted.

"It is a change of the tinges or something like that," Callaway suggested, "which is a little different from the Government standards, and you knock something off from them?" In other words he was charging that merchants paid the grower a lower price for inferior cotton but could (and did) charge buyers the full price because their grading system didn't distinguish between good and not-so-good cotton; a shipment of high-grade cotton, for which the buyer paid, would thus contain a certain amount of lower-grade cotton.

Glenny didn't deny that the merchants sometimes did pay lower rates "for the benefit of the southern producer." Despite the justification, it was a big concession, and Callaway continued the attack. "You know all of the cotton exchanges work for the benefit of the producer," he echoed, "just like the missionaries to China?"

"You need not put it just that way," complained Glenny.

"I want you to put it like this," shot back Callaway.

"But your proposition is to limit them to nine grades," Glenny objected, "and you would have a contract this year which would

13004. Cotton Exchange Building, New Orleans, La.

The New Orleans Cotton Exchange, led by its president, E. J. Glenny, was an important player in the cotton markets. Callaway argued for uniform grading standards for cotton bales.

have been unworkable." He was claiming that the strict imposition of government standards would bring the exchanges to a halt.

"Well," said Callaway reasonably, "we used to think that we could not work under the Sherman law, but we have found out that we could get along just as well." The Sherman Antitrust Act, passed in 1890, had been a game changer for American business, but as Callaway noted, by no means a game ender.

On it went. Later in his testimony, Callaway claimed that the exchange men *didn't* always protect the producer, instead taking advantage of him as well as of the buyer. The "ignorant farmer," he noted, whether black or white, "is selling cotton now and not getting its value for it" because of his failure to understand the merchants' classification systems. "An ignorant man comes in there with a bale of cotton," he declared, "and he does not stand any more chance than a snowball in hades."

"That is true in every local market," observed a representative.

Here Callaway showed his true Progressive stripes. "There is where you men of experience ought to make a law by which the ignorant man will be taken care of," he asserted. "I do not think the big fish ought to eat the little ones. I think they ought to protect the little ones." Callaway didn't mind paying the producer for his cotton. What he objected to was the merchant's appropriating the money that the producer should be getting. Protection was needed.

To bring it about, he suggested that every cotton warehouse have a government agent present to classify cotton. A Texas representative noted that under the law of his state, each warehouse already had a public weigher. "Yes," agreed Callaway. "Let that man be your classer, and give him an assistant to help him do the work, and let his certificate show his grade."

"Mr. Callaway," Representative Pat Harrison of Mississippi spoke up, "I have never heard that suggestion before, as far as I am concerned. I have never read of it. It appeals to me. I just want to ask you, is that original?"

"I have a young man in my office, about that high," said Callaway, holding up his hand, "that handles our correspondence. He got up that idea."

"Let us have his name," Glenny piped up.

"No, sir," replied Callaway, half-joking, but only half. "You all might want to hire him."

Further showing his Progressivism, Callaway suggested that in exchange for government-supervised classification, the proposed law could place a small tax on each bale of cotton, with the revenues going to a program of educating farmers to classify their cotton for themselves, and to boll-weevil control efforts as well. Once again this emphasized an important fact about Callaway. As a buyer he and cotton growers did business at arm's length. The lower the price he could pay growers, the more money he would make in the short run. But Callaway was interested in the growers' prosperity as well as his own, and the prosperity of the entire Southern cotton economy. He was happy to help out the other party in the transaction if it benefited the entire industry and kept the golden eggs coming.

To conclude his testimony, Callaway—who'd read the pending exchange regulation bills and found them both lacking—offered the committee a list of amendments that he would include in any final regulatory law, covering most of the points he'd made that day. It was a solid, well-thought-out list, and when, four months later, Congress enacted the Cotton Futures Act, many of the amendments on Callaway's list appeared at the heart of that act. They continue to be part of the current version of the law today, a century later.

~

The Cotton Futures Act was one of the last prewar measures that Congress passed. Between the time that Callaway testified in April 1914 and the enactment of the law the following August, he witnessed from within Europe the coming of an Armageddon. The United States would remain at least technically neutral for two and a half more years, but it was already feeling the war's economic effects when the Cotton Futures Act came into force.

The Great War, as it was called for a time, was the world's first full-scale industrial conflict of arms. Since the year of Callaway's birth, railroad mileage in both Europe and America had grown prodigiously, and with technology advancing at a previously unheard-of rate, industrial as well as agricultural output had increased tremendously. So, too, had the killing power of weapons. All of these things taken together meant that as the warring states mobilized for the conflict, they were able to gather, train, feed, and equip armies of unprecedented size; transport them to vast battlefields at speeds that would have been unbelievable just a century earlier; and then slaughter them almost as fast, seemingly, as they could arrive.

The defensive trench networks that sprang up in France and Belgium after Germany's invasion were, if not quite impregnable, still extraordinarily stubborn against attack. As millions of young men spent their blood in fruitless efforts to break through the enemy lines, their governments had no choice but to raise and equip more and more divisions to follow the previous ones into the maw of the western front. No one had expected that a war could chew up men and resources on such a gigantic, monstrous scale. Militarily it was a war to lay waste to countrysides and depopulate entire villages. Politically it was a war to shatter empires and knock crowns from emperors' heads. But more than this, it was a war to hamstring industries, topple economies, and bankrupt the world's richest nations.

No one had foreseen how fast the war could develop. In more recent conflicts, the financial markets could sense what was coming weeks or even months in advance and make preparations. But just as the Great War's onset took Callaway and his party by surprise—the sudden switch from peace to war during a single week in July caught the travelers scattered across Europe—so, too, were the markets on the Continent, in London, and in New York taken unaware. Even as the Callaway group fought to escape the trap that Europe had become, financial exchanges everywhere closed their doors, and an economic crisis loomed.

By the time Callaway got back to America on August 12, the cotton market was already in serious trouble, even though the war was scarcely two weeks old. In 1913 the United States exported 60 percent of its cotton crop to Europe, with a quarter of that going to Germany. In August 1913 alone, American cotton exports had amounted to a quarter of a million bales. In August 1914

Rear View of Hillside Cotton Mills, La Grange, Ga.

Established in 1915, Hillside Cotton Mill contained a variety of machinery as well as a dye house, which made possible an array of colored products.

that figure was down by 90 percent. In September 1914 the United States exported no cotton—not a single bale—to France, Belgium, Russia, Germany, or Austria, even though the previous September those countries had taken nearly a half million bales. To make matters worse, 1914 was a bumper year for cotton growers; in fact it eclipsed every previous record. The resulting raw cotton glut seemed to spell catastrophe. From the first of August to the end of December, cotton prices fell by nearly 50 percent, well below estimated production costs.

Throughout the cotton-growing South, conferences immediately convened to try to deal with the crisis, but to little effect. In the final days of August, Georgia Governor John M. Slaton announced such a conference to take place in Atlanta in early September, naming Callaway as a delegate. The conference took place on Thursday, September 3, in the Georgia Senate chamber with a hundred farmers and business leaders in attendance. At this and other conferences, heated debates often took place; farmers were urged to cut back production. But nothing could be done to stem the collapsing prices.

As soon as he returned from Europe, Callaway began advocating a policy that had been on the Populist agenda a generation earlier—a subtreasury system that provided government-backed monetary support for farmers when prices were low. "Let Bill Jones take his one bale of cotton to the warehouse and get a receipt for it," he explained.

Take the receipt to the small state bank and that bank can loan him a maximum of say 6 cents per pound. The state bank in turn can take the receipt to the national bank and get the money on it, and the secretary says that receipt, having been properly issued and authenticated, will be taken by the national bank for emergency currency. The matter of Jones selling his bale of cotton later is mere business detail that easily can be taken care of.

At the same time, Callaway was working on damage control within his own organization and community. "By all means," he was heard to say to friends, "let's keep our heads." The most pressing concern was the plight of the cotton farmers, and Callaway looked to that first. In September he convinced the boards of every mill in his organization to adopt similar resolutions that ran as follows, with the mill's name to be filled in:

WHEREAS, the interests of all of our people are identical and anything that works a hardship upon the farmers affects all other business and private interests, and the present situation calls for cooperation between all interests;

Be it therefore resolved, that the management of the _____ is hereby instructed and authorized to give preference in the purchase of such cotton as this company can use to the producers of the surrounding section, buying cotton to the extent of our resources and at as liberal prices as possible considering the prices they are able to obtain for our manufactured product.

So much for the farmers. The next problem was the mills themselves, since the war-spawned depression had hit finished goods as well as agriculture. The final months of 1914 saw American steel production fall to 50 percent of capacity; American railroad construction dropped to the lowest level since Appomattox. In the large industrial cities unemployment rates hit double digits. Quite simply the United States had never experienced, or even imagined, a scenario in which all of the other great world powers became insolvent simultaneously, but that is effectively what happened because of the British blockade of Germany and the closing of the European financial markets.

But Callaway saw opportunity in the chaos, for several reasons. The depression meant decreased construction and machinery costs, and while the machinery would last, the depression couldn't—not for long anyway. On the one hand, Callaway hoped that President Wilson had enough status and influence to negotiate a cease-fire among the warring states. In that case, with luck, the economy would bounce back quickly. On the other hand, if the war did continue, the warring states would need supplies as their stockpiles dwindled and their own productivity reached its limits, and neutral countries, as sources of food and war material for the combatants, would thus benefit economically. Either way, Callaway figured, his window of opportunity for cheap mill construction wouldn't be open for long.

Above all, Kitchener's injunction still rang in his ears. "I believe it will be a long and costly war at best," he'd told Callaway in London, "taking an enormous toll of human lives but I also believe the Allies will win. At any rate, enormous amounts of materials of all kinds will be needed, so I would advise that you go home and start running the mills you have overtime and start new ones if you can as a means of helping toward winning the war."

Cotton was crucial to modern industrial war, and Callaway knew it. The fiber was used for everything from uniforms to hospital sheets to tires to explosives. So Callaway took a risk. Armed with the million dollars of credit he'd gotten from Elkan Naumburg when he'd arrived in New York from England, in October he announced the formation of a new mill, planned to be the largest one yet in the Callaway organization, with a million dollars in capitalization and twenty thousand spindles. It would be the last, and most ambitious, mill that Callaway would personally commission.

By early December Callaway had the Truitts, Roy Dallis, Ab Perry, and a large number of other investors on board, and Hillside Cotton Mills was formally chartered. The following year it went into operation, boasting a dye house and cotton waste utilization, which Callaway had been in Europe studying as the storm of the Great War broke.

As it turned out the timing couldn't have been better. It was simply perfect. By the end of 1914, it had grown clear that the war wasn't likely to end any time soon, and that it would be terribly expensive. As 1915 opened, European buyers thus began placing huge orders in America, first for wheat, then for steel and munitions, and finally for every sort of war materiel. Europe's wheat growers were fighting in the trenches and the crop was languishing; meanwhile, in March, Kitchener told the House of Lords that as far as army demands for munitions went, "every English factory was working to its utmost power, that the orders already given were far in excess of the capacity to produce, and that deliveries of the reduced amounts were enormously in arrear." In short, the war was turning out exactly as the earl had predicted and as Callaway had anticipated.

America, as the only great power not at war, was the natural supplier to the Allies, who controlled the Atlantic and blockaded

Germany. As Allied orders with American firms grew, gold poured into the United States, and eventually both Britain and France turned to borrowing from American lenders. Few people—although Callaway was one of them—had foreseen the amazing boom, the greatest in American history up to this point, but they were quick to take advantage of it. Raw cotton as well as textiles were major beneficiaries. The German cotton trade had evaporated, although neutral Holland and Scandinavia increased their buying, almost certainly for transshipment to Germany. American mills such as Callaway's bought up the rest of the resulting surplus, since the war had opened up many new opportunities for them. First was the ravenous Allies' demands for finished cotton goods. Next came the use of cotton in the explosives industry, close to a million bales' worth a year by 1917. Then there were markets that Europe could no longer supply; by 1916 a single company could easily find itself shipping goods to a dozen markets that had never bought American textiles before. Finally, there was domestic textile consumption. The Allied gold flowing into America had greatly enriched its economy and stimulated consumer demand for goods at home. Callaway's timing had been perfect indeed.

But not everything about the war was similarly perfect. The Allied demands and other economic dislocations created production issues, even as the boll weevil, a more keenly felt problem in wartime, continued to munch its way through the South. Railroad shipment patterns accelerated and changed. Hillside, in particular, with its plans to install dyeing equipment, faced a special problem: Germany had the world's most advanced chemical industry, and its supply of aniline dyes was now completely cut off from America by the British blockade. While the basic outlook was good, there were still many war-related problems to keep Callaway busy.

There were international changes as well. The Great War was a time of huge flux; it was easily the worst upheaval of the twentieth century, the worst since the French Revolution. Had it been fought differently, or not fought at all, the world would likely have never seen the rise of Adolf Hitler, thus avoiding a second and even more destructive world war; it may never have witnessed the coming of the Soviet Union and the resulting Cold War, or the nuclear arms race. Even by 1916 it was clear that the conflict had caused New York to displace London—permanently, as it turned out—as the financial capital of the world, setting America on the road to international preeminence.

In parallel with these changes came personal ones for Callaway. His stepmother, Mary Ely Callaway, died in March 1915. The following year his nephew Cary, Howard Callaway's son, died in an elevator accident. A brighter change came though, when twenty-year-old Cason Callaway became the manager of a subsidiary of the new Hillside plant known as Valley Waste Mills. It was one of the early signs of the changing of the guard.

But Callaway had no intention of stepping down any time soon. On the contrary, he was now entering one of the most celebrated periods of his life.

One surprising turnabout took place in 1915, when the Atlanta & West Point named Callaway, of all people, as its representative in an arbitration proceeding regarding a property tax assessment. This was a mark of high esteem given the past that it had with Callaway, as well as the fact that only recently he'd been critical of its parent, the Louisville & Nashville, during the Western & Atlantic investigation. The groundwork for the entente had been laid the year before, when issues between LaGrange and the Atlanta, Birmingham & Atlantic Railroad came to a head. The Atlanta, Birmingham & Atlantic, according to its erstwhile supporters (including Callaway),

Valley Waste Mills,
La Grange, Ga.

Valley Waste Mill was started in 1917 and used waste from other mills to create new textile products.

had failed to live up to its obligations to the community. As a result, the civic leaders who'd brought the new road to La-Grange now advised citizens who'd granted it rights-of-way to ask for those rights back. For his part, Callaway told all of his mills and other businesses to resume shipment on the Atlanta & West Point. He wasn't one to hold a grudge; the presence of two roads meant—as he'd intended all along—competition and thus lower prices. If the Atlanta & West Point could provide a better deal than the Atlanta, Birmingham & Atlantic, so be it. The decision made up for many years of strife, as evidenced by the Atlanta & West Point's choice of Callaway as an arbitrator in 1915.

On the national stage, Callaway was once again summoned to Congress in January 1916. This time he was called to appear before the House Committee on Ways and Means, one of the most important committees on Capitol Hill. The issue was one of dyestuffs.

The German dye industry, like its chemical industry in general, was the best in the world in 1914, and America was heavily dependent on it. When war broke out, Germany quit selling to the Allies, and for their part, the British, with their blockade, made sure that it couldn't sell to neutrals either. This threw the American dye market into a supply crisis. By 1916 Congress was considering protective tariffs on the few dye components that businesses could find from other sources in an attempt to jump-start a domestic dyestuff industry. Callaway, as a maker of textiles that needed dyeing, was a natural witness.

By this time he was completely at ease with testifying, and the performance he gave was a folksy, plain *tour de force*, respectful but by no means deferential. It was the sort of performance to lead Nicholas Longworth, the Ohio representative who would later become Speaker of the House, to declare that Call-

away was one of the two most effective witnesses ever to appear before Congress, at least according to Hatton Lovejoy's account of the proceeding. Almost from the beginning Callaway had the committee members eating out of his hand.

"I come with an entirely different idea from these gentlemen here," he began, referring to his fellow witnesses. "They come begging for something, and I come to tell you the fix we are in, and as we have got you all hired to fix it, we ask you to do it." That statement established the tone for his entire testimony. The representatives before him weren't his masters but his and his fellow citizens' employees. The amazing thing is how the congressmen seemed not to resent his approach; in fact they clearly enjoyed Callaway's presentation.

The problem, from Callaway's point of view, was not any modest dyeing that he might want to do himself. Hillside, which would soon have a dyeing operation, had only just come online the previous month. Instead, Callaway's concern lay with his customers, who couldn't buy more textiles from him until they'd managed to dye the goods they'd already bought, and that simply wasn't happening.

"This is a very large business," Callaway told the committee.

I think we work more labor than all the dyeing plants—manufacturing and jobbing dyeing plants—in the United States; more people are dependent upon our work for their labor. And unless we can get our goods dyed—that is, unless the people who buy them from us can get dyestuffs—it is going to handicap us and hinder us, and instead of working overtime and full time and things like that, we will have to work short time, and it will be hard for us, especially right now, when it looks like probably the only thing this war was sent for was to give America the chance to get a hundred years forward in two or three years.

The room laughed at that last part, but it was a knowing laugh. Everyone there knew what the war was doing for the American economy in general.

Callaway pressed on, noting that the bottleneck in dyeing was bad for every upstream link in the cotton industry, all the way back to the farmer in his field. "It is a fact that we get more gold from our cotton crop, and have done it for years, than from any other crop we have got," he told the committee, "and it is a fact that our cotton farmers need all the American spindles to run that can run. And we want you all to get the dyestuffs here for these plants up North. We don't care how you do it. We haven't any suggestions. We want it done in a business way."

In contrast to his testimonies of 1904 and 1914, Callaway for the most part avoided technical discussion, limiting himself to hard-hitting generalities. But he kept his audience friendly by judicious humor, such as when he decried partisan squabbling. "I think well of all you gentlemen," he remarked. "I am a born American. Personally I am a Democrat, because my father was, and because all first-class folks in my country are." The witticism met with not only laughter but applause. "But I have a great many friends among the Republicans, just as fine as I ever saw. I have a great

respect for our whole Congress here. I think we have the greatest country in the world. And I really don't appreciate their sitting here and fiddling while Rome burns." Again, remarkably, came applause and laughter.

Here Callaway offered an interesting insight on his own years in office as he instructed the congressmen in their duty, including a variation on one of his favorite sayings:

If I criticize anybody I will criticize my folks most, because the most of you are my folks. There is so much good in the worst of you all, and so much bad in the best of you, that it scarcely behooves any of us to criticize you. I got a little into politics once myself, and I quit because I found out that after I had been in there a year or two I kept my ear to the ground and wanted to do what folks wanted done whether it was right or not.

Here Callaway was clearly enjoining Congress to do the right thing, by which he meant the enactment of a generally protective tariff that nevertheless took account of consumers' needs. He continued,

I am shipping goods to ports I never heard of before, and I charge them about 2 cents over the market. I do that just in order to show you that I want to protect our home trade. We have a great opportunity, if we all pull together, and I think we ought to get rid of the present political parties and have an amalgamated party for the next two or three years. We can declare the truce off just as soon as we get all the business done.

Despite all the well-accepted humor, Callaway was getting his point across. The most important thing, he noted, was to take advantage of this war that America hadn't caused and couldn't stop, a war that was enriching the country almost beyond belief. "We have got all the money there is," he proclaimed. "It is a fact. The war has been going on for a year and a half, and if we don't get out of business pretty soon we will get rich because we can not help it." Everyone loved that comment. But America, warned Callaway, and Congress, too, would have to move fast. Speed was essential. "Then the war will be over. Germany will have recovered and have built up her trade again." That was the thing to remember. "Let us quit all this foolishness; let us get down and do what is right."

At this point a representative from Connecticut raised a question. "As a great big manufacturer of cotton goods—"

"Not me," broke in Callaway. "I am a laboring man; I work for 12 hours every day." For him the distinction was huge.

"—do you prefer for two or three years to take the chances on American competition or trust to a foreign monopoly?"

"My dear sir," answered Callaway, "I am for America first on everything. I would rather pay a little more the balance of my life and have it here where we can get it." That drew another round of applause. It neatly summed up Callaway's position. America had to move quickly if it were to develop a domestic dyestuff industry, and that meant a protective tariff that would make domestic producers competitive with foreign sources. To emphasize the point, Callaway continued with one of his favorite anecdotes—the one about the hog in the trough. Normally he used the tale to warn against greed. But this was the time, he told the committee, to summon the hogs. If anything, he advised, Congress should err in the direction of too much protection. "If you will give them too much," he prophesied, "there are so blamed many who will go in there that they will produce more dyestuffs than we can use. We will sit on the fence and see them cut each others' throats." That would ensure the rise of a solid domestic dyestuff industry. "Germany can sink, and then it does not matter be-

cause we will be making 110 per cent more than we need."

Once again Congress took Callaway's advice. In September 1916 it passed a revenue act that put tariffs on coal tar products, dyes, and dyestuffs that would run for ten years, tapering off after the first five. The measure was clearly designed to protect domestic producers for a long enough time to establish themselves.

Three months after Callaway's dyestuff testimony, his public service took another step forward. At the April 1916 meeting of the American Cotton Manufacturers Association in Atlanta, he was unanimously elected as chairman of the organization's board of governors.

The occasion was quite something. North Carolina textile mill architect and engineer Stuart W. Cramer, overseeing the nominating process, made a point of pulling Callaway's leg. "For chairman of the board of governors," he announced, "your committee will nominate a man who has worked so hard for the place, Mr. Fuller E. Callaway." Everyone laughed; Callaway's work ethic was well-known. The nomination was seconded and the election duly took place, and Callaway then handed Cramer a silver dollar.

"Gentlemen," ad-libbed Cramer, "I am presented with a medal from Mr. Callaway, so you will understand what I said about his working so hard for the office, and that he was prepared." Again the room filled with laughter.

Callaway kept the joke going as he addressed the group. "I want to say about the little gift that has been presented the chairman, that it's not silver but is aluminum," he quipped. Then he poked some fun at politicians, displaying the same attitude that he'd shown in the recent congressional hearings. "Mr. President, and gentlemen, I appreciate the honor you have bestowed upon me, and since your chairman states I have worked so hard to get the place, then like all people elected I will now quit work. That, it seems,

Callaway was elected president of the American Cotton Manufacturers Association in 1917. That same year he met President Wilson and pledged the full support of the cotton industry in the war effort.

is the habit of some people, to work until they are elected and then cease working."

He continued on, making predictions about the textile market in the short run and warning what could be expected when the war ended. The short term was fine, but there was a long-term danger. "America is about the only country left to supply the world with manufactured textiles," he pointed out. "We will have to supply South America, Asia, and Africa. The longer the war lasts the scarcer goods will get, and it is always true that when goods get scarce and there are three buyers for two sellers, goods will sell higher. My suggestion is that on account of this, and the increased cost, that in making your quotations it would be a good idea to add about 1 cent to 2 cents a pound to take care of this for the next six or eight months."

That was the good news. Now for the caution. "Bear in mind the gulch we are coming to, due to a flood of cheap European goods," he warned.

I believe that after the war is over our business will probably for six months or a year be fair, but after that time look out for the gulch, for on account of the high cost of manufacturing and the large volume of goods we are making here, when Europe gets to making goods you are going to have cotton going up and goods going down, and you better add 1 cent or 2 cents for that. Get all you can, friends, for your goods now while the selling is good. Put it in a savings bank and don't let your board of directors know you have it, or they will declare a war dividend. As long as the war lasts you will get it, but if you don't put it in the bank you will "bust" when peace comes. Save it and when the crush comes, caused by the flood of cheap goods from Europe, you will be prepared to stand it. Everybody is making money now and you will need it after the war.

There is no doubt but that after the war is over and the people in Europe begin to start their factories up there will be a great demand for cotton. Now "make hay while the sun shines," for if you don't, then later on you won't stand any more show than a snowball in the fireplace.

Most of these things Callaway correctly foresaw. But some things he perhaps didn't expect. On May 23, 1917, at the annual meeting in Washington, he was elected president of the association—the first president from Georgia. That same day he and other association officials traveled to the White House, for something else had recently come to pass to draw President Wilson's attention to the textile men. The previous month the United States had declared war on Germany.

Several things had pushed the country from neutrality, pro-Allied though it was, into active hostility. The very fact of Allied indebtedness to American banks and businesses meant that America now had an economic stake in an Allied victory. Should Germany win, the United States might never get its money back from Britain and France. Germany had also grown more belligerent at sea, torpedoing American merchant ships in early 1917, knowing this would lead to war, but figuring that by attacking American vessels it could interdict the massive flow of American goods to Britain and France and strangle the Allied war effort before America could mobilize.

All of this meant that the frantic production of the textile and other industries in 1915 and 1916 was only prelude. As chairman, and now president, of the American Cotton Manufacturers Association, Callaway was in a key position to reckon with problems of supply, demand, and finance.

President Wilson sensed the nature of modern armed conflict. "The men who remain to till the soil and man the factories are no less a part of the army that is in France than the men beneath the battle flags," he declared a few days after meeting with the textile men. "It must be so with us. It is not an army that we must shape and train for war; it is a nation." This was no doubt why he met with the Callaway group.

At 2:00 p.m. on May 23, 1917, the association officials, headed by Callaway, gathered in the East Room of the White House, and Wilson, flanked by a military aide, entered. "Mr. President," said Callaway when introduced to him, "we cotton manufacturers want to offer you everything we've got." Wilson thanked him cordially.

War brought many challenges to Callaway and his family, some business-related, others personal. The Allies' voracious consumption of American products continued in 1917, but now that the United

States had entered the war, it, too, would need massive amounts of supplies. At the same time, the draft announced in May took one man in every twenty out of productive jobs for military service. All this meant both opportunity and adjustments for the mills.

The opportunities were big ones. Some civilian markets evaporated, such as the one for cotton lace, but compared to war needs, that wasn't important. Before the end of 1917, Secretary of War Newton D. Baker noted that the government had already bought 17 million blankets, 33 million yards of flannel shirting, 50 million yards of melton cloth, and more than 125 million yards of duck. The cotton crop of 1917 wasn't as large as in some recent years, but the rise in demand meant that the crop fetched the highest aggregate price in American history, good in general for the cotton regions but hard on the mills.

To keep up production as the draft went into effect, Callaway expanded his efforts, which predated the war, to recruit labor to LaGrange, especially from Appalachia. Around 1915, in conjunction with the Hillside Mill project, he built a hotel for single women, called the Martha Washington Inn, which he

As men were called to military service abroad, the Martha Washington Inn provided housing to the increasing number of women working in the mills.

Cotton Mills Employees' Garden, La Grange, Ga.

Garden plots in front of a LaGrange mill provided space for their employees and families to grow vegetables. The postcard description reads "one of the Boys and Girls Gardens...."

was happy to run at a loss since it helped keep his labor supply ample. As young men went into the armed forces, Callaway also focused on making the best use of men who weren't fit enough for the draft. To help draw them to LaGrange, he built a men's counterpart to the Martha Washington, which he named the Benjamin Franklin Inn. He also took the progressive step of hiring black workers and putting them to work in the picker rooms.

Food was a related problem. Textile production was important, but mill operatives and their families had to eat, and farmers also were subject to conscription. To see to this problem, in May 1917 Callaway bought a million sweet potato slips to supply to anyone who wanted them. He even offered premiums for the best bushel and best acre of sweet potatoes to encourage competition and improve production.

Even before America declared war, Callaway was confronting the food problem. One of his ideas was to attack the boll weevil obliquely by building up a meat industry in Georgia. He proposed to devote some of the less fertile cotton lands to the production of a mixture of corn and velvet beans. The entire crop—stalks, vines, and all—could be ground up to feed cattle and hogs, while the best land could be used to grow "early maturing varieties" of cotton of the sort he'd

sent to Kitchener, "which will make cotton before the time of year when the boll weevil gets in his deadly work; using the poorer lands for forage crops and legumes which will furnish the feed and build up the land at the same time."

Farmers and mill operatives weren't the only ones to go into the military. After America entered the war, Cason Callaway, along with Fuller's nephew Enoch, joined the navy. The armed services, like the rest of the national government, needed a lot of managerial capability during their wartime expansion, and Cason was both trained and experienced as a manager. The navy realized this and quickly put him to work where he could do the most good. Reporting to Washington, Ensign Callaway was assigned to the navy's Bureau of Supplies and Accounts. Working under Commander John M. Hancock within the bureau's Purchase Division, which now boasted fourteen times the number of personnel it had before the war, Callaway soon became chief of the division's Cotton Section.

As for Enoch, he followed in his father's footsteps. Studying medicine at Tulane, he'd graduated in 1916. In early 1918 he joined the USS *Yacona*, a former yacht refitted as an armed patrol vessel, which operated out of New York and Boston for much of the war.

The *Yacona* was in New York once when Fuller was in town on business. He was riding in a car with a friend when he spotted the vessel. "There's my nephew's ship," he remarked. "I would like to get him to come in and have supper with us."

"You can't do that," his friend observed.

"I don't see why not," Callaway answered. "I wonder if there is a message center around here."

"Yes, sir," the chauffeur spoke up. "I know where the navy message center is."

"Well, take me down there," Callaway directed.

Arriving at the message center, Callaway strode in and found a young ensign on duty. "Give me a message blank, mister," he snapped with authority.

The ensign promptly handed him a message blank. Callaway wrote out an official-sounding message to Enoch, telling him when and where the chauffeur would collect him, and signed his name. "Get this right off, mister," he ordered the ensign, who hastily complied.

Shortly thereafter Lieutenant Commander John W. Wilcox Jr., the *Yacona*'s commanding officer, summoned Enoch. "You've got orders to report ashore," he told the young medical officer.

Enoch looked at the message slip. "Hell, that's not any orders," he exclaimed. "That's my uncle!"

"Bud," Wilcox told him, "that's orders when it comes in from the message center. If I send you ashore and the man who sent that message has no authority, I won't get in any trouble about it. But if that is an admiral and I don't send you ashore, I will really be in trouble. You are going to be on that pier." And so he was.

Fuller himself certainly was not in the navy. But he did play important roles in industrial mobilization beyond that of merchant and mill owner, some of them official, some not.

"Fuller E. Callaway has enlisted," proclaimed a bankers' circular in July 1917.

He has no medals on his chest or epaulets on his shoulders, but he is a major-general in the industrial army which Uncle Sam is mobilizing. He spent practically the whole month of June in Washington (without mileage or per diem) and his plans were approved and are now in execution. He has sent out gangs of engineers to prospect the land between Dahlonega, Georgia, and Birmingham, Ala-

Cason joined the navy in 1917 and became a lieutenant (Junior Grade) in the navy's Supply Corps.

bama, for pyrite. Already one mine has been located that he believes will turn out 100,000 tons of pyrite a year.

Pyrite, also known as fool's gold, is a major source of sulfuric acid, which in turn has many applications, including explosives and—of special interest to Callaway—fertilizer. Most of America's pyrite supply had come from Europe. Now, with the U-boat campaign targeting American shipping, new sources were needed, and Frank Lane, still secretary of the interior, entreated the business community to seek them out. In particular he asked Callaway to help find and develop mines in Georgia and Alabama.

For the next two years, in addition to all of the other things he was working on, Callaway devoted a lot of his resources to pyrite. Coordinating with Lane, the United States Geological Survey, the United States Bureau of Mines, mining companies in Georgia, and many other individuals and companies, he got prospectors on the scene and helped get new mines going

Fuller's nephew Enoch served aboard the USS *Yacona* during the First World War.

as they located pyrite deposits. He also took a hand in ongoing management. He made results a priority. As the mines swung into production, he encouraged and boasted of pooling arrangements among the mines that would normally be frowned upon by the law. Under these arrangements one mine could cover another's orders in the event of underproduction, or even lend workers to other mines when needed. When the draft took away skilled laborers, Callaway wrote everyone from generals of training camps to Secretary Lane to get them back. As time passed he branched out into manganese, a key component of steel production. He also corresponded with Hoke Smith about the need for postwar tariff protection of the new pyrite industry. Before long Lane was holding up Callaway as a shining example of pyrite development.

Then there was the matter of cotton duck production. Some of the most important military uses of duck included many types of hoses (such as steam hoses and airbrake hoses), engine belts, and Pullman car diaphragms, to name a few. Before long the War Industries Board, a new federal agency designed to mobilize as well as maximize industrial output, was urging Callaway to produce as much duck as possible, to the tune of millions of pounds a week. "All of our mills have been instructed to run all looms on Government work and airbrake hose duck day and night," Callaway informed his War Industries Board contact, "and not to permit the scarcity of labor supply to interfere with duck production which is needed for oil mining, munitions factories, food products, etc." But Callaway was way ahead of the government.

Within a month or two of America's entry into the war, he'd already devised a plan to install a duck loom at the federal prison in Atlanta. This would increase duck production while simultaneously teaching the prisoners—many of them Appalachian moonshiners—a useful trade that could replace their illegal liquor production once they'd served out their terms. The government hastily approved the idea.

The strain on Callaway had to have been enormous. In December 1917, he caught a cold, which he made worse by continuing to work. By mid-January he was in such poor shape that his doctor ordered him to stop working completely. By the end of the month he'd largely recovered, but his physician insisted that he was still in need of extensive recuperation. On February 1, he and Ida departed for a month-long trip to California and other spots in the West, with his office referring only the most critically important matters to him during the break.

By spring 1918, with the American army preparing for deployment to France, Callaway was back in harness. In early May he attended the annual meeting of the American Cotton Manufacturers Association, giving a major speech as the outgoing president. The country's military effort was beginning to peak as the American Expeditionary Force began to arrive in Europe, and the meeting, as well as Callaway's remarks, was heavily concerned with the war.

"I am a mighty poor speaker, as you will discover before I get through," began Callaway, addressing an overflowing room at New York's celebrated Biltmore Hotel, "so I am not going to try and make a speech; I am just going to talk to you as man to man, and as brothers and fellows in a common cause, and that cause the one upon which our highest hopes and endeavors must be centered, since everything we hold dear is involved in the outcome of the mighty conflict now raging in Europe."

Callaway had clearly caught the spirit of wartime patriotism, seeing the conflict, as did President Wilson, as a crusade for civilization. "That we must finish this thing which the German warlords have started is apparent to all who have given any thought to the matter, I am sure," he continued. "That it must be settled right, is the determination of every true American, I am equally sure. How, then, may the cotton manufacturing industry most effectively do its part for the national defense, becomes the subject in which we are most interested."

But Callaway was aware that such enthusiasm could go too far, and he warned the convention of the danger, which he termed "patrioteering." "Selfish interests, intent only upon preserving their particular businesses, are pandering to our natural love of ease and luxury by advancing the wildest sort of panaceas for winning the war," he pointed out, promoting sales of all sorts of extravagancies by claiming that such purchases would somehow help the war effort. This, he declared, flew in the face of what Wilson and his officials were telling the country. "As I see it," announced Callaway, "the time has come for casting aside all poses and pretenses. It is not a matter of patriotism at all but one of self-preservation." The survival of civilization hung in the balance, he warned, and selfishness simply wasn't acceptable.

To achieve this, Callaway proposed a few basic ideas:

First of all, I would say that each unit of our industry must practice the virtue of self-reliance, anticipating and meeting its problems as far as possible, without burdening the Government as to finances, labor or fuel supply, or in any other way. Instead of asking help we must be prepared to give it. The Government has more than it can do with the primary problems of placing men on the firing line and getting equipment and supplies to them. It is up to us, therefore, to fill the gaps made in our labor forces through the operations of the draft and the call for skilled workers on ships and other things most vitally needed; to anticipate our needs as to fuel and other supplies, and to be ready at all times to turn our plants to the production of goods needed by the Government.

Key to this, continued Callaway, was the effective use of labor. Mill owners had to begin making use of older men and single women as well as integrating black workers, routinely putting on night shifts, and making "two blades of grass grow where one grew before." But that wasn't enough. "A factor of great importance in the handling of labor is to keep the workers and their families contented," he advised. "This means not only paying good wages, but maintaining the best living conditions possible." As an example, he then went into great detail describing how things worked in LaGrange, discussing housing; the Benjamin Franklin and Martha Washington Inns; the schools, community playgrounds, and greenhouses; and many other amenities. "I want to emphasize that all work of this nature must be in addition to paying good wages," he told his audience. "The employer who attempts to hold his workers with smaller wages in consideration of improvements or advantages in his mill will certainly fail." In fact, noted Callaway, his mills went beyond mere good wages and embraced profit sharing, which provided his operatives with "substantial bonuses" and contributed to overall satisfaction.

That brought him to a final point. "We should stop the practice of enticing labor away from each other," he cautioned. "This has gotten so bad that some families stay on the road about one-third of the time. It is an economic waste, hurtful alike to the worker and to the industry." In short, he observed, it was an inefficient use of resources. And he didn't need to tell his audience how dangerous that could be during total war.

Callaway's speech was met with great applause. By now he was more than a national textile figure; he was recognized as running a model operation.

The national government also recognized it. Frank Lane had official plans for Callaway by this time. In 1916, as war clouds began to loom over the United States, Congress had created the Council of National Defense, a body made up of several cabinet officers (Lane among them) with the mission of coordinating agricultural, industrial, and transportation resources in the event America was drawn into the conflict. Its very existence foreshadowed not only Wilson's statement about shaping a nation for war but also the whole of twentieth-century industrialized warfare. August 1918 saw the creation of a unit within the council called the Field Division, headed by Lane. This branch of the council was to coordinate the work of state, county, and municipal councils of defense that were small-scale counterparts to the national council. The Field Division also incorporated the national council's women's committees, which until then had been coordinating female contributions to state and local preparedness. As the draft removed men from the workforce, women played an increasingly vital role in the domestic war effort.

In September 1918 the council announced a governing board for the Field Division consisting of a dozen members in addition to Lane himself. Callaway was one of the twelve, and the only one who wasn't identified by a title or description on the official list. While all of the others had their businesses or institutional affiliations appended to their names, the well-known Georgian was noted simply as "Fuller Callaway, La Grange, Georgia." That was apparently enough.

Just as "La Grange" here appeared as two words, something about Callaway's own name invited frequent misspelling, especially in official records. His last name often appears as Calloway, as it had in the Supreme Court case against the Louisville & Nashville Railroad. Likewise with his middle initial. The *New York Times*, identifying him as Fuller R. Callaway when reporting on his escape from Europe in 1914, was one of several publications to make that mistake. Perhaps, especially to non-Southern ears, Callaway's enunciation of "Earle" was sometimes heard as a single "R."

Another interesting name to appear on the list of the Field Division's governing board was Miss Ida M. Tarbell, formerly of the women's committee. America's first major female journalist, an investigative reporter of the type known in the Progressive Era as muckrakers

Callaway met Ida Tarbell during his service on the Council of National Defense and at the First Industrial Conference. In 1920 Tarbell wrote an article about Callaway titled "Making American Citizens and Running Cotton Mills to Pay the Expenses," which appeared in *Red Cross Magazine*.

(although she herself disliked the term), Tarbell had achieved fame with her articles and 1904 book exposing the ruthless tactics of John D. Rockefeller's Standard Oil trust. Tarbell and Callaway likely first met while serving together on the governing board, and their paths would cross again, more than once.

The Parade of Americans was held in LaGrange on April 6, 1918 to encourage citizens to support the war effort by buying war bonds. Mrs. Ely Callaway is on the Red Cross float representing a Liberty ship.

The war couldn't last forever. At some point, if only for the grim reason that the combatants would run out of soldiers and money, it would have to end. Never had the world experienced such concentrated, massive expense in either human or economic terms. Russia, crippled by losses and revolution, had bowed out in late 1917, concluding a separate peace with the Central Powers early the following year. In the spring of 1918 the Germans, moving their freed-up eastern divisions to France, launched a major last-ditch offensive on the Western Front that strained the weakened British and French to the breaking point. But by summer, American soldiers were beginning to flood into France, countering the German buildup and slowly tipping the balance in favor of the Allies. By September it was the Allies, along with the United States (formally an Associated Power, not an Ally) who were moving to the offensive, forcing the Germans back after more than three years of static trench warfare. The German offensive of the previous spring had been the last throw of the dice; Germany had few resources left to combat the Allied surge of the late summer and autumn. In the massive Hundred Days' offensive, the American Expeditionary Force, breaking the enemy trenches and hurling the Germans back, expended more ammunition than the entire Union Army had from 1861 to 1865.

In November, with German commander Erich Ludendorff exploring the possibility of a cease-fire, came news from home: revolution was sweeping through Germany. Beginning with sailors and spreading rapidly among German workers, the revolution showed that the German population was sick of the war. Within two weeks of the first mutinies, Kaiser Wilhelm II abdicated. As Germany crumbled at home, the army's leaders had no choice but to accept the Allies' terms. The armistice went into effect at 11:00 a.m. on November 11: the eleventh hour of the eleventh day of the eleventh month. Abruptly, almost unexpectedly, the war was over. The world had forever changed.

As early as 1916 Callaway had warned that once the war ended, the economic dislocations could be as great or greater than when it began. The clock was now ticking toward the postwar depression he'd foretold, but first there was a postwar boom. There were many reasons for this boom, but the most important were Washington's continued massive deficit spending and the Allies' ongoing purchases of American goods, although as 1918 became 1919 the purchases quickly shifted from war materiel to agricultural products and civilian goods. Lack of food, clothing, and coal in Europe meant that American exports remained high for a time.

As 1919 wore on and the economy began to adjust to peacetime, the inevitable crash approached. Deficit spending slowed and then stopped, just as Europe's erstwhile soldiers began to produce their first postwar crop. Banks nationwide had lent as much as the new Federal Reserve System allowed, and they could inject no more money into the American economy. By early 1920 the depression had come in earnest, and it would linger for two years.

A major potential problem, one that had interested the Progressives even before the war, was the relationship between labor and capital. With millions of men returning to the factory from the armed forces—or rather hoping to return—and other countless millions having spent their labor to further the war effort, the issue needed addressing. President Wilson did so by calling for what he termed the First Industrial Conference, summoning it to meet in Washington in October 1919. Representatives of many interests attended, ranging from farmers' organizations to labor unions to bankers' associations, railroads, and chambers of commerce. Many of the most illustrious names of the day appear in the conference's records. Samuel Gompers attended as a representative of the American Federation of Labor; Callaway's acquaintance Ida Tarbell was on hand as a representative of women. Nearly two dozen members of the conference were listed as representatives of the public. Among them were the great financier Bernard Baruch; Charles Eliot, former president of Harvard and one of the country's most renowned educators; and Fuller E. Callaway.

For Callaway it was to be a summing-up, on the national stage, of his entire approach,

not only to business, but also to life. The conference, meeting in the stately Pan American Building, lasted for more than two weeks, and he played an active role. On the fourth day—Thursday, October 9—he introduced a simple resolution that in large measure encapsulated his entire life's outlook: "Resolved, That individual initiative and enterprise should be encouraged." The General Committee recommended its adoption. But Callaway's highest-profile contribution to the conference was a major speech he made a few minutes after introducing the resolution.

The subject under discussion was how to propagate good relations between labor and management, with an eye to learning lessons from industries in which the two groups got along well. Specifically, Frank Lane, acting as chairman of the conference, was interested in "investigating those methods which have been employed in various industries of the country where peace and harmony have prevailed."

Thomas L. Chadbourne, the leading corporate lawyer and an early proponent of multinational corporations, immediately made a suggestion. "In that behalf," he said, "might I ask whether Mr. Calloway, who probably has illustrated the method that the Chair is now discussing, perhaps, more than any other man in the United States, will not say a few words to the conference on the subject?"

Lane was enthusiastic. Given his familiarity with Callaway, he may even have set up the suggestion in advance. "I am sure it will be your pleasure, gentlemen," he announced, "to hear Mr. Calloway [sic], of Georgia, a member of the public group. Mr. Calloway, will you please step forward?" Applause filled the room.

What followed was more than just classic Callaway. It was the most perfect statement of Callaway's philosophy to be found, rendered at the apex of his public life.

"I live down in LaGrange, Georgia," he

began, "and I guess one reason why they asked me to tell you what we are doing down there is that our town is so small that almost anything we could do down there you men with large businesses should be able to use by applying the multiplication table and multiplying it at other places."

He then gave a brief history of why and how his town had built cotton mills. "It is very simple. Some twenty-odd years ago down there our country was busted, with a relapse from the Civil War and the panic of 1873," and the farmers couldn't live by growing cotton. As a result "they started building cotton mills down there, and these men moved to town as cotton mill operatives. Their position in the country had been so poor, with the low price of their products, that it elevated them even to bring them to town and work in a cotton mill, which in itself was a poorly paid occupation at that time."

He continued,

At LaGrange—it was sort of like the measles or any contagious disease. Every town wanted to build a cotton mill. They did not have anything much, and we got up a cotton mill, and we would auction off the directorships. Anybody that could take $5000 worth of stock we would make him a director; and if some widow or some one had a son with $2000 we would make the son a bookkeeper. We organized our little mill and got our home people there to working it and to going, and we worked it rather along human lines. Everybody was proud of it, and everything they had in it; and a good many of the laborers took

Callaway spoke at the First Industrial Conference in October of 1919. The conference was held at the Pan American Building in Washington, D.C. and featured prominent leaders from across the country.

stock in it, and we rather worked along the lines of the individual. We did not try to patent our people or standardize them.

I am afraid right now that one thing we will do here, and the next danger of this country now, is an attempt to standardize Americans and patent the process, like Germany did. They made a great success of it. They did get to great efficiency in their standardization and in their patents on men; but like all things that became perfect, they then explode, because this is not the world for perfect things.

I think one of the biggest things we have to look at here is not to do that, and to pay a good deal of attention to the individual. I represent the individual. I am here to represent the public—not capital and not labor; and I want to say that probably between 50 and 75 per cent of the population of America consists of the individuals who are not standardized, and who do not want to be standardized, by either capital or labor.

They are the great mass of people, that are the backbone of this country. In making our rules and regulations here we must not leave them out, because if we do they have a way of rising without any notice and righting themselves and righting you and righting the country.

I think we want to give a good deal of allowance in our plans and specifications here to the freedom of individuality, and to encourage individuality.

We find in our own business that it is one of the best things we do—to get a man interested in his own part of the work. We try to segregate our work down to where every man, nearly, will be the boss of his machine, instead of simply being a unit. In fact, in our business we have at each door a box for suggestions, and we pay a premium—not only the honor, but money—and we get very good suggestions, frequently, from persons from whom you would not think they would come.

Another point about Callaway that his speech revealed was his overriding pragmatism, the fact that circumstance and results, and not ideology, were among his first principles. "I was rather Bolshevik," he said surprisingly, "just before Mr. McKinley was elected President." He went on to say,

The capital of the country organized and practically monopolized this country. They formed all of the big trusts and all of the money trusts at that time. I didn't have any money to put into it, and I was jealous of it. I was on the outside. And they did, probably, run over some little fellows like I was, and some of the small enterprises got stepped on, like the ant when one of these big-footed men come along, and the man doesn't know he has stepped on the ant. But it is a fact, however, that they carried America forward in that period from the late nineties to 1907 a greater distance in a shorter period than any country had ever been carried before.

Then 60 or 70 or 80 per cent of the individuals whom I represent in America got tired of it, when capital got to putting its forefeet in the trough, and felt like they held the world by the tail with a downhill swing, so that you could hear them eat the slop half a mile away; and they put their left hind legs in the trough, and about 1907 we turned the trough over, and the slop went down, and the capitalist was probably discriminated against.

I was awfully against the railroads in the late nineties—and now I am sorry for them. It is just human nature. You would go down to the depot and they wouldn't pay a claim. They wouldn't tell you whether a train was late or not; they wouldn't give you a drink of water; they were just as dominant as could be. They had the world going. And then this crowd of locusts I represent rose and turned them over.

It is a fact that since 1907 labor has organized. I think organized labor has done a wonderful work for the world. I believe they have forced a great many employers, who did not mean a great deal of harm, to recognize the true situation—they have, so to speak, rung the bell and let them know we are here. Labor has now come into its best position since Adam was a boy. Now, I say to labor, do not make a mistake and put the left hind leg in the trough. I think that labor is entitled to more than they used to get. I think that labor is entitled to a good living, and when they get it I want them to use it for a good purpose. I want them to educate their children, let their women keep the houses, and the men do the work and accumulate something for a rainy day, and I believe under Mr. Gompers's leadership labor will do it, because he is a conservative man, a loyal citizen, and a full-blooded American.

Callaway also stressed the role of his own organization in seeing to it that his workers had both the opportunity and the incentive to use their resources wisely. He outlined the mills' establishment of a kindergarten and a school, the construction of a hospital, and the founding of a local YMCA with its swimming pool and other recreational and social facilities. "Among other things, we have greenhouses at every one of our mills," he noted. "I remember when we built the first greenhouse that my own objecting director objected to that. He said, 'How can you ever do that and make it pay?'" Callaway showed him how. "I proved that we could keep—and in numerous cases we did do it—that we could keep a dozen hothouses going in the mills. I remember an instance, when a family was attempted to be induced to move to Roanoke, and I remember that the wife, when the matter was put to her, objected strenuously, saying that 'No, indeed; all of my plants are here at the hothouses, and I would not think of moving.'"

Callaway also emphasized the importance of the mills' profit-sharing plans, which he described in detail. The plan, he noted, "is an entirely homemade one. This is something we built up ourselves without any definite idea in advance." But it was a useful idea, and it grew along with the mills. Everyone—every mill operative, and even the teachers in the mills' schools—took part in the plan, and Callaway swore by it, crediting it for an important fact—the lack of strikes:

Now, we have never had a strike in our lives. In the last four years we ran our mills 24 hours a day, in order to help meet the Government's needs. We were making certain special goods that had to be made—the canvas that makes the connections between the airbrakes on railroad trains, and the canvas that went into the suction hose to draw the water out of Flanders, and a great many things like that. We ran our mills 24 hours a day, and we had no trouble in getting labor. We not only did not have a strike, but in the last four years, of the worst labor turnover in the world, we have not had a man to ask us for a raise in wages; and from a second boss, at $5 a day up, with day and night shifts in various departments, we did not lose one in the four years by leaving us or by death.

We did not have one man to leave our organization, and we work 7000 people altogether; that is, from the $5 man up we did not have a man to quit us, because they had that profit sharing staring them in the face. That was one reason, and I think they were happy; they had good schools for their children, and good stores for their wives, and a good church, and the boys liked the swimming hole, and the young men and young ladies liked the Y.M.C.A. and other institutions of that kind. It was sort of like the straw that broke the camel's back. Anybody can load a camel, the Good Book says, but if you can lay the straw so that it will stabilize them and keep them satisfied—that is the point. We did not lose a one.

He moved on to a typical Callaway conclusion; built on an anecdote, it was both forceful and optimistic:

Now, another thing, a lot of my clients among this 70 or 75 per cent of the people in this country—as Bob Taylor said, representing America as a cow; you know, a cow is my favorite—that the south end of the cow, which has the bag that is milked, is owned by capital and labor, and the 60 or 70 per cent of the common people own the north, or head, end of the cow, and every now and then capital and labor will holler and say, "Hurry up and put in a little more hay."

Now, if you gentlemen do not settle this thing as it should be settled you will find that these people will rise as they have done before. They will do it without any fuss, and it will be a bloodless uprising, but they will turn things over and take charge of the country and give you the head of the cow, and you will have to get up the hay, and I do not believe that either one of you want to take that chance.

I believe we have a big opportunity here, gentlemen. I think we are going to make a success of it. I do not think we can do anything else. The truth of the business is that if all of you will do your part you are bound to make a success of it, and if you do not, and all of you go away, I think I will stay here and make a success of it myself.

I am obliged to you.

Laughing at his story of the cow, the room burst into applause as Callaway concluded.

With that, Callaway's fellow Georgian and National Farmers Union president, C. S. Barrett piped up. "Mr. Chairman, I wish to make a motion," he said. "That fellow," he said of Callaway, "lives in the greatest old country home of all the Southland. Next Saturday he is going to give an old-time Georgia barbecue. To-morrow two solid trainloads of European nabobs will pass through this town on their way, and I was wondering if we could not get an invitation to go down there and see whether he is telling the truth or not. . . . I move that we adjourn over until Monday and attend Fuller Calloway's barbecue next Saturday."

"I will invite everybody here to come there," said Callaway, "singly or en masse, any day they want to, and we will be glad to show them how we run a little country town."

The barbecue that Barrett mentioned was to be the crowning moment in Callaway's public life, a perfect complement to the speech he had just made. It had been months, if not years, in the making. It involved a meeting of the World Cotton Conference, a postwar effort to restore the world's cotton economy. The conference was scheduled to meet in New Orleans beginning the following Monday, October 13.

But Callaway had plans of his own. As Barrett had noted, a great many of the American and European dignitaries who would be attending the World Cotton Conference would be traveling to New Orleans from the East Coast. That meant their trains would be coming through LaGrange. Callaway, for quite some time, had intended that those trains stop in LaGrange for a while.

The events that Callaway had planned in LaGrange actually weren't an interruption of his duties at the First Industrial Conference. In fact, quite the opposite was true. Wilson hadn't announced the conference in Washington until mid-August, while Callaway had been involved in planning the World Cotton Conference for the better part of a year.

Two such cotton conferences had taken place before, the first in Washington in 1906 and the second in Atlanta the following year; Callaway would undoubtedly have been familiar with them. The World Cotton Conference now contemplated was an outgrowth of Callaway's realization that the end of the war would bring about major readjustments in the cotton and textile markets, and that some sections of Europe would need rebuilding while all of the Continent would be converting back to peacetime patterns of agriculture and industry. His was one of the voices that readily convinced the leadership of the National Association of Cotton Manufacturers of these things, and of the need for American cotton men to take the lead in overseeing and managing the coming changes.

Callaway himself played a huge role in moving things forward. If he wasn't the prime actor, he was certainly one of the top two or three. On January 17, 1919, barely two months after the armistice, the National Association of Cotton Manufacturers held a meeting in Washington to make plans for what it named the World Cotton Conference, to be held in New Orleans in mid-October. Among other things, the conference would address the buying, selling, growing, handling, and transportation of cotton. It would promote discussions of world cotton requirements and ways to increase and improve cotton production, including the machinery required for such increase, the international standardization of working hours, and the role of the United States as a creditor nation. This last was by no means least, since the war had promoted the United States into the first rank of nations.

From the beginning, the conference planners recognized the importance of the European textile industry and markets. The Washington meeting made a point of sending a telegram to President Wilson, who by now had arrived in France for the Paris Peace Conference, asking him to end the wartime cotton embargo to the countries neighboring Germany and Austria. (The war was still technically underway.) It also named a committee of eleven members to carry out a visit to Europe to invite cotton men there to attend the New Orleans conference. Callaway, with many such trips under his belt, was the natural choice for committee chairman.

Plans proceeded rapidly, with American textile interests responding enthusiastically. By early March more than three thousand delegates, most of them from the United States, were planning to attend. By May the anticipated number had risen to five thousand, and people were already speaking of it as "the largest gathering of representatives of the world's cotton industry in all its ramifications ever assembled."

In Europe, however, attitudes were noticeably cooler. On the Continent, preoccupied as it was by the peace negotiations and the ravages of war, textile interests were indifferent to the idea of a cotton conference. In Britain it was worse; there the cotton men were actively hostile to the notion. The editors of Britain's *Textile Recorder* confessed to believing that "our American friends were out mostly for their own interests" and penned some rather strong comments to this effect. Such were the attitudes that Callaway and his committee had to overcome.

To achieve this goal, Callaway planned out a two-month tour of Europe—conspicuously excluding Germany—to depart from New York on May 18, 1919. Some members of the committee would even remain for a

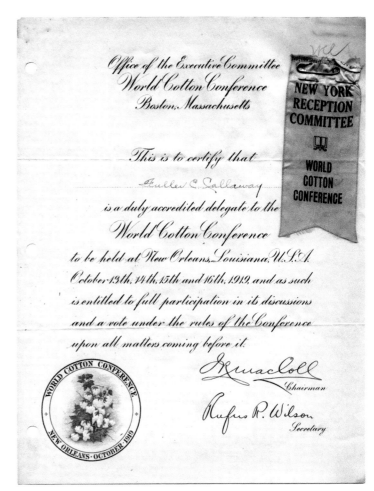

Certificate and original ribbon certifying Fuller Callaway as an accredited delegate to the 1919 New Orleans World Cotton Conference.

third month. The committee also armed itself with an elaborate pamphlet that listed the problems that the world textile industry faced and explained the desirability of holding a world conference.

The pamphlet bore clear marks of Callaway's hand. In the section that discussed travel arrangements appeared a statement that trains would transport European delegates from New York to New Orleans. "From Greenville," noted the pamphlet, "the special trains will proceed to LaGrange, Ga., the home of the Chairman of the European Commission, where an old-fashioned Georgia 'barbecue' will be tendered to the delegates by Mr. Callaway. At LaGrange will be seen cotton picking, ginning, oil milling, cotton spinning and manufacturing." Obviously such an event would take a lot of preparation in LaGrange. But first Callaway had to convince the Europeans to attend.

It was probably the most important journey to Europe that Callaway ever undertook. As was usual when he was getting ready for an important meeting, he made all possible preparations. In addition to compiling the highly persuasive pamphlet, Callaway also secured the support of Hoke Smith, and even more important, letters of introduction from Frank Lane, Secretary of War Newton Baker, and Assistant Secretary of the Navy Franklin D. Roosevelt. He contacted American embassies in advance of his arrival, and with government backing he had little trouble in getting them to arrange introductions to and meetings with various textile figures. He scheduled members of the commission to visit Rotterdam, Brussels, Ghent, Lille, Havre, and Paris, in addition to spending time in Portugal, Spain, Italy, Switzerland, and the Scandinavian countries.

The initial stop though—and the most important—would be England.

After a fast crossing, the commission headed quickly to Trafford Park, near the textile hub of Manchester. During the war a number of different industries had based themselves there, including some American factories such as Westinghouse. As such it was a natural symbol of industrial cooperation between America and Britain. Present to meet the commission were, among others, three important Englishmen: Marshall Stevens, a member of Parliament who had taken the lead in developing Trafford Park; Sir Charles W. Macara, a longtime president of the International Federation of Master Cotton Spinners and Manufacturers' Associations, and one of the most important textile men in the country; and Sir A. Herbert Dixon, Baronet, chairman of the Fine Spinners' Association and the largest textile employer in England. Sir Herbert, in particular, had his government's ear; during the war he'd chaired the Cotton Control Board established by the Board of Trade itself.

The high-profile Trafford Park meeting and further exchanges in Manchester and Liverpool were a resounding success. Within days, leading figures in the English textile world had reversed their opinions, the hostility disappearing. "British interests are bound up with the success of this projected Conference," declared Manchester's *Textile Recorder* in mid-June, the earlier suspicions it had voiced having evaporated. "There is much to be learned by enlarging our sphere of vision. Enthusiasm must be imparted into the matter, and nothing be left undone to ensure a successful issue to the deliberations of the delegates."

A major factor in this *volte-face* was Callaway himself, together with the philosophy and successes he personified. "Their Chairman is, in the writer's opinion, a real big man," stated the *Textile Recorder* of the committee and Callaway.

The welfare work he has done is remarkable in a very marked degree. He carries into his daily labour an optimism and a goodwill that are invaluable assets. He feels it is his bounden duty to use himself for the good of those he has in charge, and half an hour with him will prove to the biggest doubting Thomas in the world that there is a wonderful sedative for labour trouble and unrest in the education—social, technical, and physical—of the worker.

The tour of England was the biggest victory the commission achieved during its time in Europe, but there were other successes too.

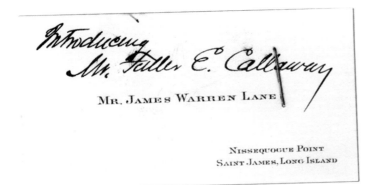

Introducing Mr. Fuller E. Callaway

MR. JAMES WARREN LANE

NISSEQUOGUE POINT
SAINT JAMES, LONG ISLAND

Card from the prominent New York businessman, James Warren Lane, introducing Fuller E. Callaway.

Fuller Callaway (holding cane) with members of the American Cotton Commission at Trafford Park, Manchester, England.

Everywhere Callaway went, apparently, people thought and spoke highly of him. Alfred Pearce Dennis, commercial attaché to the American Embassy in Rome and sometime author, was detailed to meet Callaway in Milan and to serve as his liaison to local textile men. He was so impressed by the Georgian that he later became one of Callaway's earliest biographers, devoting a chapter to him in a book he penned a few years later. Callaway, pointed out Dennis, didn't know the Italian language, but that mattered not at all. "Before he had been in the city two hours, our friend [Callaway] was surrounded by groups of fascinated Italians who swarmed about him as flies about a honey pot," he wrote later. "Some human beings have the mysterious faculty of sensing what is going on in the minds of other people and impressing their ideas and personality among their fellows. You can call it personality, human mag-

netism, but no matter where men like Callaway go they get what others have to give and bestow what others desire to receive."

It certainly worked that way in Milan and at Callaway's other stops in the summer of 1919. Dennis noted that prior to the commission's arrival, nobody in Europe cared about meeting to talk about cotton. Then Callaway arrived, and he "went back home with European cooperation pledged up to the hilt."

Everywhere he went the story was the same. By mid-June, having moved on from England to Paris, he was in contact with Pleasant A. Stovall, United States ambassador to Switzerland, who was already busily arranging meetings for him there. Stovall, a fellow Georgian, was an author and newspaperman from Augusta and Savannah, the son of a cotton broker, and a childhood friend of President Wilson. When Stovall and Callaway met, the result was much the

Callaway met Alfred Pearce Dennis at the American Embassy in Rome. Dennis, an author, later wrote an article about Callaway in *Country Gentleman Magazine* and featured him in his book *Gods and Little Fishes*, published in 1931.

same as Dennis described, and Stovall wrote to his Savannah associates of the success that Callaway achieved, which they in turn passed on to Ida:

> I recently had a very breezy visit from Fuller E. Callaway of LaGrange. He was here (Berne) working for the international conference at New Orleans. He is certainly a live wire. I think he has enlisted the sympathies of the English, French, Swiss and Italians in this convention, although he was really working against odds because it is so soon after the war. However, he has carried his point. He is a great talker and, better than that, a great worker. I enjoyed very much having him at my house and being able to help him on his way and in his work.

Callaway didn't spend all of his time in Europe on commission business. In France, probably in mid-June, he made time to visit the battlefields that had scarred the countryside and changed Europe and the world forever. One was Vimy Ridge, where the

Canadians pushed back the Germans the same month the United States entered the war. Another was Château-Thierry, the scene of one of the first actions of the American Expeditionary Force in July 1918. Today, time has done its work, and little visibly remains, although even a century later, farmers continue to plow up live shells from the old battlefields. But when Callaway visited, the wounds on the earth were still raw, with the trenches cutting through the land and the refuse of combat lying scattered about. While there he picked up spent shells and other battlefield trinkets, which the warring states of Europe had bankrupted themselves to buy but for which they no longer had any use, eventually taking them home to LaGrange with him.

That wasn't all. On June 28 Callaway was privileged to attend one of the most momentous events of the twentieth century: the signing of the Treaty of Versailles.

The world had never seen anything like the Paris Peace Conference. Even the Congress of Vienna, meeting near the conclusion of the Napoleonic Wars in 1814, was a small Eurocentric event by comparison. The Paris Peace Conference, by contrast, involved delegates from more than thirty countries around the world, meeting from January 1919 to January 1920, producing five treaties and establishing the League of Nations. The peace conference was the first episode for which a sitting American president had ever left the country; arriving in France, Wilson was greeted as almost a messiah by the people of France and Europe at large, though not by their leaders. It was at the Paris Peace Conference that T. E. Lawrence—"Lawrence of Arabia"—attended wearing an Arab keffiyeh and agal. It was here, too that an obscure visitor from French Indo-China who eventually went by the name of Ho Chi Minh arrived to seek independence for his land, known also as Vietnam, though in vain. In many ways the Paris Peace Conference was the crossroads of the twentieth century.

The most important of the agreements to come out of the peace conference was the Treaty of Versailles, which lay at the center of the crossroads. It was signed on June 28, 1919, five years to the day after the young Serb Gavrilo Princip set the war in motion by assassinating Austrian Archduke Franz Ferdinand, an event that by then seemed like something from another era. The Versailles Treaty restored peace between the Allies and Germany—for the moment. This same treaty also established the doomed League of Nations, placed formal blame for the war on Germany, and imposed massive reparations on that country that would, in the end, destroy its economy and lead to the rise of Hitler. The Treaty of Versailles, in short, set the stage for the Second World War.

But no one at Versailles knew these things would be the bitter fruit of the treaty. For them, or at least for some of them, the hope was that the treaty would make good on the naive hope that the conflict it ended had indeed been the war to end wars.

Callaway's visit to Versailles was evidently a hectic one that nevertheless spanned several days. On June 28 he scribbled a picture postcard to Fuller Jr. that read simply, "Here at the Peace Signing today." A few days later he cabled his office an equally brief message: "Seeing peace signed." He clearly knew he was witnessing an epochal moment in history; on the twenty-ninth he bought up copies of the Paris editions of several newspapers, including the *London Daily Mail* and the *New York Herald*, which he took home with him to LaGrange. He later said he would never forget the experience.

A different experience awaited Callaway when he returned to America in late July or early August. The commission's tour of Europe had been a resounding success; hundreds of cotton and textile men there had made plans to attend the New Orleans conference, joining the thousands of American attendees already committed. Now Callaway

Pleasant A. Stovall, a fellow Georgian and United States ambassador to Switzerland, helped Callaway make contacts in Europe as he encouraged European textile leaders to attend the World Cotton Conference in New Orleans.

had to turn his attention to the LaGrange exposition he'd promised them. Preparations had already begun for the affair, but now things really had to get moving. He had less than three months to get the town ready, and the clock was ticking.

Even before he got back to Georgia he was devising additional details to impress the delegates. From New York he wrote Ab Perry about some of them. "I understand that Cason has arranged to put a lot of peaches in cold storage for use of the delegates," he remarked. "It occurs to me that if water melons can be stored (I believe they do it in New York), that it will be well for you to get a lot of Wid Freeman's or Cleveland's big fine Rattlesnake watermelons and have them put in cold storage for the barbecue. This would undoubtedly make a great hit." He suggested that Perry acquire several wagonloads of them if he could.

Callaway also advised Perry to see to planting a special crop of sugar corn at Hills and Dales. "The people from England and northerners have never enjoyed the succulence

Callaway witnessed the signing of the Treaty of Versailles in the Hall of Mirrors. He sent this postcard to his son, Fuller Jr., on June 28, 1919.

321 VERSAILLES. — Jardin du Grand Trianon un jour de Grandes Eaux. — LL

of roasting ears," he opined. "If they are served Coney Island style that will be something new for them."

"I think your idea about the watermelons is excellent," Perry replied two days later. By that time he'd explored the possibility and wrote that it seemed quite feasible. "I will at once set to work to get up a lot of as fine melons as possible. Will also get Mr. Stephens to plant the corn immediately."

Perry also reported on other preparations. "Our people at the mills have already begun planning some features for this occasion," he told Callaway. "The band is practicing for dear life, and with this special incentive I hope they will achieve a creditable degree of skill by that time. It is possible that Mr. Coleman will be able to get up something special for the children to carry out."

Once Callaway got back to LaGrange, he summoned a conference of friends and associates and announced the success of the European endeavor. A few of them were worried that the community might not be up to the task of entertaining the delegates; it was a fact, for instance, that LaGrange didn't have a single building that could seat even half the expected number of visitors for a meal. But the fear was quickly suppressed. Some of the conferees, solicitous of Callaway's health,

stepped up admirably, telling him that he'd done his part and they would handle the rest.

"Thank you, friends," smiled Callaway. "I had counted on just that sort of fine cooperation, and I accept with only one condition: that I am allowed to pay all the expenses." After some resistance the others agreed. Hatton Lovejoy seemed the natural one to lead the effort, so he was half-jokingly given the title of director-general, although the job itself was quite real. The enthusiasm was infectious.

Soon other conferences were taking place, and committees were meeting to see to every detail of October 11. Lovejoy produced a master plan of five typewritten pages and oversaw the delegation of responsibilities.

The barbecue itself was to be the centerpiece of the affair, and it fell under the supervision of Chief of Police Todd Reed. It would have to be an outdoor event, and that meant that the town must gamble on having good weather that day. Hills and Dales was the obvious site; that much at least was certain. Reed set about his work, ordering young pigs of sixty to eighty pounds each, as well as lambs. In addition to the barbecue, he planned to use his own personal recipe to cook Brunswick stew, which would include the organs of the pigs as well as fifty young hens supplied by an Alabama friend of Callaway's. A large supply of biscuits was arranged for delivery from Atlanta.

Reed also planned the barbecue's entertainment, including singers and banjo pickers. Being chief of police, he also was concerned with more mundane affairs. He thus arranged not only comfort stations but a first-aid tent, the latter to be staffed by a doctor and nurse.

The mills and other businesses were preparing. Downtown, the Southern Decorating Company was busily giving the buildings and streets a facelift. The National Flag Company of Cincinnati was contracted to supply flags of more than two dozen countries ranging from Britain to Colombia and Persia, a dozen flags of each, for display in the business district and elsewhere. The order also included numerous bunting fans and, of course, dozens of American flags. Meanwhile, arrangements were made for giving the delegates tours in order for them to see every step in textile production from cotton picking to cottonseed oil production.

Despite his friends' insistence that they handle the arrangements, Callaway, too, insisted on doing some things himself. Sir Herbert Dixon was planning to attend in person. ("Fuller Callaway could persuade his satanic majesty to leave Hades if Fuller set his head to do so!" Ida reported Sir Herbert as declaring on the day of the gala.) Callaway thus took many steps to make the baronet's American visit both productive and special.

Sir Herbert, his brother, and his physician planned to arrive in New York well in advance of the conference so that they could tour both Canada and the United States, meeting the Dixons' relatives and engaging in just the sort of business that Callaway did on his own trips to Europe. Callaway took great care in arranging everything. He made reservations for the party at the Waldorf-Astoria; he wrote letters of introduction for Sir Herbert and took pains to see that they were delivered. He also contacted

Delegates en route to New Orleans enjoyed a barbeque picnic at Hills and Dales in LaGrange.

the United States Railroad Administration, the wartime government management agency, not only to secure Pullman tickets for Sir Herbert and his group, but to arrange for special attention to be given to the travelers, including pre-arranged automobile transportation at their various stops. Administration officials complied readily, helping prepare an itinerary that would take the Dixon party to Niagara Falls, Chicago, Lake Louise, Vancouver, Seattle, and San Francisco. Finally, with Sir Herbert's impending arrival in late August, Callaway asked Cunard's New York office to keep him posted on the progress and estimated arrival date of Sir Herbert's ship.

Callaway also made similar arrangements, if not quite such elaborate ones, for other visiting dignitaries during the run-up to the conference. At the same time he was coordinating preparations for Sir Herbert, he saw to it that William J. Harris, one of Georgia's senators

Cotton Conference delegates toured the Hospital of the Good Shepherd in LaGrange. This was one of Mr. Callaway's early charitable efforts.

(the other was still Hoke Smith), would host an Italian scholar in Washington. "I hope you will always call on me without hesitation whenever I can serve you or your friends in any way as it will be a genuine pleasure," Harris informed Callaway in his reply.

Then in mid-September came Wilson's summons to the First Industrial Conference. In early October, with the preparation for the LaGrange festivities entering their final stage, Callaway departed for Washington. There was no undue need for worry; his fellow citizens had everything well in hand, and he himself would be back to host the festivities. There was only one imponderable: what would the weather do on October 11?

Before dawn on the long-awaited day, two Pullman trains steamed carefully into LaGrange and onto the sidings, most of their passengers still asleep. Those passengers came from Asia, South America, North America, and Europe; the foreign visitors among them had spent days and even weeks touring New England and other parts of the United States. Three

days earlier they'd gathered in New York to embark on their journey south in the company of northeastern textile men. They'd visited Charlotte and Greenville on their way here. Now the high point of their journey was upon them.

After breakfasting aboard the trains, the delegates, their wives, their assistants and friends, and their hosts emerged expectantly onto the platforms beginning around 8:00 a.m. Immediately a sense of disappointment washed over them: the skies above LaGrange were filled with heavy, leaden-gray clouds that threatened impending rain.

But then on this day when he most needed it, the luck of Fuller Callaway came through once again. As an impressive motorcade of two hundred automobiles came rolling up to the sidings, the clouds began to dissipate. Before long the weather grew sunny and warm, almost springlike, and spirits immediately lifted. The gala at LaGrange began.

The cars were owned and driven by the Committee on Entertainment, and they would begin the day by taking the delegates on an elaborate tour of the town. Because there were so many sights to see, as well as a great number

While in LaGrange, the conference delegates also toured the Settlement Kindergarten.

of people to see them, two separate routes had been established, with all visitors scheduled to travel both routes by the end of the morning. Route A took in the Farmers Cotton Oil company, which both ginned cotton and pressed cottonseed for its oil; it then proceeded to Dunson Mills and Dixie Mills, where the guests met the youngest textile superintendent in the nation, aged twenty-four. After that came the Park Cotton Mills and the International Cotton Mills. At several of these stops the town's young ladies served fruit punch and offered cigarettes to the visitors. The drivers took care to point out churches, social services buildings, and mill operatives' homes, and they cheerfully made additional stops whenever a guest wanted a closer look at something.

Route B was a Callaway showcase. Stopping not only at Unity, Elm City, Hillside, and Valley Waste Mills, where the visitors examined raw cotton as well as textiles and conversed with the operatives, the cars made additional calls at the community greenhouses and the Episcopal Mission with its auditorium, kindergarten, playgrounds, and infirmary. After that came further stops at the Boys' and Girls' gardens as well as the public schools. Next came the Benjamin Franklin and Martha Washington Inns, the YMCA (where a community fair had been established), the new Callaway Park, and finally a drive past several churches, LaGrange Female College, and the Electric Ginnery. Most of this route concerned itself with the region called Southwest LaGrange, which Callaway had been working hard on developing in recent years.

All of this made for a full morning, but everything evidently went off without a hitch. What was more, as important as the tours were, they were merely prelude to the big event.

At 12:30 the automobiles made their way out Vernon Road, where the guests entered Hills and Dales by the east gate. Met by local Boy Scouts who served as their guides, the visitors then spent a half hour strolling through Ferrell Gardens, as well as Ida's own rose garden.

Then at one o'clock Chief Reed announced, "Ready!" and the grand barbecue began, served in a grove by the fishponds. By this time the weather was perfect, almost summer-warm. The music was provided by not one but two string bands, as well as a black choir and the brass band from the mills that had been practicing for months for the occasion. The food, new and different not just for the foreign guests but for the northerners as well, was a tremendous hit. A correspondent from the *Atlanta Journal*, in fact, trying to conduct an interview during the meal, had trouble getting one British delegate to stop eating long enough to explain why the barbecue had given him such an appetite. In the end, reported the journalist, the delegate nearly ate the plate itself.

At the end of the meal the whole party was directed to an open glade across the road so that group photographs could be taken. On the way the visitors encountered one of the most purely southern sights they could

Delegates from the 1919 World Cotton Conference explore Hills and Dales, Mr. Callaway's home in LaGrange, Georgia.

have ever hoped to see. Two black men were coming down the road, returning from a possum hunt. In addition to a hound dog, they had with them a pole holding a string of live possums. This tableau of rural Southern life entranced the Northern and foreign guests.

Some photographs were also taken in front of the grand portico of Hills and Dales, with Fuller standing at the center of the crowd. After the photography sessions, the time was 2:30, and the afternoon's outing was set to begin. It involved a trip out Hamilton Road to some cotton fields, where local citizens would demonstrate both handpicking and mechanical picking for the guests.

As Fuller led the visitors to their cars, he turned back to the house. "Ida," he called offhandedly, "have some tea ready to serve when we return."

"How many shall I prepare for?" she called back.

"Oh, just three or four hundred."

"Fine," she smiled back.

The entourage then departed for the fields. Afterward they were driven on a tour of rural Troup County to see more of Southern country life in the Cotton Belt. To add to the festivities the cars were shadowed by two military surplus airplanes flown by LaGrange citizens who had been pilots during the war.

Meanwhile, Ida and some of her neighbors were busily preparing the gallons of tea Fuller had requested. When the party returned to Hills and Dales from the country outing, Ida had not only hot tea ready but iced tea as well. The latter caused quite a sensation among the foreign visitors, who'd never before come across tea made this way. Fuller was likely taking this moment to entertain and talk business with some select few delegates in the drawing room, Sir Herbert Dixon among them.

Finally, around 6:30 p.m., the automobile procession set out for the Pullman trains. By seven o'clock all of the visitors were back aboard, where they would dine, and the trains steamed out of LaGrange. The gala event had ended. It had been a magnificent success. For weeks afterward Fuller and Ida received a seemingly endless chain of glowing thank-you notes. The chairman and secretary of the conference thanked Fuller "most heartily for the splendid entertainment extended to the foreign and Northern delegates" which "left nothing to be desired and, we are sure, will remain a delightful memory with all who were fortunate enough to enjoy it."

The head of the British delegation also gushed, thanking Callaway for "the really wonderful entertainment" provided in LaGrange. "The day was unique in every respect, and the British Delegates have severally and unanimously expressed in no halfhearted terms their thorough enjoyment in their visit."

Callaway must have been especially gratified to receive a handwritten note from Sir Herbert a few weeks later shortly before the baronet's departure for England. "I cannot adequately thank you & Mrs. Callaway for our delightful, albeit too short, stay at your beau-tiful country home," he wrote, "but believe me we appreciated your hospitality to the full & most of our talk on the train consisted of wonder & admiration of the splendid welfare conditions you were good enough to show us." He concluded by inviting the Callaways to visit him in England, where he had many things to show them in return.

October 11, 1919, built as it was not on weeks or even months of preparation, but on a generation of hard work and development, stands at the pinnacle of Callaway's public career and as one of the most important days in the history of LaGrange and Troup County. In some ways even the conference itself, opening in New Orleans the following day, was less significant. Alfred Pearce Dennis, in his chapter on Callaway, testified to the impact of October 11 in later years. On one occasion, some time after the gala, Dennis was trying to explain to a European host the location of his hometown of Princess Anne, Maryland, mentioning Baltimore by way of reference.

"Baltimore I know not," the host replied in accented English, "but tell me how far is this place from Lah Grawnge, Georgia?"

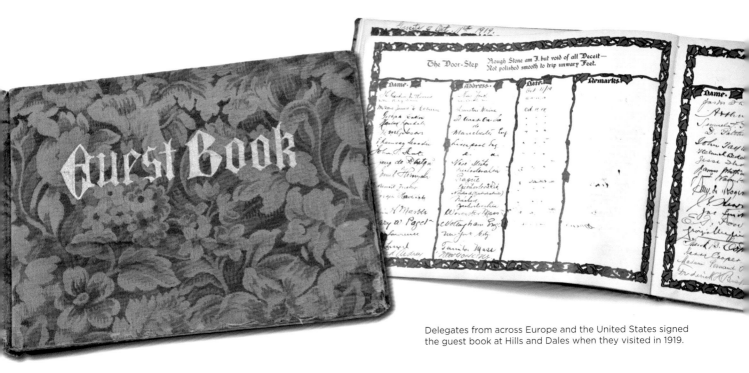

Delegates from across Europe and the United States signed the guest book at Hills and Dales when they visited in 1919.

MILL VILLAGES WERE SPREAD ACROSS LAGRANGE.
THIS 1920S VIEW OF THE VILLAGE NEAR UNITY SPINNING MILL HAD NICE SIZED LOTS
WITH GARDEN PLOTS. THE SCHOOL ON THE RIGHT IS SOUTHWEST LAGRANGE SCHOOL.

·*9*·

THE RISE OF
SOUTHWEST LAGRANGE

When Fuller Callaway testified before Congress for the first time in March 1904, he took some time to describe to the congressmen in detail his textile manufacturing operation. The testimony paints one of the most comprehensive pictures of the mills as they operated in the opening years of the new century, and of Callaway's philosophy of management.

Callaway described himself as involved with two mills, Unity and Milstead. Each mill employed around 350 workers, for a total of 700; the demographic breakdown in each mill was about 200 men, 100 women, and 50 children. Most of the operatives were white, with blacks working mainly in particular departments; practically all of the operatives were Southern. In some departments pay was by the piece. In others payment was by the day because, as Callaway explained, "you can not measure by the piece in some departments," such as in the opening room that dealt with bulk cotton. Adult piece workers earned from one to one-and-a-half dollars a day, while the adult day workers earned from seventy-five cents to three dollars per day. Older men, who did lighter jobs such as floor sweeping, earned at the seventy-five-cent rate.

The women, whom Callaway described as being "crackerjack weavers" and more attentive to their work than men, got as much as a dollar and a half per day.

As for the children, they made from forty to eighty cents a day. While child labor was slowly becoming an issue in American society as the Progressive movement gained steam, it was still very common. As many as 40 percent of all of Callaway's operatives were below age twenty-one; perhaps a quarter of all his workers were eighteen or younger, with only 10 percent or so being under age fifteen. In his testimony Callaway also pointed out several beneficial aspects of mill work when it came to children. To begin with, he employed no child under age twelve, preferring children of that age to go to school instead. The girls especially had light duties, mainly tying broken threads on the spinning frames when breakages occurred. The boys served as doffers, replacing the frames' full bobbins with empty ones, which took only about twenty minutes of each hour. In the meantime the children were free to amuse themselves as they wished in the well-lit and well-ventilated mills.

In discussing these matters, Callaway

Students enjoy recess at the original Unity School on Wilkes Street in LaGrange. The school was demolished after World War II and a new Unity School was built on Park Avenue.

hinted that, as a child, he himself had worked harder than this. "I never did go to school as much as two years in all my life," he told the committee, as well as mentioning his regular sixteen-hour work days as an adult. Furthermore, he noted that despite his own experience, he prized formal education. In fact the mills operated and largely paid for a school for the operatives' children. Georgia paid for four months' education for each child; the mills paid for an additional five months. Callaway also rotated children through his mills in two semiannual shifts, so that each child could continue to attend school either in the fall or the spring.

As for living arrangements, Callaway noted that while some operatives owned their own residences, the mill owned all immediately adjacent housing, which the operatives leased at the rate of a dollar per room per month: a two-room house for two dollars, a three-room house for three dollars, and so on. "They get 100 feet front and shade trees and sidewalks," he pointed out, "and they have a

well on the back porch. They use well water in the country, and to save them going out in the winter and catching cold it is convenient to have the well on the back porch." Additionally, noted Callaway, the mill operated "a large Union church," but over time various denominations had branched off to build their own churches near the mills.

One of the key points about this description is that it included more than just what went on within the walls of the mills. Callaway talked a good bit of his operatives' lives when they weren't on company time, and he involved himself in those lives, too. To him it was all the same.

One of his main objectives, naturally, was to make sure that these hundreds of operatives worked together as an effective team, or even as a family. For maximum efficiency, and thus maximum productivity, they must act as a single unit, a giant, coordinated organism. And to Callaway's way of thinking, that necessarily meant that their lives outside the mills, which unquestionably had an impact on how well they performed their jobs, were a legitimate area of interest to him.

Callaway wasn't alone in this view. As the Industrial Revolution reached flood tide near the turn of the century—exactly when Callaway was getting into textiles—many people were coming to see the need for greater efficiency in the factory, and many of Callaway's public statements in later years showed that he embraced the new ideas behind the efficiency movement. Fortuitously, Frederick W. Taylor, a mechanical engineer from Philadelphia, was developing the new field of scientific management—a rational approach to increasing workplace efficiency—during precisely the years that Callaway was building his mills, and Callaway's statements show that he was familiar with Taylor's concepts. But Callaway, like many other owners and managers, wanted more. As he often noted, people aren't machines. He realized early on that productivity depended to a large degree on what operatives ate, where they slept, and how they relaxed. Callaway thus sought to give operatives many opportunities for a better quality of life beyond the mills' doors, and even to direct their lives to a degree. Again, he wasn't alone in taking this approach. In fact it was so widespread among managers of Callaway's day that a later generation came up with a label for it: the slightly derogatory name *paternalism*.

The very name paternalism suggests that someone is looking out for someone else and making decisions for him because of the latter's inability to take care of himself. Broadly defined, the concept means that management sought to limit employees' freedom of action or self-determination for the employees' own good. Given the new world of the nineteenth-century factory, the interference was likely for the good of the company as well, and often the good of the company was even paramount. One of the early examples consisted of the boardinghouses established by textile

men in Lowell, Massachusetts, for female workers—the famous Lowell Mill girls—in the 1820s and 1830s. Boardinghouse life was carefully regulated: male visitors were forbidden, and the mill management enforced a 10:00 p.m. curfew.

Later came the company town, a community developed, built, and owned entirely by a corporation, which often boasted a company store where factory employees were forced to do business. The earliest and most notorious of these towns was Pullman, Illinois, built by the Pullman Company just outside Chicago in the 1880s. It was here that the deadly Pullman Strike began in 1894 before sweeping across the country. In the end a quarter of a million workers, most of them railroad employees, went on strike, rioted, and resorted to sabotage, with thirty people losing their lives before the government stepped in and broke the strike for the corporation owners.

The Pullman Strike, coming at the dawn of Callaway's textile ventures, also helped usher in a new concept of paternalism, known at the time as "welfare work." The fact was that employees were beginning to assert themselves and their rights, protesting not only bad working conditions but employers' attempts to control their lives. Ever since the first national strike—also involving the railroads, the transformative beast of industrial America—had occurred in 1877, the handwriting had been on the wall. Unions were gaining membership by tens and even hundreds of thousands, and that meant they also were gaining bargaining power. The ugliness of the Pullman Strike increased the chances that voters would make the government get involved in labor-management issues in order to protect workers' rights. Quickly, then, owners and managers began to adapt. They realized if they didn't want governments or unions telling them how to run their companies, they would need to do a better job of seeing to their employees' welfare.

The owners' main concern, other than keeping government and labor unions from interfering in their businesses, was maximizing profit. John Patterson, president and founder of the National Cash Register Company and one of America's leaders in welfare work, put it both clearly and bluntly. "We buy physical and mental labor," he explained. "If it pays to take care of a good animal that only returns physical work, how much more important is it for the employer to take care of the employee returning both physical and mental labor?" But this was only one motivation for the development of welfare work. Another was a genuine humanitarian interest in workers' quality of life.

Callaway, as a businessman par excellence, always had an eye to matters such as profit, savings, and efficiency. Inextricably interlinked with this was his concern for the general health and welfare of his workers. It ultimately meant a better bottom line for the mills, but it also meant a better life for mill operatives. He never distinguished between the two goals; to speak of one was to speak of the other. "We feel like those people are our people," he explained to members of Congress in 1904, "and there is no reason why we should not do all we can for them. We feel very kindly toward our people." That was one incentive for establishing mills in the first place, as he repeatedly stated. In the South of the 1890s, wracked by economic panic and depressed cotton prices, white farmers—poor, uneducated, and ignorant of modern health practices, but "of the highest type of character and morality and religion"—couldn't scrape out a living by farming. The mills were a way to help them make a living and to improve their quality of life, and that improved quality in turn made money for the mill owners.

The mills drew such people to LaGrange, explained Callaway, "and after getting his hand in and learning something of the business, [the operative] could make good money in the cotton mill, and eat Ferris hams and have luxuries on his table and live where they have churches and schools and electric lights on every corner." He wanted his workers to have opportunities, so long as they used those opportunities wisely. "I think that labor is entitled to more than they used to get," he declared (as he also mentioned in his speech at President Wilson's First Industrial Conference in 1919). "I think that labor is entitled to a good living, and when they get it I want them to use it for a good purpose. I want them to educate their children, let their women keep the houses, and the men to do the work and accumulate something for a rainy day."

In order to achieve these goals, Callaway engaged wholeheartedly in the welfare work model. And the first step he took was in an area where he had shortchanged himself in his youth: the matter of formal schooling.

The federal census of 1900, coming at the dawn of the Progressive era, was what first alerted the nation to the serious problem of child labor. Millions of children, often as young as four or five, were employed throughout America in dangerous jobs or in poor working conditions, with no government oversight, at wages considerably less than those of adults. The photography of sociologist Lewis Hine, which graphically revealed to Americans the plight of their children, had a huge emotional impact and helped make child labor one of Progressivism's biggest targets. "Child labor is employed simply because it is cheap and unresisting," said a textile labor leader accusingly in 1910. "There is never any danger of the child workers organizing, either among themselves or as a trade union, for the purpose of securing better conditions or higher wages." Throughout the country, states slowly began to heed such indictments and started to restrict and prohibit the use of child labor.

Emotionalism aside, the problem was never simple. While some industries and employers unquestionably used child labor abusively during the Gilded Age, the acceptability of some degree of child labor was hotly contested. And Fuller Callaway was one of those who objected to an outright ban.

He had several reasons for his views. First was the limited range of options for most children. Schooling in the South, though increasing, was still not the standard, with little in the way of compulsory attendance. If children weren't going to be in school, believed Callaway, they were better off being productive in a supervised environment than wandering around town while their parents were at work. Next was the fact that in a poor region like the South, families often needed to supplement the parents' income by having the children work. This was especially true, believed Callaway, when a parent was temporarily incapacitated due to injury or illness. As many child-labor reformers noted, the cure for child labor lay in the elimination of poverty.

Still another reason why Callaway was opposed to an outright prohibition was the fact that his mills made only limited use of child labor. With rare exceptions—essentially because someone slipped through the cracks—he didn't employ children under the age of twelve, and for the children who did work in the mills, he made sure their working conditions were good, with sufficient light, fresh air, light workloads, and frequent breaks.

This was related to still another, and very personal, reason for Callaway: he himself had worked, and worked hard, at least as early as age eight, and probably in conditions that weren't as good as the floors of his mills. He'd walked countless miles, carrying his goods from door to country door, in all seasons and weathers; he'd farmed; and he'd worked in a store. He saw nothing wrong with what he'd done. On the contrary, he'd profited by it in terms of both finance and character. What had

been good for him, he doubtless believed, wouldn't be bad for other young workers.

In 1905, with Georgia's state legislature considering a ban on child labor, Callaway went to Atlanta to testify against such a law. During the testimony he elaborated upon his views more fully, declaring that he opposed child labor laws more as a matter of principle than of practice. The House Committee on Labor and Labor Statistics allowed a total of only three hours for three opponents of the bill to speak, with Callaway as one of the three. He showed little attachment to child labor itself, and stated his belief that most other Georgia mill owners would agree with him. The larger problem, he declared, was that such a law would be the thin end of the wedge of government regulation of his business, legislation that he was sure would be instigated and driven by labor unions. Fresh from his protracted battle with the Atlanta & West Point Railroad, he stated that unions, if given the chance, were as likely to monopolize as capital. And Callaway hated monopolies.

Furthermore, asserted Callaway, mill owners in Georgia—himself among them—didn't employ children under the age of twelve. For this he gave a self-interested and thus particularly believable reason. It didn't pay. This was the central point of Callaway's argument: productivity. He didn't think that either unions or governments prized productivity, even if they did know how to achieve it. If the government wanted to pass laws at all, he observed, then those laws had to be of the right kind. "What we need," he told the committee, "are more laws to make people work and not any to keep them from working." It was apparently a persuasive argument. In the end, despite the short shrift given the labor bill's opponents, the bill failed to pass, to Callaway's relief.

Callaway and the bill's other opponents obviously put the best face they could on their own circumstances, for the plight of

Episcopal Mission, LaGrange, Ga.

The original Episcopal Mission, located on Murphy Avenue, was supported by Fuller Callaway and the mills. The mission provided health and other services to mill employees and their families who lived in Southwest LaGrange.

child workers who faced terrible conditions had grabbed the public's attention. But Callaway himself was a transitional figure. Even while defending the owner's right to hire children—at least older ones—he himself was moving away from employing them. By 1910, just a few years after his testimony on the subject in Atlanta and Washington, the *American Wool and Cotton Reporter* stated of the Callaway people that child labor "is practically unknown in any of their mills." The chief reason, the magazine pointed out, was education. "At an early age," it observed of Callaway's mills, "the children have the privilege of the day nursery and the mission, which is also a sort of primary school, where they spend the working hours, while their parents are in the mills, and when they have outgrown this, there is waiting for them the magnificent brick public school, which is situated not far from the centre of the village."

By the time of this report, Callaway had been developing educational opportunities for his operatives' children for nearly a decade. It was likely in 1903, just three years after the establishment of Unity Mills, that Callaway picked out two of the houses he'd built for operatives and turned them into a school. Ida apparently had already hired a schoolteacher well before then, Miss Fleming Ward—known

affectionately as "Miss Flemmie"—to operate a kindergarten for the mill children. Every month Ida would ask Unity's manager and other citizens for contributions with which to operate the kindergarten. At last Fuller took it over, hiring Miss Flemmie as well as her sister to run the school officially for the mill. It was the beginning of a relationship between Unity and the Wards that would last for more than twenty years. "To have the opportunity to teach, and to teach these little folks that otherwise would be left in ignorance," Miss Flemmie declared later, "can you think of a greater privilege to come to a woman?"

Others took a rather different view. This may have been one of the first mill-operated schools in the South, and it made other mill owners nervous. "What's this we hear about you teaching the children down there to read and write?" some other textile men reportedly asked Callaway. "Don't you know if you teach the children to read and write, they will never work in the mill when they grow up? You will never have any labor."

"I'll take that chance," Callaway answered them.

The question kept coming back up. "What are you going to do when the children of the mill operators grow up?" asked a Northerner. "Under the teachers they have, they are going to want better homes, better wages, and constantly higher standards of living. How are you going to hold on to them?"

"By giving them what they want!" exclaimed Callaway. "Of course they are going to improve and change. They are the finest people on earth—pure Americans. We were busted down here for a time by the aftermath of the Civil War and the panic of 1873. The people were out in the hills getting a bare living out of the ground. But they are getting up again. They will get anything they want in time."

The South-West La Grange
Public School and Playgrounds,
La Grange, Ga.

Southwest LaGrange School opened in 1916 and was used by the children of mill employees. After a fire in 1928, the building was restored as it is depicted in this S.H. Kress & Company postcard.

"But will the mills stand it?"

"The mills started with nothing," Callaway pointed out, "and look at them now. They and I began on six spools of thread. Anyone would have said all this was impossible then. But here they are. The best foundation for a business enterprise is just to set down in your mind one phrase: Everything happens that couldn't. When you've learned that, you'll believe. I found it out as I went along."

The educational enterprise, like the mills before it, grew quickly. Even as Fuller was taking over the kindergarten from Ida, he was entering into an agreement with the state government. In late 1902 Callaway and Georgia constructed a three-room school building, hiring Colonel J. P. Mooty, a well-known local educator, to run it, with the assistance of Miss Kitty King. This school would meet for ten months out of the year, free of charge to the students. The state would pay for five months of it; the cost of the other five came straight out of Callaway's pocket. With the Ward sisters overseeing around two dozen students, and Colonel Mooty and Miss King having charge of another sixty, the mill educational system was well underway.

By 1910 the mill had built a nine-room brick school building, which the textile world proclaimed as "one of the finest mill schools in the south." The following year came the founding of a training school. In 1915 Callaway formed a partnership with Chilton W. Coleman, a former head of LaGrange's Southern Female College, to develop the mill schools still further. In 1916, after visiting many other schools and conducting extensive research, Coleman opened the doors of Southwest LaGrange School, the most comprehensive educational system the mills had yet founded. Six teachers began with two hundred students; within two years both the

faculty and the student body numbers had tripled, to eighteen and six hundred respectively. Meanwhile Callaway also saw to it that Milstead in Conyers developed a school of its own. In 1918 the Southwest LaGrange curriculum was extended from primary school all the way to eighth grade. The school was about more than education; it was about community, with teachers being required to attend church as well as to make home visits to assess student living conditions. The school also took an active interest in both health and exercise. By 1920 Ida Tarbell, who possessed the highly critical eye of the social reformer, enthusiastically described the system that the mills had established:

It is not a question of getting the children to attend them; it is a question of getting them to go home!

You don't wonder when you look in on them, in their really beautiful school building, with the finest playground that I have ever seen. It consists of two terraces, each 800 feet by 200 feet, onto which every morning and afternoon for forty-minute periods, 300 or 400 children at a time are turned. They scatter to their play like the well-disciplined little soldiers they are. The game or exercise that each goes to has been settled by the most careful examination of the little body. For the weak chest, there is one thing; for the bent back, another; for anemia, another. For forty minutes, they go to it as only children can and, at the end of the period, come in flushed with health and happiness.

The school system was one of the premiere aspects of the mill's welfare work, but it was by no means the only one. The training school, in fact, came under the auspices of the LaGrange Mission, later known as the LaGrange Settlement, a major provider of social services to the mill community.

The mission was officially an organization of the Episcopal Church, but financially it was heavily backed by Baptist mill owner Callaway. Around 1906 a young Episcopal minister (much later a bishop) by the name of Henry Disbrow Phillips, newly assigned to LaGrange, conceived the idea of a mission or settlement to serve the needs of the mill community in Southwest LaGrange. The settlement movement had begun in the 1880s and had grown popular in England and America. It was based on the concept of providing, in lower-income urban settings, a headquarters for poorer citizens and workers, giving them access to food, shelter, and opportunities for education and exercise, all funded heavily by private charity.

To fund the LaGrange Mission, Phillips turned to a natural choice, Fuller Callaway, who enthusiastically agreed. Callaway not only supplied ample money but also furnished vacant houses and made other rooms available for mission activity.

The mission's first major undertaking lay in healthcare, with the establishment of the Good Shepherd Hospital. As time passed, more and more programs and activities became available. In 1911 work began on a new fourteen-bed hospital building along with the training school; Hoke Smith, once again the governor-elect, was on hand to give a speech at the groundbreaking. In 1913 the mission

The Reverend Henry Disbow Phillips conceived the idea of a settlement house for Southwest LaGrange. Fuller Callaway worked with him to create Sunday schools and provide medical and educational services for the mill employees.

was rechartered formally as the LaGrange Settlement. By 1915 it boasted a kindergarten; the Little Girls Society, which taught young girls sewing and needlework, and its counterpart for their older sisters called the Young Women's Club; the Young Boys' Club, which emphasized games and exercise; the Doffers' Club, which specialized in having its members put on skits and plays; and the Young Men's Club, sometimes called the Sword and Shield Society, which focused not merely on athletics but the notions of fair play and chivalry on the sports field.

Adults could likewise take advantage of the Men's Club and two Women's Clubs for socializing. Mothers' Meetings featured a program of physician guest speakers who gave presentations on child rearing. The settlement offered cooking and sewing classes, garden clubs, singing meetings, and more. While the Episcopal Church took great care not to push its own beliefs on settlement clientele, it nevertheless offered Sunday

The Mission of the Good Shepherd Hospital, La Grange, Ga.

The Mission of the Good Shepherd was a joint project of the Episcopal church and the mills. These buildings, which included a hospital, infirmary and nurses' home, were completed in 1911. Governor Hoke Smith attended the dedication.

school classes, Sunday afternoon Bible studies, and Sunday night worship services.

Fresh air was always a big aspect of the mill welfare programs. A wooded section of Southwest La-Grange, known as Park Woods, was long a favorite spot of operatives and their families for outdoor activity. Rather than destroy the woods to make room for new construction, the mill management took a very different direction. In June 1915 the directors of Elm City Mills conveyed an undivided one-half interest in Park Woods to Unity Mills and an undivided one-fourth interest to Hillside Mills. Fifteen months later the management of all three organizations formally resolved that the tract, now known as Callaway Park, would never be used for anything other than park or church purposes, a dedication that Fuller Callaway found quite moving. Later the park became home to a band hall that often hosted pageants, plays, and other presentations put on by the mills and their operatives, as well as frequent picnics.

For all ages the settlement offered many opportunities for healthful exercise, and Callaway and the mills added more. One was a regularly scheduled workout routine in a gymnasium built in 1919. By 1920, at 5:30 on any given afternoon, forty or fifty mill workers, male and female, blue collar and executive, might troop into the gym for an hour-long workout, leaving the stress of the day behind them when they left. "Not a grouch left," Callaway once said approvingly as he watched them go.

The settlement was popular and a great success, the training school alone producing graduates who spread throughout the South, becoming kindergarten teachers, nurses, or settlement workers themselves. The settlement's records showed that during one four-month period it had provided services to more than ten thousand souls. When it was founded, it was practically the only resource of its kind for the mill workers in Southwest LaGrange, other than the mills themselves. But over time the mills, taking the settlement as an example, added more and more offerings to their own programs. By 1920 the settlement, still enjoying considerable success, handed over the reins to the mills and dissolved itself. This left the mills in direct control of the social welfare programs. And Fuller Callaway always liked direct control.

A central feature of the mill's offerings was a YMCA, founded in 1919, which featured the gymnasium of which Callaway was so proud. The new organization offered even more ambitious programs than the settlement did, including showers, weekend trips, and personal consultations. By 1920 the mills were providing direct healthcare, including physical examinations and vaccinations, and beginning that year, a staff physician and lab assistant. The mills also made arrangements with a local dentist, Dr. F. B. Saltsman, to see to the needs of operatives and their families. To assist in extending healthcare, the mills established the Textile Benefit Association in 1919, a fund to help pay for various health services (and if

The Swimming Pool, La Grange, Ga.

The Callaway group of companies furnished numerous community amenities, including a swimming pool, ballparks, kindergarten classes, and more. This pool was in Southwest LaGrange.

necessary, funeral costs), especially when operatives faced lengthy illnesses that left them unable to work for extended periods.

Another item in which Callaway took a particular interest was housing. Starting early on, the mills built houses for its operatives to rent. In 1908 the settlement built a mission house as a residence for mill operatives, but it was essentially a safety net; long before then the mill housing of which Callaway was so proud was well established.

When it came to housing, Callaway had an eye to beauty as well as productivity, doubtless influenced in part by Ida as well as by the memory of Sarah Coleman Ferrell. The mills provided a common pasture and barns for operatives' use, encouraging each family to buy a cow and establishing a lending program to make the purchase possible. The cow was a good investment, not only readily saleable in lean times but also providing families with milk products both to eat and to sell. Callaway also saw to it that a scuppernong vine, a fig bush, and a peach tree were planted at every house, and when the Improvement Association was formed, it focused heavily not just on home improvement but on the cultivation of vegetable gardens. The mills made both flowering and vegetable plants available to operatives free

of charge. As an incentive to beautification and productivity, the association held frequent contests, many of them at community fairs, that gave prizes for the most beautiful gardens. Children were taught about nutrition in the schools, and both the settlement and the YMCA offered classes on gardening, canning, and preserving. Callaway went still further, building two community greenhouses for operatives' use. These were favorites with the mill women and aided workforce retention. In the winter, when husbands talked about moving to other mills, the wives had a typical response. "Oh, no, I can't leave my flowers," they would say, "and they will be killed if I take them out of the greenhouse!"

One of Callaway's running concerns was workforce stability. He always saw the practices of operatives migrating from job to job and mills "stealing" labor from each other as wasteful patterns that reduced Southern wealth through inefficiency. Good, pleasant homes, he believed, were key to a stable workforce. "It is through them largely that you will hold your people, satisfy them," he explained. "It isn't merely a house—that is really the last of it. It is the things that go with the house, the things that, bunched together, make a home—children, chickens, a garden, a cow. If you can sort of lead a family on until it wants them, and gets interested in using them, you stabilize it. If the children are happy in school, they won't want to leave; if the woman has a garden and flowers which she can put into a greenhouse in the winter and have them back in the spring, she won't want to leave; if a man has a cow and a place to pasture it . . . that cow will keep a man from nourishing the grouch, which might make him pull up suddenly and leave. When a man has to go after a cow at night, drive her

Callaway took a special interest in providing attractive housing for his employees. Mill villages were filled with small houses that each had room for a garden.

home, milk her and keep the calf from tipping over the pail, he is too busy to think about anything that has troubled him during the day; his grouch wears off!"

At no time did Callaway deny that there was an element of self-interest in promoting this stability, along with providing everything else that helped keep his operatives happy. But for Callaway it wasn't just self-interest. It is better described as mutual self-interest, or community self-interest. "The interests of the company and its workers are interdependent," he observed in 1918, by which time his views on labor-management relations had achieved full maturity, "and that mill which does most toward making living conditions pleasant, toward holding a stable supply of contented labor, is the one which is most likely to prosper." For that reason, he thought the term "welfare work" to be misleading.

One of the best indications that Callaway saw the mill enterprise in a cooperative light was his implementation of a profit-sharing plan in 1915. Suggestion boxes on the mill floors already allowed operatives to speak directly to the management about how to improve the way things were done, and to receive

premiums for good suggestions; profit sharing went further, giving operatives a direct stake in the mills' productivity, blurring the line between capital and labor. The arrangement wasn't limited to floor workers but included others in the organization, such as the schoolteachers. Under the plan, every employee, even those whose work couldn't be individually measured, shared in 10 percent of the mills' net profits. Those whose work could be measured often received more, sometimes as much as 60 percent of their base salaries.

Despite this and all of the other community-building efforts undertaken by the mills, there was still one major way in which the mills' employees were a separate group. It wasn't in relation to management but instead to the rest of LaGrange.

Although the overwhelming number of mill operatives were Southerners, the mills themselves were a New South phenomenon. The employees had come to LaGrange from elsewhere, largely the southern reaches of Appalachia. Often they could be distinguished from native LaGrangians by their appearance and dress. Lack of high-speed transportation meant that they had to live near the mills,

Unity Spinning Mills, La Grange, Ga.

Unity Spinning Mill was built in 1909 and manufactured twine, cord, and yarn. Note the cow in the foreground.

where they formed a sort of colony, living in mill housing and taking advantage of all of the communal mill services. These services may have brought them together, but at the same time the services made the operatives distinct from the townsfolk, who by and large didn't use the mill-sponsored facilities. While it was informally called Southwest LaGrange, most of the community—as did the mills themselves—lay outside the town on unincorporated land. Since 1856 the city limits extended in a one-mile radius centered on the courthouse square; the bulk of Southwest LaGrange lay just beyond this circle to the south and southwest, thus having no official claim on city services such as roads, sewers, or lighting.

Largely through the efforts of Callaway and other town leaders, who stressed the communal and collective nature of the mill enterprise, townsfolk showed little if any hostility toward the operatives. In that respect, LaGrange was noticeably different from many other towns where mills had sprung up. On only one occasion did any real sign of antagonism appear. In 1885, long before Callaway got involved in textiles, an assistant editor of the *LaGrange Reporter* flippantly remarked that during his recent tour of the Dixie Mill neighborhood he had been pleasantly surprised to see that the workers

were clean and clearly human, lacking the two heads that he'd expected to see. Such talk was speedily quashed.

But while there was no active hostility, there was still an awareness on everyone's part that the mills were at the heart of a separate community, divided by many things and united by few, the most important of which were physical proximity and Callaway leadership. While continuing to behave itself after its 1885 slipup, the *Reporter* nevertheless labeled much of its material as mill news, especially noting in obituaries and wedding announcements when the subjects were mill workers, and eventually running columns headed "News Items from Our Industrial Areas."

While this "otherness" of the mill community was for the most part an accepted way of life for decades, it wasn't always accepted calmly. Indeed it lay at the heart of tensions that—if not diffused—could threaten the very fabric of civic cooperation that Callaway had relied on to build the mills in the first place. At one point that fabric began to fray. Then more than a decade later, it began to come apart.

One of the first recorded instances of outright discontent between LaGrange and the mill community was rather innocuous. In January 1905 town doctors notified the public that they had in effect unionized, forming an entity known as the LaGrange Medical Association. One of the members' first actions was to set a uniform schedule of fees for medical services. One of the standard charges was aimed specifically at areas outside the LaGrange town limits. For house calls there, the doctors would impose a surcharge of fifty cents per mile in the daytime and a dollar per mile at night.

It was an odd matter to cause a reaction

from the mill community, since in 1905 much of the mill housing was still inside the town limits. But within a few days the operatives called a meeting in which they publicly denounced not only the surcharge but the entire fee schedule, characterizing it as a monopolistic money grab. The operatives also announced that they'd begun negotiating with doctors in other towns in an attempt to lure them to LaGrange.

A year later the problem remained. In one of the first whispers of collectivization to be heard from the operatives, a meeting of representatives from every mill in LaGrange—not just those of the Callaway organization—took place on January 30, 1906. "We, the mill people of LaGrange," they declared in a resolution,

feeling oppressed by the actions of the physicians in forming a combine and adopting resolutions which affected the prices of their practice, feel that we are not willing to be bound by the fetter of the doctors' sovereignty. Notwithstanding the doctors of the town are all gentlemen and we will always respect them as such, but as we have the same right to organize as physicians we take this method of defending ourselves.

The "right to organize," with its undertones of unionization, may have sounded to Callaway like a fire bell in the night. But for the time being he was apparently in the operatives' camp. Soon the mill workers announced that they would patronize a newly arrived physician who apparently planned not to join the LaGrange Medical Association, as well as give their business to another doctor who had withdrawn from it. In the meantime Callaway gave Reverend Phillips the money needed to build Good Shepherd Hospital, the timing of this endeavor surely not merely coincidental.

The fight over medical fees seemed to be the catalyst for more general discontent. In June 1905, the *Reporter* printed a complaint

that LaGrange was remiss in failing to provide a good paved street from town to Southwest LaGrange. It was the first of many sporadic complaints over the next few years about how the town skimped on basic services for the mill community. Already, the previous March, a letter from "Citizens of South, Southeast, and Southwest LaGrange" asking for a "square deal" for themselves, proposed a slate of candidates for town council that included Neal Truitt and others who were favorable to the mills. This nomination came at the same moment that another letter proposed that Callaway be elected as mayor. Still another letter, written at nearly the same time, complained that the La-Grange government had promised electric lighting for the mill two years earlier but had yet to do anything about it.

Callaway declined to run for mayor, and 1905 was his last year on the town council. But the suggestion, along with the proposed slate of candidates (of whom only Truitt won election), showed that a movement was underway to fold Southwest LaGrange into the larger community.

A year later the discontent grew even more obvious. On Tuesday, April 17, 1906, a mass meeting of eight hundred people took place to nominate candidates to the LaGrange town council. Two clear factions were present. One of them was from Callaway's mills, quite possibly encouraged to show up by the mill management. This faction, with Hatton Lovejoy as its spokesman, put forward the names of A. H. Cary and E. G. Walker, men who'd been included in the 1905 pro-mill slate, along with H. H. Childs, a Hillside investor.

Joe Dunson was there too, and right after Lovejoy nominated the mill slate, he spoke up to propose his own list of people, which included Cary and two others, E. D. Daniel and C. D. Hudson. There followed a "somewhat spirited debate" between the two groups referred to by the newspaper as the "cotton mill men" and the "bank men," aligned, respectively, with Callaway and Dunson. Accusations flew that each faction was trying to gain control of the town council in order to further its own agenda, and tempers flared.

To diffuse the situation, the attendees agreed to hold a citywide primary nine days later. Further negotiations may well have occurred, because by April 27, seven nominees rather than five were in the race. When the votes were finally counted and the results announced on May 4, the winners appeared to be a compromise group. Walker and Childs had won, while the third man was W. A. Holmes, who had been on neither group's original slate, although Cary, who had been on both slates, hadn't prevailed.

The election signaled the beginning of an uneasy truce that lasted more than a decade. During these years the mill community grew and the services offered by the mills to its people multiplied. Meanwhile, complaints to the LaGrange government from the mill operatives about bad roads and poor services continued, with Callaway often stepping in personally to fill the gaps in services in the unincorporated area. In June 1908 came the first rumblings of an idea that would have seemed a logical answer to the tension: an editorial in the *LaGrange Reporter* advocated the incorporation of Southwest LaGrange into the town proper. But nothing came of the suggestion. Perhaps the Dunson faction feared the political clout this would have given the Callaway interests, or the citizens of LaGrange were too standoffish to welcome the operatives formally into the community despite the increased tax base they would provide, or both. At any rate little more was said on the subject for years.

Then in June 1917 everything changed. By now the mills were burgeoning, with war orders pouring in. Patriotism was blooming, with the United States having declared war on the German Empire just two months earlier. Joe Dunson, likely a major opponent of

incorporation, had been dead for just over a year. Callaway, meanwhile, was fresh from a meeting at the White House during which he'd offered President Wilson all of the resources at his command. Things were suddenly in flux, and maximum efficiency was needed. All of these things perhaps explain why this was the moment when Callaway publicly announced that he was going to request incorporation of the mill community into a new town, to bear the formal name of Southwest LaGrange.

Thus ended the truce. The war had begun.

~

The reasons behind Callaway's announcement were simple enough. Although LaGrange had indeed supplied some services to the mills and mill neighborhood over the years that were supported by city revenues, Southwest LaGrange was still lacking in some important ways, particularly as to a sewer system (or rather the absence of one). Paved streets and sidewalks were also few. And LaGrange wasn't likely to address the issue for a simple, legitimate reason. When the mill interests asked the city council for help on these matters, the town council noted that LaGrange's indebtedness was close to the state-set limit for a town of its size. Simply put, there was no money available, especially for a community that wasn't even part of the town. Even if money became available through the annexation of Southwest LaGrange, it was possible that LaGrange wouldn't use taxes paid by Southwest LaGrange residents to make improvements there.

The obvious answer was to charter a separate new municipality, which would begin its life with little or no debt and which could issue bonds and impose taxes of its own. That would provide the money for sewers and roads for the mill neighborhood. It was a simple enough solution, and in July a pro-mill group, named the Committee on Public Welfare, said so in a long newspaper advertisement. The ad reminded LaGrange readers of the economic benefits the mills had brought to the town, as well as of the importance of the community spirit that was an advantage to all parties. Callaway also ran his own ad, which included his personal appeal to the fair-mindedness of La-Grange citizens. The city had been kind to the mills, he noted, but something had to be done, and soon, for the "mill folks" and "the sake of their health and better living conditions." Callaway then proposed that an incorporated Southwest LaGrange should only be an intermediate phase, a stepping-stone to an ultimate merging of the two towns (and their debts).

Once again all of this was both simple and logical. But the very fact that Callaway and the committee had to defend the incorporation proposal in such a high-profile way shows that many people in LaGrange opposed the idea, and strongly. The same newspaper edition that carried the Callaway and committee advertisements also contained an editorial by F. McLendon denouncing the proposal. While obviously this wasn't the first objection the Callaway interests had heard, it was a major one, and a typical one as well.

Simply put, McLendon felt betrayed. In his view, the town government—which he claimed was dominated by mill interests—had spent a great deal of LaGrange citizens' tax money on building up the mills. That money, he complained, could have let citizens buy more stock in the mills if it hadn't been taxed out of their pockets by the mill interests. In short, he claimed, the town had enriched the mills at taxpayers' expense, and now that the town had finally turned off the spigot, the mill was turning its back on the town.

While McLendon's arguments held a kernel of truth, they were clearly overstatements, and they also ignored the huge boost the mills gave to the local economic base. Nevertheless, whether justified or not, many La-Grange residents felt betrayed.

But the anger went both ways. While Callaway himself maintained his usual reasonable tone, Dr. Mary Brewster, head of the settlement's Good Shepherd Hospital, spoke to Callaway bluntly about the problem when he asked her to make a public statement in support of incorporation. Although in the end she opposed incorporation, Brewster strongly agreed with the need for improved services. Describing the plight of the mill operatives and the health and hygiene benefits they would get from a sewer system, Brewster accused LaGrange council members of believing "that the best part of the town, that is, the part with the handsomest houses, should receive the lion's share of all improvements." It was an impassioned but not tremendously accurate argument; it missed the point that since Southwest LaGrange wasn't legally *in* the town, LaGrange had no duty to provide services there at all, yet it had done so in many ways in the past.

The whole dispute, while unpleasant, fell into the same category as the perennial Callaway-Dunson warfare. As the community grew in size and wealth, a certain number of growing pains and differences of opinion were inevitable. In fact the remarkable thing is how few such conflicts took place, along with how long one of this size had taken to spring up.

As the summer of 1917 wore on, the fight continued, with Callaway and Ab Perry leading the efforts to drum up support for incorporation, and various interests on both sides speaking out loudly. On July 26 came a meeting between the two sides, with Callaway and other civic leaders present, in which they attempted to hammer out terms of incorporation. The attendees agreed on several important issues. The most important, other than the fact of the incorporation taking place, was that Southwest LaGrange would eventually be merged into the current city of LaGrange. Many of the remaining points of agreement concerned the bonds to be sold by the new town, specifically that they would not be sold for less than par value and not exceed a maximum interest rate set by the attendees, and that bonds could only be sold for purposes of a sewer system, street and sidewalk development, power lines, and school construction. The concern was obviously that the mill interests wouldn't use Southwest LaGrange's bond-issuing power to benefit the mills and then turn around and saddle La-Grange with debts. The group also agreed on two other issues: that the new town wouldn't reimburse the mills for money they'd already spent on existing improvements, and that LaGrange would have a representative on any Southwest LaGrange agency empowered to spend bond money.

The group then discussed the proposed membership of the new town's governing body, a council to be known as the Southwest La-Grange Commission. The attendees decided that it would have four members, three of them being Callaway; Roy Dallis; and LaGrange's city engineer, G. H. Sargent. Perry later recalled that about fifteen names were mentioned in regard to the fourth member. But in the end the main opponent to the incorporation plan, LaGrange town council member Howard Park, insisted that he himself be given the final seat. This was too much for Callaway, who simply couldn't agree. Thus with an agreement almost in place, Park walked out of the meeting and the deal fell through.

Despite the continuing opposition Callaway and the other incorporation supporters forged ahead with their plans. Within a few weeks the focus shifted to the General Assembly, where a bill to establish the new town was soon introduced. But the fight continued. A group of more than fifty opponents of the bill, headed by Park and including M. F. Lendon*, other town council members, A. H. Cary, and a number of Dunsons, published a circular purporting to state "the real facts in regard to the LaGrange situation" and arguing that the pending bill was fundamentally unfair to LaGrange taxpayers.

The circular, like the abortive July meeting, shows that the opponents weren't trying outright to stop the incorporation from going forward. In fact, claimed the circular, when LaGrange had extended lighting and water service to the mill community, "it was taken for granted and generally understood that this would become a part of greater LaGrange before 1920." The authors instead maintained that they were simply worried that if Southwest LaGrange were incorporated and proceeded to issue bonds, and then were merged into La-Grange, the bonded indebtedness would be a liability for LaGrange citizens to which they had never agreed. Infrastructure improvement in the mill community wasn't objectionable, they argued, "but we do not think that it should be done at the expense of the tax payers of LaGrange, who do not happen to be connected with Mr. Calloway's [sic] enterprises."

To protect these taxpayers, the circular recommended that the legislature add a number of provisions to the incorporation bill, many of them based on what the July meeting had agreed upon before talks failed. Among these were requirements that the new town be prohibited from selling bonds at less than par value, that they bear the same interest rates as current LaGrange bonds, and that the ad valorem tax rates of the two towns be the same. The authors did suggest that the new town reimburse the Callaway mills for the cost of the school building that it had constructed, but it also asked that $15,000 of Southwest La-Grange's bond revenues be paid to LaGrange in compensation for lighting and water equipment, "which is the property of the tax payers of LaGrange." Finally, the circular asked for the appointment of a joint commission consisting of members from both communities to oversee Southwest LaGrange bond money "to hedge against possible extravagant expenditure of the proceeds derived from the Bond issue," and that Southwest LaGrange be annexed by La-Grange at the end of 1919.

* Probably M.F. McLendon.

In the end, few of the circular's proposals were written into the law, but the authors did get one important concession, which Callaway himself had proposed. Two bills, not one, ultimately passed the legislature within two days of each other. The first, approved on August 18, 1917, declared that at midnight on December 31, 1919, a carefully delineated area around the mills—Southwest LaGrange—would be added to LaGrange. The bill also provided that as of the 1919 date the LaGrange town limits would be extended in every direction from the courthouse square from one to two miles. Perhaps most important, this bill tied its fate to that of the second. In short, it decreed that it would not go into effect unless the second bill also became law.

This second bill, passed on August 20, 1917, declared that immediately upon its passage, Southwest LaGrange would become an incorporated municipality. The metes and bounds of the new town were exactly the same as the area described in the first bill, meaning that the whole of the new town would be absorbed into LaGrange at midnight on December 31, 1919.

The second bill also gave the circular's authors one or two other things for which they'd asked. While it authorized Southwest LaGrange to issue bonds to pay for public improvements, those bonds could only be used for "lighting, water and sewer systems, streets and sidewalks, school buildings and equipment and fire house and equipment," along with allowing, though not requiring, the purchase of electrical equipment in the area that LaGrange owned. The bill also gave the circular authors one additional victory: it required the ad valorem tax rate of Southwest LaGrange to be no lower than that of LaGrange, thus guaranteeing that the citizens of the new town would pay their fair share of the improvement costs.

My dear Sir:-
     As over ninety-five percent. of the voters in Southwest LaGrange territory petition it; and as
     Over half of the tax-payers and voters in La-Grange proper approve it; and as
     It does not take an inch of LaGrange's territory---
     BUT PRIMARILY, because it will enable a work of upbuilding humanity, benefiting our entire section and hurting no one--
     I will appreciate your making sure to be present when the Southwest LaGrange Bill comes up and using all your influence to secure its passage.
               Yours truly,
                    FULLER E. CALLAWAY.
LaGrange. Ga. July 28. 1917.

Postcard from Fuller Callaway advocating the Southwest LaGrange incorporation bill.

The fight was over. The town of Southwest LaGrange had become a reality, if only for twenty-eight months, after which it became part of LaGrange. The battle had been the most unpleasant one since the Callaway-Dunson conflict of 1904. It was probably the worst in LaGrange history. But soon the affair had blown over, and the community continued to advance.

Callaway had won yet again.

≈

As 1920 began, things in LaGrange seemed better than ever before. The merger of Southwest LaGrange and the original city had gone smoothly and was greeted by the *Graphic* as the dawn of a bright future. Acrimony seemed to have evaporated. The many human resources established by the mill community were in full swing. Best of all, the visit of the World Cotton Conference delegates a few weeks earlier had been a resounding success and one of the greatest moments in the town's entire history.

But one major battle remained for Callaway to fight. As 1920 progressed, clouds once again loomed on the horizon.

Callaway had long been opposed to unions, just as he'd always spoken out against government regulation. He saw the two things as related in at least two ways, first by the fact that both of them threatened to restrict an

Students working in the Unity School sewing cottage in 1928. Sewing, cooking, and other manual training classes were added to the school in 1928.

alien to Callaway's experience but unabashedly violent. And in the wake of America's entry into the war, the same labor unrest that had fueled revolutions in Russia and then Germany became visible in the United States. As 1919 began, and with it a postwar recession, strikes swept across the nation, often accompanied by Bolshevik and anarchist rhetoric. The American labor movement had been influenced to at least some degree by such ideas for decades, but the success of the revolutions in Russia had magnified the apparent threat. Gompers, whose path had crossed Callaway's more than once over the years, roundly denounced the Bolshevik Revolution, but members of the rank and file of his organization kept voicing support for the new Soviet regime. "The workers of Russia are endeavoring to establish in their country a government of, by, and for the workers," one proposed AF of L resolution proclaimed, "and the capitalists of the world are seeking to annul their efforts. . . . We believe the workers of America have the power to prevent the capitalists of the United States from carrying out their part in the plan for the destruction of the new workingman's government of Russia." Members of the International Workers of the World, a more radical group than the AF of L, voiced even stronger support for the new Soviet government, often aligning themselves with the Socialist Party and the new American Communist Party. Soon, and largely because of the strikes, America was embroiled in the Red Scare, the belief that a Bolshevik uprising was in the American wind.

owner's control of his own business, and second by his belief that government regulation was actually, or at least potentially, a tool of labor. His address to the First Industrial Conference in the fall of 1919 showed that he had grown sympathetic to the goals of the labor movement; in that address he'd spoken in glowing terms both of the labor movement and of Samuel Gompers, the president of the American Federation of Labor. Still, Callaway had no intention of relinquishing control of his own business to either the government or to a union.

This sort of outlook on the part of capital had led to labor unrest and outright violence elsewhere during Callaway's lifetime, but not in LaGrange, a testament to Callaway's community-oriented and cooperative approach to running the mills. There had never been any union activity in the mills, and he made no secret of the fact that he didn't want any.

But in the months following the end of the Great War, the national labor scene was changing quickly and dramatically. The war had brought about the Bolshevik uprising in Russia, a revolutionary approach to the labor-capital relationship that was not only totally

This Red Scare continued for more than a year, with strikes, riots, anarchist bombings, police raids, illegal searches, and deportations of suspected radicals making the headlines month after month. In May 1920 the crisis had come to a rather whimpering end, when a national May Day uprising predicted by Attorney General A. Mitchell Palmer failed to occur. By June the hysteria was fading, although aftershocks would continue for a few months, but as luck would have it, that was the month when union organizers came to LaGrange.

On June 24, 1920, the first evidence of union activity appeared. In that day's edition *The Graphic* ran a single front-page paragraph entitled "LaGrange Should Never Be the Haven for Malcontents." In the brief item the editors stated that if "outside agitators" tried to "organize labor unions and disrupt the town," it would be an unfortunate development. The statement was obviously a response to exactly that, for five days later Callaway got some disturbing news from mill manager James Newsome.

That same day, Newsome told Callaway, two union representatives (apparently affiliated with the United Textile Workers of America, itself a branch of the AF of L) had shown up at Deloach's Store near the Unity Mill. "They told Mr. Deloach that they had been here two or three days and that they would remain here six or eight weeks," Newsome reported. "That they intended to organize every industry and business in LaGrange. That it would probably take a long time to do it but they had strong backing behind them." They had tried to rent office space from J. G. Truitt, but since Truitt refused, they said they would build a union hall. Two years earlier the UTWA had managed to unionize the neighboring town of Columbus, and in 1919 a wave of textile strikes in Georgia and the Carolinas had helped usher in high unionization rates throughout the region. LaGrange seemed to be next on the list.

Given Callaway's insistence on control of his own business, as well as the themes of community and cooperation that had long existed in LaGrange, the town likely wouldn't

have responded well to union overtures at any point before this. But coming when it did, in the wake of the Red Scare and at a time when the town was putting the strife of the Southwest LaGrange affair behind it, the organizers stood even less chance than they would have in calmer times. The fact that Callaway's operatives had no major issues reduced that chance still further. The mill strikes in surrounding regions, moreover, had sounded an early warning, so Callaway was ready. Acting together with the Board of Trade, which was now evolving into the LaGrange Chamber of Commerce, he began to coordinate a citywide antiunion effort in which most of the town's business leaders joined.

On July 10, Callaway wrote a number of civic leaders, asking them to prepare commentaries to be published in the local newspaper to help in "saving our city from the plague of labor unionism" that was threatening to infect LaGrange. The response was quite positive. One or two local residents, notably clergymen, declined to write such articles and even suggested that unions weren't as evil as they'd been made out to be. Another correspondent, Ethel Thomas, who edited the mill newspaper *The Shuttle*, did see unions as a threat but responded that she thought a high-profile antiunion campaign was the wrong tactic. "I have always contended that newspapers in publishing accounts of agitation," she told Ab Perry, "created excitement and *more* agitation, and that it was good advertising for those who seek publicity or notoriety." Despite this advice, Callaway and the chamber went ahead with the campaign.

The union organizers came unprepared, which proved yet another handicap. They apparently relied heavily on making personal contacts and distributing broadsides. Only one of two ubiquitous broadsides dealt with textile unionization; the other advocated the unionization of carpenters, and was apparently chosen because it was illustrated. In addition to this *The Graphic* occasionally published letters from some local residents who favored at least the possibility of unionizing.

In response came a flood of editorial contributions from the citizens whom Callaway and the chamber had contacted. The main themes they focused on were the familiar ones: a heritage of and the need for cooperation within a tight-knit community among capital, management, and labor; the value of self-rule and local control, as opposed to influence from union outsiders who might not have LaGrange's best interests at heart; and the evil, selfish nature of unions.

In light of the unrest of the preceding year, some of these arguments were quite strident. Only the postwar labor unrest and a fear of revolution can explain the tone of these writings in light of Callaway's statements in support of the union movement the previous October. In short, the Red Scare was not yet over in LaGrange; instead it was reaching its peak. "There is no soil here to grow this IWW, Bolshevik gang," one writer swore. S. H. Dunson, half brother of Joe Dunson, was solidly in agreement with Callaway on this issue, warning of a cloud hanging over the town that threatened to raise "a wind storm, a cyclone, a tornado" that had the potential to turn LaGrange into "a veritable Hell on Earth." Dunson then went on to describe the threat as "the silent, slimy, and treacherous monster in sheep's clothing that is masked under the dignified name 'American Federation of Labor.'" *The Shuttle* even published an apparently unsolicited letter from a resident of Phenix City, Alabama, who warned LaGrange readers that if they allowed the unions a foothold, those unions would "come in and tear this community up as others I have been in have been torn up."

The Chamber of Commerce even went so far as to hire an Atlanta publicity firm to supply antiunion editorials and graphic cartoons. The editorials harped on the same themes that had been developed by local writers and Call-

away himself. LaGrange, argued the publicity pieces, should be under the control of its own citizens, not that of union bosses who could call a national strike "because the local union in Smithtown, Michigan, has had a quarrel with the shop foreman." Local, internal cooperation, stated the editorials, were far preferable to such an arrangement. Echoing Callaway's statements at the First Industrial Conference, they encouraged an approach in which every mill operative was "an individual—not a cog in a wheel," and observed that, in such a system, citizens like Joe Dunson and Callaway had independently worked their way to the top. The same route was open to "every doffer boy in a LaGrange mill"—if the unions weren't allowed to interfere.

The cartoons supplied by the publicists, echoing S. H. Dunson's writings, were dark and ominous. One of them portrayed a specter labeled "unionism" looming over the happy and contented citizens of LaGrange; another, still darker, showed a mill operative sprawled out on the street in view of his horrified family, victim of a brick labeled "strike violence," with a devil labeled "unionism" congratulating the worker who had thrown the brick. Another cartoon, tapping into recent wartime sentiments, portrayed "labor autocracy" as a giant kaiser-like figure in a *pickelhaube* dictating, "You *do* this! You *do* that! You *cannot* do so and so! You *must* do—" to a small figure labeled "individual worker."

In contrast to such hyperbole, Callaway's own public comments on the subject were relatively restrained. Echoing his comments of the previous October, Callaway conceded that in some circumstances unions could be good, even necessary. The problem, he stated, was that unions could be perverted into "instruments of selfishness, tyranny and lawless oppression." That was presently the case, he argued: the modern union was trying "to set up an oligarchy superior to the law itself . . . under which the ambitions and

Machinery in early textile mills increased speed, but production still required extensive labor, as evidenced by several rows of young women hand-looming moonbeam rugs.

individuals are held down to the level of the least capable and ambitious."

In contrast to such an approach, wrote Callaway, was the one that he'd always favored and had long preached: "the ideal relationship of justice for all the interest affected—labor, capital, management, and the customer." Again he used a phrase that had become a favorite of his. If a business were to last, he wrote, all of those elements had to cooperate in a spirit of "enlightened self-interest." The alternative, he warned, could well be the "death of enterprise in our fair city" since investors "will not put their money where there is to be strife and division."

The hint was probably sufficient. But to underscore it, a notice appeared around this time in all of the Callaway mills. The notice stated that the mills had always used nonunion labor, and that it was in their best interests to keep following this policy. "Employees continuing in our employ," read the notice, "do so with the agreement between us and each of them that they are not members of Labor Unions and that they will not become members of a Textile or Labor Union while in our employment."

Barely a month after the union organizers arrived in LaGrange, the antiunion campaign came to a successful end. On July 30 Callaway himself wrote the Atlanta publicity firm, noting that the antiunion effort was wrapping up. In this letter he noted that the management at each of his mills had been able to secure "personally signed pledges from every one of their employees" that they would refrain from joining a union.

The crisis had blown over as quickly and completely as it had come. Fifteen years later, after Fuller Callaway had passed from the stage, the union question would arise once more, this time against the backdrop of the economic disaster of the Great Depression, a disaster that Callaway himself predicted. But for now Callaway had prevailed. For twenty-five years he'd worked to create a stable, profitable mill community with high standards of living for all of its residents, building on the achievements of more than a decade and a half before that as a merchant. His victory over the unionization effort in 1920 had ended the same way as all of his earlier battles: with success.

FULLER CALLAWAY WANDERING THE LAND SURROUNDING HIS NEW HOME.
BEYOND THE OVERGROWN AGRICULTURAL TERRACES THE NEWLY COMPLETED
NEEL REID-DESIGNED CALLAWAY HOME IS VISIBLE.

· 10 ·

THE FINAL YEARS

"On July 15th Callaway had a birthday," reported the trade magazine *Cotton* in September 1921. "He does this about once a year, although he has been advised by some of his lady acquaintances that if he doesn't quit it he will find himself growing old some day."

Actually Callaway had been feeling the effects of his chronic overextension, if not age, well before 1921. Photographs of him taken in 1919 show him holding a cane, which he'd adopted as a jaunty aspect of his attire some years earlier, but which at some point he likely began to rely upon. In January 1920 he was being mentioned as a successor to his friend Frank Lane, who was about to leave the post as secretary of the interior, for the remaining year of the Wilson administration. But Callaway let it be known that, if offered the job, he would decline the appointment. He gave his usual reasons of commitment to the mills and his other LaGrange positions, but declining energy and worsening health likely played a role in the decision.

By the middle of 1920, just before the unionization battle began in LaGrange, Callaway's health issues had become a real concern. In May he traveled to Johns Hopkins

Hospital. Some of his European friends might be more familiar with LaGrange than with Baltimore, but the hospital, a branch of the Johns Hopkins School of Medicine, had already revolutionized healthcare since its founding three decades earlier; Callaway likely could have found no better hospital in the world. He spent five weeks there in the care of Lewellys F. Barker, former chief physician of the hospital, undergoing an extraordinary range of tests and treatment, including a thorough dental examination, an electrocardiogram (a cutting-edge technology that had only a few years earlier required two rooms full of equipment to record), and, of all things, a psychiatric evaluation, another cutting-edge development in medicine. (The latter concluded, rather predictably, that Callaway had a "very buoyant personality with mood at continuously high level with no apparent tendency to depression.") No doubt because of this personality, as had so often been the case, Barker and Callaway quickly became friends as well as doctor and patient.

The records indicate that Callaway's chief concerns were excitability and nervousness, no doubt related to a more ominous development

Dr. Lewellys Barker, a nationally recognized physician at Johns Hopkins, provided medical care to both Fuller and Ida.

was happily reporting that he had lost twenty pounds. "I believe there are other benefits," he told his friend Sir Herbert Dixon in a letter describing the stay, "not the least of which is the knowledge gained as to how to take care of myself."

As part of that knowledge, Callaway almost immediately began planning another trip to Europe in the spring and summer of the following year. The World Cotton Conference would be meeting in England in June 1921, and Callaway hoped to attend. But this would be largely a vacation, with both Ida and Fuller Jr. accompanying him. He also made some major plans to change his lifestyle in the immediate future. Shortly after Callaway's stay at Johns Hopkins concluded, his new friend Dr. Barker suggested that Fuller and Ida join him for a vacation in his native Ontario. Barker owned a place at Go Home Bay, located on the much larger Georgian Bay; the latter contained a number of small islands, many of them for sale. Callaway, accepting Barker's invitation, began to consider buying one of the islands and spending a few months there each summer.

By July 1920 the plans were in place. Fuller, Ida, and Fuller Jr. would catch a train to Atlanta, spend the day there, and then travel to Savannah, where they would take the steamer *City of St. Louis* to New York. Fuller liked the Savannah Line ships, and on this occasion he arranged specially to have the bridal suite, the most luxurious accommodations aboard. From New York the Callaways would head to Georgian Bay and spend at least a week or two exploring the region and visiting with the Barkers. Following this stay they would return to New York via Montreal, Lake Champlain, Lake George, and Albany, and from there they would return to LaGrange via Washington.

that Callaway had noticed for the past few years: high blood pressure. Physicians had been able to diagnose hypertension for two decades by 1920, and they recognized its dangers, but they still had few treatments for it, chief among them being reduced sodium intake. Barker diagnosed episodes of tachycardia and he also concluded that Callaway was overweight; the treatment he prescribed was a healthful diet emphasizing fruit and green vegetables along with the avoidance of starchy foods. He also prescribed rest after meals, a strict 10:00 p.m. bedtime, and more exercise. Callaway, he advised, should gradually work up to two half-hour walks per day, once in the morning and once again in the afternoon.

By the time he left the hospital, Callaway

That was the plan, at least. But the big birthday party was not in 1921, the *Cotton* article notwithstanding; it was on July 15, 1920, when Fuller turned fifty. As Fuller planned the vacation, LaGrange was plotting quite a surprise celebration, and someone—perhaps Ida, perhaps a knowing Fuller—had seen to it that the family wouldn't set out on the trip until the morning of the sixteenth.

The festivities took place on the evening of the fifteenth in the YMCA gymnasium in Southwest LaGrange (still called by its old name in spite of the recent merger with La-Grange). Four long tables filled the huge room, occupied by two hundred guests, many of them from out of town. At the head table, placed crosswise to the other four, sat the Callaways, Dr. Spencer Tunnell of the First Baptist Church, and toastmaster Hatton Lovejoy. Behind the head table was a large birthday cake sporting fifty candles.

A number of speakers made brief comments, embarrassing Callaway terribly by describing some of the behind-the-scenes good deeds he'd done over the years. As he squirmed uncomfortably, Ida's eyes sparkled. Many letters and telegrams had arrived bearing the good wishes of national civic and political leaders, and the gym was filled with excellent orchestral music as well as offerings from the American Industries quartet. The meal was provided by the Kunzes, a German couple affiliated with the YMCA. The high point of the evening came when Callaway was presented with a silver loving cup, which bore an inscription:

Fuller and Ida used this travel brochure in 1920 during their trip to Ontario. They spent part of their vacation with Dr. Barker.

On his fiftieth Birthday This cup is presented to

Fuller E. Callaway

Somewhat in recognition of the creative genius, the wisdom, the strength, the courage and ability which have been the predominating factors in the wonderful development of the city of LaGrange, and through which he has won the just encomium

"The First Citizen of LaGrange"

But more especially is it hoped that this cup will be an abiding token of the deep and sincere affection of those who have been drawn and bound to him by a magnetism, a memory never failing, an interest never ending for those so fortunate as to be named his friends.

The following morning the excursion began, as the Callaways embarked on the Atlanta-bound train, accompanied by a number of friends who had come down from the capital for the party the day before. All was well, or so it seemed.

About halfway through the trip, Ely Callaway, who was also returning to Atlanta, approached the three vacationers. "Sister Ida," he asked, "have you got any whiskey?"

It was an outlandish request. "Whiskey?" replied Ida, scandalized. "Ely, you know I haven't got any whiskey." Something must be very wrong for Ely to have asked such a question. "What's the matter?"

"I'm just as sick as a dog," moaned Ely. But there was nothing to do for it.

By the time the train pulled into Atlanta, the travelers had realized that something ominous was happening. Two or three others who'd come down for the party had also gotten sick. Concerned, the vacationers headed to the Piedmont Hotel, which they'd be using as their base for the day, but by the time they arrived both Fuller and Ida were showing symptoms as well. Fuller Jr., who'd been allowed to go out with friends instead of attending the party, was fine. That was perhaps the main clue. Something had been wrong with the food at the party.

Back in LaGrange, a number of attendees had fallen deathly ill even as the sickness had swept through the Atlanta-bound train. For a time, in this postwar era, people suspected that the German Kunzes had deliberately poisoned the fare, but that idea soon died down. It was far more likely a simple but potentially deadly case of spoilage.

To keep from upsetting her ailing husband, Ida tried not to let on that she, too, was sick. In Fuller's case there was no hiding it; the food poisoning had hit him quite hard. As soon as he got to the hotel room, he sent for the house physician, who gave him some medicine and departed. Then Fuller, as he

sometimes did, called up a second doctor, who also gave him some medicine, and then a third doctor, who gave him still more.

The train to Savannah was scheduled to leave that evening. Illness or not, Callaway meant to be on it. The bridal suite on the *City of St. Louis* was waiting. As evening approached, he dragged himself up and began dressing, though he could hardly manage it.

"Let's give up the trip," Ida begged him. "Let's stay and get well." But Callaway wouldn't hear of it. The couple, with young Fuller in tow, tottered down to the lobby, where Ida collapsed into a chair while Fuller saw to the bill. Suddenly Fuller went down, his money flying in one direction and his cane in another, his head striking the floor.

Several people immediately rushed over to help, lifting Callaway's legs, loosening his tie, and rubbing his wrists. He was out cold, but within two or three minutes he came to. Still lying on the floor, he pulled out his pocket watch and checked it. "We've got 25 minutes to catch the train," he announced.

Somehow, likely carried along by Fuller's sheer stubbornness, the travelers made it. Ida fell into the berth, not even bothering to undress. By the following morning, Fuller had recovered enough to call on several friends with his son. But that evening, once Fuller and Ida finally arrived in the much-anticipated bridal suite, they stayed there for the whole of the three-day trip to New York, no doubt like many other couples who'd had occasion to stay in the suite, but for very different reasons.

Fortunately no one died from the food poisoning, but apparently some victims had close calls. The Callaways themselves took several more days to recuperate, reversing their itinerary and staying in New York several days, due also in part to scheduling difficulties. No doubt the extra time there came as a relief to Ida. From LaGrange, Ab Perry acknowledged receipt of the change of plan, and nine days after the party he reported that

ON HIS FIFTIETH BIRTHDAY
THIS CUP IS PRESENTED TO

Fuller E. Callaway

SOMEWHAT IN RECOGNITION OF THE CREATIVE GENIUS
THE WISDOM THE STRENGTH THE COURAGE AND THE ABILITY
WHICH HAVE BEEN THE PREDOMINATING FACTORS IN THE
WONDERFUL DEVELOPMENT OF THE CITY OF LA GRANGE
AND THROUGH WHICH HE HAS WON THE JUST ENCOMIUM
"THE FIRST CITIZEN OF LA GRANGE"
YET MORE ESPECIALLY IS IT HOPED THAT THIS CUP
WILL BE AN ABIDING TOKEN OF THE DEEP AND
SINCERE AFFECTION OF THOSE WHO HAVE BEEN DRAWN
AND BOUND TO HIM BY A MAGNETISM UNBROKEN
A MEMORY NEVER FAILING AN INTEREST NEVER TIRING
A LOYALTY AND FIDELITY NEVER ENDING FOR THOSE
FORTUNATE AS TO BE NAMED HIS FRIENDS

239

most of the victims, himself included, were up and about. "All of the sufferers are now out of danger," he was happy to write. "Terrible as it was, there was much to be thankful for that all have lived through this awful experience." He also remarked how glad he was to have received encouraging letters and telegrams from Callaway. "We hope that your entire vacation trip will be marked by only happy experiences and will prove of the greatest benefit to all," he concluded.

Meanwhile, in New York and Ontario, the Callaways were finally enjoying their vacation. On July 25 the travelers steamed up the Hudson to Albany; from there they journeyed to Lake George, where they remained for a few days. On August 12 they joined the Barkers for three days, doubtless touring nearby islands. August 19 found them at Penetanguishene on Georgian Bay, lodging at the Minnicoganashene, a summer resort renowned for its fishing and boating. The Callaways, by now completely recovered, met and entertained a number of new friends, as evidenced by bills for extra dinners, and enjoyed the excellent fishing, as shown by charges for a rowboat and worms. (Ida, in particular, loved to fish.) "Like Minnicog fine," Fuller telegraphed his office. "Will likely stay here until August 27." Then came the meandering journey south, via Niagara, New York City, and Washington. By mid-September the Callaways had returned home. "All three were greatly benefited by our vacation in Canada," declared Fuller.

Nevertheless he wasn't getting any younger, and despite his claim that the vacation had helped, Ida later noted that his general health wasn't improving. Within a couple of weeks after returning from Canada, Fuller then took another step down the road to retirement, a step he'd likely been contemplating for some months.

On Wednesday September 15, 1920, a joint stockholders' meeting of the Unity, Elm City, and Hillside Mills took place at the LaGrange National Bank. That same day came a meeting of the Textile Benefit Association. These were followed the next day in Atlanta by the annual meeting of the Milstead Mill. The mills' financial reports, coming at the end of a turbulent postwar year, were nevertheless all quite good—so good, in fact, that the companies all declared substantial dividends, despite Callaway's dim view of the practice.

But that was only part of the news. The biggest item was that at these meetings, Callaway resigned his positions as corporate officer. To succeed him, the boards elected twenty-four-year-old Cason Callaway as treasurer of Unity and Elm City, and president of Hillside and Milstead. Fuller, meanwhile, was elected chairman of the boards of all of the mills. The Textile Benefit Association, for its part, followed suit, establishing the new position of chairman of the board and electing Callaway to that seat as well. Clearly all these shuffles were designed to keep Callaway involved while sharply reducing his day-to-day workload.

The elevation of Cason to such key positions was by no means a case of nepotism. For more than a decade he'd learned the mills' operation and the textile business from the ground up, in a way even his father never had. He'd also gotten an education fitted to the job, and he'd had valuable managerial experience in the navy during the war. To add to this he was already vice president of the Cotton Manufacturers Association of Georgia. He was, in Fuller's estimation, "a good risk."

Making this shift must have run counter to Callaway's entire worldview; his nature simply demanded that he work hard and be in charge. But his health left him no choice. He'd been burning the candle at both ends far too long for his own good. But in public he showed no sign of any disappointment— quite the opposite. The saving grace was that while he had to be in command, as part of his

Fuller Callaway attended the meeting of the Cotton Manufacturers Association of Georgia in Atlanta on May 16, 1922. Fuller is on the second row in the center. His son Cason is next to him on the left.

leadership he'd always found it easy to delegate. "You can make a fast-running horse poor with hard work," he gamely observed that autumn. "I have had to forbid one of our men to do certain parts of his work. He is a big man, but he won't let himself be big. He wants to do everything."

By the same token he refused to do his employees' work for them, as Ely Callaway had learned decades earlier, when as the new credit manager for the department store, he asked Fuller to make a decision for him. Just as Callaway loathed having responsibility without authority, as he'd initially had at Milstead, he thought authority without responsibility equally bad. Ida and Fuller Jr. both recounted a typical story on occasion. Once while Fuller was having lunch in the Waldorf, he received a telegram from the mills' cotton buyer in LaGrange. The buyer wanted to know Fuller's opinion on cotton prices and whether the agent should buy, since Fuller, in New York, could presumably get more up-to-date information on the market. Telling the bellboy to wait, Fuller turned the telegram over and wrote out a reply, which his son later claimed became the most

famous telegram in textile history. "Some think it's going up, some think it's going down," it read. "I think so too. Whatever you do will be wrong. Act quick!" Fuller made sure to send the telegram collect.

This outlook meant that as far as Fuller was concerned, Cason was now in charge. Fuller knew it and he accepted it, but it took longer for others to accept it as well. For months people kept approaching Fuller regarding issues of mill operation, effectively making end runs around Cason. They almost certainly intended no disrespect; it was simply that Fuller, who'd been in charge of things for a quarter of a century, was still there, and still possessed all of his experience as well as his wisdom.

But the practice irked Fuller, since he knew it put his son in the hated position of having responsibility without authority. The father hinted broadly to some people that he expected them to go to Cason; as early as October 1920 he'd written a World Cotton Conference official that he should "follow in a way the example of the Directors of our companies by saddling on to the young chap anything in the way of real work that you might be counting upon the old man to do." One day in 1921, while he and Hatton Lovejoy were working on a major business matter in the Waldorf, another such request arrived. It was one too many. Fuller discussed the problem with Lovejoy; then as the attorney watched, he sat down and hand-wrote a letter ordering that no more mill questions be brought to him. Everything, he declared, should be directed to Cason. That largely ended the problem.

Thus did Fuller remove himself from day-to-day mill operations. But that didn't mean that he stopped working. In the next few years several matters and new projects occupied his attention.

Surely one of the most gratifying was a wave of national publicity. Because of the many positions he'd held during the war, he'd come into the public eye. Early in his acquaintance with Ida Tarbell during his service on the Council of National Defense and the First Industrial Conference, he'd piqued her interest. "What do you do in LaGrange?" she asked him soon after they met.

"We make American citizens," he told her, "and run cotton mills to pay the expenses."

Such an outlook enticed her to journey to LaGrange after the war. Callaway showed her around the mill community as she interviewed him. In August 1920 her glowing article on Callaway and his operation (Tarbell, a noted critic of corporate America, rarely glowed) appeared in *Red Cross Magazine*. Its title was, aptly, "Making American Citizens and Running Cotton Mills to Pay the Expenses." Two months later in the *American Magazine* came another highly favorable profile entitled "The Homely Wisdom of Fuller E. Callaway," this one written by Helen Christine Bennett. All this was in addition to the *Who's Who in America* entries on Callaway that had appeared for the past few years. These profiles, particularly the Bennett and Dennis writings, contained a wealth of Callaway's thoughts about life and business.

Throughout the interviews Callaway continued to stress the theme of cooperation that he saw as utterly essential to the success LaGrange had achieved. "Callaway, you are a great philanthropist," Bennett exclaimed as she considered the mills' housing, churches, hospital, schools, greenhouses, and gardens. "Do you know that?"

"Philanthropist—nothing!" Callaway answered. "It's business." To be precise, it was a business in which everybody involved won. It was a recipe for success that would bring more success, as Callaway emphasized for Bennett in an anecdote. He told of meeting an acquaintance on the street recently. "Hello, Callaway," he'd said. "What are you starting now?"

"Oh, I don't know," Callaway had replied casually.

"Well," the acquaintance said with a grin, "put me down for a hundred shares."

While Callaway acknowledged his own reduced role in his businesses, he didn't give his health issues as the reason, at least in the Bennett piece. "Men over fifty ought to stop a good share of active work and become seed gardens," he shared, then explained,

We used the Greer Almanac a good deal when I was a boy, used it for crop information. Men are a good deal like the Greer Almanac used to describe the earth. "You want plenty of humus," the old almanac said, "and the earth should be friable and fertile." Now, when a man gets to be fifty he's worn out a good deal of that humus, and he isn't nearly as friable and fertile as he was. But, on the other hand, he's much easier to handle because he's in good shape. His hedges are all trimmed, his stones are all out, and he's worn pretty level. I have a notion that about this time a man ought to be promoted to a kind of emeritus position in business and let in those young fellows—friable and fertile and full of humus—on a good part of the work. The older man (I'm doing it myself at fifty) ought to get down to

R. M. S. "Canopic."

In the spring of 1921 Fuller, Ida, and Fuller Jr. traveled from New York to Genoa aboard the White Star liner *Canopic*.

WHITE STAR LINE

NEW YORK BOSTON FOR MEDITERRANEAN

FIRST CLASS HOLD NOT WANTED

the office late, if he wants to, and play golf afternoons, and keep himself fit to help the young fellows. His best usefulness is to listen to their plans and say: "That's good—let's try it!" or, "Now, I wouldn't do that. I tried that twenty years back and it didn't work."

Despite these observations, as well as his decisive actions in shifting authority to Cason, Fuller still had trouble adjusting to the idea that he was no longer able to work as hard as before, and he still did what he could. In August 1920 he wrote a public letter endorsing Hoke Smith in his bid for reelection to the U.S. Senate. Also around this time, in response to a request from Sir Herbert, he penned a thoughtful memoir on the methods and importance of co-operation among capital, labor, and management. In mid-September 1920, just as he was stepping down from the mills, he received word that he'd been elected as chairman of the World Cotton Conference's executive committee, which he accepted with the proviso that it be arranged that "if I am unable to carry on nothing will be allowed to suffer thereby."

The Canadian trip perhaps helped in the short run, but barely four months later Callaway needed another break. In early 1921 he and Ida traveled to Florida for a longish vacation, perhaps visiting Nassau as well. "The trip was enjoyable for us both," Fuller reported to a friend in mid-March, "but I find I am not yet

well enough to undertake active work." The solution, he hoped, lay in the planned European trip, during which he and his family would see the sights and visit some of the friends they had made during the LaGrange festivities of October 1919. "Mrs. Callaway, Fuller Jr., and I are planning to sail from New York on the steamer *Canopic* of the White Star Line for Genoa to be absent about three months," he told a Tennessee acquaintance.

But Callaway was constitutionally unable to leave the work entirely at home. He made extensive plans to conduct business on the European trip. He made no secret of the fact that he planned to attend the World Cotton Conference, although he did declare that he would be "merely taking the very quiet part an on-looker instead of one of the leaders." The planned departure date was in mid-April, and as soon as he returned from Florida he started getting things in order. He secured letters of credit for himself as well as for Ida and Fuller Jr., his own amounting to the hefty sum of ten thousand dollars and the others made out for one thousand dollars (a princely sum considering that young Fuller was still only fourteen years old). In the wake of the Great War, European states now required passports; Callaway got them from the State Department in late March. While he was at it he also procured letters of

Callaway BEACON

A photo of Fuller, Ida, and Fuller Jr. after a successful fishing trip, was featured on the front of the *Callaway Beacon* on July 10, 1950. The photo dates from about 1920.

introduction from Herbert Hoover, the new secretary of commerce and a figure well-known throughout Europe for his energetic wartime and postwar relief activities, heading up both the Food Administration and the American Relief Administration. Callaway also got a letter of introduction from Charles Evans Hughes, President Warren G. Harding's new secretary of state. Meanwhile, he was conferring with World Cotton Conference officials, making plans to call on several of the conference's key figures. Clearly the business of the trip was beginning to outweigh the other aspects. Other than the letters of credit for young Fuller and Ida, one of Fuller's few concessions was to write letters to friends and acquaintances to ask for their recommendations for the better hotels in some of the cities the family would be visiting.

The *Canopic* was scheduled to leave New York for Genoa, by way of Boston, the Azores, Gibraltar, and Naples, on April 20. But almost on the eve of their departure from LaGrange, on April 11, Ida's mother, Olivia Cason, suffered a major stroke, dying two days later.

The scheduled April 12 departure was obviously out of the question. But Ida was not only mourning the loss of her mother, she was also harboring serious concerns about Fuller's health. Some of her comments in retrospect suggest that she knew or believed that his condition was more serious than he himself knew, although she thought he perhaps suspected. So for the sake of his health, she selflessly insisted that the European tour go on as scheduled. Within a few days, with the shadow of her mother's death still hovering, she and her family set out for New York.

It was likely during the family's brief stay there that an interesting episode took place. One evening the two Fullers were walking through the Waldorf's famed Peacock Alley when the son noticed a man glancing at his father. As the two travelers stopped by the cigar counter for Fuller to make a purchase, the man came up to them. "Aren't you Fuller Callaway of LaGrange, Georgia?" he asked.

Callaway wasn't surprised. He seemed to expect the question. "Yes," he answered. "I wondered if you would remember me. I saw you sitting in Peacock Alley."

"I'll never forget you!" the stranger exclaimed. He turned to the cigar counter. "Give me the biggest box of cigars, the kind Mr. Callaway smokes, that you have," he told the salesman, who quickly complied. The stranger then presented the cigars, together with a five-dollar bill, to Callaway.

Fuller Callaway's angling permit from his 1920 trip to Canada.

A postcard of Waterport Street, Gibraltar. Ida sent this postcard to a friend during the Callaways' 1921 trip to Europe.

"You are the 100th man to pay me back," declared Callaway while his son looked on. "Every one."

Soon young Fuller understood. During the dark summer of 1914, when Fuller and Howard Callaway and Sam Austin were trying to escape London in the first days of the war, he'd given a gold sovereign and his business card to each of a hundred Americans at the Hotel Cecil who hadn't been able to secure any gold of their own. Over the years, Fuller now explained to his son, each of these men had sought him out and repaid the favor, often with a cane, a hat, or a box of cigars, always telling Callaway—as the cigar-stand acquaintance now did—the story of how they'd used the sovereign. This man was the final one; the sovereigns were now all accounted for. Young Fuller never forgot the episode.

The *Canopic* steamed on time with the Callaways aboard. But while the trip abroad would generally be good, other shadows besides the death of Ida's mother awaited. When the ship called for a day at Gibraltar, the Callaways eagerly planned to see the sights, but while there Fuller suffered what Ida termed "a slight attack of apoplexy." While she wrote that he soon recovered, the event clearly did nothing to lessen her worries about his health.

A day or two later the *Canopic* arrived in Italy and the real tour began—fourteen countries over the next three months. The family spent the first half of May exploring the Italian peninsula, spending time in Genoa, Naples, Rome, and Florence.

During the latter half of May, the family moved on to Switzerland, taking in both Lucerne and Zurich. It surely wasn't mere coincidence that the Textile Institute was holding its annual spring conference in Basel at the same time the Callaways were touring the country; Fuller probably dropped in for at least a day, perhaps longer, although by then his work plans may have been changing.

Thus far, despite the Gibraltar incident, Callaway seemed in acceptable health and good spirits. From Florence he wrote a single letter to Cason, Ab Perry, and mill executive Barry J. King, "Three in One," he titled it, "Just for Fun." The message was short: "No quick heart. No trouble. No World Cotton Conference," he reported. "Am thankful and believe you all are going to lose a *detail worrier & worker*. Trip is simply splendid. All three enjoying it."

The news was welcome in LaGrange, producing many letters to Callaway in response. "Your 'three in one' note of May fifteenth has just come to hand, and has gone the rounds of the office, bringing much joy to all," replied Ab Perry a few weeks later. "For while we hate to think of seeing less of our beloved Chief at the office, we are resigned to doing so as a necessary means to your living longer. . . . We were all so glad to know," he added, "that you decided not to go to the World Cotton Conference."

A week after his "three in one" letter, Fuller telegraphed Cason in Philadelphia, where the young executive was attending a meeting of both the American and the Georgia Cotton Manufacturers Associations. "Greetings to friends," the elder Callaway cabled. "Suggest spinners accumulate reserve stock cotton while plentiful as Joseph did corn in Egypt," signing the telegram "Fuller-corn." The timing of the cable suggests that he indeed attended the Textile Institute conference, hearing something that made him suggest the extra purchases to Cason.

He was answered by a telegram from Cason: "Thanks Philadelphia cable," it read. "Elected president [of Georgia] association. Cable regarding mother's cough. If not well, suggest week's rest in bed." Ida, not wanting him to worry, sent a message of her own. "Cough well. All happy. Congratulations."

In early June the Callaways moved on to Vichy, one of the high points of the trip. Over the years Fuller had developed quite a liking for Vichy water; despite its sodium content. Dr. Barker had even permitted Callaway to drink some with lemon juice before breakfast each morning. After having to pay to get the water shipped to LaGrange, Callaway was looking forward to drinking all of it he wanted right at the source. Cason, among others, prophesied that Fuller would likely have to drink so much of it while there that "he would have to be poured back into the spring." But Dr. P. DesGeorges, whom Fuller consulted at Vichy, quickly vetoed the idea, forbidding him any of the water. Cason and the others back home had a good laugh at the irony when they heard about it, but in Vichy, neither Ida nor young Fuller was laughing. According to DesGeorges, Fuller's blood pressure was so high that he was in danger of having a stroke at any time. Apparently keeping the information from Fuller, probably to avoid precipitating the very stroke he was trying to avert, the physician told Ida to come up with some way to keep Fuller at Vichy for at least two weeks.

Ida handled the situation by telling Fuller that the water was benefiting her, which she, in fact, believed it was. This sufficed to extend the Vichy stay for the two weeks DesGeorges had called for. The rest did Fuller a noticeable

amount of good. Then the family was off again. Throughout France the Callaways roamed, sometimes by train, sometimes by boat, sometimes by carriage; making new friends along the way; Fuller arranging and scheduling things for the group, taking in museums, cathedrals, and parks; engaging local guides at each stop; and sometimes covering hundreds of miles in a day. One thing he particularly enjoyed doing was taking his wife and son to places he'd scouted out on previous trips.

During the stay in Vichy, Fuller definitively decided not to try attending the World Cotton Conference even as a passive observer,

Fuller, Ida, and Fuller Jr. visited St. Neot Parish, Cornwall, during their 1921 European trip. Here they saw the St. Callaway stained-glass window for the first time.

The Callaway stained glass window at St. Neot Parish, Cornwall, inspired Ida to add the "Ora Pro Me" motto to the garden.

but that didn't mean he would avoid a lengthy stay in England. Late June found the family touring Germany. It was Fuller's first visit to the country since the thunderous summer of 1914. The timing was interesting; almost on the same day Congress was passing the Knox-Porter Resolution, which formally ended the state of war between the United States and Germany, although a German-American peace treaty wouldn't be in place until the end of August. By July 2, however, the day the resolution passed, the Callaways had departed Berlin, completed visits to Wiesbaden and Hamburg, moved on through Brussels, and at last arrived in London.

During July the Callaways traveled throughout England, visiting many places and friends. One of the latter was Alfred P. Dennis, Callaway's friend from the Italian embassy who was now a commercial attaché in London. Another was Sir Frank Warner, KBE, a silk and velvet manufacturer and one of England's

foremost authorities on the silk industry. Several months earlier, upon learning that the Callaways would be visiting, he'd sent Fuller a "scrap of 'Canterbury Muslin,' the invention of John Callaway which had made Canterbury famous and prosperous in the early 18th century." Fuller was quite interested in the cloth and its significance, and this may well have been the spur that caused the family to explore the Callaway roots in July. This exploration led to Cornwall, where the Callaways found the family stained-glass window at St. Neot Church, inspiring Ida to include the "Ora pro me" inscription in her garden.

One friend the Callaways wouldn't be visiting was Sir Herbert Dixon. The baronet and textile giant had died the previous December, overtaxed by his work during the war; the news had "deeply shocked and grieved" Callaway when he'd received the cable on the very day of Sir Herbert's death. But life went on. Despite Sir Herbert's absence, the Callaways made sure that Manchester was on their itinerary. In fact they were there on July 15, Fuller's fifty-first birthday, where several leading members of the World Cotton Conference hosted a banquet to celebrate the occasion.

A few weeks earlier, during the Philadelphia meeting of the Georgia Cotton Manufacturers Association, several members got the idea of sending Callaway a special birthday present. As one humorous report had it, the Philadelphia attendees "became greatly perturbed because someone suggested that Callaway had gone abroad and that perhaps in his haste had neglected to carry with him his cane, or his 'stick' as our British cousins know it. Therefore, when the suggestion was made to send some little token of remembrance to this absent member, a 'stick' was the unanimous choice." A committee was thus established, the gift procured, and a member who planned to attend the World Cotton Conference delegated to deliver it. The member gave it to Frank Nasmith, one of the banquet's hosts, and as a high point of the evening, Nasmith presented it to Callaway. The cane sported a gold band bearing the inscription:

Presented to Fuller E. Callaway, Esq.,
Georgia Cotton Manufacturers Association
As a token of their
Appreciation, Esteem and Respect.

At the Manchester station a minor incident took place; Ida, holding the gift cane, her purse, and several packages, dropped the cane and the purse while boarding the train. The items fell from the platform down onto the tracks. Young Fuller immediately jumped between the cars and onto the tracks to retrieve the items, giving Ida a scare. Luckily the train didn't start moving until he had gotten back up onto the platform.

When Fuller Callaway traveled to London, he often stayed at the Hotel Cecil, located between the Thames and the Strand.

After the Manchester visit the Callaways returned to London for the final days of July, basing themselves at the Hotel Cecil, where the Callaway party had stayed as war loomed in August 1914. On August 6 they steamed for New York, arriving there ten days later and just missing Hatton Lovejoy, who'd been in town working on matters at J. H. Lane. But other friends awaited them on the dock, and as the ship approached, the welcoming party could see Callaway standing on deck, surrounded by acquaintances, holding his cane and smiling.

In the months that followed his return from Europe, Callaway, unable to help himself, returned to a work schedule that his various doctors would have condemned, although it was not what it had been in the old days. Throughout the rest of 1921 and most of 1922, he focused on two projects in particular. The first was a country club for La-Grange. Having been entertained in many clubs over the past several years, he'd come to believe that the community could benefit from the amenities of one. It would be good, recreationally speaking, for its members, and it would be a good business asset as well. Forty thousand dollars were quickly subscribed for the project, which would be called

HIGHLAND COUNTRY CLUB, LA GRANGE, GA.—14

Highland Country Club, La Grange, Georgia

In 1922 Fuller Callaway helped found Highland Country Club. He donated 207 acres of land and secured the services of Neel Reid to design the clubhouse. The golf course was designed by the noted Donald Ross.

the Highland Country Club, with a number of Callaways, Dunsons, and Truitts among the subscribers, together with Roy Dallis, Ab Perry, and Hatton Lovejoy.

Lovejoy took the lead in securing a charter, which he did in January 1922. Callaway himself donated outright the 207 acres of land for the club, located not far north of Hills and Dales. At his urging, the younger men more directly involved in the club's founding sought out considerable talent to design the facilities. For the clubhouse they engaged Neel Reid's architectural firm; to design a nine-hole golf course, they approached Donald Ross, the celebrated Scottish-born course designer. The club soon boasted other amenities as well, including tennis courts and a swimming pool. The subscribers thoughtfully made provisions for the younger, up-and-coming men in the community by requiring only membership dues, with no initiation fee.

One humorous passage by an early chronicler of the club noted, quite accurately, that it was designed from the start to be family oriented. For that reason, notes the account, there was a "definite agreement that there was to be no drinking in sight of the youngsters," although legally, given Prohibition, there should have been no drinking at all. Nevertheless,

continues the account, club members winked at "a little nip on occasion" in the locker room, with anyone who'd taken too many nips being "quietly taken to his home."

By 1922 Callaway was also involved in a much more complex undertaking, his second major post-European project. The textile market was bad in the early 1920s, a running concern for Callaway and others in the industry, and Callaway felt the need to have as much contact directly with buyers as possible in order to offset the hard times. Working with Cason, he came up with a plan for the mills to establish their own selling agency. Callaway's relationship with the J. H. Lane Company had been in place for nearly a quarter of a century, and on the whole it hadn't been bad; Callaway and Coit Johnson of Lane were good friends. But Lane was still an independent concern, and there had been friction more than once. "Dammit," the normally cheerful Callaway had been heard to say of Lane on occasion, "the tail is wagging the dog."

In April 1922 the mills' boards began officially planning to establish a new selling agency; by the end of the month they'd gone public with the news. All the evidence suggests that the split between Lane and the mills was amicable. One stated reason was that some of the older Lane people who'd handled the Callaway accounts were, like Callaway himself, cutting back on their workloads as they neared retirement. But the split, as well as the establishment of the new firm, was still quite complex despite the goodwill. The arrangement, in which Fuller Callaway played a quite active role, involved some though not all of the aspects of a stock swap. A good many of the mills' investors evidently owned Lane stock, and the mills encouraged them to sell this stock to the new selling agency or exchange their stock for shares in the new company. This new agency—named, appropriately, Callaway Mills, Inc.—would then borrow start-up money against the value of the Lane stock it held. The indications are that Callaway Mills would then sell the stock back to Lane.

Callaway Mills, Inc. was established on July 1, 1922, and quickly began operations. The stock exchanging process continued for several months afterward, as Callaway, Lovejoy, and Johnson worked on securing an equitable deal for all parties. By the end of the year, most of the work had been done. But it came at further cost to Fuller Callaway's health. In August, suffering from a new spell of poor health, Callaway checked in to the famed Battle Creek Sanatorium in Battle Creek, Michigan, where he would spend time over several summers in the near future, for rest and medical tests.

Battle Creek, which during its life hosted such patients as Mary Todd Lincoln, Warren G. Harding, Henry Ford, and Amelia Earhart, was a health resort that operated according to Seventh-Day Adventist health principles that provided a natural fit for Callaway's needs. The workup he received there confirmed the cardiac and blood pressure problems that had been found at Johns Hopkins two years earlier, and the Battle Creek doctors prescribed the same diet and lifestyle changes. The doctors also noted that Callaway's tonsils weren't in the best shape, a problem that continued to bother him in the coming months.

Despite the need to take it easy, even while at Battle Creek, Callaway exchanged a flurry of cables with Cason regarding the new selling agency, and he followed his stay there with a trip directly to New York. Small wonder, then, that even after returning to La-Grange, Callaway remained in poor health. To make matters worse, Ida was also suffering from a serious illness, which culminated in the removal of one of her kidneys that same August.

The following spring both Fuller and Ida presented themselves at Johns Hopkins for thorough workups, including a careful examination of Fuller's tonsils. While Dr. Barker reported that Ida was coming along quite nicely, seeing "no signs whatever of the trouble for which she was operated upon," Fuller's condition still worried the physician.

Fuller Callaway acquired this electric light bath from the Battle Creek Sanatorium.

Callaway visited the Battle Creek Sanatorium in Michigan for rest, therapy, and medical tests.

One of the doctors who examined him reported a "very definite chronic infection of the tonsils" and recommended that he have them removed. But Fuller was still overweight, and in light of his hypertension, Barker advised against surgery. "We rather dislike to put a man with increased blood pressure through a surgical operation unless it is imperatively necessary," he explained.

The weight problem was also an issue. For at least two years various doctors both in Europe and America had been telling Callaway to watch what he ate, prescribing strict diets light on meats and fats, and rich in cereals, fruits, and vegetables. But the diet was hard for him to stick to. He loved food too much and he chewed too quickly. By this time, in an effort to stick to the diet, he moved himself and Pope to a separate table in the Hills and Dales dining room, since Pope, too, was on a special diet. That way, hoped Fuller, the two men could control their eating. But it didn't work. Fuller would gobble up all of the food he'd been served, and then he'd slide his chair over to the main table and start visiting with everyone there. As he visited, he'd begin "tasting" whatever dishes had been served at the main table. The "tasting" soon got out of hand, and before long the diet was over.

Despite this weakness, Callaway knew that he had to be careful, and he showed this in other ways. In September 1923 he received a

letter from Georgia Governor Clifford Walker dated Tuesday the eleventh. "You will notice from the papers that I have taken the liberty to name you as a member of the Tax Committee which is to take under consideration the needs of the State Government and the reformation of the tax system," the governor informed him. He clearly knew that Callaway wasn't well; nevertheless he continued, "I hope you will be good enough to suspend judgment as to your ability to render a partial service on this Committee until I can confer with you on Thursday."

It wasn't quite out of the blue. Five days earlier Walker had apparently spoken to Callaway by telephone, requesting a meeting. Perry, speaking for Callaway, had then written Walker a cautionary letter that suggested Callaway was taking his physicians' warnings seriously. "Mr. Callaway has been unwell for some time and is still finding it necessary to spend only short periods at the office," Perry explained, "and to limit his activities to only the most necessary duties." The trip to Atlanta that Callaway was contemplating, Perry informed Walker, might not even be possible.

In answer to this came the appointment, which Walker made public. As a result of the announcement, one attorney who would be working with the commission even sent Callaway a tax proposal for his review and began sounding him out as to his preferred meeting schedule. In light of all this, Walker's actions come across as a heavy-handed insistence bordering on rudeness, an attempt to force the hand of an ill man who had never enjoyed being bossed around even on his best days. Perhaps Walker presumed to do this because of Callaway's brief service at the National Cotton Conference on Boll Weevil Control the previous February, an appointment Callaway had accepted from Walker's predecessor, Thomas W. Hardwick. But Walker handled things badly, and Callaway didn't stand for it. Indications are that he telephoned Walker immediately after receiving the September 11 letter to decline the appointment, and that even then Walker continued to press him. Then, on Thursday, September 13, the day Walker had hoped to meet with him, Callaway sent the governor a pointed letter. "In answer to your kind favor of the 11th," he wrote, "I am sorry to say that I am obliged to ask that you consider my declination as final." Perhaps Callaway was sorry, but in light of Walker's approach, not as sorry as he might have been otherwise. "Much as I regret this I have no choice, really, as the state of my health is forcing me to give up a large part of my regular work." Again his regret was likely genuine, at least to a degree; his statements indicate that Barker and the other doctors were at last getting through to him. But Walker's handling of the affair probably helped Callaway accept the change in lifestyle.

Another event of just a few weeks before also probably helped, and may have contributed to Callaway's impatience with Walker. In late July 1923, Pope Callaway died of kidney failure. On Saturday, July 28, he was stricken suddenly in the morning, expiring the following Tuesday. It was a hard blow. "He had made his home with us for about twenty-five years," Fuller wrote his distant English relation John Callaway, "and his going away was indeed a great shock." It would have been a shock in any event, but Pope's kidney failure raised the specter of Ida's own recent affliction. It was an inevitable reminder to both Fuller and Ida of their own mortality, an event that Fuller likely took as a warning that he must take better care of himself.

By December 1923, less than half a year after Pope's death, Howard Callaway had retired from business and moved in with Fuller and Ida in the wake of his own wife's demise. "All through my life," Fuller told Howard around this time, "you have been the very

Fuller (left) and his brother Pope standing on the terrace at Hills and Dales. Pope lived at Hills and Dales from 1916 until his death in 1923.

best brother that any boy, youth, or man could have, and I am deeply grateful for your love and the unfailing sympathy and understanding you have always shown." Ida, too, was happy to have him; given the resemblance between Howard and Fuller, she began referring to them as "my twins."

Howard's arrival was one more sign that times were changing, but by then Fuller hardly needed it. By October he'd already decided, in the words of Ab Perry, "to give up entirely all detailed work and will only come to the office twice weekly for short periods of consultation."

In October, when Perry announced this decision, both Fuller and Ida returned to Johns Hopkins for a month of treatment under Dr. Barker's care. "At last Mrs. Callaway and I are going to do what you have been recommending for some time," Fuller wrote to his friend Barker. "We are coming to you for a stay of a number of weeks under your direction." The couple had taken several vacations and made several hospital visits in the preceding two years, so Fuller's comment indicates that this latest sojourn to Baltimore would be for some special purpose, likely centered around rest and dieting. "We are coming to you," he continued, "because of our implicit faith in your great ability; believe if anyone can set us on the road to health, you can."

This was quite an admission from the normally upbeat Fuller, and he followed it with another confession that was more remarkable still. He informed Barker that he wanted to begin treatment as soon as possible. "I am nervous and run down," he stated plainly, "and believe it will be bad for me to be subjected to delays or disappointment in this regard."

All of this suggests that the autumn of 1923 was a turning point in Fuller Callaway's life. Certainly he seemed to think so. But despite his resolution, he still didn't let go entirely. While in Baltimore he kept in touch with Perry by telegram, with Perry responding by letter. Ida also kept Perry informed— perhaps surreptitiously—of Fuller's condition during the stay. Apparently Callaway was serious about making major changes, the correspondence with Perry excepted. As soon as he got to Johns Hopkins, Ida told Perry, he slowed down. "I was afraid that he would have a hard time of it to start with," Perry replied, "because he had kept going and thinking about the business much too long." Everybody, it seemed, agreed on this. Now it seemed things were finally changing. "It is a great relief," Perry declared, "to know that Mr. Callaway has already begun to mend and that it is being made so pleasant and satisfactory to you both."

Returning to LaGrange in early November, Fuller declared that he felt much improved. Things were going to be different now, or at least that was the plan. He was under strict orders from Barker as to his diet and daily routine. He was to go to the office only two days a week, and he was to work only for two hours on those days. It was now a life-or-death matter, if it hadn't been before, and Fuller's statements show that he took Barker's warning seriously, but it still went against the grain. Fuller Jr. later claimed that despite Barker's instructions, his father still contrived to get to the office every day until his death, even though he did much less work. "Perhaps it is just as well that my health prevents me from taking an active part," he wrote somewhat wistfully to the executives of the Callaway Mills selling agency the following spring, forcing himself to look on a bright side that he now often mentioned. "It gives our younger men an opportunity to master the business and for each one to show the degree of his resourcefulness and ability." Still he couldn't help but give advice, even when it was only of a general sort. "I consider that the present furnishes you and our other young men *the* opportunity of your lives, as well as the supreme test of your respective abilities," he told the executives. "I shall count upon our being able to demonstrate superior ability in getting business, and so faring better than our competitors."

Aside from the textile mills, Callaway had many other interests, and these helped fill the vacuum left by his restricted office hours. One of these was his church. Callaway had joined the Baptist church around the age of ten, and he'd been involved in it ever since. "I believe everything in the Bible—every word of it," he once told Alfred P. Dennis. He had no interest at all in religious modernism, and by way of compliment, Dennis described Callaway as having a

Callaway acquired his favorite horse, Jim, in 1920 and was frequently seen riding him around LaGrange and the surrounding countryside.

thirteenth-century theological mind. "I never dispute with anyone about religion," Callaway also proclaimed to Dennis. "I am like my old Aunt Judy who was making pickles one day in the kitchen and had set a bowl of hot pickles outside to cool. One of our smart young men about town"—and Callaway didn't mean *that* as a compliment—"dropped in to tell her that he had been reading some of the infidel writings and had decided to give up his belief in the Bible. Aunt Judy did not think it worth while to argue with him," he concluded. "All she did was to throw the bowl of pickles in his face."

In a more restrained way Fuller told Ida that he sinned every day "unintentionally," as he put it, "but that he asked the Lord to forgive him every night; and that when he died he was going to knock at the Mercy Gate and ask Saint Peter to let him in, as the Lord's Mercy would be the only Gate through which he could enter."

In practice Callaway always wanted his employees to follow the Golden Rule. As usual he had an anecdote to show what he meant—or in this case, what he didn't mean. He told the story of a clerk who showed his customer a bolt of cloth; she asked to see a better quality item. The clerk then showed her the same grade of cloth but quoted more than twice the price as the first bolt, and the customer bought it.

"I told you to sell by the Bible," the owner told the clerk in disapproval once the customer had left.

"I did," protested the clerk. "She was a 'stranger' and I 'took her in.'" The story was good, even though in Callaway's eyes the clerk's behavior was bad.

Callaway generously supported his church as well as the Episcopal-affiliated LaGrange Settlement. Often he did so behind the scenes. In addition to contributing openly to every ministry his church carried on, he also gave large discretionary sums to its pastors, provided only that the pastors withhold the donor's name. But in the fall of 1923 he made one very public contribution when he subscribed two of the windows that the church was replacing, requesting that the name Callaway be placed on one and Cason be inscribed on the other. Then in the following year, acting either directly or through the Relief Association, Fuller and Ida donated thousands of dollars to the needy.

Hills and Dales, along with agricultural concerns, also drew Callaway's attention. In the early 1920s Callaway wrote to the federal Department of Agriculture, asking for every sort of pamphlet on horticulture and crop growth. Of course he'd always been interested in these things, but the interest naturally grew as he spent more time at home and his exercise took him around the estate. He still walked, in keeping with his doctors' instructions. Often he walked the whole one and a quarter miles to his office. But he'd also acquired a favorite new horse named Jim, whom he rode throughout the nearby countryside. For trips with Ida he also bought a new car, which the couple enjoyed.

On at least one occasion though, someone expressed disapproval of the horse. One day as Fuller rode Jim across a small plank bridge on the farm, a plank broke. Jim went down, injuring Fuller's knee in the process.

A few days later, when Fuller was able to ride again, he took Jim to the golf course. He was watching the golfers, as he often liked to do, when they came across Sam Austin, the mill executive who'd shared Fuller's and Howard's adventures in wartime Europe back in 1914. Austin paused his golf game for a chat.

"Mr. Callaway," Austin greeted him, "I heard Jim fell down on you the other day."

"Yes, he fell down," confirmed Callaway, "but it didn't hurt him a bit and he got up all right."

It wasn't Jim that Austin was worried about. "I don't like that, Mr. Callaway," he replied. "I don't like Jim falling down; he's liable to hurt you. If you go down to the stable some morning and find old Jim has been chloroformed," he said, all innocence, "don't blame me."

By this time Callaway and Jim were good friends. Thinking with his usual speed, Callaway came up with a humorous response that got his point across. "Sam," he observed, "did I have you chloroformed the first time you fell down on me?" The story got around, and nobody else ever made a death threat against Callaway's equine friend.

There were other pleasant episodes besides Callaway's new pastoral life. The family continued to vacation in Florida in the winters, often going on excursions from Miami in the family car. Callaway also kept up his correspondence with family and friends, often slipping in a little business as well. Lewellys Barker, perhaps because of his association with the Callaways, once asked Fuller's advice on a potential textile investment he was considering with another Georgia company, which Fuller was happy to give: "Opinions as to the future are decidedly at variance.... Personally I would not care for the common stock at $200 per share."

In the summer of 1924 came a pleasant development. Alfred Pearce Dennis, Callaway's friend from the Italian and London embassies, now returned to Washington, wrote a longish article on Callaway for *Country Gentleman Magazine*, an old and prestigious agricultural publication. "I hope you like the article," Dennis wrote Callaway, enclosing the galley proofs of the piece. "I could not make it as laudatory as my affection for you prompted, otherwise it might have lost its judicial quality and have been considered only the eulogy of a friend." The article later went on to become a chapter in Dennis's book *Gods and Little Fishes*, published in 1931.

Callaway fell upon the galleys immediately, writing Dennis as soon as he finished going over them. "Dear Dr. Dennis," he wrote,

Words fail me in trying to express my appreciation of your article written for the Country Gentleman of August 16th. As I have read it over I have first of all been impressed with its literary quality, the keen sympathy in interpretation of motives and purposes which it reflects but what touches me particularly is the consciousness of having won such dear partial friendship. This I appreciate more than I can tell you and let me assure you that it is most heartily reciprocated. I have greatly enjoyed the privilege of knowing you, a feeling which is shared by all of my family. We want you and Mrs. Dennis to give us the pleasure of visiting us as often and for as long as may be convenient.

Another solace for Callaway was his family. Among other things, he took an interest in genealogy. "For some time past I have been accumulating genealogical data regarding the Callaway and the Howard families," he told Cason in April 1924. "I hope in time to get everything together for a complete record. If I should not be spared

Ida and Fuller's granddaughter Virginia (Jinks) with her Great Dane, Rex.

to do this I want to ask that you see to it that the data gathered is preserved and if possible and you are so inclined I should be glad for you to finish what I have started in this direction."

Fuller's interest in genealogy likely went back at least to the 1921 visit to Cornwall. Certainly he corresponded with his distant kinsman John Callaway, whom he and Howard both knew from 1914, after the 1921 trip, although not all of the exchange was on pleasant subjects, for John Callaway, too, was ill. "I can appreciate what it means to suffer poor health," Fuller commiserated, "because I have been in bad shape for some time past myself. My trouble is high blood pressure and

Ida Cason Callaway with grandchildren Virginia (Jinks) and Howard (Bo) in the garden at Hills and Dales in about 1930.

exhausted nervous forces." Nevertheless, Callaway seemed to enjoy the correspondence. And if his interest in family history had been piqued by the Cornwall journey, it was likely also strengthened by a wholly happy development: the arrival of his first grandchildren.

For all of his hard work Cason was fun-loving, and into his early twenties he showed no desire to settle down, preferring to share a freewheeling bachelor's life with his older friend Chilton Coleman, the head of the Southwest LaGrange School. This was fine up to a point, but by the time the war ended and Cason had come home from the navy, he was nearly twenty-five years old and his father was getting concerned, perhaps having Pope's lifelong bachelorhood in mind. One day Callaway spotted the two friends. "Doggone your procrastinating times," he told them lightly but seriously, "it's high time you married. You're both getting more particular and less desirable all the time."

The message seemed to sink in, at least with Cason. Not long afterward, while attending a party in Atlanta, he met Virginia Hollis Hand. She would have been nineteen, or very close to it, at the time; her father, fittingly enough, owned a mercantile business in Pelham, Georgia. The two were quite taken with each other, and on April 3, 1920, they were married in Pelham. This sign of growing stability on Cason's part was likely an event that factored into Fuller's decision to hand the reins over to him later that year.

On August 21, 1921, on one of Ida's "happiest days," Virginia Hand "Jinks" Callaway was born. She was the first grandchild and a special treat for Fuller and Ida, who had only boys. Then on July 17, 1924, came the first grandson, Cason Jewell Callaway Jr., who quickly became Fuller Sr.'s "pal." On April 2, 1927, he was followed by Howard Hollis (Bo) Callaway, named in part for his maternal grandmother.

With the arrival of these grandchildren, wrote Ida, "our happiness seemed complete. . . . Our cup of joy overflowed."

By this time Fuller Jr. also was coming of age. In the fall of 1924 he was seventeen, although one family acquaintance declared, "He has the poise of a man of twenty-five" as well as "the fine modesty of his father and mother." That year he matriculated at Georgia Tech, inaugurating a long and important relationship between the school and the Callaway family.

Although Fuller Jr. was off at school a good bit for the rest of his father's life, his strongest recollections of Fuller Sr. were from this period. By this time the elder Fuller was having significant dental trouble, and he had his dentist extract the problem teeth, which had gold fillings. "Don't throw away those teeth," ordered Callaway, true to form; the gold was valuable. He had the dentist retrieve it, and Callaway then had the gold melted down into two rings, one for each of his sons. "I want you always to wear these," he told them. "If you ever do anything that I wouldn't approve of, I'll bite you."

Young Fuller also recounted how family and friends conspired to keep Callaway's health as sound as possible. One tactic was to arrange a schedule whereby a different family member or business executive would happen to drop by every afternoon to sit and talk with Callaway. Ministers and close family friends also called in the afternoons. Within a matter of weeks Callaway spotted the pattern, but he enjoyed the visits, so he went along with the ruse. Roy Dallis, who according to Ida was the last surviving investor in the original mill other than Callaway himself, was a particularly welcome guest. Young Fuller was on the schedule as well, despite frequently being away at Georgia Tech; it was during his own afternoon visits that he really came as an adult to know his father. One of the many conversa-

Two of Fuller and Ida's five grandchildren standing together. Howard (Bo) is with his older brother Cason Jr. (Caso).

tions that stayed with him was the one in which Fuller Sr. predicted the 1929 stock market crash.

The business executives were under strict instructions not to share any news during their visits that Callaway might find distressing. Most of the time they were able to comply, but on occasion Callaway still managed to find out something disturbing that had been kept from him. He would then get distressed and excited, and an angina attack would often follow.

Try as they might—and try as he might—there was simply no way to divorce Callaway entirely from work, or at least an interest in

While the Callaway Auditorium was not built until the 1940s, more than a decade after Fuller's death, the idea of an auditorium was suggested to Fuller by the city's lack of a proper venue to host the great orator, William Jennings Bryan.

work. The very thought of stopping completely made him feel helpless. By around 1926, when walking to town had gotten to be too much for him, he and Ida would take the car in the mornings, calling on various mills and offices. At first Callaway would walk around the mill premises, but eventually he was reduced to sitting in the car as Barry King or someone else came out to give him a report on whatever was going on.

One project that Callaway gave some thought to in his final years was a town auditorium. Decades before, during the heyday of William Jennings Bryan, the great Democratic orator had come to LaGrange. Although voting for Bryan when he was the Democratic nominee in the 1896 presidential election, Callaway was no Bryan

supporter; Bryan's "soft money" policies were anathema to him. But despite this the two men had struck up a friendship, likely based on their common social and moral views. In later years Bryan made a speech at the railroad depot in 1911, and he visited Hills and Dales more than once. On one occasion, at Callaway's urging, he'd given an address. Callaway was chagrined that the town had no facility with enough seats for the important event; Bryan had to speak in a gymnasium that could seat only seventy-five people, and after the address Callaway announced his hope that one day the town would be able to afford an auditorium where great speakers would appear. The auditorium, boasting two thousand seats, finally became a reality in the early 1940s under young Fuller's leadership; still, the idea began with his father.

Callaway also participated in some major business developments in late 1927 and early 1928, when Cason oversaw the chartering of no less than five new mills. Among them were Valley Waste Mills, which had been using cotton waste productively as part of Hillside for many years; Valway Rug Mills, which focused on the specialized process of rug weaving; Rockweave Mills, another Hillside offshoot that produced goods related to the laundry trade; Oakleaf Mills, yet another Hillside spin-off that turned out flannel and cord; and Truline, which produced cotton breeches. It was the most ambitious mill expansion and reorganization to date, and while Cason of course oversaw it, his father took a huge interest in it, attending several directors' meetings in early 1928.

Once these projects were well underway, Fuller at last—or so it seemed to Ida—resigned himself to his end. The key moment, she believed, was when the stock certificates he'd bought in the new corporations were brought in for him to sign, with Cason's

Just over eighteen months after Fuller Callaway's death, the Callaway Memorial Clock Tower was dedicated. The tower was designed by Ed Ivey and Lewis Crook and modeled after the Campanile in St. Mark's Square in Venice, Italy.

Located on a hill overlooking southwest LaGrange, the dedication of the Callaway Memorial was held on October 15, 1929. Throngs of friends and mill employees attended the ceremony.

name appearing on them as president and Fuller Jr.'s as treasurer. For Callaway the moment symbolized the completion of his work. "He had always said that he hoped to see the boys both established in business," Ida wrote. The names of both of them on those certificates meant the fulfillment of that hope.

But for her part Ida was not yet resigned to being parted from her husband. "Now Fuller," she told him, "you must live to see our bright little grandson, Cason Jr., established in business." But to that Fuller would

only shake his head. "My task is almost finished," he answered. "Cason Sr. and Fuller Jr. will have to attend to that."

One afternoon around this time—probably in the latter part of 1927—it was young Fuller's day to make an afternoon call on his father. That summer the elder Callaway's brother Howard had died; it was another reminder of the turning of the wheel. Callaway knew well by then that his own time, too, was short. "Son," he told his namesake, "you know I haven't got much longer to live and when I die, people are going to say wasn't

The Pullman Car, dedicated to Fuller E. Callaway Sr. Standing left to right are Fuller E. Callaway Jr., Alice Hand Callaway, Virginia Hand Callaway, and Cason Callaway.

Callaway a fool; worked himself to death; burned the candle at both ends, but . . . if I had my life to live over again and could start out knowing everything that I know today, even knowing what I've learned by experience, I wouldn't do one, single thing different from what I did."

That prompted young Fuller to ask him a question. "Father," he spoke up, "of all the things you've done, what are you the most proud of?"

The answer perhaps surprised him, but probably, knowing his father, it didn't. "Well, not putting them in any order," replied Callaway, "I saved your uncle Pope from being a drunkard. I gave your uncle Howard the last few years of his life in hap-

piness. Third, I've always been true to your mother." The stores, the mills, the banking, the national roles as industrial leader: none of them made the list.

On the night of February 11, 1928, with the new mills safely incorporated and the stock certificates signed, Callaway had a restless night. "The next morning, however," Ida recounted, "he was very bright and talkative while waiting for his breakfast. Then, suddenly, he lay back and folded his hands across his breast; and his great, loving heart beat no more. I am glad and thankful," she added, "that the messenger came thus peacefully and in the fresh vigor and promise of the early morning." Fuller Earle Callaway was fifty-seven years old.

Callaway had two favorite anecdotes concerning death, greed, and generosity. One was a simple statement; he often remarked that he'd never seen a shroud that had pockets. Money was to be used for good, not hoarded. He also often told a story of a friend of his who served as the administrator of an estate, and Ida retold the story in her account of Fuller's life:

Somebody asked how much money the man left. The friend replied, "He left it all." Fuller said that if one could carry gold to heaven, it would just be in the way, for it would make a pile to stumble over, as the streets were already paved with gold; and if he didn't go to heaven the gold would melt! "This world," he went on, "is a fiery furnace, into which we, like Shadrach, Meshach and Abednego, were thrown for the fire to refine the gold and burn out the dross in us."

The funeral took place on the morning of February 14. A host of around fifty Callaway organization directors served as an honorary escort; among them were at least

In the years following Fuller's death, a special ceremony was held annually on July 15 at the Callaway monument. In 1932 Cason (center) and Fuller Jr. (right) present a special award to a longtime mill employee.

The Callaway mausoleum at Hill View Cemetery was encircled with flowers after Fuller's death on February 12, 1928.

two Dunsons, as well as C. V. "Neal" Truitt. The pallbearers included Chilton Coleman, Barry King, Sam Austin, Hatton Lovejoy, and Ab Perry. A name conspicuous by its absence among the pallbearers was that of Roy Dallis; Callaway's good friend and indispensable aide had predeceased him by about three weeks. The mayor of LaGrange issued a proclamation asking for all businesses to close their doors for the day—an honor, if an ironic one. Callaway would probably have disapproved. He may have felt differently though about the Fuller E. Callaway memorial holiday, held by the mills on Saturday, July 14, at Callaway Park to mark Callaway's birthday, complete with bands, athletic contests, and plenty of food, with parallel celebrations taking place in Manchester and at Milstead.

Some funerals signify an end. Callaway's was only a transition. LaGrange would continue on the trajectory he'd set it on for decades after his death. When he was born in the summer of 1870, the town was little different from the frontier community it had been at its inception, forty-odd years before. It was Fuller E. Callaway, along with his generation, that made it into a New South textile and commercial center. That didn't change with his death. The only thing that changed was the generation in charge, as Cason and Fuller E. Callaway Jr. now moved to the forefront.

The Callaway story was only beginning.

(Facing page) Henry Augustus Lukeman completed this Carrara marble bust of Fuller Callaway in 1929, one year after his death. Lukeman is well known for his work on Stone Mountain and several important pieces on display in Washington, D.C. and New York.

NOTES

·1·
THE YOUNG ENTREPRENEUR

3 **make a way for himself, and soon.:** Donna Jean Whitley, "Fuller E. Callaway and Textile Mill Development in LaGrange, 1895-1920," Ph.D. Diss., Emory University, 1984, 6-8; Ida Cason Callaway, "Memories of Fuller Earle Callaway Sr. of LaGrange, Georgia Written by His Wife, Ida Cason Callaway," unpublished manuscript, Callaway Family Papers, Troup County Archives, LaGrange, Georgia, 1929, pp. 15-16; "Fuller Earle Callaway," undated manuscript, Callaway Family Papers, Troup County Archives, LaGrange, Georgia.

3 **And he meant to make use of it.:** James Saxon Childers, "Three Spools of Thread: The Life-Story of Fuller E. Callaway." Unpublished manuscript, Callaway Family Papers, Troup County Archives, LaGrange, Georgia, 2-4; Fuller E. Callaway Jr., interview by James Saxon Childers, July 16, 1953, Callaway Family Papers, Troup County Archives, LaGrange, Georgia, 12.

3 **he was practically rich.:** http://www.measuringworth.com/calculators/uscompare/result.php# (last visited May 24, 2013); Jonathan Hughes, *American Economic History*, 3rd ed. (Glevview, Ill: Scott, Foresman and Co., 1990), 257-62.

3 **tears a seamless web.:** Frederic William Maitland, "A Prologue to a History of English Law," 14 *L. Qtrly. Rev.* 13 (1898).

4 **especially in Cornwall and London.:** Charles Wareing Bardsley, *A Dictionary of English and Welsh Surnames with Special American Instances* (London: Henry Frowde, 1901), 156; Whitley, "Fuller E. Callaway," pp. 1-2; Childers, "Three Spools of Thread," pp. 21-23; Ida Cason Callaway, "Memories," pp. 5-6.

4 **the motto of the LaGrange Callaways.:** 5 *Callaway Family Association Journal* 26-27 (1980); see pages 148, 247-48, *infra*; see also 2 *Callaway Family Association Journal* 24 (1977).

5 **when Flanders Callaway married Jemima.:** Lyman Copeland Draper, *The Life of Daniel Boone*, ed. Ted Franklin Belue (Mechanicsville, Pa.: Stackpole Books, 1998), 411-22; Meredith Mason Brown, *Frontiersman: Daniel Boone and the Making of America* (Baton Rouge: Louisiana State University Press, 2008), 106-12; John Bakeless, *Daniel Boone: Master of the Wilderness* (Lincoln: University of Nebraska Press, 1989), ch. 8.

5 **whose mothers were Callaways.:** Ely R. Callaway, scrapbook, Callaway Family Papers, Troup County Archives, LaGrange, Georgia, 1-4.

5 **were all Baptist ministers.:** Whitley, "Fuller E. Callaway," pp. 1-2; Allen Daniel Candler & Clement A. Evans, eds., *Georgia; Comprising Sketches of Counties, Towns, Events, Institutions, and Persons Arranged in Cyclopedic Form* (Atlanta: State Historical Association, 1906), 295-96.

6 **Enoch's father-in-law Abner Reeves.:** http://www.giddeon.com/wilkes/bios/callaway-enoch.shtml (last visited May 24, 2013); S. G. Hillyer, *Reminiscences of Georgia Baptists* (Atlanta: Foote & Davis Co., 1902), 117-19, 121-25.

6 **men make plans and God laughs.:** Cf. Proverbs 16:9.

6 **He was ordained the following year.:** Luke 1:5-22; Whitley, "Fuller E. Callaway," pp. 2-3.

7 **made the whole system work.:** Hughes, *American Economic History*, pp. 188-89.

8 **the wrong time to be born.:** Hughes, *American Economic History*, pp. 255-57; Whitley, "Fuller E. Callaway," pp. 5-6; Fuller E. Callaway Jr., interview by James Saxon Childers, July 16, 1953, Callaway Family Papers, Troup County Archives, LaGrange, Georgia, pp. 11-12; Harold M. Mayer & Richard C. Wade *Chicago: Growth of a Metropolis* (Chicago: The University of Chicago Press, 1969), 124.

9 **when he later learned the whole story.:** Ida Cason Callaway, "Memories,"pp. 10-11.

9 **which is what brings success.":** Ibid., pp. 12-13; cf. Helen Christine Bennett, "The Homely Wisdom of Fuller E. Callaway," *American Magazine* Oct. 1920, 16, 100.

10 **You will never get any in through your head.' ':** Alfred Pearce Dennis, *Gods and Little Fishes* (Indianapolis; Bobbs-Merrill Co., 1931), 262.

10 **in exchange for his goods.:** Childers, "Three Spools of Thread," pp. 26-27.

10 **three whole spools of it for a nickel.:** Ibid., pp. 19-20; Fuller E. Callaway Jr., interview by James Saxon Childers, July 16, 1953, Callaway Family Papers, Troup County Archives, LaGrange, Georgia, p. 12. Callaway later claimed his initial stock to have been six spools. See page 219, *infra*.

10 **you've got your ball.":** Ida Cason Callaway, "Memories," prologue; cf. Bennett, "The Homely Wisdom of Fuller E. Callaway," pp. 100, 105.

10 **labor is the source of value.:** See Adam Smith, *An Inquiry into the Nature and Causes of the Wealth of Nations*, book 1, ch. 5, paras. 1-2.

10 **branching out into needles and scissors.:** Fuller E. Callaway Jr., interview by James Saxon Childers, July 16, 1953, Callaway Family Papers, Troup County Archives, LaGrange, Georgia, p. 12.

10 **giving away the bride.:** Whitley, "Fuller E. Callaway," p. 7.

12 **"one would not be missed.":** Ibid.; Ida Cason Callaway, "Memories," p. 14.

12 **in his business ventures.:** Whitley, "Fuller E. Callaway," pp. 3, 10.

12 **a fixture in West Georgia.:** Childers, "Three Spools of Thread," pp. 47-48, 50.

12 **groundwork for his later successes.:** Ida Cason Callaway, "Memories," p. 19; Childers, "Three Spools of Thread," p. 18.

12 **he found one: a farm.:** Fuller E. Callaway Jr., interview by James Saxon Childers, July 16, 1953, Callaway Family Papers, Troup County Archives, LaGrange, Georgia, pp. 12-13.

12 **every city in the country.":** Henry Steele Commager, ed., *Documents of American History*, 7th ed., vol. 1 (New York: Appleton Century Crofts, 1963), 627.

12 **he would keep these things in mind throughout his career.:** "Address by Fuller Callaway Sr. to the Washington Labor Conference," *Southern Textile Bulletin*, Oct. 16, 1919; cf. Ida Cason Callaway, "Memories," p. 43 (rendering the quotation as a "hard way to make a poor living, and a poor way to make a hard living"); Ida M. Tarbell, "Making American Citizens and Running Cotton Mills to Pay the Expenses," *Red Cross Magazine*, Aug. 1920, 58, 59.

13 **if you can find him.":** Fuller E. Callaway Jr., interview by James Saxon Childers, July 16, 1953, Callaway Family Papers, Troup County Archives, LaGrange, Georgia, p. 13.

13 **pleased with himself.:** Tarbell, "Making American Citizens," p. 59.

13 **quite an experience.:** Fuller E. Callaway Jr., interview by James Saxon Childers, July 16, 1953, Callaway Family Papers, Troup County Archives, LaGrange, Georgia, p. 13.

15 **a deliberate idler.":** Ibid., pp. 13-14; Tarbell, "Making American Citizens," p. 59.

15 **The lesson wasn't lost on young Fuller.:** See Smith, *History of Troup County*, p. 124; Fuller E. Callaway Jr. interview by James Saxon Childers, July 16, 1953, Callaway Family Papers, Troup County Archives, LaGrange, Georgia, pp. 13-14.

· 2 ·
THE PROPRIETOR

17 **the stock phrase "love and affection.":** Fuller Earle Callaway—His Father Proves His Mettle (n.d.), Callaway Family Papers, Troup County Archives, LaGrange, Georgia.

17 **in the deed itself.:** Ibid.

18 **declared himself "made.":** Ida M. Tarbell, "Making American Citizens and Running Cotton Mills to Pay the Expenses," *Red Cross Magazine*, Aug. 1920, 58, 59; see page 13, *supra*.

18 **the banker reputedly answered.:** Tarbell, "Making American Citizens," p. 59.

18 **"Your overdraft is good for $1000.":** Fuller E. Callaway Jr., interview by James Saxon Childers, July 16, 1953, Callaway Family Papers, Troup County Archives, LaGrange, Georgia, p. 14; Clifford L. Smith, *History of Troup County* (Atlanta: Foote & Davies Co., 1933), 127.

18 **where it normally should be.:** See *Ga. Laws*, volumes for years 1882-1891 inclusive, under headings of private acts and joint resolutions.

19 **which he presumably did.:** Fuller Earle Callaway—His Father Proves His Mettle (n.d.), Callaway Family Papers, Troup County Archives, LaGrange, Georgia.

19 **at the age of eighteen, he did it.:** Information for *The National Cyclopedia of American Biography*, Callaway Family Papers, Troup County Archives, LaGrange, Georgia.

19 **what appealed to him.:** Notes on visit with Ely R. Callaway at his office, Administration Building, Callaway Mills Company, LaGrange, Georgia, July 3, 1951, Callaway Family Papers, Troup County Archives, LaGrange, Georgia; Fuller Earle Callaway (Early Life—Boyhood, and the Mercantile Period) (n.d.), Callaway Family Papers, Troup County Archives, LaGrange, Georgia.

19 **on five hundred dollars.":** Ida Cason Callaway, "Memories of Fuller Earle Callaway Sr. of LaGrange, Georgia Written by His Wife, Ida Cason Callaway," unpublished manuscript, Callaway Family Papers, Troup County Archives, LaGrange, Georgia, 1929, p. 23.

20 **a carload of tinware on ninety days' credit.:** Notes on visit with Ely R. Callaway at his office, Administration Building, Callaway Mills Company, LaGrange, Georgia, July 3, 1951, Callaway Family Papers, Troup County Archives, LaGrange, Georgia; Fuller E. Callaway Jr., interview by James Saxon Childers, July 16, 1953, Callaway Family Papers, Troup County Archives, LaGrange, Georgia, p. 15. Fuller E. Callaway Jr. stated the terms to have been seventy days. Ibid.

20 **asked where I was moving.":** Fuller E. Callaway Jr., interview by James Saxon Childers, July 16, 1953, Callaway Family Papers, Troup County Archives, LaGrange, Georgia, p. 15.

20 **Callaway's Famous Mammoth Five-and-Ten Cent Store to open its doors.:** Donna Jean Whitley, "Fuller E. Callaway and Textile Mill Development in LaGrange, 1895-1920," Ph.D. Diss., Emory University, 1984, 26; Fuller Earle Callaway (Early Life—Boyhood, and the Mercantile Period) (n.d.), Callaway Family Papers, Troup County Archives, LaGrange, Georgia.

21 **a cheap form of advertising.:** Fuller E. Callaway Jr., interview by James Saxon Childers, July 16, 1953, Callaway Family Papers, Troup County Archives, LaGrange, Georgia, p. 19.

21 **Another was his grand opening.:** Whitley, "Fuller E. Callaway," p. 29; Notes on a Conference with Mr. Henry D. Glanton, (n.d.), Callaway Family Papers, Troup County Archives, LaGrange, Georgia.

21 **I used to have one every month.":** Fuller E. Callaway Jr., interview by James Saxon Childers, July 16, 1953, Callaway Family Papers, Troup County Archives, LaGrange, Georgia, p. 15.

21 **both died wealthy men.:** Ibid.; *Atlanta Centennial Year Book: 1837-1937* (Atlanta: G. Murphy, 1937), 101; http://www.conklinmetal.com/History.aspx (last visited May 24, 2013).

22 **specialization had come into fashion.:** Ralph M. Hower, *History of Macy's of New York 1858-1919: Chapters in the Evolution of the Department Store* (Cambridge: Harvard Univerity Press, 1943), 77-83.

22 **passing the savings on to his customers.:** Ibid., pp. 51-52, 82-83, 86-87; William Leach, *Land of Desire: Merchants, Power, and the Rise of a New American Empire* (New York: Vintage Books, 1993), 16-17.

23 **turning over his stock at a fast pace.:** Fuller E. Callaway Jr., interview by James Saxon Childers, July 22, 1953, Callaway Family Papers, Troup County Archives, LaGrange, Georgia, p. 11.

23 **no demand to have them supplied.":** Leach, *Land of Desire*, p. 37.

23 **try their chances climbing the pole.:** Ibid., pp. 42, 46-47; Helen Christine Bennett, "The Homely Wisdom of Fuller E. Callaway," *American Magazine* Oct. 1920, 16, 100; Fuller E. Callaway Jr., interview by James Saxon Childers, July 16, 1953, Callaway Family Papers, Troup County Archives, LaGrange, Georgia, p. 21.

23 **the crowds would be at Callaway's door.:** Fuller E. Callaway Jr., interview by James Saxon Childers, July 22, 1953, Callaway Family Papers, Troup County Archives, LaGrange, Georgia, p. 18.

23 **for each dollar a customer spent.:** Fuller E. Callaway Jr., interview by James Saxon Childers, July 16, 1953, Callaway Family Papers, Troup County Archives, LaGrange, Georgia, p. 21.

24 **"Our prices are strictly low.":** "County's Times of Old," *LaGrange News*, May 24, 1958.

24 **still rare in Callaway's.:** Hower, *History of Macy's*, p. 51.

24 **customer credit problems.:** See Strasser, *Satisfaction Guaranteed*, p. 70.

24 **to the end of the First World War.:** See ibid., p. 69; Whitley, "Fuller E. Callaway," pp. 27-28.

25 **more use as a verb than as a noun.:** Strasser, *Satisfaction Guaranteed*, p. 73.

25 **the buyer's perceived ability to pay.:** Hower, *History of Macy's*, p. 89; Strasser, *Satisfaction Guaranteed*, pp. 73-74.

26 **an inexperienced (and thus a relatively low-paid) staff.:** See Strasser, *Satisfaction Guaranteed*, p. 204.

26 **the price was seventy-five cents.:** Ibid., p. 74.

26 **an extension of this policy.:** Fuller E. Callaway Jr., interview by James Saxon Childers, July 22, 1953, Callaway Family Papers, Troup County Archives, LaGrange, Georgia, pp. 5, 11.

27 **as if it were bursting with stock.:** John N. Ingham ed., *Biographical Dictionary of American Business Leaders*, vol. 1 (Westport, Conn: Greenwood Press, 1983), 131-32; Fuller E. Callaway Jr., interview by James Saxon Childers, July 16, 1953, Callaway Family Papers, Troup County Archives, LaGrange, Georgia, p. 15.

27 **His success was beginning to build on itself.:** Fuller E. Callaway Jr., interview by James Saxon Childers, July 16, 1953, Callaway Family Papers, Troup County Archives, LaGrange, Georgia, p. 15.

28 **Business was booming.:** Ibid., p. 16.

29 **an older, established Callaway once said.:** Bennett, "The Homely Wisdom of Fuller E. Callaway," p. 100.

29 **The modern spectacle known as the department store.:** See Leach, *Land of Desire*, pp. 20-26; ibid., chs. 2-3.

29 **he had fourteen employees.:** Fuller E. Callaway Jr., interview by James Saxon Childers, July 16, 1953, Callaway Family Papers, Troup County Archives, LaGrange, Georgia, p. 19; Fuller E. Callaway Jr., interview by James Saxon Childers, July 22, 1953, Callaway Family Papers, Troup County Archives, LaGrange, Georgia, p. 19.

29 **with his mass purchase of quart jars.:** Ida Cason Callaway, "Memories," pp. 25-26; Fuller E. Callaway Jr., interview by James Saxon Childers, July 22, 1953, Callaway Family Papers, Troup County Archives, LaGrange, Georgia, pp. 18-19.

29 **his counterpart the corporate buyer.:** Leach, *Land of Desire*, p. 19; Hower, *History of Macy's*, p. 86; Strasser, *Satisfaction Guaranteed*, pp. 60-65.

30 **the best prices for his retail concern.:** Fuller E. Callaway Jr., interview by James Saxon Childers, July 16, 1953, Callaway Family Papers, Troup County Archives, LaGrange, Georgia, pp. 19-20.

30 **that small a man.":** Bennett, "The Homely Wisdom of Fuller E. Callaway," p. 105.

30 **buyers in thirty-six states.:** Ibid.; Fuller E. Callaway Jr., interview by James Saxon Childers, July 16, 1953, Callaway Family Papers, Troup County Archives, LaGrange, Georgia, p. 20.

32 **where Abner Callaway had once taught.:** Ida Cason Callaway, "Memories," pp. 21-22, 31; Charles Edgeworth Jones, *Contributions to American Educational History*, No. 5, *Education in Georgia* (Washington: Government Printing Office, 1889), 71-74.

32 **higher education of females in the Southern states.":** Jones, *Education in Georgia*, p. 72; I. M. E. Blandin, *History of Higher Education of Women in the South Prior to 1860* (New York: Neale Publishing Co., 1909), 141-47.

32 **introduced the two of them at a college function.:** Ida Cason Callaway, "Memories," pp. 21-22.

32 **energy, enthusiasm, and good humor.:** Fuller E. Callaway Jr., interview by James Saxon Childers, July 22, 1953, Callaway Family Papers, Troup County Archives, LaGrange, Georgia, p. 25; Whitley, "Fuller E. Callaway," pp. 44-45.

32 **an exotic treat in West Georgia.:** Fuller E. Callaway Jr., interview by James Saxon Childers, July 16, 1953, Callaway Family Papers, Troup County Archives, LaGrange, Georgia, p. 17; Whitley, "Fuller E. Callaway," pp. 39-40; Ida Cason Callaway, "Memories," pp. 19, 22.

32 **It was no respecter of persons.":** Ida Cason Callaway, "Memories," p. 22.

32 **the contents always irked the school's professors.:** Ibid.

34 **the best day's work we ever did.":** Fuller E. Callaway Jr., interview by James Saxon Childers, July 16, 1953, Callaway Family Papers, Troup County Archives, LaGrange, Georgia, pp. 17-18; Ida Cason Callaway, "Memories," p. 27.

34 **how mother put up with it.":** Fuller E. Callaway Jr., interview by James Saxon

Childers, July 16, 1953, Callaway Family Papers, Troup County Archives, LaGrange, Georgia, p. 18.

34 **usually got home around midnight.:** Ibid., pp. 18, 23.

34 **I get up an hour *before* day.":** Fuller Earle Callaway—Sayings (n.d.), Callaway Family Papers, Troup County Archives, LaGrange, Georgia; cf. Ida Cason Callaway, "Memories," pp. 29-30, in which the protagonist is a loafer named Juno Body.

34 **sending hot meals to her husband there.:** Fuller E. Callaway Jr., interview by James Saxon Childers, July 22, 1953, Callaway Family Papers, Troup County Archives, LaGrange, Georgia, p. 28; Fuller E. Callaway Jr., interview by James Saxon Childers, July 16, 1953, Callaway Family Papers, Troup County Archives, LaGrange, Georgia, p. 18.

34 **and economize.:** Alfred Pearce Dennis, *Gods and Little Fishes* (Indianapolis; Bobbs-Merrill Co., 1931), 264; cf. Ida Cason Callaway, "Memories," p. 42, which, surprisingly, quotes Fuller as saying "*Early* to bed" (emphasis added) and, unsurprisingly and in a ladylike manner, omits the strong language. Other sources substitute "advertise" for "economize." See, e.g., Fuller Earle Callaway—Stories and Maxims (n.d.), Callaway Family Papers, Troup County Archives, LaGrange, Georgia.

34 **moved into a house of their own.:** Early Married Life of Mr. and Mrs. Fuller Callaway (n.d.), Callaway Family Papers, Troup County Archives, LaGrange, Georgia; Ida Cason Callaway, "Memories," p. 28; Fuller E. Callaway Jr., interview by James Saxon Childers, July 16, 1953, Callaway Family Papers, Troup County Archives, LaGrange, Georgia, p. 18.

35 **"Let's *stay* able.":** Ida Cason Callaway, "Memories," p. 29; Fuller Earle Callaway—Stories and Maxims (n.d.), Callaway Family Papers, Troup County Archives, LaGrange, Georgia.

35 **an excellent investment—in his marriage.:** Fuller Earle Callaway—Stories and Maxims (n.d.), Callaway Family Papers, Troup County Archives, LaGrange, Georgia.

36 **you're my partner.":** Ibid.

36 **the last conversation the couple ever had about money.:** Fuller E. Callaway Jr., interview by James Saxon Childers, July 16, 1953, Callaway Family Papers, Troup County Archives, LaGrange, Georgia, p. 18; cf. Ida Cason Callaway, "Memories," p. 28.

36 **in her later years.**: Ida Cason Callaway, "Memories," p. 28.

36 **and the husband was the one.**: E.g., John E. Cribbet, *Principles of the Law of Property* (Westbury: Foundation Press, 1975), 86; cf. William Blackstone, *Commentaries on the Laws of England*, vol. 1 (Oxford: Clarendon Press, 1765), 430-31.

36 **much of that mindset remained.**: See, e.g., Huff v. Wright, 39 Ga. 41 (1869); see generally Sandra R. Zagier Zayac & Robert A. Zayac, Jr., "Georgia's Married Women's Property Act: An Effective Challenge to Coverture," 15 *Tex. J. Women & L.* 81 (2005).

37 **the last moss scraping the couple ever had.**: Fuller E. Callaway Jr., interview by James Saxon Childers, July 16, 1953, Callaway Family Papers, Troup County Archives, LaGrange, Georgia, pp. 23-24.

37 **what he termed "Mortgage Avenue."**: Bennett, "The Homely Wisdom of Fuller E. Callaway," pp. 16, 105; Ida Cason Callaway, "Memories," p. 28; Fuller Earle Callaway—Stories and Maxims (n.d.), Callaway Family Papers, Troup County Archives, LaGrange, Georgia; Fuller E. Callaway Jr., interview by James Saxon Childers, July 16, 1953, Callaway Family Papers, Troup County Archives, LaGrange, Georgia, pp. 18-19.

37 **never having met a man he didn't like.**: *Saturday Evening Post*, Nov. 6, 1926.

37 **a beehive of activity.**: Fuller E. Callaway Jr., interview by James Saxon Childers, July 22, 1953, Callaway Family Papers, Troup County Archives, LaGrange, Georgia, pp. 32-33.

38 **what had become the family business.**: Fuller E. Callaway Jr., interview by James Saxon Childers, July 16, 1953, Callaway Family Papers, Troup County Archives, LaGrange, Georgia, pp. 18-19.

38 **"I thank you for some stew, brother Fuller," he gasped.**: Fuller E. Callaway Jr., interview by James Saxon Childers, July 22, 1953, Callaway Family Papers, Troup County Archives, LaGrange, Georgia, pp. 5-6.

38 **"Now you won't have to go in the back yard."**: Ibid.

39 **he always remembered the moment as a valuable experience.**: Notes on visit with Ely R. Callaway at his office, Administration Building, Callaway Mills Company, LaGrange, Georgia, July 3, 1951, Callaway Family Papers, Troup County Archives, LaGrange, Georgia.

39 **Fuller would sometimes absent-mindedly call Ida "Ab."**: Ida Cason Callaway, "Memories," p. 60.

39 **very much like a son to Callaway.**: http://www.trouparchives.org/man/ms057.htm (last visited Apr. 28, 2010); Hatton Lovejoy Papers 1912-1922, Callaway Family Papers, Troup County Archives, LaGrange, Georgia; Fuller Earle Callaway—Mr. Hatton Lovejoy (n.d.), Callaway Family Papers, Troup County Archives, LaGrange, Georgia.

40 **how he had gotten to know Hatton Lovejoy.**: Fuller Earle Callaway—Mr. Hatton Lovejoy (n.d.), Callaway Family Papers, Troup County Archives, LaGrange, Georgia. This account states clearly that Callaway met Lovejoy around 1897 through the LaGrange Board of Trade, but that agency did not exist until 1902. Whitley, "Fuller E. Callaway," pp. 119-21.

40 **build this store and operate it for us."**: Fuller E. Callaway Jr., interview by James Saxon Childers, July 22, 1953, Callaway Family Papers, Troup County Archives, LaGrange, Georgia, p. 19.

40 **a little frog in a big pond."**: Ibid.

41 **the sort of thing that LaGrange businessmen had been hoping for.**: Whitley, "Fuller E. Callaway," p. 66.

41 **some sort of connection seems likely.**: Ibid., p. 67.

41 **local investment capital.**: Ibid., pp. 67-69; Smith, *History of Troup County*, pp. 109, 117; Fuller Earle Callaway (Early Life—Boyhood, and the Mercantile Period) (n.d.), Callaway Family Papers, Troup County Archives, LaGrange, Georgia.

42 **one of the mill's largest non-affiliated investors.**: Whitley, "Fuller E. Callaway," pp. 69-70; Fuller E. Callaway Jr., interview by James Saxon Childers, July 16, 1953, Callaway Family Papers, Troup County Archives, LaGrange, Georgia, p. 25.

42 **But then the trouble began.**: Smith, *History of Troup County*, p. 117; Whitley, "Fuller E. Callaway," p. 71.

42 **they'd taken the money and left.**: Fuller Earle Callaway (Early Life—Boyhood, and the Mercantile Period) (n.d.), Callaway Family Papers, Troup County Archives, LaGrange, Georgia; Fuller E. Callaway Jr., interview by James Saxon Childers, July 16, 1953, Callaway Family Papers, Troup County Archives, LaGrange, Georgia, p. 25.

42 **Dixie was a white elephant.**: Whitley, "Fuller E. Callaway," p. 72; Fuller Earle Callaway (Early Life—Boyhood, and the Mercantile Period) (n.d.), Callaway Family Papers, Troup County Archives, LaGrange, Georgia; Fuller E. Callaway Jr., interview by James Saxon Childers, July 16, 1953, Callaway Family Papers, Troup County Archives, LaGrange, Georgia, p. 25.

42 **to try to salvage the mill.**: Fuller Earle Callaway (Early Life—Boyhood, and the Mercantile Period) (n.d.), Callaway Family Papers, Troup County Archives, LaGrange, Georgia.

43 **more than fifty percent of the voting stock.**: Fuller E. Callaway Jr., interview by James Saxon Childers, July 16, 1953, Callaway Family Papers, Troup County Archives, LaGrange, Georgia, p. 25.

43 **shipped it down to LaGrange.**: Ibid.; Ida Cason Callaway, "Memories," p. 42; Fuller Earle Callaway (Early Life—Boyhood, and the Mercantile Period) (n.d.), Callaway Family Papers, Troup County Archives, LaGrange, Georgia.

43 **one good piece of machinery.**: Fuller E. Callaway Jr., interview by James Saxon Childers, July 16, 1953, Callaway Family Papers, Troup County Archives, LaGrange, Georgia, p. 25; Fuller Earle Callaway (Early Life—Boyhood, and the Mercantile Period) (n.d.), Callaway Family Papers, Troup County Archives, LaGrange, Georgia; Whitley, "Fuller E. Callaway," p. 74.

43 **a major step towards recovery.**: Fuller E. Callaway Jr., interview by James Saxon Childers, July 16, 1953, Callaway Family Papers, Troup County Archives, LaGrange, Georgia, p. 26; Whitley, "Fuller E. Callaway," pp. 74-75.

43 **advising others to get out as well.**: Fuller E. Callaway Jr., interview by James Saxon Childers, July 16, 1953, Callaway Family Papers, Troup County Archives, LaGrange, Georgia, p. 26; Whitley, "Fuller E. Callaway," pp. 74-76.

43 **"I cut my eye teeth getting that mill in better condition."**: Ida Cason Callaway, "Memories," p. 42.

· 3 ·
COTTON

45 **dangerous place for Northern investments.**: *Atlanta Herald*, Mar. 14, 1874.

46 **had built another mill in LaGrange.**: Clifford L. Smith, *History of Troup County* (Atlanta: Foote & Davies Co., 1933), 115-16.

46 **By 1880 it was happening.**: Ibid., p. 111; Broadus Mitchell, *The Rise of Cotton Mills in the South* (Columbia: University of South Carolina Press, 2001), 115 n.115.

46 **proudly donned.**: Alice Galenson, *The Migration of the Cotton Textile Industry from New England to the South: 1880-1930* (New York: Garland Publishing Co., 1985), 75-76.

47 **to operate for nearly a century.**: See Thomas H. Martin, *Atlanta and its Builders: A Comprehensive History of the Gate City of the South*, vol. 2 (Atlanta: Century Memorial Publishing Co., 1902), 461-67; Galenson, *Cotton Textile Industry*, pp. 75-78.

47 **Booker T. Washington.**: Paul E. Bierley, *The Incredible Band of John Philip Sousa* (Urbana: University of Illinois Press, 2006), 20; Edward L. Ayers, *The Promise of the New South: Life After Reconstruction* (New York: Oxford University Press, 1992), 322-26.

47 **the pool of potential mill workers grew fast.**: Ayers, *The Promise of the New South*, pp. 113-15; Galenson, *Cotton Textile Industry*, pp. 129-32, 117-19; Ben F. Lemert, *The Cotton Textile Industry of the Southern Appalachian Piedmont* (Chapel Hill: University of North Carolina Press, 1933), 32-33.

47 **made borrowing easier.**: Galenson, *Cotton Textile Industry*, pp. 62-69.

48 **came from the South.**: Ibid., pp. 80-83.

48 **a pool from which managers might be drawn.**: Ayers, *The Promise of the New South*, pp. 104-05; Mitchell, *The Rise of Cotton Mills in the South*, pp. 106-07.

48 **he had to become a mill president.**": Mitchell, *The Rise of Cotton Mills in the South*, p. 157.

48 **the national commodities and credit markets, it was he.**: Ibid., pp. 106-07.

48 **The Southerners who best fit the description were merchants.**: Ibid., pp. 251-52.

48 **but we got up a cotton mill.**": Ida M. Tarbell, "Making American Citizens and Running Cotton Mills to Pay the Expenses," *Red Cross Magazine*, Aug. 1920, 58, 59.

49 **"we will see what we can do.**": Fuller E. Callaway Jr., interview by James Saxon Childers, July 16, 1953, Callaway Family Papers, Troup County Archives, LaGrange, Georgia, p. 26.

50 **Callaway already had an option on the property.**: Ida Cason Callaway, "Memories of Fuller Earle Callaway Sr. of LaGrange, Georgia Written by His Wife, Ida Cason Callaway," unpublished manuscript, Callaway Family Papers, Troup County Archives, LaGrange, Georgia, 1929, pp. 42-43.

50 **to national and international markets.**: Fuller Earle Callaway—The Cotton Manufacturing Period (n.d.), Callaway Family Papers, Troup County Archives, LaGrange, Georgia.

50 **The next step was to raise capital.**: Ibid.

50 **but more was needed.**: Conversations Between Fuller E. Callaway Jr. and Hatton Lovejoy—Reference Book on Life of Fuller E Callaway Sr., July 20, 1953, p. 2, Callaway Family Papers, Troup County Archives, LaGrange, Georgia; Fuller E. Callaway Jr., interview by James Saxon Childers, July 16, 1953, Callaway Family Papers, Troup County Archives, LaGrange, Georgia, p. 26. Another source claims that Callaway only invested $5,000. See Conversations Between Fuller E. Callaway Jr. and Hatton Lovejoy—Reference Book on Life of Fuller E Callaway Sr., July 20, 1953, p. 2, Callaway Family Papers, Troup County Archives, LaGrange, Georgia.

51 **than would have been possible otherwise.**: Fuller Earle Callaway—The Cotton Manufacturing Period (n.d.), Callaway Family Papers, Troup County Archives, LaGrange, Georgia.

51 **"I couldn't find anybody else who would put $100 into it."**: Ibid.; Fuller E. Callaway Jr., interview by James Saxon Childers, July 16, 1953, Callaway Family Papers, Troup County Archives, LaGrange, Georgia, p. 26.

51 **running it just the way he wished.**: Conversations Between Fuller E. Callaway Jr. and Hatton Lovejoy—Reference Book on Life of Fuller E Callaway Sr., July 20, 1953, p. 2, Callaway Family Papers, Troup County Archives, LaGrange, Georgia; Fuller Earle Callaway—The Cotton Manufacturing Period (n.d.), Callaway Family Papers, Troup County Archives, LaGrange, Georgia; Fuller E. Callaway Jr., interview by James Saxon Childers, July 16, 1953, Callaway Family Papers, Troup County Archives, LaGrange, Georgia, p. 27.

51 **The finer goods they left, for the time being, to New England.**: See Galenson, *Cotton Textile Industry*, pp. 4-6, 49-50, 56-59.

51 **the cycling and nascent automobile industries.**: Steven Klepper & Kenneth L. Simons, "Technological Extinction of Industrial Firms: An Inquiry into Their Nature and Causes" (unpublished paper, 1997, available at http://www.rpi.edu/~simonk/pdf/te.pdf (last visited May 24, 2013)), pp. 25-27, tbl. 6; see Smith, *History of Troup County*, p. 120; see also Steven Klepper & Kenneth L. Simons, "Technological Extinction of Industrial Firms: An Inquiry into Their Nature and Causes," 6 *Industrial and Corporate Change* 379 (Mar. 1997).

52 **who wanted to buy its products.**: John Moody, *The Truth About the Trusts: A Description and Analysis of the American Trust Movement* (New York: Moody Publishing Co., 1904), xiii-xiv.

52 **would soon raise duck prices.**: New York Times, Aug. 2, 1899; ibid., Aug. 26, 1899.

52 **a massive amount of confidence in Callaway.**: Fuller E. Callaway Jr., interview by James Saxon Childers, July 16, 1953, Callaway Family Papers, Troup County Archives, LaGrange, Georgia, p. 26.

52 **that it ever made.**: Ibid., p. 27; Fuller Earle Callaway—Sayings (n.d.), Callaway Family Papers, Troup County Archives, LaGrange, Georgia.

53 **stuffed the money in a rat hole.**": Conversation between Fuller E. Callaway Jr., James Saxon Childers, and Maurine Childers Concerning Life of Fuller E. Callaway Sr., July 22, 1953, Callaway Family Papers, Troup County Archives, LaGrange, Georgia, p. 9.

53 **a modest dividend policy.**: Fuller Earle Callaway—Sayings (n.d.), Callaway Family Papers, Troup County Archives, LaGrange, Georgia.

53 **a few weeks or months later at low interest rates.**: Frank K. Houston, "Commercial Paper: Its Uses Part I," *The Financier*, vol.109 (May 12, 1917), 1235, 1235-36, 1251-53.

54 **a firm rivaled only by Goldman-Sachs.**: *The New Yorker*, Dec. 7 1957, pp. 42-44.

54 **when the mill was first established.**: Fuller Earle Callaway—Stories and Maxims (n.d.), Callaway Family Papers, Troup County Archives, LaGrange, Georgia; Fuller E. Callaway to F. Coit Johnson, Dec. 24, 1909, Callaway Family Papers, Troup County Archives, LaGrange, Georgia; Fuller E. Callaway to Frank Wolf, Dec. 27, 1909, Callaway Family Papers, Troup County Archives, LaGrange, Georgia.

55 **another of his most capable lieutenants.**: Fuller Earle Callaway—Audits (n.d.), Callaway Family Papers, Troup County Archives, LaGrange, Georgia.

56 **it would have to open another mill.**: Fuller Earle Callaway—The Cotton Manufacturing Period (n.d.), Callaway Family Papers, Troup County Archives, La-Grange, Georgia.

57 **eventually they gained a controlling interest.**: Conversations Between Fuller E. Callaway, Jr. and Hatton Lovejoy—Reference Book on Life of Fuller E Callaway Sr., July 20, 1953, p. 3, Callaway Family Papers, Troup County Archives, LaGrange, Georgia; Ida Cason Callaway, "Memories," p. 45; Fuller Earle Callaway—The Cotton Manufacturing Period (n.d.), Callaway Family Papers, Troup County Archives, La-Grange, Georgia; Donna Jean Whitley, "Fuller E. Callaway and Textile Mill Development in LaGrange, 1895-1920," Ph.D. Diss., Emory University, 1984, pp. 102-03.

58 **and above all ambitious.**: Lucian Lamar Knight, *A Standard History of Georgia and Georgians*, vol. 5 (Chicago: Lewis Publishing Co., 1917), 2302-03; Forrest Clark Johnson, III, *Histories of LaGrange and Troup County Georgia*, vols. 1 & 2 (LaGrange: Family Tree, 1987), 126, 256; Smith, *History of Troup County*, p. 118.

59 **Callaway's $100 monthly salary.**: Fuller Earle Callaway—The Cotton Manufacturing Period (n.d.), Callaway Family Papers, Troup County Archives, LaGrange, Georgia , Conversation Between Fuller E. Callaway Jr. and Hatton Lovejoy, July 20, 1953, pp. 2-3, Callaway Family Papers, Troup County Archives, LaGrange, Georgia; Fuller E. Callaway Jr., interview by James Saxon Childers, July 16, 1953, Callaway Family Papers, Troup County Archives, LaGrange, Georgia, p. 27.

59 **"which has now been satisfactorily adjusted."**: Fuller E. Callaway Jr., interview by James Saxon Childers, July 16, 1953, Callaway Family Papers, Troup County Archives, LaGrange, Georgia, pp. 27-28; Fuller Earle Callaway—The Cotton Manufacturing Period (n.d.), Callaway Family Papers, Troup County Archives, LaGrange, Georgia , Conversation Between Fuller E. Callaway Jr. and Hatton Lovejoy, July 20, 1953, p. 2, Callaway Family Papers, Troup County Archives, LaGrange, Georgia.

60 **until his death in 1946.**: "Georgia Power Company History," http://www.georgiapower.com/news/heritage/history.asp (last visited Apr. 28, 2011); "Georgia Power Company/Southern Company," *New Georgia Encyclopedia*; "Business: Electricitizens," *Time*, June 18, 1928; Allen D. Candler & Clement A. Evans, *Georgia: Comprising Sketches of Counties, Towns, Events, Institutions, and Persons, Arranged in Cyclopedic Form*, vol. 1 (Atlanta; State Historical Association, 1906), 73-74; Lucian Lamar Knight, *A Standard History of Georgia and Georgians*, vol. 4 (Chicago: The Lewis Publishing Co., 1917), 1946.

60 **exactly the skills that Callaway needed.**: "Georgia Power Company/Southern Company," *New Georgia Encyclopedia*; James H. Tate, *Keeper of the Flame: The Story of Atlanta Gas Light Company 1856-1985* (Atlanta: Atlanta Gas Light Co., 1985), 45.

60 **at least under certain conditions.**: James C. Bonbright & Gardiner C. Means, *The Holding Company: Its Public Significance and Its Regulation* (New York: McGraw-Hill Book Co., 1932), 7-10, 55-57; see Trust Company of Georgia v. Georgia, 35 S.E. 323, 329-30 (Ga. 1900); see also Cox v. Hardee, 68 S.E. 932, 935 (Ga. 1910).

61 **on a single network.**: Bonbright & Means, *The Holding Company*, pp. 90-93; Richard D. Cudahy & William D. Henderson, "From Insull to Enron: Corporate (Re)Regulation After the Rise and Fall of Two Energy Icons," 26 *Energy L. J.* 35 54-55 (2005).

61 **via a stock swap.**: Tate, *Keeper of the Flame*, pp. 45-47; Bonbright & Means, *The Holding Company*, pp. 95-98.

61 **He explained what he had in mind.**: Fuller E. Callaway Jr., interview by James Saxon Childers, July 16, 1953, Callaway Family Papers, Troup County Archives, LaGrange, Georgia, p. 28.

62 **his silencing of the opposition.**: Ibid., pp. 27-28; *Travels and Explorations of the Jesuit Missionaries in New France 1610-1791*, ed. Reuben Gold Thwaites, vol. 59 (Cleveland: Burrows Bothers Co., 1899), 128-29; Sean Michael Rafferty & Rob Mann, *Smoking and Culture: The Archaeology of Tobacco Pipes in Eastern North America* (Knoxville: University of Tennessee Press, 2004), xiii ("The calumet's role as a facilitating device led to the misleading colloquial term peace pipe. This slang tells only half the story of the calumet, as not all social interactions that the calumet ritual enabled were peaceful; there was a calumet of war as well.").

62 **what their charters specifically allowed.**: Henry O. Taylor, *A Treatise on the Law of Private Corporations*, 3rd ed. (Philadelphia: Kay & Brother, 1894), § 265 & n.2, pp. 228-29; James Willard Hurst, *The Legitimacy of the Business Corporation in the Law of the United States, 1780-1970* (Charlottesville: University Press of Virginia, 1970), 4-18.

62 **the wife of Joe Dunson.**: Johnson, *Histories of LaGrange and Troup County Georgia*, vols. 1 & 2, pp. 126-27, 514-15.

63 **later generations would recall little of it.**: Fuller E. Callaway Jr., interview by James Saxon Childers, July 16, 1953, Callaway Family Papers, Troup County Archives, LaGrange, Georgia, p. 29; Knight, *A Standard History of Georgia and Georgians*, vol. 5, p. 2303.

63 **never touching them until the day he died.**: Bonbright & Means, *The Holding Company*, pp. 18-20; Fuller E. Callaway to Textile Manufacturer, Charlotte, N.C., Dec. 17, 1909, Callaway Family Papers, Troup County Archives, LaGrange, Georgia; Fuller E. Callaway Jr., interview by James Saxon Childers, July 16, 1953, Callaway Family Papers, Troup County Archives, La-Grange, Georgia, p. 29.

64 **more than $315,000.**: Smith, *History of Troup County*, p. 118; Fuller Earle Callaway—The Cotton Manufacturing Period (n.d.), Callaway Family Papers, Troup County Archives, LaGrange, Georgia.

64 **rather than woven cloth.**: Smith, *History of Troup County*, p. 118; Ida Cason Callaway, "Memories," pp. 58, 112.

64 **had finally come to fruition.**: Whitley, "Fuller E. Callaway," p. 150.

64 **still underway and gaining more ground.**: Galenson, *Cotton Textile Industry*, pp. 2-4.

64 **one of the world's first commercial railroads.**: Fuller Earle Callaway—The Cotton Manufacturing Period (n.d.), Callaway Family Papers, Troup County Archives, LaGrange, Georgia; Regina P. Pinkston, *Historical Account of Meriwether County 1827-1974* (Greenville, Georgia: Gresham Printing Co., 1974), 180, 228, 356-57; Christian Wolmar, *Blood, Iron, and Gold: How the Railroads Transformed the World* (New York: PublicAffaris, 2010), 1-3.

64 **he usually preferred the post of treasurer.**: Fuller Earle Callaway—The Cotton Manufacturing Period (n.d.), Callaway Family Papers, Troup County Archives, LaGrange, Georgia; Ida Cason Callaway, "Memories," p. 112; "Atlanta, Birmingham & Atlantic Railroad,"

http://www.railga.com/atlbirmatl.html (last visited May 24, 2013); Fuller E. Callaway to Textile Manufacturer, Charlotte, N.C., Dec. 17, 1909, Callaway Family Papers, Troup County Archives, LaGrange, Georgia.

65 **which it sold to potential residents at seventy-five dollars per acre.**: "Excerpts from Minutes of Meeting with Stockholders of Manchester Cotton Mills Held January 12, 1909," Callaway Family Papers, Troup County Archives, LaGrange, Georgia; Pinkston, *Historical Account of Meriwether County*, p. 227.

65 **with others following his lead.**: "Excerpts from Minutes of Meeting with Stockholders of Manchester Cotton Mills Held January 12, 1909," Callaway Family Papers, Troup County Archives, LaGrange, Georgia; Fuller E. Callaway to Textile Manufacturer, Charlotte, N.C., Dec. 17, 1909, Callaway Family Papers, Troup County Archives, LaGrange, Georgia; Fuller E. Callaway to O. A. Barnard, Mar. 19, 1910, Callaway Family Papers, Troup County Archives, LaGrange, Georgia.

66 **store these narrow looms in our warehouse.**": Fuller E. Callaway to O. A. Barnard, Mar. 19, 1910, Callaway Family Papers, Troup County Archives, La-Grange, Georgia; Fuller E. Callaway to O. A. Barnard, Mar. 24, 1910, Callaway Family Papers, Troup County Archives, LaGrange, Georgia.

66 **the new mill went into production, and the crisis was past.**: Fuller Earle Callaway—The Cotton Manufacturing Period (n.d.), Callaway Family Papers, Troup County Archives, LaGrange, Georgia; Fuller E. Callaway et al. to Stockholders of Manchester Mills, Sept. 14, 1911, Callaway Family Papers, Troup County Archives, LaGrange, Georgia.

66 **This time there was no serious complaint.**: Fuller E. Callaway et al. to Stockholders of Manchester Mills, Sept. 14, 1911, Callaway Family Papers, Troup County Archives, LaGrange, Georgia.

67 **a likely governor of Georgia.**: Knight, *A Standard History of Georgia and Georgians*, vol. 5, p. 2302; Smith, *History of Troup County*, p. 119.

· 4 ·
BUILDING A
MODERN LaGRANGE

69 **low-friction tracks, which allow energy efficiency.**: John Moody, *The Rail-*

road Builders: A Chronicle of the Welding of the States (New Haven: Yale University Press, 1921), 2.

69 **a number of small-scale steam locomotives.**: Ibid., pp. 6-9.

69 **the most important commodity this rail line hauled was raw American cotton.**: Ibid., pp. 1-3.

69 **fully half of American railroad freight tonnage.**: Charles Lee Raper, *Railway Transportation: A History of its Economics and of its Relation to the State* (New York: G. P. Putnam's Sons, 1912), 226.

69 **symbioses among coal, iron, and the railroad.**: Wolmar, *Blood, Iron, and Gold*, p. 233.

70 **making it available for investment.**: Ibid., p. 235.

70 **and Callaway was often one of them.**: Peter T. Maiken, *Night Trains: The Pullman Systems in the Golden Years of American Rail Travel* (Baltimore: Johns Hopkins University Press, 1992), 8.

70 **with Fuller missing only a single day's work.**: See page 33, *supra*.

70 **forty percent of the world's total.**: Raper, *Railway Transportation*, pp. 186-87.

70 **planned for little rural Troup County:** Clifford L. Smith, *History of Troup County* (Atlanta: Foote & Davies Co., 1933), 108-11.

70 **business away from competitors.**: Herbert Hovenkamp, *Enterprise and American Law, 1836-1937* (Cambridge: Harvard University Press, 1991), 153-56.

71 **short-haul/long-haul distinction.**: Hovenkamp, *Enterprise and American Law*, pp. 152-56; Joseph Henry Beale & Bruce Wyman, *Railroad Rate Regulation with Special Reference to the Interstate Commerce Commission under the Acts to Regulete Commerce*, 2nd ed. (New York: Baker, Voorhis & Co., 1915), § 781, pp. 699-700, § 785, pp. 705-07.

71 **people such as Callaway in La-Grange—joined in as well.**: Dennis Sven Nordin, *Rich Harvest: A History of the Grange, 1867-1900* (Jackson: University Press of Mississippi, 1974), 215.

71 **they were subject to this state regulation.**: See Munn v. Illinois, 94 U.S. 113 (1877).

71 **a matter for federal, and not state, regulation.**: See Wabash, St. Louis & Pacific Railway Company v. Illinois, 118 U.S. 557 (1886).

72 **to require rate adjustments.**: Interstate Commerce Act, 24 Stat. 379, ch. 104, Feb. 4, 1887.

72 **when it first got to LaGrange.**: Maury Klein, *History of the Louisville & Nashville Railroad* (Louisville: University Press of Kentucky, 2003), 347-52; *Eleventh Annual Report of the Interstate Commerce Commission* (Washington: Government Printing Office, 1897), 105.

72 **its powerful parent company, the Louisville & Nashville.**: Klein, *History of the Louisville & Nashville Railroad*, pp. 179-80.

73 **they suggested that Callaway look to the ICC for relief.**: Callaway v. Atlanta & West Point R.R. Co., July 24, 1895, Public Service Commission, Hearing Reporter, vol. 2-8400, p. 278, Georgia Archives, Record Group 17; *Twenty-Second Report of the Railroad Commission of Georgia* (Atlanta: Geo. W. Harrison, Franklin Printing & Publishing Co., 1894), 3.

73 **a clear violation of the U.S. Statutes.**": Forrest Clark Johnson, III, *Histories of LaGrange and Troup County Georgia*, vols. 1 & 2 (LaGrange: Family Tree, 1987), 381; F. M. Longley to Judson C. Clements, July 26, 1895, National Archives, Record Group 134, Box 219, Docket 431, Inserts for Correspondence.

73 **he was thus naturally very interested in Callaway's cause.**: Lucian Lamar Knight, *A Standard History of Georgia and Georgians*, vol. 6 (Chicago: Lewis Publishing Co., 1917), 3045; New York Times, Jan. 14, 1911.

73 **which Callaway then submitted to the commission.**: Petition, Calloway v. Louisville & Nashville Railroad Co., Oct. 16, 1895, National Archives, Record Group 134, Box 220, Docket 431. Interestingly, the spelling "Calloway" appears throughout most of the federal litigation.

73 **challenged the Atlanta & West Point's rates to LaGrange on all of these grounds.**: Interstate Commerce Act, §§ 1-4, 24 Stat. 379, 379-80, ch. 104, Feb. 4, 1887; Petition, Calloway v. Louisville & Nashville Railroad Co., Oct. 16, 1895, National Archives, Record Group 134, Box 220, Docket 431.

73 **it missed the legal deadline for filing an answer.**: [Edward A. Moseley] to Atlanta & West Point Railroad Co., Nov. 21, 1895, National Archives, Record Group 134, Box 219, Docket 431, Correspondence.

74 **West Point and its parent, the Louisville & Nashville had delayed the reply.**: George C. Smith to Edward A. Moseley, Nov. 25 , 1895, National Archives, Record Group 134, Box 219, Docket 431, Correspondence.

74 **they have had 90 days time.":** Fuller E. Callaway to Judson C. Clements, Oct. 3, 1896, National Archives, Record Group 134, Box 219, Docket 431, Correspondence.

74 **much less my shipping it to Hogansville.":** Testimony, Calloway v. Louisville & Nashville Railroad Co., Nov. 9, 1896, National Archives, Record Group 134, Box 219, Docket 431.

74 **a Confederate artillery officer.**: "Biography of Edmund Dillahunty Baxter," http://www.baxtersbattery.5u.com/custom2.html (last visited May 24, 2013).

75 **in exchange for concessions to Southern elsewhere.**: Testimony, Calloway v. Louisville & Nashville Railroad Co., Nov. 9, 1896, National Archives, Record Group 134, Box 219, Docket 431.

75 **not to any favoritism or discrimination.":** H. T. Newcomb, *The Federal Courts and the Orders of the Interstate Commerce Commission* (Washington: Press of Gibson Brothers, 1905), 143-44.

75 **the railroad had yet to file its final arguments.**: Fuller E. Callaway to Judson C. Clements, Feb. 26, 1897, National Archives, Record Group 134, Box 219, Docket 431, Correspondence; Judson C. Clements to Fuller E. Callaway, Mar. 2, 1897, National Archives, Record Group 134, Box 219, Docket 431, Correspondence.

75 **as soon as a decision is rendered.":** Fuller E. Callaway to Judson C. Clements, Dec. 16, 1897, National Archives, Record Group 134, Box 219, Docket 431, Correspondence.

75 **and others doing business at LaGrange.":** Calloway v. Louisville & Nashville Railroad Co., 7 ICC 431, 453 (1897).

75 **made the railroad's claim that its rates were reasonable "seem almost absurd.":** Ibid., p. 454.

75 **the commission recommended its own rate schedule, advising the railroad to adopt it.**: Calloway v. Louisville & Nashville Railroad Co., Order, Dec. 31, 1897, National Archives, Record Group 134, Box 219, Docket 431.

75 **and what, if any, steps you have taken in the matter.":** Edward A. Moseley to Fuller E. Callaway, Feb. 12, 1898, National Archives, Record Group 134, Box 219, Docket 431, Inserts for Correspondence.

76 **"In fact we have been paying slightly higher rates.":** Fuller E. Callaway to Edward A. Moseley, National Archives, Record Group 134, Box 219, Docket 431, Inserts for Correspondence.

76 **unless they are made to do so," he declared.**: Ibid.

76 **to enforce its orders when necessary.**: Interstate Commerce Act, 24 Stat. 379, 384-85, § 16, ch. 104, Feb. 4, 1887; George M. Chandler, "The Interstate Commerce Commission—The First Twenty-Five Years," 16 *Transportation L.J.* 53, 56 (1987).

76 **the railroads' continued violation of the order.**: Certificate of Service, Interstate Commerce Commission v. Louisville & Nashville Railroad Co., July 25, 1898, National Archives, Record Group 134, Box 220, Docket 431.

76 **the injunction that Callaway wanted.**: Interstate Commerce Commission v. Louisville & Nashville Railroad Co., 102 F. 709, 709-10 (S. D. Ala. 1899).

76 **refusing to enforce the ICC's order.**: Louisville & Nashville Railroad Co. v. Interstate Commerce Commission, 108 F. 988, 988 (5th Cir. 1901).

77 **But again, Callaway didn't have any choice.**: Newcomb, *The Federal Courts and the Orders of the Interstate Commerce Commission*, p. 7; Interstate Commerce Commission v. Clyde Steamship Company, 181 U.S. 29 (1901); East Tennessee, Virginia and Georgia Railway Company v. Interstate Commerce Commission, 181 U.S. 1 (1901).

77 **for Callaway to win under those terms.**: Interstate Commerce Commission v. Louisville & Nashville Railroad Co., 190 U.S. 273, 279, 285 (1903). For the thoughts of the commissioners on the courts' handling of the case, see *Seventeenth Annual Report of the Interstate Commerce Commission* (Washington: Government Printing Office, 1903), 70-74.

77 **"very much exercised" over the whole issue of freight rates,:** Ida Cason Callaway, "Memories of Fuller Earle Callaway Sr. of LaGrange, Georgia Written by His Wife, Ida Cason Callaway," unpublished manuscript, Callaway Family Papers, Troup County Archives, LaGrange, Georgia, 1929, p. 46.

77 **to run the new line straight through LaGrange.**: Atlanta & West Point Railroad Co. v. Atlanta, Birmingham & Atlantic Railroad Co., 54 S.E. 736, 741 (Ga. 1906); Fuller Earle Callaway—The New Railroad, Callaway Family Papers, Troup County Archives, LaGrange, Georgia; Smith, *History of Troup County*, pp. 110-11; Fuller E. Callaway et al. to Subscribers to fund for securing Right of Way and Terminals for the Atlantic & Birmingham Railway, Apr. 28, 1905, Callaway Family Papers, Troup County Archives, LaGrange, Georgia.

77 **"This is the date of the new birth of LaGrange.":** "Fuller Earle Callaway," n.d., Callaway Family Papers, Troup County Archives, LaGrange, Georgia.

78 **"and I'd like to see our city ruined in the same manner.":** Ibid.

78 **in actual use for railroad purposes.**: See City Council of Augusta v. Georgia Railroad & Banking Co., 26 S.E. 499 (Ga. 1895).

78 **the Atlanta & West Point wanted to prevent that.**: Atlanta & West Point Railroad Co. v. Atlanta, Birmingham & Atlantic Railroad Co., 52 S.E. 320, 320-21 (Ga. 1905).

79 **seeking a right of way through the city of LaGrange.":** Ibid., p. 322.

79 **in Fulton County Superior Court, asking for another injunction.**: Atlanta & West Point Railroad Co. v. Atlanta, Birmingham & Atlantic Railroad Co., 54 S.E. 736, 737 (Ga. 1906).

79 **by then the railroad had been using the land for decades.**: Ibid., pp. 737-43.

79 **it wanted to monopolize rail transportation to and from LaGrange.**: Ibid., p. 743.

79 **continuing to act with its newfound haste.**: Ibid., pp. 737, 743.

80 **with other public use of the street.**: Ibid., pp. 745-47.

80 **Its whole tendency would be to exclude others ....":** Ibid., pp. 736, 747.

80 **because Callaway himself now wanted them.**: Order, Calloway v. Louisville & Nashville Railroad Co., Oct. 3, 1903, National Archives, Record Group 134, Box 220, Docket 431; [Edward A. Moseley] to Fuller E. Callaway, Oct. 24, 1904, National Archives, Record Group 134, Box 220, Docket 431; [Edward A. Moseley] to Fuller E. Callaway, Nov. 2, 1904, National Archives, Record Group 134, Box 220, Docket 431; A. R. Smith to Edward A. Moseley, Mar. 5, 1905, National Archives, Record Group 134, Box 220, Docket 431;

Judson C. Clements to Fuller E. Callaway, Aug. 3, 1906, National Archives, Record Group 134, Box 220, Docket 431.

80 **without a need to resort to the courts for enforcement.**: Judson C. Clements to Fuller E. Callaway, Aug. 3, 1906, National Archives, Record Group 134, Box 220, Docket 431; Hepburn Act, 34 Stat. 584, ch. 104, June 29, 1906.

80 **a disastrous effect upon the negotiations.**": Fuller E. Callaway to Judson C. Clements, Aug. 6, 1906, National Archives, Record Group 134, Box 220, Docket 431.

81 **in accordance with the laws of Georgia.**": Condemnation, Atlanta, Birmingham & Atlantic Railroad Co. v. Atlanta & West Point Railroad Co., Superior Court, Troup County, Ga., Mar. 27, 1906.

81 **in the blank space contained in the form, was Fuller E. Callaway.**: Ibid.

82 **more then twelve years earlier.**: Calloway v. Louisville & Nashville Railroad Co., 12 ICC 581 (1907); Calloway v. Louisville & Nashville Railroad Co., Oct. 8, 1907, National Archives, Record Group 134, Box 220, Docket 431.

82 **nearly every bank in the South had closed its doors.**: Richard Franklin Bensel, *The Political Economy of American Industrialization, 1877-1900* (New York: Cambridge University Press, 2000), 93, 97.

82 **three times the number of banks per capita.**: Benjamin J. Klebaner, *American Commercial Banking: A History* (Boston: Twayne Publishers, 1990), 61, 75.

82 **Congress passed the National Bank Acts.**: Act of Feb. 25, 1863, 12 Stat. 665, ch. 58; National Bank Act of 1864, 13 Stat. 99, ch. 106, June 3, 1864.

82 **a run on the bank in the first place.**: Klebaner, *American Commercial Banking*, pp. 64-65, 68.

82 **only sixty-nine of them were in the former Confederacy.**: Ibid., pp. 66-67; Bensel, *American Industrialization*, p. 97.

82 **a 10 percent federal tax on their bank notes.**: Act of Mar. 3, 1865, 13 Stat. 469, 484, § 6; Klebaner, *American Commercial Banking*, p. 67.

82 **the town's new textile ventures of the late 1800s.**: Smith, *History of Troup County*, pp. 127-28.

83 **to invigorate its economy and break out of the cycle.**: Bensel, *American Industrialization*, pp. 91-92.

83 **sometimes in blocks as small as**

$100.: See page 51, *supra.*

84 **between seven** AM **and nightfall.**: Act of June 3, 1864, 13 Stat. 99, 101, ch. 106, § 7; "Notes of a Conference with Mr. Henry D. Glanton, who Started with Mr. Callaway's Organization at the Time of Organization of the LaGrange National Bank, the First Banking Institution in the Organization," n.d., Callaway Family Papers, Troup County Archives, LaGrange, Georgia; Smith, *History of Troup County*, p. 128.

84 **trouble at the Unity Mill around this same time.**: Johnson, *Histories of LaGrange and Troup County Georgia*, vols. 1 & 2, pp. 127, 256; Smith, *History of Troup County*, pp. 127-28; "Fuller Earle Callaway: The Cotton Manufacturing Period," n.d., Callaway Family Papers, Troup County Archives, LaGrange, Georgia; see pages 57-59, *supra.*

84 **financing the purchase through the mortgage process.**: "Fuller Earle Callaway: The Cotton Manufacturing Period," n.d., Callaway Family Papers, Troup County Archives, LaGrange, Georgia; Hatton Lovejoy to J. A. Perry, Aug. 30, 1951, Callaway Family Papers, Troup County Archives, LaGrange, Georgia; Edward L. Symons, Jr., "The 'Business of Banking' in Historical Perspective," 51 *Geo. Wash. L. Rev.* 676, 715-16 (1983); National Bank Act of 1864, 13 Stat. 99, 107-08, ch. 106, § 28, June 3, 1864; Act of Dec. 23, 1913, 38 Stat. 273, ch. 6, §§ 34, 38.

84 **a local election approved the new plant's construction.**: Smith, *History of Troup County*, pp. 113, 116; Hatton Lovejoy to J. A. Perry, Aug. 30, 1951, Callaway Family Papers, Troup County Archives, LaGrange, Georgia.

84 **the new LaGrange Insurance Agency.**: "Fuller Earle Callaway: The Cotton Manufacturing Period," n.d., Callaway Family Papers, Troup County Archives, LaGrange, Georgia.

84 **a new electrically-powered gin.**: Smith, *History of Troup County*, p. 124; "Fuller Earle Callaway: The Cotton Manufacturing Period," n.d., Callaway Family Papers, Troup County Archives, LaGrange, Georgia.

85 **the insurance policy covered the entire loss.**: "Fuller Earle Callaway: The Cotton Manufacturing Period," n.d., Callaway Family Papers, Troup County Archives, LaGrange, Georgia.

85 **they found nothing but closed doors.**: Joseph French Johnson, "The Crisis and Panic of 1907," 23 *Political Science*

Quarterly 454, 461 (1908); cf. Alexander D. Noyes, "A Year after the Panic of 1907," 23 *Quarterly Journal of Economics* 185, 191 (1909); Robert F. Bruner, *The Panic of 1907: Lessons Learned from the Market's Perfect Storm* (New York: John Wiley & Sons, 2009), 2.

85 **two of Callaway's most important projects outside the textile industry itself.**: Bruner, *Panic of 1907*, chs. 5-7.

85 **balancing the sheets of every bank in the community against each other.**: Richard H. Timberlake, "The Central Banking Role of Clearinghouse Associations," 16 *Journal of Money, Credit and Banking* 1, 2-3 (1984).

86 **end the panic by pooling their resources.**: Gary Gorton, "Clearinghouses and the Origin of Central Banking in the United States," 45 *Journal of Economic History* 277, 279-82 (1985).

86 **the disastrous copper scheme.**: Gorton, Clearinghouses," pp. 282-83.

87 **sound currency, and plenty of it, both on deposit and in circulation.**: "Notes of a Conference with Mr. Henry D. Glanton, who Started with Mr. Callaway's Organization at the Time of Organization of the LaGrange National Bank, the First Banking Institution in the Organization," n.d., Callaway Family Papers, Troup County Archives, LaGrange, Georgia.

· 5 ·
THE MIDDLE YEARS:
FAMILY AND TRAVEL

89 **The son thus took the name of Cason Jewell Callaway.**: "Fuller Earle Callaway," Callaway Family Papers, Troup County Archives, LaGrange, Georgia 1-19; "A Son is Born," Callaway Family Papers, Troup County Archives, LaGrange, Georgia.

89 **the highest office any woman could attain.**": Ida Cason Callaway, "Memories of Fuller Earle Callaway Sr. of LaGrange, Georgia Written by His Wife, Ida Cason Callaway," unpublished manuscript, Callaway Family Papers, Troup County Archives, LaGrange, Georgia, 1929, 35.

90 **McKinley's two-time Democratic opponent, William Jennings Bryan.**: Ibid., p. 36.

90 **which Fuller probably found quite encouraging.**: Ibid., pp. 36-37.

90 **when the boy was only six years old.**: Ibid., p. 43.

90 the former upset and the latter embarrassed.: Donna Jean Whitley, "Fuller E. Callaway and Textile Mill Development in LaGrange, 1895-1920," Ph.D. Diss., Emory University, 1984, 45.

90 during Christmas he would sell fireworks.: Ida Cason Callaway, "Memories," p. 38.

90 "Put all boys who have coughs to work in a cotton mill!": Ibid., p. 39; "Byssinosis," 24 Chest 674 (1953).

91 an important foundation for his later successes.: North Carolina and its Resources (Winston: M. I. & J. C. Stewart, 1896), 260; A Handbook of the Best Private Schools of the United States and Canada (Boston: Porter E. Sargent, 1915), 92.

91 you can save something on your fare coming and going by doing so.": Fuller E. Callaway to Cason J. Callaway, Sept. 9, 1909, Callaway Family Papers, Troup County Archives, LaGrange, Georgia; Fuller E. Callaway to Cason J. Callaway, Dec. 2, 1909, Callaway Family Papers, Troup County Archives, LaGrange, Georgia.

91 being able to sleep all the way to LaGrange.: Fuller E. Callaway to Cason J. Callaway, Dec. 2, 1909, Callaway Family Papers, Troup County Archives, LaGrange, Georgia.

91 but at least the family was together again.: "A Visit to Cason at Asheville," Callaway Family Papers, Troup County Archives, LaGrange, Georgia; "The Life and Works of Mr. Fuller E. Callaway, Senior," Callaway Family Papers, Troup County Archives, LaGrange, Georgia, p. 4.

91 Bingham's recent sports victory over the rival Mooney school.: Fuller E. Callaway to Cason J. Callaway, Dec. 6, 1909, Callaway Family Papers, Troup County Archives, LaGrange, Georgia.

93 to have our children journey on the same road with us," she wrote.): Ida Cason Callaway, "Memories," p. 39; "LaGrange Boy Honored," LaGrange Reporter, Oct. 24, 1911; Ida Cason Callaway, "Memories," p. 39.

93 at Eastman Business College in Poughkeepsie, New York.: "Cason J. Callaway," Callaway Family Papers, Troup County Archives, LaGrange, Georgia.

93 he could learn how to handle adversity.: Ibid.

93 a few weeks after his twenty-second birthday.: Ibid.

93 instead of 'buy, buy!' ': Ida Cason Callaway, "Memories," p. 37.

93 have you got any loose change about you?": Ibid.

94 Callaway opted to go ahead and pay for the mounting.: Ibid., p. 48.

94 which end of the bee stung.": Ibid., p. 38.

94 the Elm City plant's basement furnace room.: Ibid., pp. 38-39; LaGrange Rotary Bulletin, June 15, 1938; http://www.callawayfoundation.org/fuller_callaway_jr.php (last visited May 24, 2013).

95 a cousin of the Callaway family through Wilkes County connections.: Louis D. Newton, "Pastor Tunnell Observes Fifth Anniversary at LaGrange," The Christian Index, Sept. 11, 1924; Robert B. Wallace, Jr., Dress Her in White and Gold: A Biography of Georgia Tech and of the Men Who Led Her (Atlanta: The Georgia Tech Foundation, 1969), 140.

95 his widow also came to live with the Callaways.: Fuller E. Callaway Jr., interview by James Saxon Childers, July 16, 1953, Callaway Family Papers, Troup County Archives, LaGrange, Georgia, pp. 19, 25; Ida Cason Callaway, "Memories," p. 29; "Mr. Howard Callaway Comes to Live with the Family," Callaway Family Papers, Troup County Archives, LaGrange, Georgia; "The Life and Works of Mr. Fuller E. Callaway, Senior," Callaway Family Papers, Troup County Archives, LaGrange, Georgia, p. 15.

96 it was a one-floor house.: Fuller E. Callaway Jr., interview by James Saxon Childers, July 16, 1953, Callaway Family Papers, Troup County Archives, LaGrange, Georgia, pp. 19, 25.

96 particularly to Atlanta and later to Memphis.: Ibid., p. 24; "Death of Mr. Pope F. Callaway," Callaway Family Papers, Troup County Archives, LaGrange, Georgia; LaGrange Graphic, Aug. 3, 1923.

96 a rather wild place, in the way that could feed Pope's own wildness.: Tim Sharp, Memphis Music before the Blues (Charleston: Arcadia Publishing, 2007), chs. 5-6; J. P. Young, Standard History of Memphis, Tennessee (Knoxville: H. W. Crew & Co., 1912), 231-36.

96 Pope agreed to the bargain.: Fuller E. Callaway Jr., interview by James Saxon Childers, July 16, 1953, Callaway Family Papers, Troup County Archives, LaGrange, Georgia, p. 24.

97 imparting a sense of urgency to customers, which drew them to the stores.: "The Life and Works of Mr. Fuller E. Callaway, Senior," Callaway Family Papers, Troup County Archives, LaGrange, Georgia, p. 7; "Fuller Earle Callaway—Brother Pope Comes Back," Callaway Family Papers, Troup County Archives, LaGrange, Georgia.

97 the Fuller E. Callaway Company, which specialized in wholesale dry goods.: "Fuller Earle Callaway—Brother Pope Comes Back," Callaway Family Papers, Troup County Archives, LaGrange, Georgia.

98 Fuller used it to buy his wedding suit.: Fuller E. Callaway Jr., interview by James Saxon Childers, July 16, 1953, Callaway Family Papers, Troup County Archives, LaGrange, Georgia, p. 24.

98 on the whole his investments paid off.: "Fuller Earle Callaway—Brother Pope Comes Back," Callaway Family Papers, Troup County Archives, LaGrange, Georgia.

98 the nation's first commercial radio station, 600 miles away.: Amateur Radio Stations of the United States, edition June 30, 1920 (Washington: Government Printing Office, 1920), 132; "Fuller Earle Callaway—Fuller E. Callaway Jr., is Born," Callaway Family Papers, Troup County Archives, LaGrange, Georgia.

98 the manager of Hills and Dales and the garden that Ida loved.: "Death of Mr. Pope F. Callaway," Callaway Family Papers, Troup County Archives, LaGrange, Georgia; LaGrange Graphic, Aug. 3, 1923.

99 that was what Pope did, to everyone's delight.: "Value Received Through Pleasure to Friends," Callaway Family Papers, Troup County Archives, LaGrange, Georgia.

99 his sister-in-law Ida.: Fuller E. Callaway to Mr. and Mrs. William S. Witham, Aug. 6, 1923, Callaway Family Papers, Troup County Archives, LaGrange, Georgia; "Death of Mr. Pope F. Callaway," Callaway Family Papers, Troup County Archives, LaGrange, Georgia; LaGrange Graphic, Aug. 3, 1923; Fuller E. Callaway Jr., interview by James Saxon Childers, July 16, 1953, Callaway Family Papers, Troup County Archives, LaGrange, Georgia, p. 24-25.

99 not even coming close to offsetting the loss.: "Buying Experience in Speculation," Callaway Family Papers, Troup County Archives, LaGrange, Georgia. 5-154-55.

99 unburdened, went to sleep.: Ida Cason Callaway, "Memories," pp. 32-33.

100 take that left hind leg of yours out of the trough—quick!": Helen Christine Bennett, "The Homely Wisdom of Fuller E. Callaway," *American Magazine*, Oct. 1920, 16, 105.

100 "but we need it to stand the drought of August.": Ibid., pp. 105-06.

100 to buy too soon and sweat over the mistake.": Fuller E. Callaway to _____, 1923, Callaway Family Papers, Troup County Archives, LaGrange, Georgia.

101 BEFORE YOU INVEST, INVESTIGATE.": "Buying Experience in Speculation," Callaway Family Papers, Troup County Archives, LaGrange, Georgia; "The Life and Works of Mr. Fuller E. Callaway, Senior," Callaway Family Papers, Troup County Archives, LaGrange, Georgia, p. 14.

101 Most people do just the opposite.": Conversation between Fuller E. Callaway Jr., James Saxon Childers, and Maurine Childers Concerning Life of Fuller E. Callaway Sr., July 22, 1953, Callaway Family Papers, Troup County Archives, LaGrange, Georgia, p. 19.

101 "the crowd is always wrong.": Ibid., p. 22.

101 When everybody is selling, buy. When everybody is buying, sell.": Bennett, "The Homely Wisdom of Fuller E. Callaway," p. 106; Conversation between Fuller E. Callaway Jr., James Saxon Childers, and Maurine Childers Concerning Life of Fuller E. Callaway Sr., July 22, 1953, Callaway Family Papers, Troup County Archives, LaGrange, Georgia, p. 22; Ida Cason Callaway, "Memories," p. 51.

101 the bursting of the Florida land bubble in 1925 and 1926.: Ida Cason Callaway, "Memories," p. 47; Conversation between Fuller E. Callaway Jr., James Saxon Childers, and Maurine Childers Concerning Life of Fuller E. Callaway Sr., July 22, 1953, Callaway Family Papers, Troup County Archives, LaGrange, Georgia, p. 21; see generally William Frazer & John J. Guthrie, *The Florida Land Boom: Speculation, Money, and the Banks* (Westport: Quorum Books, 1995).

101 it's coming; get ready. It's going to crash wide open.": Conversation between Fuller E. Callaway Jr., James Saxon Childers, and Maurine Childers Concerning Life of Fuller E. Callaway Sr., July 22, 1953, Callaway Family Papers, Troup County Archives, LaGrange, Georgia, pp. 20-21.

101 that particular stock dropped by well over 90 percent.: Ibid., p. 22.

101 hit the bed I was asleep. It doesn't pay to worry over anything.": Bennett, "The Homely Wisdom of Fuller E. Callaway," p. 109.

102 a remarkable ability to remember things.: Hatton Lovejoy to James S. Childers, Apr. 7, 1954, Callaway Family Papers, Troup County Archives, LaGrange, Georgia.

102 Callaway always gave the right answers.: Fuller E. Callaway Jr., interview by James Saxon Childers, July 16, 1953, Callaway Family Papers, Troup County Archives, LaGrange, Georgia, p. 3.

102 This system greatly reduced the chance that anything would slip through the cracks.: "The Truth About Mr. Callaway's Memory," Callaway Family Papers, Troup County Archives, LaGrange, Georgia; Conversation between Fuller E. Callaway Jr., James Saxon Childers, and Maurine Childers Concerning Life of Fuller E. Callaway Sr., July 22, 1953, Callaway Family Papers, Troup County Archives, LaGrange, Georgia, p. 35.

102 his employees would leave him alone so he could concentrate.: "Rehearsing," Callaway Family Papers, Troup County Archives, LaGrange, Georgia; Hatton Lovejoy to James S. Childers, Apr. 7, 1954, Callaway Family Papers, Troup County Archives, LaGrange, Georgia.

102 he was as ready as possible for any argument he might come up against.: Hatton Lovejoy to James S. Childers, Apr. 7, 1954, Callaway Family Papers, Troup County Archives, LaGrange, Georgia.

103 without using a slide rule.: Fuller E. Callaway Jr., interview by James Saxon Childers, July 16, 1953, Callaway Family Papers, Troup County Archives, LaGrange, Georgia, pp. 3-4; Conversation between Fuller E. Callaway Jr., James Saxon Childers, and Maurine Childers Concerning Life of Fuller E. Callaway Sr., July 22, 1953, Callaway Family Papers, Troup County Archives, LaGrange, Georgia, p. 31.

103 gathering dust for months or even years.: Conversation between Fuller E. Callaway Jr., James Saxon Childers, and Maurine Childers Concerning Life of Fuller E. Callaway Sr., July 22, 1953, Callaway Family Papers, Troup County Archives, LaGrange, Georgia, pp. 11-12.

103 more aggressive in their hunt for new business.: Ibid., p. 12.

103 just another of his tales, intended to make light of the mannerism.: Ibid., p.

27; Ida Cason Callaway, "Memories," pp. 53-54.

103 very few employees ever left the Callaway businesses.: Hatton Lovejoy to James S. Childers, Apr. 7, 1954, Callaway Family Papers, Troup County Archives, LaGrange, Georgia.

103 the problem of its outmoded narrow looms.: See pages 65-66, *supra*.

104 to adopt this spirit and attitude toward me of late.: Fuller E. Callaway to O. A. Barnard, Dec. 13, 1909, Callaway Family Papers, Troup County Archives, LaGrange, Georgia; Fuller E. Callaway to Dr. F. M. Ridley, Sr., Dec. 13, 1909, Callaway Family Papers, Troup County Archives, LaGrange, Georgia; Fuller E. Callaway to Park A. Dallis, Dec. 13, 1909, Callaway Family Papers, Troup County Archives, LaGrange, Georgia; Fuller E. Callaway to O. A. Barnard, Dec. 14, 1909, Callaway Family Papers, Troup County Archives, LaGrange, Georgia.

104 the recent epidemic of criticism.": Fuller E. Callaway to F. Coit Johnson, Dec. 13, 1909, Callaway Family Papers, Troup County Archives, LaGrange, Georgia.

104 since the desired end was accomplished.: Fuller E. Callaway to O. A. Barnard, Dec. 13, 1909, Callaway Family Papers, Troup County Archives, LaGrange, Georgia.

104 the splendid results that have been and may be accomplished through cooperation team work.: Fuller E. Callaway to F. Coit Johnson, Dec. 17, 1909, Callaway Family Papers, Troup County Archives, LaGrange, Georgia.

105 his father would buy extra clothes at his destination if he needed them.: Conversation between Fuller E. Callaway Jr., James Saxon Childers, and Maurine Childers Concerning Life of Fuller E. Callaway Sr., July 22, 1953, Callaway Family Papers, Troup County Archives, LaGrange, Georgia, p. 34; Conversation between Fuller E. Callaway Jr., James Saxon Childers, and Maurine Childers Concerning Life of Fuller E. Callaway Sr., July 22, 1953, Callaway Family Papers, Troup County Archives, LaGrange, Georgia, p. 29; "Fuller Earle Callaway," Callaway Family Papers, Troup County Archives, LaGrange, Georgia; Fuller E. Callaway Jr., interview by James Saxon Childers, July 16, 1953, Callaway Family Papers, Troup County Archives, LaGrange, Georgia, p. 8; Hatton Lovejoy to James S. Childers, Apr. 7, 1954, Callaway Family Papers, Troup County Archives, LaGrange, Georgia.

105 **he would often use it to point and gesture.**: Conversation between Fuller E. Callaway Jr., James Saxon Childers, and Maurine Childers Concerning Life of Fuller E. Callaway Sr., July 22, 1953, Callaway Family Papers, Troup County Archives, LaGrange, Georgia, p. 29.

106 **his father would produce one from a pocket.**: Ibid., pp. 31, 32, 34; Fuller E. Callaway Jr., interview by James Saxon Childers, July 16, 1953, Callaway Family Papers, Troup County Archives, LaGrange, Georgia, p. 8.

106 **I never could have done what I did."**: Fuller E. Callaway Jr., interview by James Saxon Childers, July 16, 1953, Callaway Family Papers, Troup County Archives, LaGrange, Georgia, p. 8; Conversation between Fuller E. Callaway Jr., James Saxon Childers, and Maurine Childers Concerning Life of Fuller E. Callaway Sr., July 22, 1953, Callaway Family Papers, Troup County Archives, LaGrange, Georgia, p. 34.

106 **and wore the new one out the door.**: Fuller E. Callaway Jr., interview by James Saxon Childers, July 16, 1953, Callaway Family Papers, Troup County Archives, LaGrange, Georgia, p. 8.

106 **the Waldorf staff, with whom he became a great favorite.**: Ibid., pp. 8, 19-20; "Fuller Earle Callaway," Callaway Family Papers, Troup County Archives, LaGrange, Georgia.

106 **seventeen years on Cash Street when we could afford to live on Mortgage Avenue."**: Bennett, "The Homely Wisdom of Fuller E. Callaway," p. 105.

106 **Can give possession latter part of January.' '**: Fuller E. Callaway to *The LaGrange Reporter*, Dec. 24, 1909, Callaway Family Papers, Troup County Archives, LaGrange, Georgia.

107 **just shy of age forty, in the prime of his life and career.**: "The Life and Works of Mr. Fuller E. Callaway, Senior," Callaway Family Papers, Troup County Archives, LaGrange, Georgia, p. 5; "Living on 'Cash Street," Callaway Family Papers, Troup County Archives, LaGrange, Georgia; "Four Forty-Year-Old Letter Books," Callaway Family Papers, Troup County Archives, LaGrange, Georgia; Forrest Clark Johnson, III, *Histories of LaGrange and Troup County Georgia*, vols. 1 & 2 (LaGrange: Family Tree, 1987), 496.

107 **And that is what he did in the end.**: Ida Cason Callaway, "Memories," p. 49.

108 **more information than the other party thought he did, worked in his favor.**: Ibid., p. 50.

109 **and hope to establish this condition for good."**: Ibid., pp. 50-54.

109 **Once again his family told him that he had to take a break.**: "Fuller Earle Callaway," Callaway Family Papers, Troup County Archives, LaGrange, Georgia.

110 **about the progress in Manchester as well as with more routine matters.**: _____ to Fuller E. Callaway, July 28, 1909, Callaway Family Papers, Troup County Archives, LaGrange, Georgia.

110 **away up the list in point of beauty."**: Mateel Howe, "The Exposition," *The Independent*, June 24, 1909, pp. 1368, 1369.

110 **Callaway would likely have found it a valuable experience.**: "Fuller Earle Callaway," Callaway Family Papers, Troup County Archives, LaGrange, Georgia.

110 **setting out on his journey north he was already very run down from overwork.**: Ida recalled the fateful New York trip to have happened in 1913, but the bulk of evidence suggests that 1911 is the correct year.

111 **And in 1911 there were no antibiotics.**: See generally John Riddell, "The Incidence Of Erysipelas," *British Medical Journal*, vol. 2, No. 3906 (Nov. 16, 1935), 94; Stella Kathleen Kenny, "Erysipelas: A Few Observations," *American Journal of Nursing*, vol. 8 (Sep., 1908), 976.

112 **in hopes that the waters there would reduce his blood toxicity.**: Ida Cason Callaway, "Memories," pp. 63-65; "Mr. Callaway Suffers Serious Illness While in New York and Finally Goes Abroad in May, 1911," Callaway Family Papers, Troup County Archives, LaGrange, Georgia.

112 **He'd been studying it since at least 1904.**: W. E. Cotton & Sons to E. J. Robertson, Aug. 22, 1904, Callaway Family Papers, Troup County Archives, LaGrange, Georgia; "Utilization of Waste," Callaway Family Papers, Troup County Archives, LaGrange, Georgia.

112 **other products that don't require a high tensile strength.**: See generally Thomas Thornley, *Cotton Waste: Its Production, Manipulation, and Uses* (London: Scott, Greenwood & Son, 1912); United States Department of Commerce, *Foreign Markets for Cotton Linters, Batting, and Waste* (Washington: Government Printing Office, 1918).

112 **Callaway wanted to go there and see the operation for himself.**: "Utilization of Waste," Callaway Family Papers, Troup County Archives, LaGrange, Georgia.

112 **will come home stronger in every way than for years."**: Fuller E. Callaway to _____, June 10, 1911, "Letters from 1911 Trip to Europe," Callaway Family Papers, Troup County Archives, LaGrange, Georgia.

113 **he'd been pulling his leg, but he never got around to it.**: Ida Cason Callaway, "Memories," pp. 65-66.

113 **where he traveled among the Norwegian fjords.**: Fuller E. Callaway to _____, June 23, 1911, "Letters from 1911 Trip to Europe," Callaway Family Papers, Troup County Archives, LaGrange, Georgia.

113 **engaging himself heavily in research for his own enterprises.**: *The LaGrange Reporter*, Aug. 18, 1921.

113 **did not try to put on any 'language' airs.**: "Callaway Happy to be Back in Dear Old Georgia Hills," *Atlanta Constitution*, Aug. 20, 1911.

114 **between England and India by more than 4,000 miles, nearly halving travel time.**: Frederick Hooper and James Graham, *The Import and Export Trade, or, Modern Commercial Practice* (London: Macmillan and Co., 1905), 171.

115 **hardly any difficulty, comparatively small risk, and insignificant loss to the victors."**: Winston S. Churchill, *The River War: An Historical Account of the Reconquest of the Soudan*, rev. ed. (London: Longmans, Green, and Co., 1902), 300.

115 **only forty-eight of his own men killed and fewer than 500 wounded.**: Harold E. Raugh, *The Victorians at War, 1815-1914: An Encyclopedia of British Military History* (Santa Barbara: ABC-CLIO, 2004), 257.

115 **when the American cotton supply dried up as a result of the war.**: "Mr. Callaway's Trip to Egypt and the Holy Land," Callaway Family Papers, Troup County Archives, LaGrange, Georgia; see, e.g., George R. Gliddon, *A Memoir on the Cotton of Egypt* (London: James Madden & Co., 1841); Louis B. Grant, "Cotton in Egypt," *Reports from the Consuls of the United States*, No. 144, Sept. 1892 (Washington: Government Printing Office, 1892), 112; W. Lawrence Balls, *The Cotton Plant in Egypt* (London: Macmillan and Co., 1912).

116 **that of Lord Kitchener himself.**: "Mr. Callaway's Trip to Egypt and the Holy

Land," Callaway Family Papers, Troup County Archives, LaGrange, Georgia; "A Hotel With History," http://www.shepheard-hotel.com/history.html (last visited May 24, 2013); *A Handbook for Travellers in Egypt, Including Descriptions of the Course of the Nile to the Second Cataract, Alexandria, Cairo, the Pyramids, and Thebes, the Overland Tranit to India, the Penninsula of Mount Sinai, the Oases, &c.* (London: John Murray, 1873), 124; see generally Nina Nelson, *Shepheard's Hotel* (New York: Macmillan, 1960).

116 **he doubted that even these credentials would be good for more than a handshake.**: "Mr. Callaway's Trip to Egypt and the Holy Land," Callaway Family Papers, Troup County Archives, LaGrange, Georgia; Conversation between Fuller E. Callaway Jr., James Saxon Childers, and Maurine Childers Concerning Life of Fuller E. Callaway Sr., July 22, 1953, Callaway Family Papers, Troup County Archives, LaGrange, Georgia, p. 1.

116 **dazzled the man into admitting him to Kitchener's inner sanctum.**: Ida Cason Callaway, "Memories," pp. 67-68; Conversation between Fuller E. Callaway Jr., James Saxon Childers, and Maurine Childers Concerning Life of Fuller E. Callaway Sr., July 22, 1953, Callaway Family Papers, Troup County Archives, LaGrange, Georgia, p. 1.

117 **Callaway even stayed in Kitchener's home as his guest for a time.**: John Pollock, *Kitchener: Architect of Victory, Artisan of Peace* (New York: Carroll & Graf, 2001), xxi-xxii, 402, 438; Conversation between Fuller E. Callaway Jr., James Saxon Childers, and Maurine Childers Concerning Life of Fuller E. Callaway Sr., July 22, 1953, Callaway Family Papers, Troup County Archives, LaGrange, Georgia, p. 2.

117 **in light of the needs of war production.**: See generally Grant, "Cotton in Egypt," pp. 112-20; W. D. Hunter, *The Control of the Boll Weevil, Including Results of Recent Investigations* (Washington: Government Printing Office, 1905); A. Henry McMahon to Sir Edward Grey, Dec. 22, 1915, Colonial Office series 23, PRO, The National Archives of the UK (TNA); Sir George Arthur, *The Life of Lord Kitchener*, vol. 2 (London: The Macmillan and Co., 1920), 322-27.

118 **"Plant it and try it."**: Alfred Pearce Dennis, *Gods and Little Fishes* (Indianapolis; Bobbs-Merrill Co., 1931), 265-66; Conversation between Fuller E. Callaway Jr., James Saxon Childers, and Maurine Childers Concerning Life of Fuller E. Callaway Sr., July 22, 1953, Callaway

Family Papers, Troup County Archives, LaGrange, Georgia, pp. 1-2; Ida Cason Callaway, "Memories," p. 68; Frederick J. Tyler, *Varieties of American Upland Cotton* (Washington: Government Printing Office, 1910), 115.

118 **on the next stage of his journey, a tour of the Holy Land.**: "Mr. Callaway's Trip to Egypt and the Holy Land," Callaway Family Papers, Troup County Archives, LaGrange, Georgia.

118 **I was right" about Christ's immersion, which gave Fuller a good laugh.**: Ibid.; Ida Cason Callaway, "Memories," pp. 66-67.

118 **The Truitt strain had beaten the pink boll worm by a full two weeks.**: Dennis, *Gods and Little Fishes*, p. 96.

119 **forebear of Dun and Bradstreet, to identify the major players in the field.**: "Mr. Callaway's Trip to Egypt and the Holy Land," Callaway Family Papers, Troup County Archives, LaGrange, Georgia.

119 **Cologne, Hamburg, and Berlin. His timing couldn't have been much worse.**: Ibid.; Fuller E. Callaway to John H. Callaway, Nov. 5, 1922, Callaway Family Papers, Troup County Archives, LaGrange, Georgia.

121 **became acute during the final days of the month, and the mobilizations began.**: See generally Laurence Lafore, *The Long Fuse: An Interpretation of the Origins of World War I* (Philadelphia: Lippincott, 1965).

122 **making his way, like Howard, across the channel to England.**: *New York Times*, Aug. 1, 1914; The Sun, Aug. 13, 1914.

123 **he had "forced the British Empire to issue two new forms of currency."**: Conversation between Fuller E. Callaway Jr., James Saxon Childers, and Maurine Childers Concerning Life of Fuller E. Callaway Sr., July 22, 1953, Callaway Family Papers, Troup County Archives, LaGrange, Georgia, p. 3; Josephus Nelson Larned, *The New Larned History for Ready Reference, Reading and Research*, vol. 2 (Springfield, Mass: C. A. Nichols Publishing Co., 1922), 858; Alexander Dana Noyes, *Financial Chapters of the War* (New York: Charles Scribner's Sons, 1916), 34-45.

123 **He did this as many as a hundred times.**: Conversation between Fuller E. Callaway Jr., James Saxon Childers, and Maurine Childers Concerning Life of Fuller E. Callaway Sr., July 22, 1953, Callaway Family Papers, Troup County Archives, LaGrange, Georgia, p. 3.

123 **where he was waiting for developments during much of August 4.**: Pollock, *Kitchener*, pp. 75-76, 372-73.

124 **We will need every yard of goods we can get."**: Fuller E. Callaway Jr., interview by James Saxon Childers, July 16, 1953, Callaway Family Papers, Troup County Archives, LaGrange, Georgia, p. 10; Pollock, *Kitchener*, pp. 373-75.

125 **lying down when necessary to hold places for the other two.**: Conversation between Fuller E. Callaway Jr., James Saxon Childers, and Maurine Childers Concerning Life of Fuller E. Callaway Sr., July 22, 1953, Callaway Family Papers, Troup County Archives, LaGrange, Georgia, p. 4; *New York Times*, Aug. 13, 1914.

125 **had doubtless never looked so fine to Callaway, or to anyone else aboard.**: Conversation between Fuller E. Callaway Jr., James Saxon Childers, and Maurine Childers Concerning Life of Fuller E. Callaway Sr., July 22, 1953, Callaway Family Papers, Troup County Archives, LaGrange, Georgia, p. 4; *New York Times*, Aug. 13, 1914.

125 **"I'll take it."**: Fuller E. Callaway Jr., interview by James Saxon Childers, July 16, 1953, Callaway Family Papers, Troup County Archives, LaGrange, Georgia, p. 10.

· 6 ·
HILLS AND DALES

127 **something about the social and economic status of the family that lives in it.**: James Grady, *Architecture of Neel Reid in Georgia* (Athens: University of Georgia Press, 1973), xvii; Medora Field Perkerson, *White Columns in Georgia* (New York: American Legacy Press, 1952), 245.

128 **lands to the west belonging to the Creek Nation until a few years later.**: Treaty with the Creeks, Jan. 8, 1821, Proclamation, Mar. 2, 1821, 7 Stat. 215.

128 **History, especially that of the Classical world, would also have been required.**: Christine Donhardt, "Ferrell Gardens: A Designed Landscape of the 19th Century," M.L.A. thesis, University of Georgia, 2007, 7-11.

129 **Sarah's new husband becoming a lawyer.**: Ibid., pp. 12, 15-16.

129 **things fell into place for what was to come.**: Ibid., p. 17.

129 **she inaugurated her work on the garden the following year.**: *LaGrange Reporter*, May 28, 1888.

129 she made no mention of illness as a motivation for her garden work.: Donhardt, "Ferrell Gardens," pp. 34-35; see *LaGrange Reporter*, May 28, 1888.

130 largely through the influence of one of her teachers.: Donhardt, "Ferrell Gardens," pp. 11-12.

130 The arrangement also gave Sarah ideas about how to create her garden.: Ibid., pp. 19-21.

131 then over time worked downward from there.: Ibid., pp. 35-36.

131 hundreds of thousands of dollars in modern terms.: *LaGrange Reporter*, May 31, 1888.

131 Labyrinth Avenue; Magnolia Avenue; and the Valley.: Donhardt, "Ferrell Gardens," p. 42.

131 mentioned in the Book of Isaiah.: Isaiah 41:19; ibid., 60:13.

131 a great renaissance of the practice in England.: Donhardt, "Ferrell Gardens," p. 57; William R. Mitchell, Jr., *J. Neel Reid, Architect, of Hentz, Reid & Adler and the Georgia School of Classicists* (Atlanta: Georgia Trust for Historic Preservation, 1997), 47: Brent Elliott, "Historical Revivalism in the Twentieth Century: A Brief Introduction," *Garden History* 28.1, "Reviewing the Twentieth-Century Landscape," (Summer 2000), 7-31, 19. See generally Miles Hadfield, *Topiary and Ornamental Hedges: Their History and Cultivation* (London: Adam & Charles Black, 1971).

131 As a result, the labyrinth was removed.: Donhardt, "Ferrell Gardens," p. 64.

131 the flowers that never would in other climates grow.'": Frank M. Ridley, *In Memory of Sarah Coleman Ferrell* (Atlanta: Ward and Darrington, 1904), 13.

132 the role of God in the world.: Donhardt, "Ferrell Gardens," pp. 61-62.

132 which Ida Callaway much later identified as a collection plate.: Ibid., pp. 65-66.

132 in one corner, a pulpit.: Ibid., p. 67.

133 the original shape of the latter sculpture is now lost.: Earle S. Draper, "The Gardens at Hills and Dales," *House Beautiful*, May 1932, 372, 416; Donhardt, "Ferrell Gardens," pp. 67-68.

133 or the waters of baptism.: Donhardt, "Ferrell Gardens," pp. 67-68.

133 was not a church member.: Ibid., pp. 74-75.

133 as it progresses from birth to resurrection.: *Mackey's National Freemason, October 1872 to September 1873* (Whitefish, Montana: Kessinger Publishing, 2003), 132.

133 represents eternity for Freemasonry.: Albert Gallatin Mackey & William James Hughan, *An Encyclopedia of Freemasonry and its Kindred Sciences*, vol. 1 (New York: The Masonic History Co., 1913), 151.

133 determine the correctness of angles.: Ibid., pp. 186-87.

134 some day we will have wings.": Ruth Bradfield Slack, "History of Ferrell Gardens," Lecture to the Garden Club of America, Apr. 1932, p. 2, Troup County Archives, LaGrange, Georgia; Constance Knowles Draper, "Ferrell Gardens," n.d., p. 6, Draper Collection, Box 1, Folder 6, Cherokee Garden Library, Atlanta History Center.

134 representing to the Masonic mind all of life's anxieties.: Craig M. Wright, *The Maze and the Warrior: Symbols in Architecture, Theology, and Music* (Cambridge: Harvard University Press, 2001), 206-16; Mackey & Hughan, *An Encyclopedia of Freemasonry*, p. 420.

134 the Masonic seeking of enlightenment and knowledge.: Benedict XVI, *The Spirit of the Liturgy* (San Francisco: Ignatius Press, 2009), 67-69; Mackey & Hughan, *An Encyclopedia of Freemasonry*, p. 226.

134 the wine drunk at the wedding at Cana and at the Last Supper.: John 2:8-11; e.g., Mark 14:22-25; see Donhardt, "Ferrell Gardens," p. 64.

134 Sarah's youngest son, who died of fever during the Civil War.: Donhardt, "Ferrell Gardens," pp. 62-67.

134 Among these are myrtle, fir, and pine trees;: Isaiah 41:19; ibid., 60:13.

134 the tiel tree mentioned in Isaiah;: Ibid., 41:19; ibid., 6:13; Donhardt, "Ferrell Gardens," pp. 73-74.

134 the cypress, from which Noah built his ark;: Genesis 6:14.

134 bay trees : Psalms 37:35.

134 and roses: Isaiah 35:1; Song of Solomon 2:1.

135 as he entered Jerusalem in triumph.: John 12:13; Exodus 30:23-26; e.g., Matthew 26:30.

135 the inspiration for all of Sarah's work at "The Terraces.": Donhardt, "Ferrell Gardens," p. 72.

135 the pine, and the box tree together … .": Isaiah 41:19.

135 she lined her driveways with them.: Donhardt, "Ferrell Gardens," p. 71.

135 By Ida's day it had grown to sixty feet tall.: Ibid., p. 72; Exodus 37; Ida Cason Callaway, "Memories of Fuller Earle Callaway Sr. of LaGrange, Georgia Written by His Wife, Ida Cason Callaway," unpublished manuscript, Callaway Family Papers, Troup County Archives, LaGrange, Georgia, 1929, pp. 66, 94.

136 the tropics, Europe, Africa, and Asia.: Donhardt, "Ferrell Gardens," pp. 68-70.

136 she often sent flowers from her garden to the sick.: Ibid., pp. 6, 27.

136 a great many couples became engaged there.: Ibid., p. 48; Ida Cason Callaway, "Memories," p. 92.

136 their noisy and boisterous conduct.": *LaGrange Reporter*, Feb. 18, 1870.

136 a parade ground, park, and cemetery.: Ibid., Mar. 21, 1890.

137 [I]t will save my wife the worry of an intolerable nuisance.": Ibid., Mar. 17, 1893.

137 "mar its beauty and pilfer its treasures.": Ibid., June 23, 1893.

137 the prettiest or most improved plants, gardens, and yards.: Donna Jean Whitley, "Fuller E. Callaway and Textile Mill Development in LaGrange, 1895-1920," Ph.D. Diss., Emory University, 1984, 214-16; see page 222, *infra*.

137 her own deceased son Palmon Ernest Ferrell.: See Ridley, *In Memory of Sarah Coleman Ferrell*, p. 9.

137 he loved the garden more than anyone except for the Ferrells themselves.: Ida M. Tarbell, "Making American Citizens and Running Cotton Mills to Pay the Expenses," *Red Cross Magazine*, Aug. 1920, 58, 76.

137 for every one she'd been able to make before he opened the store.: Ida Cason Callaway, "Memories," p. 91.

137 Callaway would remember the conversation.: Tarbell, "Making American Citizens," p. 76.

137 the property rapidly went downhill.: "A Hundred Years a-Growing: The Ferrell Gardens in Georgia," *Harpers Bazaar*, Aug. 1940, 85, 114.

137 **Fuller Callaway bid on it and bought it for $8,150.**: *Atlanta Georgian*, Dec. 6, 1911.

138 **crew of laborers and a foreman working under him.**: Donhardt, "Ferrell Gardens," pp. 40-41.

138 **he had a penchant for "owning all the land that 'jines me."**: "Beginning of Building of Residence on the Ferrell Place," Callaway Family Papers, Troup County Archives, LaGrange, Georgia.

138 **hiring an architectural firm.**: LaGrange Reporter, Jan. 16, 1914; Mitchell, *J. Neel Reid, Architect*, p. 226.

138 **but ultimately he returned to Georgia.**: Grady, *Architecture of Neel Reid in Georgia*, pp. x-xi.

139 **something reminiscent of the Renaissance,**: Mitchell, *J. Neel Reid, Architect*, p. 46.

139 **Callaway's acquaintants soon referred to the new home as an Italian villa.**: Grady, *Architecture of Neel Reid in Georgia*, p. 44; Mitchell, *J. Neel Reid, Architect*, p. 46; Harry L. Williams to Fuller E. Callaway, May 11, 1916, Callaway Family Papers, Troup County Archives, LaGrange, Georgia.

139 **that sacred portion of the globe dedicated to one's self.**: Charles A. Platt, *Italian Gardens* (New York, Harper & Brothers, 1894), 6-7.

139 **Old South plantation roots.**: Mitchell, *J. Neel Reid, Architect*, p. 46.

139 **a large staff of servants.**: Grady, *Architecture of Neel Reid in Georgia*, pp. xv-xvii.

140 **a sunroom of an elongated shape that Reid often favored.**: Ibid., p. 46.

140 **a more relaxed design than the southern and eastern elevations.**: Ibid., pp. 44-46.

140 **he didn't try to hide it, either.**: "Beginning of Building of Residence on the Ferrell Place," Callaway Family Papers, Troup County Archives, LaGrange, Georgia; see Grady, *Architecture of Neel Reid in Georgia*, pp. xv-xvii.

140 **the deal was acceptable to everyone.**: "Beginning of Building of Residence on the Ferrell Place," Callaway Family Papers, Troup County Archives, LaGrange, Georgia.

141 **the Atlanta, Birmingham & Atlantic Railroad.**: Material Required for Residence of Fuller E. Callaway, Apr. 21, 1915, Callaway Family Papers, Troup County Archives, LaGrange, Georgia.

141 **thus finalizing the name and membership of the their firm.**: Mitchell, *J. Neel Reid, Architect*, p. 208.

141 **boasting a red pantile roof.**: Grady, *Architecture of Neel Reid in Georgia*, p. 45.

142 **not a damn' one of 'em looks like him!"**: "A Notice that was *Not* Issued," Callaway Family Papers, Troup County Archives; Perkerson, *White Columns in Georgia*, p. 246. Ida Callaway tells a different version of the story: "A woman who once visited the gardens remarked, 'The place is full of statues of old man Ferrell, but not a one looks like him!'" Ida Cason Callaway, "Memories," p. 98.

142 **an eighteenth century French theme.**: Grady, *Architecture of Neel Reid in Georgia*, p. 46.

143 **But Reid ultimately convinced him, and at last Fuller gave in.**: Ida Cason Callaway, "Memories," p. 60; Alfred Pearce Dennis, *Gods and Little Fishes* (Indianapolis; Bobbs-Merrill Co., 1931), 269-70.

144 **he never got his torture chair.**: Ida Cason Callaway, "Memories," pp. 60-62.

144 **that's about the kind of a thing they would like."**: Dennis, *Gods and Little Fishes*, p. 269.

144 **for a time he thought that the deadline might be met.**: Fuller E. Callaway to J. P. Stevens Engraving Company, May 12, 1916, Callaway Family Papers, Troup County Archives, LaGrange, Georgia.

145 **Callaway finally nailed down the date: June 15, 1916.**: J. P. Stevens Engraving Company to Fuller E. Callaway, Mar. 29, 1916, Callaway Family Papers, Troup County Archives, LaGrange, Georgia; Fuller E. Callaway to Chas. T. Wurm, June 3, 1916, Callaway Family Papers, Troup County Archives, LaGrange, Georgia.

145 **a good time never to be forgotten."**: William S. Witham Jr. to Fuller E. Callaway, June 6, 1916, Callaway Family Papers, Troup County Archives, LaGrange, Georgia.

145 **one of the finest events that LaGrange had ever seen.**: Fuller. E. Callaway to Chas. T. Wurm, June 3, 1916, Callaway Family Papers, Troup County Archives, LaGrange, Georgia.

146 **"No ice water!"**: "A Notice that was *Not* Issued," Callaway Family Papers, Troup County Archives; cf. Ida Cason Callaway, "Memories," p. 98: "'It looks like the folks would keep a cup in the park to drink out of.'"

146 **are asked not to apply for permits.**: "Notice," Callaway Family Papers, Troup County Archives.

148 **the dead, closed hand of a little child?"**: Ida Cason Callaway, "Memories," pp. 97-98.

148 **matching bed that read "St. Callaway" and "ora pro me."**: Ibid., p. 97; see page 4, *supra*.

·7·
LIFE AS A
PUBLIC FIGURE:
LOCAL AND STATE

151 **the newest member of the LaGrange City Council.**: Minute Book, LaGrange City Council, July 5, 1894, Troup County Archives, LaGrange, Georgia, p. 179.

151 **from 1895 to 1897, his brother Enoch was mayor.**: Ibid., Apr. 4, 1895, p. 186.

152 **he eventually joined Callaway and Dunson as a regular on the committee.**: Ibid., May 7, 1897, p. 207; ibid., Dec. 11, 1900, p. 304.

152 **refuse jobs to people who hadn't been duly vaccinated.**: Ibid., Nov. 8, 1898, p. 224; ibid., Jan. 4, 1905, p. 386.

152 **fire would have badly damaged not only Dunson but the town's economy.**: Clifford L. Smith, *History of Troup County* (Atlanta: Foote & Davies Co., 1933), 117; Minute Book, LaGrange City Council, June 4, 1903, Troup County Archives, LaGrange, Georgia, p. 341.

152 **peddling without a license on the streets of LaGrange.**: Minute Book, LaGrange City Council, Dec. 11, 1900, Troup County Archives, LaGrange, Georgia, p. 267.

152 **a merry-go-round to drum up business for his store.**: Ibid., Mar. 20, 1905, p. 392; see page 23, *supra*.

153 **all of which the council passed in 1901.**: Minute Book, LaGrange City Council, Apr. 3, 1901, Troup County Archives, LaGrange, Georgia, pp. 276-77; ibid., May 15, 1901, p. 283.

153 **lagged behind their creation on paper.**: Ibid., Dec. 6, 1899, pp. 245-49; ibid., Sept. 24, 1902, p. 316.

153 **mainly street lights—by the early 1890s.**: Smith, *History of Troup County*, p. 116; Minute Book, LaGrange City Council, July 1, 1900, Troup County Archives, LaGrange, Georgia, pp. 252-54.

153 **a fight over the lighting issue.**: Minute Book, LaGrange City Council, May 2, 1901, Troup County Archives, LaGrange, Georgia, p. 281; ibid., Oct. 25, 1901, p. 291.

154 **the establishment of a city lighting department—the only councilman to do so.**: Smith, *History of Troup County*, p. 117; Minute Book, LaGrange City Council, May 10, 1904, Troup County Archives, LaGrange, Georgia, p. 360; ibid., June 17, 1904, p. 363; ibid., Aug. 4, 1904, p. 369.

154 **to be used for the retirement of general debts.**: Minute Book, LaGrange City Council, July 6, 1904, Troup County Archives, LaGrange, Georgia, pp. 364-65.

154 **the board reinstated him.**: See pages 58-59, *supra*.

155 **Yours Sincerely J. E. Dunson**: Minute Book, LaGrange City Council, Aug. 4, 1904, Troup County Archives, LaGrange, Georgia, p. 369; ibid. Aug. 5, 1904, p. 370.

156 **withdraw your resignation, We are Yours Sincerely**: Ibid., Aug. 5, 1904, p. 370.

156 **the respect that you have so generously expressed in your letter.**: Ibid., Aug. 11, 1904, p. 371.

156 **the voters approved the bond issue in September.**: Ibid., Sept. 23, 1904, p. 374.

156 **the Atlanta & West Point would later sue to protect.**: See pages 78-82, *supra*.

156 **no suggestion in the record that he lacked Dunson's backing.**: Minute Book, LaGrange City Council, Mar. 20, 1905, Troup County Archives, LaGrange, Georgia, p. 392.

157 **to say nothing of the Atlanta, Birmingham & Atlantic Railroad.**: "Fuller Earle Callaway," *Who's Who in America*, http://www.marquiswhoswho.com/about-us (last visited May 24, 2013); Smith, *History of Troup County*, p. 116.

157 **which the Supreme Court decided in May 1903.**: See page 77, *supra*; Interstate Commerce Commission v. Louisville & Nashville Railroad Co., 190 U.S. 273 (1903).

158 **another indispensable component of the southern textile industry.**: Fuller E. Callaway Jr., interview by James Saxon Childers, July 22, 1953, Callaway Family Papers, Troup County Archives, LaGrange, Georgia, p. 30; *Eight Hours for Laborers on Government Work: Hearings Before the Committee on Labor of the House of Representatives, February 4, 11, 18, 25, March 3, 4, 10, 17, 22, 23, 24, 25, and 26,* *1904* (Washington: Government Printing Office, 1904), 316-18.

158 **the two cotton mills I am connected with.**: *Eight Hours for Laborers on Government Work*, p. 317.

159 **still in its infancy.**: Ibid., p. 318. See generally Witold Rybczynski, *Waiting for the Weekend* (New York: Penguin Books, 1992).

159 **"But that is one of our natural resources."**: *Eight Hours for Laborers on Government Work*, p. 318.

159 **The whole thing, as Callaway presented it, was inequitable.**: Ibid.

160 **they are going on with finer grades."**: Ibid., p. 319.

160 **"We would rather prefer to control our own business."**: Ibid., p. 327.

160 **His audience laughed appreciatively.**: Ibid.

160 **only Caldwell, Hughes, and Hearst voting to pass it.**: "Labor Measures Before Congress," *American Federationist*, vol. 11 (May 1904), 404; *Elkhart Weekly Truth*, Apr. 7, 1904; *Mansfield News*, Apr. 7, 1904; *New York Times*, Apr. 9, 1904.

160 **the Progressives, who saw the railroads as enemies.**: Interstate Commerce Commission v. Louisville & Nashville Railroad Co., 190 U.S. 273 (1903); Atlanta & West Point Railroad Co. v. Atlanta, Birmingham & Atlantic Railroad Co., 54 S.E. 736 (Ga. 1906); "Fuller Earle Callaway—The New Railroad," Callaway Family Papers, Troup County Archives, LaGrange, Georgia; Smith, *History of Troup County*, pp. 110-11; Fuller E. Callaway et al. to Subscribers to Fund for Securing Right of Way and Terminals for the Atlanta & Birmingham Railway, Apr. 28, 1905, Callaway Family Papers, Troup County Archives, LaGrange, Georgia.

161 **a third house of the Georgia legislature.**: Dewey W. Grantham, Jr., *Hoke Smith and the Politics of the New South* (Baton Rouge: Louisiana State University Press, 1958), 146.

161 **the railroads were making too much money anyway.**: Lucian Lamar Knight, *A Standard History of Georgia and Georgians*, vol. 2 (Chicago: The Lewis Publishing Co., 1917), 1088-89.

161 **the commission ruled against the businesses, refusing to impose port rates.**: Grantham, *Hoke Smith*, pp. 132-33; *Atlanta Constitution*, May 11, 1905.

161 **Hoke Smith as a potential "trust-buster" governor.**: Grantham, *Hoke Smith*, pp. 132-33; *Atlanta Journal*, May 21, 1905.

161 **In early June he announced that he was running for governor.**: "Hoke Smith," *New Georgia Encyclopedia*; Grantham, *Hoke Smith*, pp. 132-39.

161 **an abortive attempt to get the commission to help him.**: See pages 72-73, *supra*; Callaway v. Atlanta & West Point R.R. Co., July 24, 1895, Public Service Commission, Hearing Reporter, vol. 2-8400, p. 278, Georgia Archives, Record Group 17; *Twenty-Second Report of the Railroad Commission of Georgia* (Atlanta: Geo. W. Harrison, Franklin Printing & Publishing Co., 1894), 3.

161 **having represented the city in a waterworks case in 1898.**: Minute Book, LaGrange City Council, Mar. 2, 1898, Troup County Archives, LaGrange, Georgia, p. 216.

162 **Smith hated railroads, Brown charged, because he made his living suing them.**: Grantham, *Hoke Smith*, pp. 146, 180-81; "Hoke Smith," *New Georgia Encyclopedia*; Knight, *A Standard History of Georgia and Georgians*, 2:1088-89.

162 **one of his first acts would be to fire Joe Brown.**: Grantham, *Hoke Smith*, p. 146.

163 **we demand the immediate righting of these wrongs by the Railroad Commission.**: Knight, *A Standard History of Georgia and Georgians*, 2:1064.

163 **of about 165,000 votes cast, Smith won nearly 100,000.**: *Atlanta Constitution*, Aug. 23, 1906; *Weekly Times Enterprise* and *South Georgia Progress*, Aug. 31, 1906.

163 **one into which Callaway would be drawn.**: Grantham, *Hoke Smith*, pp. 182-83.

163 **Candler-Overstreet Act, which achieved his goal of revamping the Railroad Commission.**: Ibid., pp. 163-65, 181-82; Knight, *A Standard History of Georgia and Georgians*, 2:1070; *Thirty-Seventh Report of the Railroad Commission of Georgia* (Atlanta: Foote & Davies Co., 1909), 397-403.

163 **the modern Public Service Commission, although that name would not come until later.**: *Thirty-Seventh Report of the Railroad Commission of Georgia*, pp. 397-403; "Georgia Public Service Commission," *New Georgia Encyclopedia*.

163 **The other was Fuller E. Callaway.**: *Thirty-Seventh Report of the Railroad Commission of Georgia*, p. 399; *Atlanta Georgian*, Aug. 26, 1907.

164 **ably, amiably, and yet fearlessly, there is no room for doubt.":** *Atlanta Georgian*, Aug. 26, 1907.

164 **will undoubtedly give the people good service on the board.":** *Atlanta Constitution*, Aug. 27, 1907.

164 **from where Smith sat, Callaway seemed the ideal man for the job.:** *Atlanta Georgian*, Aug. 26, 1907.

164 **the Manchester Development Company, which was consuming a great deal of his energy.:** See pages 64-66, *supra*; *Atlanta Constitution*, June 7, 1906; *Atlanta Georgian*, Jan. 29, 1907.

164 **he expressly refused to stay on the commission for any particular length of time.:** Knight, *A Standard History of Georgia and Georgians*, 2:1074; *Atlanta Georgian*, Aug. 26, 1907.

165 **chosen by the governor to replace the banished Joe Brown.:** Knight, *A Standard History of Georgia and Georgians*, 2:1087; *Atlanta Constitution*, Aug. 27, 1907.

165 **customers, who "must foot all the bills.":** *Atlanta Constitution*, Aug. 27, 1907.

165 **Georgia's motto, "by wisdom, by justice, and by moderation … .":** Ibid.

166 **so that Callaway could carefully draft the final resolution.:** *Atlanta Georgian*, Aug. 26, 1907; *Atlanta Constitution*, Aug. 27, 1907.

166 **neither did it say that it wouldn't do so in the future.:** *Atlanta Georgian*, Aug. 27, 1907.

166 **would be remiss in his place as a public official to accept the same.":** Ibid., Aug. 27, 1907.

166 **to whom issued, upon what account issued, and between what stations.":** *Atlanta Constitution*, Aug. 28, 1907; *Thirty-Fifth Annual Report Part 1 of the Railroad Commission of Georgia for the Year Ended October 15, 1907* (Atlanta: The Franklin-Turner Co., 1908), 22-23.

167 **"we will issue a special order for their enlightenment.":** *Atlanta Georgian*, Oct. 31, 1907.

167 **a June order requiring railroads to reduce their passenger rates.:** *Thirty-Fifth Annual Report Part 1 of the Railroad Commission*, pp. 14, 78-80; Grantham, *Hoke Smith*, p. 59.

167 **to order some freight rate reductions.:** *The Outlook*, Sept. 7, 1907.

167 **Callaway managed to ride out the storm fairly well due to his wise deci-**

sions,: See pages 85-87, *supra*.

167 **support for him began waning.:** Grantham, *Hoke Smith*, pp. 170-71; see generally Robert F. Bruner & Sean D. Carr, *The Panic of 1907: Lessons Learned from the Market's Perfect Storm* (New York: John Wiley & Sons, 2007).

167 **he became something of an irritant over the next few weeks.:** *Atlanta Constitution*, Apr. 19, 1908; ibid., May 4, 1908.

167 **an example of discriminatory rates during his battle with the Atlanta & West Point.:** See pages 72-75, *supra*.

167 **his ongoing concern all of his other time commitments.:** *Atlanta Constitution*, May 4, 1908; ibid., May 8, 1908; ibid., May 31, 1908.

168 **now and then he would sign letters to family with the name "Fullercorn.":** Fuller E. Callaway Jr., interview by James Saxon Childers, July 16, 1953, Callaway Family Papers, Troup County Archives, LaGrange, Georgia, pp. 5-6; see, e.g., Fullercorn [Fuller E. Callaway] to Cason Callaway [cable], n.d., 1921, Callaway Family Papers, Troup County Archives, LaGrange, Georgia.

168 **How much stock does he hold in said railroad, either legally or equitably?:** *Atlanta Constitution*, May 31, 1908.

168 **the victor there winning by only 12,000 votes.:** Ibid., June 7, 1908.

168 **he'd ousted from the Railroad Commission the previous year, Joseph M. Brown.:** Knight, *A Standard History of Georgia and Georgians*, 2:1088-93; Grantham, *Hoke Smith*, pp. 186-93.

169 **several Atlanta businesses filed petitions requesting port rates as well.:** *Thirty-Seventh Annual Report of the Railroad Commission of Georgia*, p. 262.

169 **abruptly tendered his resignation, to be effective at the end of the month.:** *Atlanta Georgian*, Mar. 15, 1909.

169 **the executive committee of the Georgia Bankers' Association.:** *Atlanta Constitution*, Nov. 7, 1908; *Atlanta Constitution*, Mar. 7, 1909.

169 **the same for many years, yet the cost of handling has been reduced.":** *Atlanta Georgian*, Apr. 5, 1909.

170 **making Georgia manufacturers' products more desirable to Georgia buyers.:** *Atlanta Constitution*, Apr. 25, 1909.

170 **his own mills were beneficiaries of that policy.:** Ibid., May 7, 1909.

170 **they may be reasonably expected not to have anything interesting to say for publication.":** Ibid., Mar. 25, 1909.

170 **Governor Smith, who appointed him as a member of the commission.":** Ibid., May 9, 1909.

171 **the overriding reason for his departure.:** *Atlanta Georgian*, May 12, 1909.

171 **one of the ablest men of his time.:** *Atlanta Constitution*, May 14, 1909.

171 **Smith made no secret of his displeasure.:** *Atlanta Georgian*, Apr. 24, 1909; *Atlanta Constitution*, Apr. 25, 1909.

171 **Smith had known of the transactions and hadn't cared until McLendon betrayed him.:** *Atlanta Georgian*, June 18, 1909; Grantham, *Hoke Smith*, pp. 194-95.

171 **low railroad rates at Manchester, although nothing came of the charge.:** *Atlanta Georgian*, Jan. 23, 1911.

171 **the discomfited politicians laid their heads together to compass his defeat.":** *Atlanta Constitution*, Aug. 7, 1910; *Atlanta Constitution*, Aug. 19, 1910.

171 **Georgia's citizens, who returned Smith to office in that year's rematch against Brown.:** Grantham, *Hoke Smith*, pp. 197-204.

172 **elected vice president of the Georgia Industrial Association.:** Fuller E. Callaway to Philip Cook, Dec. 22, 1909, Callaway Family Papers, Troup County Archives, LaGrange, Georgia; Fuller E. Callaway to James M. Donald, Feb. 2, 1910, Callaway Family Papers, Troup County Archives, LaGrange, Georgia; *Atlanta Constitution*, Jan. 29, 1910; ibid., June 20, 1910.

172 **"getting Troup County out of the mud.":** "The Life and Works of Mr. Fuller E. Callaway, Senior," (n.d.), p. 5, Callaway Family Papers, Troup County Archives, LaGrange, Georgia.

172 **set up by the Atlanta Chamber of Commerce.:** *Atlanta Constitution*, Nov. 16, 1913.

172 **papers weren't averse to quoting Callaway on these matters.:** See e.g., ibid., Sept. 12, 1913.

172 **when he did, people paid attention.:** Donald F. Anderson, *William Howard Taft: A Conservative's Conception of the Presidency* (Ithaca: Cornell University Press, 1973), 79.

173 **moments later the men were back on the train.:** *Atlanta Constitution*, Jan. 30, 1910.

173 on anticipated prices of cotton and other agricultural products.: Ibid.

173 in April he announced a major investigation.: " 'Where the Common People Could Speculate': The Ticker, Bucket Shops, and the Origins of Popular Participation in Financial Markets, 1880-1920," 93 *Journal of American History* 335, 355 (2006); *Galveston Daily News*, Apr. 19, 1910; *New York Times*, May 6, 1910.

173 thereby denying the exchange's reason for existence.: *Galveston Daily News*, Apr. 19, 1910.

174 reputation for high integrity, was a great tribute.: *Atlanta Constitution*, Sept. 12, 1913; ibid., Sept. 23, 1913; "John M. Slaton," *New Georgia Encyclopedia*.

174 breach of contract, which the company decisively won.: Georgia v. Western & Atlantic Railroad Co., 76 S.E. 577 (Ga. 1912); Georgia v. Western & Atlantic R. Co., 715 S.E. 1055 (Ga. 1911); *Atlanta Constitution*, Nov. 17, 1912; *Atlanta Constitution*, Oct. 23, 1913. See generally James Houstoun Johnston, *Western & Atlantic Railroad of the State of Georgia* (Atlanta: Georgia Public Service Commission, 1931); "Western & Atlantic Railroad," http://www.railga.com/watl.html (last visited May 24, 2013).

174 some other entity, persuaded him to sign on.: *Atlanta Constitution*, Aug. 7, 1913; ibid., Sept. 23, 1913.

174 the commission ultimately rejected the proposal.: Ibid., Sept. 23, 1913; ibid., Dec. 12, 1913; ibid., Jan. 15, 1914; ibid., Oct. 23, 1913; ibid., July 15, 1915.

174 the group lacked authority to speak for the state.: Ibid., July 23, 1914; Maury Klein, *History of the Louisville & Nashville Railroad* (Louisville: University Press of Kentucky, 2003), 192-93, 294-95; "Louisville & Nashville Railroad," http://www.railga.com/ln.html (last visited May 24, 2013).

175 "with broad duties and powers.": *Atlanta Constitution*, July 23, 1914.

175 which Callaway had been serving, and Callaway himself.: Ibid., Nov. 25, 1915.

175 in the state of Georgia," he happily declared.: Ibid., Nov. 26, 1915.

175 regret that I am unable to serve with them.: Ibid., Nov. 27, 1915; *Atlanta Journal*, Dec. 4, 1915.

· 8 ·

LIFE AS A PUBLIC FIGURE: CALLAWAY, THE GREAT WAR AND THE NATIONAL STAGE

177 by the president to be secretary of the treasury.: Arthur S. Link, *Woodrow Wilson and the Progressive Era 1910-1917* (New York: Harper Torchbooks, 1954), 27-30.

177 had recommended that Wilson nominate him as Indian commissioner.: Ida Cason Callaway, "Memories of Fuller Earle Callaway Sr. of LaGrange, Georgia Written by His Wife, Ida Cason Callaway," unpublished manuscript, Callaway Family Papers, Troup County Archives, LaGrange, Georgia, 1929, pp. 70-72.

177 the Red men that they cannot ply their trade.": *Atlanta Constitution*, Apr. 2, 1913; ibid., Apr. 27, 1913.

177 Native Americans and millions of acres of land.: Francis Paul Prucha, *The Great Father: The United States Government and the American Indians*, vol. 2 (Lincoln: University of Nebraska Press, 1984), 865, 1217; Laurence F. Schmeckebier, *The Office of Indian Affairs: Its History, Activities and Organization* (Baltimore: The Johns Hopkins Press, 1927), 293, 311, 313-14.

177 below cabinet level, directly responsible to Lane.: Schmeckebier, *The Office of Indian Affairs*, pp. 270-71, 293.

178 the story would be different.: *Atlanta Constitution*, Apr. 27, 1913.

178 in light of recent swings in cotton rates,: See pages 172-73, *supra*.

178 influence the regulation that was nearly certain to happen.: I. Newton Hoffmann, "The Cotton Futures Act," 23 *Journal of Political Economy* 465, 479-81 (May 1915); *Regulation of Cotton Exchanges: Hearings before the Committee on Agriculture House of Representatives Sixty-Third Congress Second Session Regarding Various Bills Relative to the Regulation of Cotton Exchanges April 22 to 25, 1914* (Washington: Government Printing Office, 1914), 2, 281, 283.

178 the bales would be unsuitable for milling.: Hoffmann, "The Cotton Futures Act," pp. 471-73; *Regulation of Cotton Exchanges*, pp. 25-30.

178 his first congressional hearing a decade before.: See pages 157-60, *supra*.

179 five dollars to anyone who could find his cow.: *Regulation of Cotton Exchanges*, pp. 55-56; see page 9, *supra*.

179 then we will lose our 'riggers.' ": *Regulation of Cotton Exchanges*, p. 51.

179 This from a man who hated speculating.: Ibid.

180 by no means a game-ender.: Ibid., pp. 26-27.

180 "You all might want to hire him.": Ibid., p. 60.

181 the law today, a century later.: Ibid., pp. 64-65; Act of Aug. 18, 1914, 38 Stat. 693, ch. 255, §§ 5, 6; 7 U.S.C. § 15B(f)(1) (2008).

181 bankrupt the world's richest nations.: See generally John Keegan, *The First World War* (New York: Alfred A. Knopf, 1999); Martin Gilbert, *The First World War: A Complete History* (New York: Henry Holt and Co., 1994).

181 closed their doors, and a financial crisis loomed.: Alexander D. Noyes, *The War Period of American Finance 1908-1925* (New York: G. P. Putnam's Sons, 1926), 53-56; see pages 121-25, *supra*.

182 had taken nearly a half-million bales.: Noyes, *War Period of American Finance*, pp. 64-65.

182 nearly fifty percent, well below estimated production costs.: Harold U. Faulkner, *The Decline of Laissez Faire 1897-1917* (New York: Rinehart & Co., 1951), 390; Noyes, *War Period of American Finance*, pp. 65-66

182 farmers were urged to cut back production.: [Americus] *Times-Recorder*, Aug. 30, 1914; *Atlanta Constitution*, Aug. 29, 1914; *Atlanta Constitution*, Sept. 4, 1914.

182 business detail that easily can be taken care of.: *Atlanta Constitution*, Aug. 25, 1914.

182 "let's keep our heads.": "Fuller E. Callaway—The Country at War," Callaway Family Papers, Troup County Archives, LaGrange, Georgia.

182 they are able to obtain for our manufactured product.: Ibid.

183 Germany and the closing of the European financial markets.: Noyes, *War Period of American Finance*, pp. 94-96.

183 with luck, the economy would bounce back quickly.: *Raleigh Observer*, Aug. 27, 1914.

183 materiel for the combatants, would thus benefit economically.: Noyes, *War Period of American Finance*, p. 94.

183 **as a means of helping toward winning the war.":** "Fuller E. Callaway—He Starts a New Mill," Callaway Family Papers, Troup County Archives, LaGrange, Georgia; see pages 123-24, *supra.*

183 **Naumberg when he'd arrived in New York from England,:** See page 125, *supra.*

183 **most ambitious, mill that Callaway would personally commission.:** *Atlanta Journal,* Oct. 17, 1914; Donna Jean Whitley, "Fuller E. Callaway and Textile Mill Development in LaGrange, 1895-1920," Ph.D. Diss., Emory University, 1984, 150.

183 **as the storm of the Great War broke.:** Clifford L. Smith, *History of Troup County* (Atlanta: Foote & Davies Co., 1933), 119-20.

183 **deliveries of the reduced amounts were enormously in arrear.":** Noyes, *War Period of American Finance,* p. 110.

184 **stimulated consumer demand for goods at home.:** Ibid., pp. 123-24.

184 **the changing of the guard.:** "Fuller Earle Callaway," Callaway Family Papers, Troup County Archives, LaGrange, Georgia; "Fuller Earle Callaway—Sorrows," Callaway Family Papers, Troup County Archives, LaGrange, Georgia; Ida Cason Callaway, "Memories," p. 108.

184 **during the Western & Atlantic investigation.:** See pages 174-75, *supra.*

185 **choice of Callaway as an arbitrator in 1915.:** Whitley, "Fuller E. Callaway," p. 140; Ida Cason Callaway, "Memories," p. 73.

185 **at least according to Hatton Lovejoy's account.:** Hatton Lovejoy to James S. Childers, Apr. 7, 1954, Callaway Family Papers, Troup County Archives, LaGrange, Georgia.

185 **we ask you to do it.":** *To Establish the Manufacture of Dyestuffs, Hearing before the Committee on Ways and Means, House of Representatives, Sixty-Fourth Congress, First Session, on H. R. 702 A Bill to Provide Revenue for the Government and to Establish and Maintain the Manufacture of Dyestuffs* (Washington: Government Printing Office, 1916), 70.

186 **a hundred years forward in two or three years.:** Ibid., p. 75.

186 **We want it done in a business way.":** Ibid.

186 **folks wanted done whether it was right or not.:** Ibid., p. 76.

186 **as soon as we get all the business done.:** Ibid., p. 78.

187 **let us get down and do what is**

187 **right.":** Ibid., pp. 78-80.

187 **110 per cent more than we need.":** Ibid., p. 80.

187 **for a long enough time to establish themselves.:** Act of Sept. 8, 1916, 39 Stat. 756, 793-94, ch. 463.

188 **a snowball in the fireplace.:** *Proceedings of the Twentieth Annual Convention of the American Cotton Manufacturers Association Held at Atlanta, Georgia April 4 and 5, 1916* (1916), 156-58.

188 **the first president from Georgia.:** "Wilson Greets Cotton Mill Men," *Journal of Commerce,* May 24, 1917; "Cotton Manufacturers in Washington," *Mill News,* May 31, 1917.

189 **before America could mobilize.:** Paul Kennedy, *The Rise and Fall of the Great Powers* (New York: Random House, 1987), 268, 271; Robert D. Schulzinger, *American Diplomacy in the Twentieth Century* (New York: Oxford University Press, 1990), 79-80; Samuel Flagg Bemis, *A Diplomatic History of the United States,* rev. ed. (New York: Henry Holt and Co, 1942), ch. 32.

189 **and train for war; it is a nation.":** James Ciment, ed., *The Home Front Encyclopedia: United States, Britain, and Canada in World Wars I and II,* vol. 3 (Santa Barbara: ABC-CLIO, 2007), 1134, 1136.

189 **Wilson thanked him cordially.:** "Wilson Greets Cotton Mill Men," *Journal of Commerce,* May 24, 1917.

189 **it too would need massive amounts of supplies.:** Noyes, *War Period of American Finance,* p. 219.

189 **productive jobs for military service.:** Ibid.

189 **compared to war needs, that wasn't very important.:** George Soule, *Prosperity Decade: From War to Depression: 1917-1929* (New York: Rinehart & Co., 1947), 61.

189 **more than 125 million yards of duck.:** Noyes, *War Period of American Finance,* p. 220.

189 **for the cotton regions but hard on the mills.:** Ibid., pp. 223-24.

190 **putting them to work in the picker rooms.:** Whitley, "Fuller E. Callaway," p. 150; *Macon Telegraph,* June 2, 1917.

190 **sweet potatoes to encourage competition and improve production.:** *Athens Banner,* May 9, 1917.

190 **and build up the land at the same time.":** *Atlanta Constitution,* Nov. 13, 1916.

190 **Callaway soon became chief of the**

division's Cotton Section.: Fuller Earle Callaway—Cason, Oldest Son, is Put in Harness," Callaway Family Papers, Troup County Archives, LaGrange, Georgia; "Cason J. Callaway, Callaway Family Papers, Troup County Archives, LaGrange, Georgia; Historical Branch, War Plans Division, General Staff, *A Handbook of Economic Agencies of the War of 1917* (Washington: Government Printing Office, 1919), 371-72.

190 **New York and Boston for much of the war.:** Biographical Note, Dr. and Mrs. Enoch Callaway Jr. Papers, Callaway Family Papers, Troup County Archives, LaGrange, Georgia; *Dictionary of American Naval Fighting Ships,* vol. 8 (Washington: Naval History Division, Department of the Navy, 1976).

191 **be on that pier." And so he was.:** Conversation between Fuller E. Callaway Jr., James Saxon Childers, and Maurine Childers Concerning Life of Fuller E. Callaway Sr., July 22, 1953, Callaway Family Papers, Troup County Archives, LaGrange, Georgia, pp. 14-15.

191 **100,000 tons of pyrite a year.:** *Southern Banker,* July 1917.

191 **help find and develop mines in Georgia and Alabama.:** Fuller E. Callaway Scrapbook, Callaway Family Papers, Troup County Archives, LaGrange, Georgia.

192 **as a shining example of pyrite development.:** 1918 Box, 1918 Pyrite Box, Fuller E. Callaway Papers, Callaway Family Office, LaGrange, Georgia.

192 **mining, munitions factories, food products, etc.":** Callaway to Spencer Turner, May 8, 1918, 1918 Box, Fuller E. Callaway Papers, Callaway Family Office, LaGrange, Georgia.

192 **The government hastily approved the idea.:** *The Southern Banker,* July 1917.

192 **most critically important matters to him during the break.:** J. A. Perry to Chas. A. Wickersham, Jan. 10, 1918, 1918 Box, Fuller E. Callaway Papers, Callaway Family Office, LaGrange, Georgia; _____ [J. A. Perry?] to D. C. Collins, Feb. 4, 1918, Pyrite Box, Fuller E. Callaway Papers, Callaway Family Office, LaGrange, Georgia.

194 **how dangerous that could be during total war.:** *Proceedings of the Twenty-Second Annual Convention of the American Cotton Manufacturers Association Held at New York May 1, 2, and 3, 1918* (Charlotte: Queen City Printing Co., 1918), 49-54.

194 **an increasingly vital role in the domestic war effort.**: *Third Annual Report of the United States Council of National Defense for the Fiscal Year ended June 30 1919* (Washington: Government Printing Office, 1919), 61.

194 **LaGrange, Georgia." That was apparently enough.**: Ibid., p. 62.

194 **Supreme Court case against the Louisville & Nashville Railroad.**: Interstate Commerce Commission v. Louisville & Nashville Railroad Co., 190 U.S. 273 (1903).

194 **one of several publications to make that mistake.**: See, e.g., *New York Times*, Aug. 13, 1914; *Proceedings of the National Academy of Sciences of the United States of America, 1919*, vol. 5 (Washington: Home Office of the Academy, 1919), 606.

195 **John D. Rockefeller's Standard Oil trust.**: Ida M. Tarbell, *The History of the Standard Oil Company* (New York: McClure, Phillips & Co., 1905).

195 **the entire Union Army had from 1861 to 1865.**: Allan R. Millett & Peter Maslowski, *For the Common Defense: A Military History of the United States of America* (New York: The Free Press, 1984), 342-58.

195 **the war was over. The world had forever changed.**: Ibid.; Gilbert, *The First World War*, ch. 25.

196 **American exports remained high for a time.**: Soule, *Prosperity Decade*, pp. 87-88.

196 **it would linger for two years.**: Ibid., pp. 97-100.

196 **most renowned educators; and Fuller E. Callaway.**: *Proceedings of the First Industrial Conference (Called by the President) October 6 to 23, 1919* (Washington: Government Printing Office, 1920), 5-7.

196 **The General Committee recommended its adoption.**: Ibid., pp. 68, 103.

198 **from whom you would not think they would come.**: Ibid., pp. 69-70.

198 **a full-blooded American.**: Ibid., pp. 71-72.

199 **I would not think of moving.' "**: Ibid., pp. 72-73.

199 **We did not lose a one.**: Ibid., pp. 73-75.

200 **the room burst into applause as Callaway concluded.**: Ibid., p. 77.

200 **show them how we run a little country town."**: Ibid.

200 **announced the conference in Wash-**ington until mid-August,: *Iowa City Citizen*, Aug. 11, 1919.

200 **Callaway would obviously have been very familiar with them.**: "Fourth World Cotton Conference," *Textiles: A Monthly Technical Journal*, vol. 19 (July 1921), 11.

200 **role of the United States as a creditor nation.**: *Naugatuck Daily News*, Jan. 17, 1919; *Warren Evening Times*, Jan. 17, 1919.

201 **the natural choice for committee chairman.**: *Galveston Daily News*, Jan. 18, 1919; *Naugatuck Daily News*, Jan. 17, 1919; *Boston Evening Globe*, May 24, 1919.

201 **world's cotton industry in all its ramifications ever assembled."**: *Galveston Daily News*, Mar. 6, 1919; *Casa Grande Dispatch*, May 30, 1919.

201 **the cotton men were actively hostile to the notion.**: Alfred Pearce Dennis, *Gods and Little Fishes* (Indianapolis: Bobbs-Merrill Co., 1931), 260.

201 **and penned some rather strong comments to this effect.**: *Textile Recorder*, June 14, 1919, p. 41.

201 **ginning, oil milling, cotton spinning and manufacturing."**: "World Cotton Conference New Orleans, La., U.S.A., Oct. 13, 14, 15, & 16, 1919. A Pamphlet of Information Issued and Circulated by the European Commission of the World Cotton Conference, Liverpool, May, 1919," Callaway Family Papers, Troup County Archives, LaGrange, Georgia.

202 **Italy, Switzerland, and the Scandinavian countries.**: Fuller E. Callaway to Pleasant A. Stovall, June 3, 1919, Callaway Family Papers, Troup County Archives, LaGrange, Georgia; Pleasant A. Stovall to Fuller E. Callaway, June 11, 1919, Callaway Family Papers, Troup County Archives, LaGrange, Georgia; Dennis, *Gods and Little Fishes*, pp. 260-62; *The Southern Banker*, June 1919.

202 **industrial cooperation between America and England.**: Michael Stratton & Barrie Stuart Trinder, *Book of Industrial England* (London: B. T. Batsford, 1997), 88; see generally Robert Nicholls, *Trafford Park: The First Hundred Years* (Chichester: Phillimore, 1996).

202 **established by the Board of Trade itself.**: *Manchester Guardian*, May 31, 1919; *New York Times*, July 24, 1915; *American Wool and Cotton Reporter*, Dec. 30, 1920, p. 4463 (65); Hubert D. Henderson, *The Cotton Control Board* (Oxford: Clarendon Press, 1922), 9.

202 **a successful issue to the deliberations of the delegates."**: *Textile Recorder*, June 14, 1919, pp. 42-43.

202 **technical, and physical—of the worker.**: Ibid., p. 43.

203 **to give and bestow what others desire to receive."**: Dennis, *Gods and Little Fishes*, pp. 260-62.

203 **home with European cooperation pledged up to the hilt."**: Ibid., p. 260.

204 **help him on his way and in his work.**: Taylor A. [Whitfield?] to Ida Callaway, July 31, 1919, Callaway Family Papers, Troup County Archives, LaGrange, Georgia.

204 **eventually taking them home to LaGrange with him.**: "Fuller E. Callaway on European Conditions," Callaway Family Papers, Troup County Archives, LaGrange, Georgia.

204 **Europe at large, though not by their leaders.**: Robert H. Ferrell, *Woodrow Wilson and World War I 1917-1921* (New York: Harper & Row, 1985), 135-42.

204 **Peace Conference was the crossroads of the twentieth century.**: Malcolm Brown, *T. E. Lawrence* (New York: New York University Press, 2003), 101-02; Sophie Quinn-Judge, *Ho Chi Minh: The Missing Years; 1919-1941* (Berkeley: University of California Press, 2002), 11-28.

205 **had indeed been the war to end wars.**: See generally David A. Andelman, *A Shattered Peace: Versailles 1919 and the Price We Pay Today* (New York: John Wiley & Sons, 2008); Margaret MacMillan, *Paris 1919: Six Months That Changed the World* (New York: Random House, 2002); Alan Sharp, *Consequences of Peace: The Versailles Settlement: Aftermath and Legacy 1919-2010* (London: Haus Publishing Ltd., 2010).

205 **joining the thousands of American attendees already committed.**: Dennis, *Gods and Little Fishes*, p. 260; [Americus] *Times-Recorder*, Oct. 15, 1919; *Galveston Daily News*, Mar. 6, 1919.

206 **Coney Island style that will be something new for them."**: Callaway to J. A. Perry, July 26, 1919, Callaway Family Papers, Troup County Archives, LaGrange, Georgia.

206 **something special for the children to carry out."**: J. A. Perry to Callaway, July 28, 1919, Callaway Family Papers, Troup County Archives, LaGrange, Georgia.

207 **to be staffed by a doctor and nurse.**:

"Fuller E. Callaway," Callaway Family Papers, Troup County Archives, LaGrange, Georgia.

207 **and, of course, dozens of American flags.**: Ibid.

207 **textile production from cotton picking to cottonseed oil production.**: Ida Cason Callaway, "Memories," pp. 80-81; *Program Entertainment of Delegates to World Cotton Conference (New Orleans, October 13-16, 1919) LaGrange, Georgia October 11, 1919,* Callaway Family Papers, Troup County Archives, LaGrange, Georgia.

207 **Sir Herbert as declaring on the day of the gala.)**: Ida Cason Callaway, "Memories," p. 80.

207 **estimated arrival date of Sir Herbert's ship.**: Fuller E. Callaway to W. A. McCusker, Aug. 20, 1919, Callaway Family Papers, Troup County Archives, LaGrange, Georgia; Fuller E. Callaway to Frank B. Hayne, Aug. 20, 1919, Callaway Family Papers, Troup County Archives, LaGrange, Georgia; Fuller E. Callaway to Mark L. Requa, Aug. 20, 1919, Callaway Family Papers, Troup County Archives, LaGrange, Georgia; [E. D. Cook] to F. R. Perry, Aug. 11, 1919, Callaway Family Papers, Troup County Archives, LaGrange, Georgia; E. D. Cook to Fuller E. Callaway, Aug. 11, 1919, Callaway Family Papers, Troup County Archives, LaGrange, Georgia; [E. D. Cook] to Niel Mooney, Aug. 12, 1919, Callaway Family Papers, Troup County Archives, LaGrange, Georgia; Fuller E. Callaway to Sir Herbert Dixon, Aug. 20, 1919 (letter 1 of 2), Callaway Family Papers, Troup County Archives, LaGrange, Georgia; Fuller E. Callaway to Sir Herbert Dixon, Aug. 20, 1919 (letter 2 of 2), Callaway Family Papers, Troup County Archives, LaGrange, Georgia; Fuller E. Callaway to Passenger Office, Cunard Line, New York City, Aug. 14, 1919, Callaway Family Papers, Troup County Archives, LaGrange, Georgia.

208 **Harris informed Callaway in his reply.**: William J. Harris to Fuller E. Callaway, Aug. 14, 1919, Callaway Family Papers, Troup County Archives, LaGrange, Georgia.

208 **the high point of their journey was upon them.**: "The World Cotton Conference," *Cotton* (Nov. 1919), 17; *Program Entertainment of Delegates to World Cotton Conference*; *Atlanta Journal,* Oct. 12, 1919.

208 **leaden-gray clouds that threatened impending rain.**: *Atlanta Journal,* Oct. 12, 1919.

209 **had been working hard on developing in recent years.**: "The World Cotton Conference," *Cotton* (Nov. 1919), 17; *Program Entertainment of Delegates to World Cotton Conference*; "Fuller Earle Callaway," Callaway Family Papers, Troup County Archives, LaGrange, Georgia; *Atlanta Journal,* Oct. 12, 1919.

209 **Ferrell Gardens, as well as Ida's own rose garden.**: "The World Cotton Conference," *Cotton* (Nov. 1919), 17; *Program Entertainment of Delegates to World Cotton Conference.*

209 **the delegate nearly ate the plate itself.**: *Atlanta Journal,* Oct. 12, 1919.

210 **rural Southern life entranced the Northern and foreign guests.**: "The World Cotton Conference," *Cotton* (Nov. 1919), 17.

210 **"Fine," she smiled back.**: Ida Cason Callaway, "Memories," pp. 80-81.

210 **LaGrange citizens who had been pilots during the war.**: Ibid.; *Atlanta Journal,* Oct. 12, 1919.

210 **the drawing room, Sir Herbert Dixon among them.**: Ida Cason Callaway, "Memories," p. 81; A. Herbert Dixon to Fuller E. Callaway, Nov. 9, 1919, Callaway Family Papers, Troup County Archives, LaGrange, Georgia.

211 **with all who were fortunate enough to enjoy it.**": James R. MacColl and Rufus R. Wilson to Fuller E. Callaway, Oct. 28, 1919, Callaway Family Papers, Troup County Archives, LaGrange, Georgia.

211 **no halfhearted terms their thorough enjoyment in their visit.**": Secretary, British Delegation to Fuller E. Callaway, Oct. 13, 1919.

211 **he had many things to show them in return.**: A. Herbert Dixon to Fuller E. Callaway, Nov. 9, 1919, Callaway Family Papers, Troup County Archives, LaGrange, Georgia.

211 **far is this place from Lah Grawnge, Georgia?**": Dennis, *Gods and Little Fishes,* p. 259.

, 9 ,
THE RISE OF SOUTHWEST LAGRANGE

213 **a dollar and a half per day.**: *Eight Hours for Laborers on Government Work: Hearings Before the Committee on Labor of the House of Representatives, February 4, 11, 18, 25, March 3, 4, 10, 17, 22, 23, 24, 25, and 26, 1904* (Washington: Government Printing Office, 1904), 318, 327, 319; see pages 157-60, *supra.*

213 **the well-lit and well-ventilated mills.**: *Eight Hours for Laborers on Government Work,* pp. 320, 325, 326.

214 **his regular sixteen hour work days as an adult.**: Ibid., pp. 327, 331.

214 **despite his own experience, he prized formal education.**: Ibid., p. 327.

214 **attend school either in the fall or the spring.**: Ibid., pp. 312, 326.

214 **convenient to have the well on the back porch.**": Ibid., p. 321.

214 **off to build their own churches near the mills.**: Ibid.

215 **management enforced a ten P.M. curfew.**: Thomas Dublin, "Women, Work, and Protest in the Early Lowell Mills; 'The Oppressing Hand of Avarice Would Enslave Us,' " 16 *Labor History* 99 (1975).

215 **broke the strike for the corporation owners.**: See generally Almont Lindsey, *The Pullman Strike: The Story of a Unique Experiment and of a Great Labor Upheaval* (Chicago: The University of Chicago Press, 1942).

216 **the employee returning both physical and mental labor?**": Andrea Tone, *The Business of Benevolence: Industrial Paternalism in Progressive America* (Ithaca: Cornell University Press, 1997), 64.

216 **We feel very kindly toward our people.**": *Eight Hours for Laborers on Government Work,* p. 321.

216 **churches and schools and electric lights on every corner.**": Ibid., p. 328; *Proceedings of the First Industrial Conference (Called by the President) October 6 to 23, 1919* (Washington: Government Printing Office, 1920), 69, 72-73.

216 **accumulate something for a rainy day … .**": *Proceedings of the First Industrial Conference,* p. 72.

216 **helped make child labor one of progressivism's biggest targets.**: *New York Times,* Nov. 4, 1940.

216 **the purpose of securing better conditions or higher wages.**": John Golden, "Children in the Textile Industry," 35 (Supp.) *Annals of the American Academy of Political and Social Science* 42, 42 (1910).

217 **wandering around town while their parents were at work.**: Donna Jean Whitley, "Fuller E. Callaway and Textile Mill Development in LaGrange, 1895-1920," Ph.D. Diss., Emory University, 1984, pp. 201-02; Everett W. Lord, "Inadequate

Schools," 35 (Supp.) *Annals of the American Academy of Political and Social Science* 33, 33 (1910).

217 **for child labor lay in the elimination of poverty.**: Whitley, "Fuller E. Callaway," p. 201; see, e.g., Golden, "Children in the Textile Industry," pp. 45-46.

217 **fresh air, light workloads, and frequent breaks.**: *Eight Hours for Laborers on Government Work*, pp. 325-27.

217 **the bill failed to pass, to Callaway's relief.**: *Atlanta Constitution*, July 15, 1905; ibid., Aug. 2, 1905; *Eight Hours for Laborers on Government Work*, pp. 325-27.

218 **situated not far from the centre of the village.":** *American Wool and Cotton Reporter*, May 19, 1910, 750 [d].

218 **a greater privilege to come to a woman?":** Ida Cason Callaway, "Memories of Fuller Earle Callaway Sr. of LaGrange, Georgia Written by His Wife, Ida Cason Callaway," unpublished manuscript, Callaway Family Papers, Troup County Archives, LaGrange, Georgia, 1929, pp. 43-44; Fuller E. Callaway Jr., interview by James Saxon Childers, July 16, 1953, Callaway Family Papers, Troup County Archives, LaGrange, Georgia, p. 31; Ida M. Tarbell, "Making American Citizens and Running Cotton Mills to Pay the Expenses," *Red Cross Magazine*, Aug. 1920, 60-61.

219 **I found it out as I went along.":** Fuller E. Callaway Jr., interview by James Saxon Childers, July 16, 1953, Callaway Family Papers, Troup County Archives, LaGrange, Georgia, p. 31; "Fuller Callaway Rose from Porter to Mill Magnate," *Daily News Record*, Feb. 14, 1928; Helen Christine Bennett, "The Homely Wisdom of Fuller E. Callaway," *American Magazine* Oct. 1920, 16, 114.

219 **the mill educational system was well underway.**: Whitley, "Fuller E. Callaway," pp. 192-93.

219 **one of the finest mill schools in the south.":** *American Wool and Cotton Reporter*, May 19, 1910, 750 [d].

219 **the founding of a training school.**: "Making Better Men and Women," *Cotton*, Nov. 1915, pp. 7 "The Life and Works of Mr. Fuller E. Callaway, Senior," Callaway Family Papers, Troup County Archives, LaGrange, Georgia, p. 6.

220 **flushed with health and happiness.**: Fuller Earle Callaway—Putting Plans for Southwest LaGrange into Effect (n.d.), Callaway Family Papers, Troup County Archives, LaGrange, Georgia; Notes on a

Meeting with Mrs. Herberta Herring Weathersbee, Affectionately Known to Her Many Friends Young and Old as "Miss Berta," Now Serving as Principal of Southwest LaGrange School, to Which She has Given 35 Years of Service, (n.d.), Callaway Family Papers, Troup County Archives, LaGrange, Georgia; *Macon Telegraph*, June 2, 1917; Tarbell, "Making American Citizens," p. 61.

220 **made other rooms available for Settlement activity.**: Whitley, "Fuller E. Callaway," pp. 194-98.

220 **a speech at the groundbreaking.**: Ida Cason Callaway, "Memories," pp. 55-56; *LaGrange Reporter*, Apr. 14, 1911.

221 **afternoon Bible studies, and Sunday night worship services.**: Whitley, "Fuller E. Callaway," p. 204.

221 **and their operatives, as well as frequent picnics.**: Fuller Earle Callaway—Callaway Park (n.d.), Callaway Family Papers, Troup County Archives, LaGrange, Georgia; Excerpt from Minutes of Meeting of Directors of Elm City Cotton Mills, LaGrange, Georgia, Held June 16, 1915, Callaway Family Papers, Troup County Archives, LaGrange, Georgia; Excerpt from Minutes of Annual Meeting of Stockholders of Elm City Cotton Mills Held September 15, 1916, Callaway Family Papers, Troup County Archives, LaGrange, Georgia; Resolution for the Directors of the Unity Cotton Mills, Elm City Cotton Mills, and Hillside Cotton Mills, Sept. 13, 1916, Callaway Family Papers, Troup County Archives, LaGrange, Georgia; Fuller Earle Callaway—Dedication of Callaway Park (n.d.), Callaway Family Papers, Troup County Archives, LaGrange, Georgia; Whitley, "Fuller E. Callaway," pp. 216-17.

221 **Callaway once said approvingly as he watched them go.**: Whitley, "Fuller E. Callaway," pp. 197-201; Tarbell, "Making American Citizens," p. 70.

221 **provided services to more than 10,000 souls.**: Whitley, "Fuller E. Callaway," p. 198.

221 **Fuller Callaway always liked direct control.**: Ibid., pp. 205-06; *LaGrange Graphic*, July 29, 1920.

222 **that left them unable to work for extended periods.**: Whitley, "Fuller E. Callaway," pp. 210-12.

222 **of which Callaway was so proud was well established.**: *Eight Hours for Laborers on Government Work*, pp. 320-21.

222 **classes on gardening, canning, and**

preserving.: Whitley, "Fuller E. Callaway," p. 213.

222 **if I take them out of the greenhouse!":** Ida Cason Callaway, "Memories," pp. 56-57, 75-76; Whitley, "Fuller E. Callaway," pp. 212-15; *Proceedings of the Twenty-Second Annual Convention of the American Cotton Manufacturers Association held at New York May 1, 2, and 3, 1918* (Charlotte: Queen City Printing Co., 1918), 52.

222 **wasteful patterns that reduced southern wealth through inefficiency.**: *Proceedings of the Twenty-Second Annual Convention of the American Cotton Manufacturers Association*, pp. 53-54.

223 **his grouch wears off!":** Tarbell, "Making American Citizens," p. 70.

223 **the term "welfare work" to be misleading.**: *Proceedings of the Twenty-Second Annual Convention of the American Cotton Manufacturers Association*, p. 51.

223 **as much as sixty percent of their base salaries.**: Fuller Earle Callaway—The Other Mills (n.d.), Callaway Family Papers, Troup County Archives, LaGrange, Georgia; *Proceedings of the First Industrial Conference*, pp. 70, 73-74; 1-46; 5-161; 6-95.

223 **distinguished from native LaGrangians by their appearance and dress.**: Whitley, "Fuller E. Callaway," p. 222.

224 **services such as roads, sewers, or lighting.**: Clifford L. Smith, *History of Troup County* (Atlanta: Foote & Davies Co., 1933), 51; Whitley, "Fuller E. Callaway," pp. 221-22.

224 **Such talk was speedily quashed.**: Whitley, "Fuller E. Callaway," p. 222; *LaGrange Reporter*, Oct. 25, 1885.

224 **"News Items from Our Industrial Areas.":** Whitley, "Fuller E. Callaway," pp. 222-23.

224 **a dollar per mile at night.**: Ibid., pp. 235-36; *LaGrange Reporter*, Jan. 20, 1905.

225 **an attempt to lure them to LaGrange.**: *LaGrange Reporter*, Jan. 27, 1905; Whitley, "Fuller E. Callaway," p. 237.

225 **we take this method of defending ourselves.**: *LaGrange Reporter*, Jan. 27, 1905.

225 **the timing of this endeavor surely not merely coincidental.**: Whitley, "Fuller E. Callaway," p. 238; *LaGrange Reporter*, Feb. 10, 1906.

225 **skimped on basic services for the mill community.**: Whitley, "Fuller E. Call-

away," pp. 239-40; *LaGrange Reporter*, June 2, 1905.

225 **to fold Southwest LaGrange into the larger community.**: Whitley, "Fuller E. Callaway," pp. 242-44; *LaGrange Reporter*, Mar. 3, 1905; Smith, *History of Troup County*, p. 54; *LaGrange Reporter*, Feb. 24, 1905; Minute Book, LaGrange City Council, May 8, 1905, Troup County Archives, LaGrange, Georgia, pp. 398-99; see page 156, *supra*.

226 **to further its own agenda, and tempers flared.**: Whitley, "Fuller E. Callaway," pp. 244-45; *LaGrange Reporter*, Apr. 20, 1906.

226 **who had been on both slates, hadn't prevailed.**: Whitley, "Fuller E. Callaway," pp. 245-48 *LaGrange Reporter*, May 4, 1906.

226 **the gaps in services in the unincorporated area.**: Whitley, "Fuller E. Callaway," p. 250.

226 **all of the resources at his command.**: Forrest Clark Johnson, III, *Histories of LaGrange and Troup County Georgia*, vols. 1 & 2 (LaGrange: Family Tree, 1987), 256; see page 189, *supra*.

227 **merging of the two towns (and their debts).**: Whitley, "Fuller E. Callaway," p. 264; Fuller E. Callaway Jr., interview by James Saxon Childers, July 22, 1953, Callaway Family Papers, Troup County Archives, LaGrange, Georgia, pp. 23-24; *LaGrange Graphic*, July 19, 1917.

227 **the mill was turning its back on the town.**: Whitley, "Fuller E. Callaway," pp. 255-56; *LaGrange Graphic*, July 19, 1917.

227 **the lion's share of all improvements."**: Whitley, "Fuller E. Callaway," pp. 267-72; Mary Brewster to Fuller E. Callaway, n.d., Fuller E. Callaway Papers, Callaway Family Office, LaGrange, Georgia; Mary Brewster to Fuller E. Callaway, July 18, 1917, Fuller E. Callaway Papers, Callaway Family Office, LaGrange, Georgia; Mary Brewster to Fuller E. Callaway, July 20, Fuller E. Callaway Papers, Callaway Family Office, LaGrange, Georgia.

228 **out of the meeting and the deal fell through.**: Whitley, "Fuller E. Callaway," pp. 275-77; Memorandum, July 26, 1917, Fuller E. Callaway Papers, Callaway Family Office, LaGrange, Georgia.

228 **fundamentally unfair to LaGrange taxpayers.**: "We Desire to Be Heard: The Real Facts in Regard to LaGrange Situation: Is the Proposed Bill to Incorporate 'South-West LaGrange' Fair to Tax Payers of LaGrange?" Troup County Archives, n.d.

(ca. Aug. 1917).

228 **be annexed by LaGrange at the end of 1919.**: Ibid.

229 **unless the second bill also became law.**: Act of Aug. 18, 1917, 1917 *Ga. Laws* 705, 705-07.

229 **would pay their fair share of the improvement costs.**: Act of Aug. 20, 1917, 1917 *Ga. Laws* 866, 866-72.

229 **dawn of a bright future.**: Whitley, "Fuller E. Callaway," p. 288; *LaGrange Graphic*, Jan. 1, 1920.

230 **at least potentially, a tool of labor.**: *Eight Hours for Laborers on Government Work*, p. 327; *Atlanta Constitution*, July 15, 1905; ibid., Aug. 2, 1905; see page 217, *supra*.

230 **the president of the American Federation of Labor.**: See page 198, *supra*.

230 **the destruction of the new workingman's government of Russia."**: Philip S. Foner, *History of the Labor Movement in the United States*, vol. 8, *Postwar Struggles 1918-1920* (New York: International Publishers, 1987), 49-51; *Report of the Proceedings of the Thirty-ninth Annual Convention of the American Federation of Labor* (Washington: The Law Reporter Printing Co., 1919), 246.

230 **a Bolshevik uprising was in the American wind.**: See generally Ann Hagedorn, *Savage Peace: Hope and Fear in America, 1919* (New York: Simon & Schuster, 2007); Robert K. Murray, *Red Scare: A Study in National Hysteria, 1919-1920* (Minneapolis: University of Minnesota Press, 1955).

231 **it would be an unfortunate development.**: Whitley, "Fuller E. Callaway," p. 294.

231 **high unionization rates throughout the region.**: James Newsome to Fuller E. Callaway, June 29, 1920, Callaway Family Papers, Troup County Archives, LaGrange, Georgia; George S. Mitchell, *Textile Unionism and the South* (Chapel Hill: University of North Carolina Press, 1931), 10.

231 **good advertising for those who seek publicity or notoriety."**: Ethel Thomas to Ab Perry, July 5, 1920, Callaway Family Papers, Troup County Archives, LaGrange, Georgia.

232 **residents who favored at least the possibility of unionizing.**: Broadsides, Callaway Family Papers, Series I: Business Papers, subsection A: Business Correspondence, Box 11, File 8, July 1920, Troup County Archives, LaGrange, Georgia; see Whitley, "Fuller E. Callaway," pp. 303-04.

232 **this IWW, Bolshevik gang," one**

writer swore.: Whitley, "Fuller E. Callaway," p. 300.

232 **dignified name 'American Federation of Labor.' "**: Johnson, *Histories of LaGrange and Troup County Georgia*, vols. 1 & 2, pp. 254-56, 258; Whitley, "Fuller E. Callaway," p. 300.

232 **others I have been in have been torn up."**: Whitley, "Fuller E. Callaway," pp. 302-03.

232 **Michigan has had a quarrel with the shop foreman."**: Ibid., p. 307.

232 **if the unions weren't allowed to interfere.**: *Proceedings of the First Industrial Conference*, pp. 70-71; Whitley, "Fuller E. Callaway," p. 307; *LaGrange Graphic*, July 22, 1920.

232 **a small figure labeled "individual worker."**: Illustrations, 1920 Box, Fuller E. Callaway Papers, Callaway Family Office, LaGrange, Georgia; Whitley, "Fuller E. Callaway," pp. 307-10.

233 **where there is to be strife and division."**: Whitley, "Fuller E. Callaway," pp. 301-02.

233 **a Textile or Labor Union while in our employment."**: Ibid., pp. 314-15.

233 **that they would refrain from joining a union.**: Fuller E. Callaway to Dudley Glass, July 30, 1920, Fuller E. Callaway Papers, Callaway Family Office, LaGrange, Georgia.

233 **Great Depression, a disaster that Callaway himself predicted.**: Conversation between Fuller E. Callaway Jr., James Saxon Childers, and Maurine Childers Concerning Life of Fuller E. Callaway Sr., July 22, 1953, Callaway Family Papers, Troup County Archives, LaGrange, Georgia, pp. 20-21; see page 101, *supra*.

· 10 ·
THE FINAL YEARS

235 **he will find himself growing old some day."**: *Cotton*, Sept. 1921, p. 822.

235 **at some point he likely began to rely upon.**: *The Drapers' Record*, June 7, 1919; *The Drapers and Drapery Times*, June 7, 1919; Fuller E. Callaway Jr., interview by James Saxon Childers, July 22, 1953, Callaway Family Papers, Troup County Archives, LaGrange, Georgia, p. 29.

235 **worsening health likely played a role in the decision.**: *Atlanta Constitution*, Jan. 16, 1920.

235 **more familiar with LaGrange than with Baltimore,**: See page 211, *supra*.

235 **quickly became friends as well as doctor and patient.**: Fuller. E. Callaway to Sir A. Herbert Dixon, June 21, 1920, Callaway Family Papers, Troup County Archives, LaGrange, Georgia; Francis R Dieuaide to Fuller E. Callaway, Aug. 19, 1922, Callaway Family Papers, Troup County Archives, LaGrange, Georgia; Lewellys F. Barker, "Report of Diagnostic Study of Mr. Fuller Callaway, LaGrange, Georgia," June 30, 1920, Callaway Family Papers, Troup County Archives, LaGrange, Georgia; Diagnosis of Fuller E. Callaway, n.d. (ca. June 8, 1920), Callaway Family Papers, Troup County Archives, LaGrange, Georgia.

236 **in the morning and once again in the afternoon.**: Lewellys F. Barker, "Report of Diagnostic Study of Mr. Fuller Callaway, LaGrange, Georgia," June 30, 1920, Callaway Family Papers, Troup County Archives, LaGrange, Georgia; see generally Nicolas Postel-Vinay, ed., *A Century of Arterial Hypertension 1896-1996* (Chichester: John Wiley & Sons, 1996); P. M. Esunge, "From Blood Pressure to Hypertension: The History of Research," *Journal of the Royal Society of Medicine* 84(10) 621, 621 (Oct. 1991).

236 **as to how to take care of myself."**: Fuller. E. Callaway to Sir A. Herbert Dixon, June 21, 1920, Callaway Family Papers, Troup County Archives, LaGrange, Georgia.

236 **both Ida and Fuller, Jr. accompanying him.**: Fuller E. Callaway to Frank Nasmith, July 9, 1920, Callaway Family Papers, Troup County Archives, LaGrange, Georgia; *Official Report, World Cotton Conference, Liverpool, June 13, 14, 15, 1921; Manchester, June 16 to 22, 1921* (Manchester: Executive Committee, 1921).

236 **islands and spending a few months there each summer.**: North Winship to Fuller E. Callaway, Mar. 23, 1921, Callaway Family Papers, Troup County Archives, LaGrange, Georgia; Fuller. E. Callaway to Lewellys F. Barker, July 23, 1920 Callaway Family Papers, Troup County Archives, LaGrange, Georgia; Albert Grigg to Lewellys F. Barker, June 7, 1920 Callaway Family Papers, Troup County Archives, LaGrange, Georgia; Lewellys F. Barker to Fuller E. Callaway, June 14, 1920, Callaway Family Papers, Troup County Archives, LaGrange, Georgia.

236 **from there they would return to LaGrange via Washington.**: Itinerary of Mr. and Mrs. Fuller E. Callaway and Fuller, Jr., on Summer Vacation Trip (1920), Callaway Family Papers, Troup County Archives, LaGrange, Georgia; Fuller E. Callaway Jr., interview by James Saxon Childers, July 22, 1953, Callaway Family Papers, Troup County Archives, LaGrange, Georgia, p. 7.

237 **those so fortunate as to be named his friends.**: Ida Cason Callaway, "Memories of Fuller Earle Callaway Sr. of LaGrange, Georgia Written by His Wife, Ida Cason Callaway," unpublished manuscript, Callaway Family Papers, Troup County Archives, LaGrange, Georgia, 1929, p. 86; *LaGrange Graphic*, July 22, 1920; *The Shuttle*, July 23, 1920.

238 **But there was nothing to do for it.**: Fuller E. Callaway Jr., interview by James Saxon Childers, July 22, 1953, Callaway Family Papers, Troup County Archives, LaGrange, Georgia, pp. 7-8;

238 **Something had been wrong with the food at the party.**: Ibid.

238 **but for very different reasons.**: Ibid.; Fuller Earle Callaway, Vacation in Canada, Summer of 1920, Callaway Family Papers, Troup County Archives, LaGrange, Georgia; J. A. Perry to Fuller E. Callaway, July 24, 1920 Callaway Family Papers, Troup County Archives, LaGrange, Georgia; Ida Cason Callaway, "Memories," pp. 86-87.

240 **will prove of the greatest benefit to all," he concluded.**: Fuller E. Callaway to Lewellys F. Barker, July 23, 1920 Callaway Family Papers, Troup County Archives, LaGrange, Georgia; Fuller Earle Callaway, Vacation in Canada, Summer of 1920, Callaway Family Papers, Troup County Archives, LaGrange, Georgia; J. A. Perry to Fuller E. Callaway, July 24, 1920, Callaway Family Papers, Troup County Archives, LaGrange, Georgia.

240 **benefited by our vacation in Canada," declared Fuller.**: Fuller Earle Callaway, Vacation in Canada, Summer of 1920, Callaway Family Papers, Troup County Archives, LaGrange, Georgia; Minnicoganashene Summer Hotel receipt, Aug. 21, 1920, Callaway Family Papers, Troup County Archives, LaGrange, Georgia; Lewellys F. Barker to Fuller E. Callaway, Aug. 10, 1920, Callaway Family Papers, Troup County Archives, LaGrange, Georgia; Fuller E. Callaway Jr., interview by James Saxon Childers, July 22, 1953, Callaway Family Papers, Troup County Archives, LaGrange, Georgia, p. 27; Enderby Press and Walker's Weekly, Sept. 23, 1909; Fuller E. Callaway to Fuller E. Callaway, Aug. 16, 1920, Callaway Family Papers, Troup County Archives, LaGrange, Georgia.

240 **Ida later noted that his general health wasn't improving.**: Ida Cason Callaway, "Memories," p. 109.

240 **despite Callaway's dim view of the practice.**: *The Shuttle*, Sept. 24, 1920; *The LaGrange Reporter*, Sept. 20, 1920; see page 53, *supra*.

240 **"a good risk."**: "The Life and Works of Mr. Fuller E. Callaway, Senior," Callaway Family Papers, Troup County Archives, LaGrange, Georgia, p. 13; "Fuller Earle Callaway—Cason, Oldest Son, is Put in Harness," Callaway Family Papers, Troup County Archives, LaGrange, Georgia; *Cotton*, Nov. 1920; *LaGrange Reporter*, Sept. 20, 1920; Conversations Between Fuller E. Callaway Jr. and Hatton Lovejoy—Reference Book on Life of Fuller E Callaway Sr., July 20, 1953, p. 4, Callaway Family Papers, Troup County Archives, LaGrange, Georgia.

241 **He wants to do everything."**: Helen Christine Bennett, "The Homely Wisdom of Fuller E. Callaway," *American Magazine* Oct. 1920, 16, 109.

241 **he asked Fuller to make a decision for him.**: See pages 38-39, *supra*.

241 **Fuller made sure to send the telegram collect.**: Ida Cason Callaway, "Memories," p. 57; Fuller E. Callaway Jr., interview by James Saxon Childers, July 22, 1953, Callaway Family Papers, Troup County Archives, LaGrange, Georgia, p. 9.

242 **That largely ended the problem.**: Fuller. E. Callaway to Rufus R. Wilson, Oct. 19, 1920, Callaway Family Papers, Troup County Archives, LaGrange, Georgia; Conversations Between Fuller E. Callaway Jr. and Hatton Lovejoy—Reference Book on Life of Fuller E Callaway Sr., July 20, 1953, p. 4, Callaway Family Papers, Troup County Archives, LaGrange, Georgia.

242 **"and run cotton mills to pay the expenses."**: Ida M. Tarbell, "Making American Citizens and Running Cotton Mills to Pay the Expenses," *Red Cross Magazine*, Aug. 1920, 59, 60.

242 **Running Cotton Mills to Pay the Expenses."**: Tarbell, "Making American Citizens," p. 59.

242 **this one written by Helen Christine Bennett.**: Bennett, "The Homely Wisdom of Fuller E. Callaway," p. 16.

242 **Callaway answered. "It's business."**: Ibid.

242 **"put me down for a hundred shares.":** Ibid., p. 110.

243 **tried that twenty years back and it didn't work.":** Ibid.

243 **nothing will be allowed to suffer thereby.":** *Atlanta Journal*, Aug. 13, 1920; "Welfare Work in the Cotton Industry," Callaway Family Papers, Troup County Archives, LaGrange, Georgia; Fuller E. Callaway to Rufus R. Wilson, Sept. 20, 1920, Callaway Family Papers, Troup County Archives, LaGrange, Georgia.

243 **about three months," he told a Tennessee acquaintance.:** Frederic E. Kip to Fuller E. Callaway, Feb. 5, 1921, Callaway Family Papers, Troup County Archives, LaGrange, Georgia; Fuller E. Callaway to Alex Bonnyman, Mar. 19, 1921, Callaway Family Papers, Troup County Archives, LaGrange, Georgia; "Fuller Earle Callaway—Mr. and Mrs. Callaway and Fuller, Jr., Go Abroad in 1921," Callaway Family Papers, Troup County Archives, LaGrange, Georgia.

245 **some of the cities the family would be visiting.:** Fuller E. Callaway to Frank Nasmith, Mar. 21, 1921, Callaway Family Papers, Troup County Archives, LaGrange, Georgia; *Textile World Journal*, Feb. 19, 1921; *Atlanta Journal*, Apr. 1, 1921; Fuller E. Callaway to The LaGrange National Bank, Apr. 6, 1921, Callaway Family Papers, Troup County Archives, LaGrange, Georgia; Michael Marrus, *The Unwanted: European Refugees in the Twentieth Century* (New York: Oxford University Press, 1985), 92-93; Charles E. Hughes to Diplomatic and Consular Officers of the United States of America, Mar. 29, 1921, Callaway Family Papers, Troup County Archives, LaGrange, Georgia; Fuller E. Callaway to Herbert Hoover, Mar. 23, 1921, Callaway Family Papers, Troup County Archives, LaGrange, Georgia; Herbert Hoover to Fuller E. Callaway, Mar. 30, 1921, Callaway Family Papers, Troup County Archives, LaGrange, Georgia; Fuller E. Callaway to Herbert Hoover, Apr. 4, 1921, Callaway Family Papers, Troup County Archives, LaGrange, Georgia; Fuller E. Callaway to Rufus R. Wilson, Apr. 7, 1921, Callaway Family Papers, Troup County Archives, LaGrange, Georgia; Frederic E. Kip to Fuller E. Callaway, Feb. 5, 1921, Callaway Family Papers, Troup County Archives, LaGrange, Georgia; North Winship to Fuller E. Callaway, Mar. 23, 1921, Callaway Family Papers, Troup County Archives, LaGrange, Georgia.

245 **suffered a major stroke, dying two days later.:** Itinerary of Steamer *Canopic* of White Star Line, Apr. 20, 1921, Callaway Family Papers, Troup County Archives, LaGrange, Georgia; Fuller E. Callaway to H. H. Barnard, Apr. 14, 1921, Callaway Family Papers, Troup County Archives, LaGrange, Georgia; Fuller E. Callaway to H. H. Barnard [cable], Apr. 12, 1921, Callaway Family Papers, Troup County Archives, LaGrange, Georgia; "Fuller Earle Callaway—Mr. and Mrs. Callaway and Fuller, Jr., Go Abroad in 1921," Callaway Family Papers, Troup County Archives, LaGrange, Georgia; Ida Cason Callaway, "Memories," pp. 31, 37.

245 **she and her family set out for New York.:** Ida Cason Callaway, "Memories," pp. 81-82; "Fuller Earle Callaway—Mr. and Mrs. Callaway and Fuller, Jr., Go Abroad in 1921," Callaway Family Papers, Troup County Archives, LaGrange, Georgia.

246 **Young Fuller never forgot the episode.:** Fuller E. Callaway Jr., interview by James Saxon Childers, July 22, 1953, Callaway Family Papers, Troup County Archives, LaGrange, Georgia, p. 4; see page 123, *supra*.

246 **did nothing to lessen her worries about his health.:** Ida Cason Callaway, "Memories," p. 81; Memorandum Follow-Up, Apr. 8, 1921, Callaway Family Papers, Troup County Archives, LaGrange, Georgia.

246 **in Genoa, Naples, Rome, and Florence.:** [Fuller E. Callaway] to Fuller E. Callaway [cable], May 7, 1921, Callaway Family Papers, Troup County Archives, LaGrange, Georgia; F. Coit Johnson to Fuller E. Callaway, May 24, 1921, Callaway Family Papers, Troup County Archives, LaGrange, Georgia; Fuller E. Callaway to Cason Callaway et al., May 15, 1921, Callaway Family Papers, Troup County Archives, LaGrange, Georgia.

246 **by then his work plans may have been changing.:** "Textile Institute Spring Conference, 1921," Fuller E. Callaway Sr., 1921 box, Fuller E. Callaway Papers, Callaway Family Office, LaGrange, Georgia.

246 **Trip is simply splendid. All three enjoying it.":** "Fuller Earle Callaway—Mr. and Mrs. Callaway and Fuller, Jr., Go Abroad in 1921," Callaway Family Papers, Troup County Archives, LaGrange, Georgia; *Textile World Journal*, Feb. 19, 1921; Fuller E. Callaway to Cason Callaway et al., May 15, 1921, Callaway Family Papers, Troup County Archives, LaGrange, Georgia; Fuller E. Callaway Jr., interview by James Saxon Childers, July 22, 1953, Callaway Family Papers, Troup County Archives, LaGrange, Georgia, p. 17.

246 **decided not to go to the World Cotton Conference.":** J. A. Perry to Fuller E. Callaway, June 9, 1921, Callaway Family Papers, Troup County Archives, LaGrange, Georgia.

247 **signing the telegram "Fullercorn.":** Fullercorn [Fuller E. Callaway] to Cason Callaway [cable], n.d., 1921, Callaway Family Papers, Troup County Archives, LaGrange, Georgia.

247 **"Cough well. All happy. Congratulations.":** "Fuller Earle Callaway—Mr. and Mrs. Callaway and Fuller, Jr., Go Abroad in 1921," Callaway Family Papers, Troup County Archives, LaGrange, Georgia; *Cotton*, Sept. 1921, p. 822; Fullercorn [Fuller E. Callaway] to Cason Callaway [cable], n.d., 1921, Callaway Family Papers, Troup County Archives, LaGrange, Georgia; Fuller E. Callaway to Cason J. Callaway, May 23, 1921, Callaway Family Papers, Troup County Archives, LaGrange, Georgia.

247 **would have to be poured back into the spring.":** Ida Cason Callaway, "Memories," pp. 81-82; "Fuller Earle Callaway—Mr. and Mrs. Callaway and Fuller, Jr., Go Abroad in 1921," Callaway Family Papers, Troup County Archives, LaGrange, Georgia; J. A. Perry to Fuller E. Callaway, June 9, 1921, Callaway Family Papers, Troup County Archives, LaGrange, Georgia.

247 **keep Fuller at Vichy for at least two weeks.:** Ida Cason Callaway, "Memories," pp. 81-82; "Fuller Earle Callaway—Mr. and Mrs. Callaway and Fuller, Jr., Go Abroad in 1921," Callaway Family Papers, Troup County Archives, LaGrange, Georgia; P. DesGeorges, diagnosis and prescription, June 15, 1921, Callaway Family Papers, Troup County Archives, LaGrange, Georgia.

247 **places he'd scouted out on previous trips.:** Ida Cason Callaway, "Memories," pp. 81-82; "Fuller Earle Callaway—Mr. and Mrs. Callaway and Fuller, Jr., Go Abroad in 1921," Callaway Family Papers, Troup County Archives, LaGrange, Georgia; Fuller E. Callaway Jr., interview by James Saxon Childers, July 22, 1953, Callaway Family Papers, Troup County Archives, LaGrange, Georgia, p. 28.

248 **and at last arrived in London.:** Joint Resolution of July 2, 1921, 42 Stat. 105, ch. 40; _____ to Fuller E. Callaway [cable], June 23, 1921, Callaway Family Papers, Troup County Archives, LaGrange, Georgia; _____ to Fuller E. Callaway [cable], June 28, 1921, Callaway Family Papers, Troup County Archives, LaGrange, Georgia; F. Coit Johnson to Fuller E. Callaway, July

19, 1921, Callaway Family Papers, Troup County Archives, LaGrange, Georgia.

248 "ora pro me" inscription in her garden.: Fuller E. Callaway to Alfred P. Dennis, Apr. 4, 1921, Callaway Family Papers, Troup County Archives, LaGrange, Georgia; Alfred P. Dennis to Fuller E. Callaway, Feb. 21, 1921, Callaway Family Papers, Troup County Archives, LaGrange, Georgia; Fuller E. Callaway to Sir Frank Warner, Mar. 11, 1921, Callaway Family Papers, Troup County Archives, LaGrange, Georgia; *Journal of the Textile Institute Proceedings*, vol. 21, Issue 20, 1930, pp. 40-41; Sir Frank Warner, *The Silk Industry of the United Kingdom* (London: Dranes [1921]); Ida Cason Callaway, "Memories," p. 97; see pages 4 and 148, *supra*.

249 a banquet to celebrate the occasion.: *American Wool and Cotton Reporter*, Dec. 16, 1920, p. 4296 (50); Fuller E. Callaway to Frank Nasmith, Dec. 10, 1920, Callaway Family Papers, Troup County Archives, LaGrange, Georgia.

249 Appreciation, Esteem and Respect.: *Cotton*, Sept. 1921, p. 822; Ida Cason Callaway, "Memories," p. 83.

249 until he had gotten back up onto the platform.: Ida Cason Callaway, "Memories," p. 83.

249 surrounded by acquaintances, holding his cane and smiling.: *Cotton*, Sept. 1921, p. 822.

250 requiring only membership dues, with no initiation fee.: Donald J. Ross, *Golf Has Never Failed Me: The Lost Commentaries of Legendary Golf Architect, Donald J. Ross* (Chelsea, Michigan: Sleeping Bear Press, 1996), 1-6; William R. Mitchell, Jr., *J. Neel Reid, Architect, of Hentz, Reid & Adler and the Georgia School of Classicists* (Atlanta: Georgia Trust for Historic Preservation, 1997), 236; "Highland Country Club," Callaway Family Papers, Troup County Archives, LaGrange, Georgia; Cason J. Callaway, Scrapbook, Callaway Family Papers, Troup County Archives, LaGrange, Georgia.

250 many nips being "quietly taken to his home.": "Highland Country Club," Callaway Family Papers, Troup County Archives, LaGrange, Georgia.

250 "the tail is wagging the dog.": Fuller E. Callaway to F. Coit Johnson, June 6, 1922, Callaway Family Papers, Troup County Archives, LaGrange, Georgia; *Daily News Record*, Aug. 17, 1921; *Daily News Record*, Aug. 17, 1921; "Fuller Earle Callaway—The Mills Establish Their Own Selling Agency," Callaway Family Papers, Troup County Archives, LaGrange, Georgia; *Daily News Record*, Apr. 29, 1922.

251 Mills would then sell the stock back to Lane.: *Daily News Record*, Apr. 29, 1922; J. H. Lane Co. to Fuller E. Callaway, June 20, 1922, Callaway Family Papers, Troup County Archives, LaGrange, Georgia; F. Coit Johnson to Fuller E. Callaway, Oct. 9, 1922, Callaway Family Papers, Troup County Archives, LaGrange, Georgia; Fuller E. Callaway to F. Coit Johnson, Oct. 19, 1922, Callaway Family Papers, Troup County Archives, LaGrange, Georgia; Kellogg, Emery, Inness-Brown & Cuthell to Hatton Lovejoy, Sept. 13, 1922, Callaway Family Papers, Troup County Archives, LaGrange, Georgia.

251 removal of one of her kidneys that same August.: M. A. Mortensen to Fuller E. Callaway, Sept. 8, 1922, Callaway Family Papers, Troup County Archives, LaGrange, Georgia; F. Coit Johnson to Fuller E. Callaway, Oct. 9, 1922, Callaway Family Papers, Troup County Archives, LaGrange, Georgia; Cason Callaway to Fuller E. Callaway [cable], Aug. 22, 1922 (1), Callaway Family Papers, Troup County Archives, LaGrange, Georgia; Cason Callaway to Fuller E. Callaway [cable], Aug. 22, 1922 (2), Callaway Family Papers, Troup County Archives, LaGrange, Georgia; Fuller E. Callaway to Cason Callaway [cable], Aug. 22, 1922, Callaway Family Papers, Troup County Archives, LaGrange, Georgia; Wm. H. Turner to J. A. Perry, Oct. 11, 1922, Callaway Family Papers, Troup County Archives, LaGrange, Georgia; Fuller E. Callaway to John H. Callaway, Nov. 5, 1922, Callaway Family Papers, Troup County Archives, LaGrange, Georgia.

252 unless it is imperatively necessary," he explained.: Fuller E. Callaway to Harry G. White, June 6, 1923, Callaway Family Papers, Troup County Archives, LaGrange, Georgia; Lewellys F. Barker to Fuller E. Callaway, May 19, 1923, Callaway Family Papers, Troup County Archives, LaGrange, Georgia; Report of Diagnostic Study of Mrs. Fuller Callaway, La Grange, Ga., May 22, 1923, Callaway Family Papers, Troup County Archives, LaGrange, Georgia.

252 before long the diet was over.: Fuller E. Callaway Jr., interview by James Saxon Childers, July 22, 1953, Callaway Family Papers, Troup County Archives, LaGrange, Georgia, pp. 28-29.

252 until I can confer with you on Thursday.": Clifford Walker to Fuller E. Callaway, Sept. 11, 1923, Callaway Family Papers, Troup County Archives, LaGrange, Georgia.

252 Perry informed Walker, might not even be possible.: Fuller E. Callaway [A. J. Perry] to Clifford Walker, Sept. 8, 1923, Callaway Family Papers, Troup County Archives, LaGrange, Georgia.

252 sounding him out as to his preferred meeting schedule.: A. S. Bussey to Fuller E. Callaway, Sept. 11, 1923, Callaway Family Papers, Troup County Archives, LaGrange, Georgia.

253 probably helped Callaway accept the change in lifestyle.: *Rome Herald*, Feb. 16, 1923; Fuller E. Callaway to Clifford Walker, Sept. 14, 1923, Callaway Family Papers, Troup County Archives, LaGrange, Georgia; see J. A. Perry to Arthur S. Bussey, Sept. 12, 1923, Callaway Family Papers, Troup County Archives, LaGrange, Georgia; see, e.g., [Athens] *Banner-Herald*, Sept. 9, 1923.

253 warning that he must take better care of himself.: Fuller E. Callaway to John H. Callaway, Nov. 5, 1923, Callaway Family Papers, Troup County Archives, LaGrange, Georgia; *LaGrange Graphic*, Aug. 2, 1923; ibid., Aug. 3, 1923; Fuller E. Callaway Jr., interview by James Saxon Childers, July 16, 1953, Callaway Family Papers, Troup County Archives, LaGrange, Georgia, pp. 24-25.

253 she began referring to them as "my twins.": "Mr. Howard Callaway Comes to Live with the Family," Callaway Family Papers, Troup County Archives, LaGrange, Georgia; Fuller E. Callaway to Howard Callaway, Dec. 26, 1924, Callaway Family Papers, Troup County Archives, LaGrange, Georgia; Louis D. Newton, "Pastor Tunnell Observes Fifth Anniversary at LaGrange," *The Christian Index*, Sept. 11, 1924.

253 twice weekly for short periods of consultation.": Fuller E. Callaway to John H. Callaway, Nov. 5, 1923, Callaway Family Papers, Troup County Archives, LaGrange, Georgia; J. A. Perry to John H. Callaway, Oct. 29, 1923, Callaway Family Papers, Troup County Archives, LaGrange, Georgia.

254 subjected to delays or disappointment in this regard.": Fuller E. Callaway to Lewellys F. Barker, Sept. 25, 1923, Callaway Family Papers, Troup County Archives, LaGrange, Georgia.

254 so pleasant and satisfactory to you both.": J. A. Perry to Fuller E. Callaway, Oct. 1, 1923, Callaway Family Papers, Troup County Archives, LaGrange, Georgia; [J. A. Perry] to Mrs. Fuller E. Callaway, Oct. 8, 1923, Callaway Family Papers, Troup County Archives, LaGrange, Georgia.

254 **so faring better than our competitors.":** Fuller E. Callaway Jr., interview by James Saxon Childers, July 16, 1953, Callaway Family Papers, Troup County Archives, LaGrange, Georgia, p. 37; Fuller E. Callaway to W. A. Drieler et al., Apr. 17, 1924, Callaway Family Papers, Troup County Archives, LaGrange, Georgia.

255 **to throw the bowl of pickles in his face.":** Alfred Pearce Dennis, *Gods and Little Fishes* (Indianapolis; Bobbs-Merrill Co., 1931), 268-69.

255 **the only Gate through which he could enter.":** Ida Cason Callaway, "Memories," p. 19.

256 **in Callaway's eyes the clerk's behavior was bad.:** Ibid., p. 25.

256 **provided only that the pastors withhold the donor's name.:** Ibid., p. 19.

256 **donated thousands of dollars to the needy.:** _____ to Fuller E. Callaway, Oct. 31, 1923, Callaway Family Papers, Troup County Archives, LaGrange, Georgia; S. Y. Austin to Fuller E. Callaway, Nov. 13, 1923, Callaway Family Papers, Troup County Archives, LaGrange, Georgia; Meeting of Trustees, Relief Association, Oct. 16, 1924, Callaway Family Papers, Troup County Archives, LaGrange, Georgia.

256 **a death threat against Callaway's friend.:** Fuller E. Callaway Jr., interview by James Saxon Childers, July 16, 1953, Callaway Family Papers, Troup County Archives, LaGrange, Georgia, p. 37; "Fuller Earle Callaway," Callaway Family Papers, Troup County Archives, LaGrange, Georgia.

256 **common stock at $200 per share.").:** "Fuller Earle Callaway," Callaway Family Papers, Troup County Archives, LaGrange, Georgia; Fuller E. Callaway to Fuller E. Callaway [cable], Jan. 4, 1924, Callaway Family Papers, Troup County Archives, LaGrange, Georgia; J. A. Perry to Fuller E. Callaway, Jan. 5, 1924, Callaway Family Papers, Troup County Archives, LaGrange, Georgia; Fuller E. Callaway to Lewellys F. Barker, Oct. 16, 1924, Callaway Family Papers, Troup County Archives, LaGrange, Georgia.

257 *Gods and Little Fishes*, **published in 1931.:** Alfred P. Dennis to Fuller E. Callaway, Aug. 7, 1924, Callaway Family Papers, Troup County Archives, LaGrange, Georgia; Dennis, *Gods and Little Fishes*, ch. 8.

257 **often and for as long as may be convenient.:** Fuller E. Callaway to Alfred P. Dennis, Aug. 9, 1924, Callaway Family Papers, Troup County Archives, LaGrange, Georgia.

257 **to finish what I have started in this direction.":** Fuller E. Callaway to Cason J. Callaway, Apr. 18, 1924, Callaway Family Papers, Troup County Archives, LaGrange, Georgia.

258 **high blood pressure and exhausted nervous forces.":** Fuller E. Callaway to John H. Callaway, Nov. 5, 1923, Callaway Family Papers, Troup County Archives, LaGrange, Georgia.

258 **getting more particular and less desirable all the time.":** "Fuller Earle Callaway," Callaway Family Papers, Troup County Archives, LaGrange, Georgia.

258 **hand the reins over to him later that year.:** Ibid.; http://www.callawaygardens.com/about-us/history/virginia-callaway (last visited May 24, 2013).

259 **[O]ur cup of joy overflowed.":** Ida Cason Callaway, "Memories," pp. 40-41.

259 **important relationship between the school and the Callaway family.:** Louis D. Newton, "Pastor Tunnell Observes Fifth Anniversary at LaGrange," *The Christian Index*, Sept. 11, 1924; see pages 94-95, *supra*.

259 **I'll bite you.":** Fuller E. Callaway Jr., interview by James Saxon Childers, July 22, 1953, Callaway Family Papers, Troup County Archives, LaGrange, Georgia, p. 18.

259 **predicted the 1929 stock market crash.:** Ida Cason Callaway, "Memories," pp. 100, 104-05; Fuller E. Callaway Jr., interview by James Saxon Childers, July 22, 1953, Callaway Family Papers, Troup County Archives, LaGrange, Georgia, p. 21; see page 101, *supra*.

259 **an angina attack would then often follow.:** Fuller E. Callaway Jr., interview by James Saxon Childers, July 16, 1953, Callaway Family Papers, Troup County Archives, LaGrange, Georgia, pp. 35-36.

260 **give him a report on whatever was going on.:** Ida Cason Callaway, "Memories," p. 100.

260 **still, the idea began with his father.:** Fuller Earle Callaway—Stories and Maxims (n.d.), Callaway Family Papers, Troup County Archives, LaGrange, Georgia; Ida Cason Callaway, "Memories," p. 36; "Building of Callaway Auditorium," Callaway Family Papers, Troup County Archives, LaGrange, Georgia; see pages 89-90, *supra*.

260 **attending several directors' meetings in early 1928.:** Ida Cason Callaway, "Memories," pp. 100, 109-10; Clifford L. Smith, *History of Troup County* (Atlanta: Foote & Davies Co., 1933), 119-21.

261 **the fulfillment of that hope.:** Ida Cason Callaway, "Memories," p. 110.

261 **will have to attend to that.":** Ibid.

262 **none of them made the list.:** Fuller E. Callaway Jr., interview by James Saxon Childers, July 22, 1953, Callaway Family Papers, Troup County Archives, LaGrange, Georgia, pp. 24-25.

262 **Fuller Earle Callaway was fifty-seven years old.:** Ida Cason Callaway, "Memories," p. 101.

263 **burn out the dross in us.":** Fuller E. Callaway Jr., interview by James Saxon Childers, July 22, 1953, Callaway Family Papers, Troup County Archives, LaGrange, Georgia, p. 16; Ida Cason Callaway, "Memories," pp. 57-58.

264 **Callaway would probably have disapproved.:** Forrest Clark Johnson, III, *Histories of LaGrange and Troup County Georgia*, vols. 1 & 2 (LaGrange: Family Tree, 1987), 236; Ida Cason Callaway, "Memories," pp. 104-05; *LaGrange Reporter*, Feb. 13, 1928.

264 **parallel celebrations taking place in Manchester and at Milstead.:** Ida Cason Callaway, "Memories," pp. 116-18.

INDEX

Italicized page numbers refer to illustrations

ILLUSTRATION & PHOTO CREDITS

A complete list of credits appears below. Unless otherwise noted, all photographs and illustrations are courtesy of Troup County Archives. All object and portrait photos were taken by Lee Cathey unless otherwise noted.

ST.CALLAWY ORA PRO ME